Approaches to International Education

Approaches to International Education

EDITED BY

Earl L. Backman

Director
Center for International Studies
University of North Carolina
at Charlotte

AMERICAN COUNCIL ON EDUCATION ● MACMILLAN PUBLISHING COMPANY
NEW YORK

Collier Macmillan Publishers
LONDON

Macmillan Publishing Company
A Division of Macmillan, Inc.
866 Third Avenue, New York, N. Y. 10022

Collier Macmillan Canada, Inc.

Library of Congress Catalog Card Number: 83-15849

Printed in the United States of America

printing number
1 2 3 4 5 6 7 8 9 10

Library of Congress Cataloging in Publication Data
Main entry under title:

Approaches to international education.

   (The American Council on Education/Macmillan series
on higher education)
   Bibliography: p. 346
   1. International education—United States—Case
studies. 2. Universities and colleges—United States—
Curricula. I. Backman, Earl L. II. American Council on
Education. III. Series.
LC1090.A67 1984   370.11′5   83-15849
ISBN 0-02-901360-7

Contents

v

Foreword

In a speech given before the House of Commons in 1940, Winston Churchill warned: "If we open a quarrel between the past and the present, we shall find that we have lost the future." Those who cling to a romanticized interpretation of Jefferson's famous warning against "entangling alliances" with foreign nations would do well to heed the words of Paul Valéry, who remarked, "The trouble with our times is that the future is just not what it used to be."

In theory, few oppose the arguments that our nation should possess an educational system producing at least a minimal cadre of experts about other peoples and cultures, as well as professionals in business and government who can transact negotiations across national borders; that we should have scientists and technicians who can extend and share human knowledge on a global basis; and finally, that America must have citizens knowledgeable enough to support tough leadership decisions and policies in a dangerous and complicated world.

But in fact such schools, experts, and citizens are precisely what we do not have. Thus few Americans appreciate the magnitude of their nation's many involvements in a very interconnected world. As a people, our perception and vision of the world seem to stop at our shoreline. To be sure, we are aware of a "they" out there, but we understand very little how "they" interact with our lives, let alone how interdependent our world has become.

Despite skyrocketing prices at the gas pump, a 1977 Gallup Poll showed that more than half of the general public were totally unaware that we must import part of our precious petroleum supplies, and fewer than ten percent knew that more than half of our energy requirements came from foreign sources. Similarly, in 1980, as the rest of the world struggled to survive a faltering economy that was closely linked with balance-of-payments problems and highly sensitive to deteriorating international trading patterns, a Roper poll revealed that 49 percent of Americans surveyed believed that foreign trade was either irrelevant or harmful to the United States. They held this conviction despite the fact that one out of three acres of farmland in this country produces for export, and that fully 25 percent of our economy is involved in either exports or imports.

"The business of America is business," Calvin Coolidge once said. But too many of us forget that much of our business is with "them." Between 1950 and 1979, American exports increased from $10 billion to $377 billion. One out of six manufacturing jobs in this country is directly dependent on foreign trade.

Clearly, maintaining healthy trade is vital to our economic circumstances. Yet only 250 or so of America's 300,000 business firms account for over 80 percent of America's exports. Such a lopsided ratio is evidence that thousands of companies are somewhat distrustful—or even unaware—of foreign markets. The sorry result is that countless opportunities are being lost to create jobs, strengthen the dollar, and stem inflation by improving America's balance-of-payments. Because relatively few American businessmen understand the culture, the customs, or even the language of the buyer, America's competitive edge is often lost in the tough realities of international buying and selling.

Fortunately, throughout the country, school officials, parents' associations, community action and civic groups, politicians on the local, state, and national levels, educators, and other professionals are organizing themselves in an effort to bring about change.

This volume is a compilation of seventeen effective and practical examples of successful efforts to internationalize higher education. It serves an important national purpose, and arrives opportunely as educators begin the complicated yet necessary task of building American competence in world affairs and thus freeing us from our self-imposed, hobbling parochialism.

Unlike so many treatises dedicated to the subject of international education, this publication is short on rhetoric and long on practical, realizable examples. It is, in brief, a case study book unlike any other in the field, and is intended to provide university administrators, international educators, governmental personnel, foundations, and others with an in-depth look at seventeen quite different models of structuring international activities on a campus. These approaches have been tested and have proved workable—that is their ultimate virtue. The reader is not subjected to an abstract survey and should not expect that all possible options are treated here. What is more useful than any abstract array of catalog samplings is the fact that the institution itself is the focus; moreover, each chapter has been designed to provide essentially the same categories of information, so that the reader can examine historical evolution, organizational structure, funding problems, and programmatic components in a variety of models. As a consequence each case may be read in its entirety, or a particular phenomenon such as administrative organization may be cross-referenced. For committed readers, then, who wish to design a meaningful international program in their own institutional settings, this book is of the "how to" variety. It will save such readers the trouble of reinventing the wheel, no matter how unusual the materials they have been provided with.

Indeed, colleges and universities are not alike, a fact which the structure of this study amply demonstrates. Three types of institutions are treated, first in an overview statement, then by example: state universities, private colleges and universities, and community colleges. In each section the reader will find both comparisons and contrasts.

One commonality, refreshing in its honesty, is the specific enunciation of strengths and weaknesses related to establishing and maintaining an effective international program. The "bottom line" for success is clear, namely that an institution must have an authentic commitment to the task at hand, someone in charge, a visible international office, and a very determined faculty. If top institutional officials are uninvolved, and if the faculty is lukewarm, the structure flawed, and the funding inadequate, the odds against educational innovation are extremely high.

Finally, no one institution possesses in equal balance all the common ingredients in an international program: foreign students; student exchanges; study abroad programs; faculty exchanges; faculty development opportunities; English-language teaching facilities; campus-based international activities; outreach projects; and development assistance programs. Rather, each institution has its own ethos, history, professional and financial resources, and most likely several if not all of the ingredients listed above. For determined educators at many of these institutions, there *is* a will to serve this nation's pressing need for a greater number of globally literate citizens and future leaders. For these very critical educators, there is now a first-rate guide to successful international programming— *Approaches to International Education*. It is a most worthwhile text whose time has certainly come, and whose utility is clearly apparent.

Dr. Rose Lee Hayden
Executive Director
National Council on Foreign
    Language and International Studies

About the Contributors

Earl L. Backman currently serves as director of the Center for International Studies at the University of North Carolina at Charlotte. He is the author of numerous articles and papers about international education, a recipient of more than forty grants, and a frequent consultant to institutions of higher learning as well as private and public educational associations and agencies.

Barbara B. Burn is presently director of international programs at the University of Massachusetts at Amherst, and formerly the executive director of the President's Commission on Foreign Languages and International Studies. She is the author of *Expanding the International Dimension of Higher Education* (1980) and numerous other works on international exchanges, foreign students, and higher education.

Maryélise Suffern Lamet serves as overseas study coordinator for the International Programs Office at the University of Massachusetts at Amherst.

Raymond L. Cravens is professor of government and former dean of public service and international programs at Western Kentucky University. He also currently serves as president of the Kentucky Council for International Education.

Edward Baum is associate professor of political science and former associate provost for international studies at Ohio University. He was one of the founders of the National Committee of International Studies and Program Administrators (NCISPA), serving as its chairman from 1978 to 1980, and is a frequent consultant to the US Department of Education.

John V. Lombardi serves as dean of international programs and is a professor of history at Indiana University. He is the author of six books, including *Venezuela: The Search for Order, the Dream of Progress;* the recipient of more than ten grants and fellowships; and a frequent contributor to books on Venezuela and Latin American history.

Joseph Jones is dean of the graduate school and director of international programs at Texas Southern University. He was been awarded several grants in international studies and is actively involved in training projects overseas.

Thomas A. Breslin is the former associate dean of international affairs at Florida International University. He is the author of several articles in the field of Asian studies, as well as a book entitled *China, American Catholicism, and the Missionary* (Pennsylvania State University Press, 1980).

Thomas E. Gouttierre is the director of international studies and programs at the University of Nebraska at Omaha (UNO). He previously served as executive director of the Afghan-American Educational Commission in Kabul, Afghanistan.

Jeana Dunn McKinney is director of international student services at Warren Wilson College and has served as chairperson for Region VII of the National Association for Foreign Student Affairs. She is active in Partners of the Americas and serves on their board of directors in North Carolina.

Joseph V. Navari is director of international programs and adjunct professor of history at Linfield College. He is active in the National Association of Foreign Student Affairs and has received both a Fulbright-Hayes Fellowship and a DAAD Research Fellowship in Germany.

Lewis M. Hoskins is professor emeritus of history and former director of international programs at Earlham College (1962–1981). He has had extensive overseas experience, particularly in China and Africa.

Richard B. Rosen is a professor of history and director of the Development Office, and was formerly director of international studies at Utica College of Syracuse. A recipient of several grants, he also is active professionally in the Association for Asian Studies.

Kenneth W. Stein is an assistant professor of Near Eastern history and director of the International Studies Center at Emory University. He has written numerous scholarly articles concerning Palestinian Arab society during and after the Mandate and contributed frequent articles on contemporary Middle Eastern history and politics. He is presently the executive director and moderator of a semimonthly public television program in Georgia entitled *"World in Review."*

Mordechai Rozanski is a former assistant professor of Asian history and director of the Office of International Education at Pacific Lutheran University. He currently serves as director of international education at Adelphi University. He has received more than a dozen grants in international education, is a frequent consultant to universities and colleges, and has written many articles on China and Asian history.

G. Elisabet Bailey serves as director of international studies and instructor of speech at Pima Community College at Tucson, Arizona. She has been awarded international grants from the Department of Education and is involved in developing outreach programs for the international business community.

Lynda Icochea is an associate professor of Spanish language and literature, as well as director of the Center for International Studies at Bergen Community College in Paramus, New Jersey. As a Hispanic-Indian, she serves as a consultant for many civic and educational groups.

Howard A. Berry currently serves as coordinator of the International College at Rockland Community College. A frequent consultant on international education, he has considerable overseas experience both as an administrator and a consultant.

Introduction

A nation's welfare depends in large measure on the intellectual and psychological strengths that are derived from perceptive visions of the world beyond its own boundaries. On a planet shrunken by the technology of instant communications, there is little safety behind a Maginot Line of scientific and scholarly insolationism. In our schools and colleges as well as in our public media of communications, and in the everyday dialogue within our communities, the situation cries out for a better comprehension of our place and our potential in a world that, though it still expects much from America, no longer takes American supremacy for granted.[1]

The late twentieth-century world into which college and university students are graduating is becoming increasingly international. During the past two decades the United States has been involved in world problems that have previously appeared, on the surface, irrelevant to American growth and prosperity. If the United States is to meet the challenges outlined in the Report of the President's Commission on Foreign Language and International Studies, we must alter our thinking. World problems such as trade relations, the allocation and conservation of resources, overpopulation, hunger, environmental quality, energy, poverty, lack of adequate communication, inflation, and the quest for peace all require international solutions.

Education in the United States must have a strong international dimension in today's increasingly interdependent world. As Tonkin and

Edwards (1981) state, every citizen, not just the international specialists, must understand how our local and national concerns relate to the larger world and how present-day realities dictate a harmonizing of our own aspirations with those of other nations and peoples. The democratic principles of consent has always made it essential that Americans understand what they are voting for. Only if we have an informed citizenry can we induce our leaders to follow a wise course in their dealings with the rest of the globe. Today, when a military command can trigger the destruction of our entire civilization and when both local and national decisions have a strong impact on the world beyond our own boundaries, it is imperative that the public better understand what values and what human necessities are at stake in our foreign relations and in our international conduct.[2]

With advanced technology, everyday events in any nation can directly affect another nation; each has become an interrelated part of a world society. Therefore, citizens of all nations need to understand their citizenship in relation to global concerns as well as to local or national issues.

The world has changed radically during the past thirty years; if Americans are to cope with the changing environment, the higher education community should—in fact, *must*—take the lead in developing international education programs. Students, faculty members, and staff, as well as the local community, need the opportunity to understand and experience the interaction of our society with other societies.

The field of international education (broadly defined to include international studies, global education, foreign language study, exchanges, study abroad, area studies, comparative education, and the like) no longer finds itself at the receiving end of large public and private disbursements. Massive federal assistance, significant state resources, and benevolent private support will not in the near future be allocated for the development of international programs at institutions of higher learning. Minimal funding, moral support, and great encouragement from institutional leaders may be the most that can be expected in the 1980s. Therefore the question is: How does an institution of higher learning that commits itself to international education on campus use its existing resources to best advantage?

Many other questions remain. How can an institution promote initially the idea of a program in international education? What local resources can be adduced? Where can an institution find assistance in planning its program? By what means can existing academic units work together in creating a new international program? To such questions outside consultants, institutional associations, and federal agencies sometimes provide answers. But more often than not, their advice is insufficient or inappropriate to specific institutional needs. Therefore, administrators and faculty members become frustrated with the many problems that obstruct the development of an international commitment. Happily, however, some institutions of all kinds have managed to put all the pieces together, define their institutional goals and objectives, put into place a structure that fits their particular needs, and, through a combination of methods, support international activities. This book describes in detail seventeen different case studies on how campuses can successfully institutionalize an international commitment.

Approaches to International Education appears at a time when a number of other books on international education have recently been published. Some of these offer a well-detailed rationale for the inclusion of international programs in the curriculum (Tonkin and Edwards, 1981); others are oriented toward developing international education specifically at the secondary level (Becker, 1979); while still others describe national trends and seek to define ways of instituting international programs at colleges and international universities (Burn, 1980).[3] Some books, such as *The Tongue-Tied American* (Simon, 1980), focus on a specific aspect of international education, while others, such as Harari's latest book, *Internationalizing the Curriculum on the Campus* (1981), are designed to assist institutions in assessing their degree of commitment to international education and to present practical guidelines in developing an international program. These books have significantly heightened institutional awareness of the need for commitment to international education; in the broadest sense, they present the various components of such a commitment.

However, the present book is the first truly practical text on how to establish international programs. It incorporates the specific detail that administrators need. Its major purpose is to answer fundamental questions about developing an international program and at the same time to provide tested models of development. While examining in detail seventeen different approaches to "internationalizing" a campus, readers can determine what aspects of a particular model are pertinent for their institution.

Although this book is a case study of several approaches, it is emphatically not a survey of international education. It makes no attempt to present the seventeen most ideal or successful international models in the United States. The programs included were not selected (nor are they held up) as the only appropriate models for emulation. Quite the contrary; scores of other institutions have developed ways to strengthen the international dimension on their respective campuses. However, the institutions of higher education selected for this book have firmly committed themselves to international education. These institutions have designated someone to be responsible for coordinating international education, and they have each established a visible international office with a defined list of responsibilities. On the other hand, they differ considerably in the actual coordination of international education on their campuses. Some have highly centralized programs whereby all international activities are coordinated through a central office. Others have a highly decentralized approach in which one office handles curriculum, another foreign student advising, a third exchange programs, etc. It is important to note that there is no single approach that is ideal for every type of institution. The case studies presented in this book are drawn from community colleges, small private colleges, and private universities, as well as small, medium, and large state universities.

Each international program described addresses similar issues so that comparisons may be drawn. For example, readers from a community college can closely examine three different approaches to developing an international program at a two-year institution. Furthermore, because each chapter contains the same kind of analysis, readers can focus on a single area to see how various institutions treat that issue. For instance, all chapters discuss the structure of an international program; and thus an institution in the process of developing an international program can examine seventeen different ways such a program might be organized. Each chapter contains most or all of the following elements: a brief institutional description; a brief historical account of the development of the international program; a discussion of organization and an organizational chart, if available; a statement of mission or an articulation of commitment to international education; a detailed program description; an analysis of the strengths and weaknesses of this institutional approach; and a strategy for the 1980s.

The raison d'etre for this book is to help institutions of higher education develop appropriate international education programs. To accomplish this goal, those institutions that have made international commitments share the keys to their success. In all seventeen models presented in this book, two criteria for success exist: an institutional commitment from the highest administrative officers and a determined faculty willing to internationalize the curriculum. Although other factors are certainly important as well, without administrative commitment and commitment from faculty leadership total institutional efforts are unlikely to succeed. The case for an international component in American education has been made time and time again. Yet relatively few institutions have made the necessary commitment required to educate and train future leaders about the world in which they will find themselves. If American students are to live in an international world, their education must have an international perspective. The goal of this book is to assist colleges and universities in the United States in accomplishing this task.

Earl L. Backman

Notes

1. *Strength Through Wisdom: A Critique of U.S. Capability. A Report to the President from the President's Commission on Foreign Language and International Studies* (Washington, DC: US Government Printing Office, 1979), p. 2.
2. Humphrey Tonkin and Jane Edwards, *The World in the Curriculum* (New Rochelle, NY: Change Magazine Press, 1981), p. 6.
3. See James M. Becker, ed., *Schooling for a Global Age* (New York: McGraw-Hill, 1979); and Barbara B. Burn, *Expanding the International Dimension of Higher Education* (San Francisco: Jossey-Bass, 1980).

Approaches to International Education

PART I

State Universities

STATE-SUPPORTED UNIVERSITIES have been the driving force in international education at postsecondary institutions. Although international activities at some institutions date back to the 1900s, the major push for international involvement at state universities began after World War II. For example, Michigan State University, long recognized as one of the few large American universities with an effective centralized international program, has for twenty-five years made a commitment to international education. The concern of higher education over international awareness and understanding developed after 1945, as did public concern for international affairs. After World War II, the United States could no longer consider itself geographically isolated and was deeply involved in rebuilding economies of war-damaged countries. At the same time, however, state-supported universities were ill-prepared to "produce" the needed experts in languages, cultures, and politics of other nations.

The unique role that the United States played in the late 1940s was a positive factor in the development of international programs, particularly at major state universities. Two other factors contributed significantly to the growth in international activities. The first was the expanding role of universities in developmental assistance. Several large institutions entered into contracts in the early 1950s with the Federal Operations Administration, and after 1960 with the Agency for International Development. Throughout the 1960s and the 1970s, universities have played a key role in the US development assistance plan. Title XII of the Foreign Assistance Act of 1975, for example, was designed to encourage American agricultural universities to work collaboratively with less developed countries in solving problems of hunger and inadequate agricultural production.

1

The impact of this developmental assistance on the part of many state universities, particularly the agricultural institutions, has been felt in several ways on campuses. Faculty members have been engaged for several years in conducting research and contributing assistance abroad, activities resulting in a new cadre of experts with language ability and a knowledge of the cultures and politics of less-developed countries. Developmental assistance has meant money for institutional growth, and furthermore it has stimulated research in agricultural sciences, fostered faculty exchange, and brought thousands of foreign students and scholars to US institutions.

A second factor instrumental in the growth of international activities was the support given to develop international and area studies. Initiated through private foundations such as Carnegie, Rockefeller, and Ford, new thrusts were made by many institutions to train and educate Americans in the knowledge of other countries and geographic areas. Throughout the 1950s and 1960s support was given to launch area studies programs, provide advanced graduate training and doctoral fellowships, and stimulate language instruction.

Following the launch of Sputnik, the federal government, under the National Defense Act of 1958 (title VI of NDEA), supported area studies centers and foreign language programs. Although the government allocated less money per year for this program than did the Ford Foundation ($11 million and $18 million, respectively), it nevertheless awarded almost $230 million during its first twenty years. Title VI was designed to create a resource base of specialists in languages and area studies and to update knowledge of geographical areas of the world; by 1970 more than a hundred area studies centers were operating at universities across the country.

Although the NDEA title VI centers have significantly affected doctorate-granting institutions (one of the five types of institutions listed in the taxonomy developed by the Carnegie Commission on Higher Education), they have had little impact on comprehensive universities (753 institutions that award few or no doctoral degrees, have master's programs, and offer at least one professional program in addition to liberal arts). All but one area study program financed by the federal government have been located at a doctorate-granting institution. Of equal significance to comprehensive state universities (although much smaller in scope) have been undergraduate international studies programs, which support curricular changes in general education. These federally supported programs were initiated from the 1972 title VI amendments. Since 1972 more than a hundred awards have been made to strengthen international studies and foreign languages at the undergraduate level.

Support for international activities has also affected small- and medium-sized state universities. The greatest impact has been on curriculum, with new international courses added, existing courses revised, and interdisciplinary approaches developed. Faculty development activities (for example, workshops, institutes, release time, and travel) have also been strongly endorsed.

Postwar support from private foundations and the federal government for international programs has encouraged the growth of such efforts at state universities. As significant as this support has been, it has greatly eroded during the past five to ten years. Ford Foundation support ended in the early 1970s, and appropriations by the federal government for title VI have never closely approximated the authorized level of $75 million. The various programs of title VI have not only lost ground as a result of inflation, but have also been reduced in real dollars. Even less money would be available if Congress heeded the requests of the administration. The prognosis for increased federal support of international activities is not promising. In 1981 the allocation for title VI was $28 million (the highest level achieved); by 1982 it had fallen to $26.8 million (because the citizens' education amendment of 1976, designed to promote international awareness in communities, was not funded); and the administration recommended a budget of $12.6 million for fiscal year 1983. Under this proposed budget, no new grants for developing programs in international and foreign language studies—grants for undergraduate programs— would be made. In addition, the number of national centers receiving grants would be reduced to fifty in 1983–84 and fellowship awards would be cut from 905 to 330. Although Congress did not support the proposals of the administration and decided instead to appropriate additional funds, reliance on federal funding for international programs will continue to be risky at best.

The first section of this book presents eight case studies of international programs located at state-supported institutions. In light of reduced support from private foundations and the federal government, these models present a good case for a balanced financial base. More importantly, they argue for strong institutional commitment and a diversified programing focus. The institutions discussed are in many ways typical of midsized comprehensive universities and large doctorate-granting institutions. They were selected because of their extensive commitment to international education and because their approach, in part, can be replicated by similar institutions.

The international program at the *University of North Carolina at Charlotte* began in the early 1970s, but was not institutionalized until 1975 with the creation of the Center for International Studies. It represents a highly centralized approach at a midsized university. The activities sponsored by the coordinating unit include: foreign students, intensive English language training, study abroad, academic programs, faculty development, student and faculty exchange, community outreach, and campus programing. A highly diversified funding base, strong institutional commitment, and a high percentage of faculty participation characterize this program.

Increasing foreign student enrollment and overseas study abroad programs provided the impetus for the establishment of the International Programs Office at the *University of Massachusetts at Amherst*. With strong support from the president's office, this institution of 25,000 students made a strong commitment to centralizing and coordinating international activities. The University of Massachusetts at Amherst illustrates how a large university can create an independent unit to administer international programs without threatening existing academic and service units. Eight major functions are coordinated through one central office: foreign student services, overseas study and exchange programs, work and travel advising, overseas fellowship/scholarship services, campus awareness programs, community outreach, faculty involvement, and development of the international component in all programs. Strengths of the international program at this university include solid support throughout the institution, a long tradition of international involvement, and positive links with other university administration units.

The international program at *Western Kentucky University* illustrates a commitment that evolved from an area focus. In the late 1960s the university developed an interdisciplinary Latin American studies program, followed by a certification program in 1969 and a minor in Latin American Studies in 1971. By 1976 a Latin American Studies Center had been established and designated as a language and area studies center by the US Office of Education. Concurrent with this focus was the development of an emphasis designed to infuse international content into general education course offerings. A grant from the Office of Education's undergraduate strengthening program launched this effort. From the momentum of these two efforts came study abroad programs, exchange programs, international projects involving technical assistance, and greater centralization of the total institutional effort for international programs.

The fourth case study describes the twenty-year evolution of the Center for International Studies at *Ohio University*. As early as the 1950s the institution was involved in successful education development projects in cooperation with the US International Cooperation Administration. Out of these early efforts arose three area studies programs centered on Africa, Latin America, and Southeast Asia. With twenty-six agreements involving research, contracts, exchanges, or staff development with overseas institutions as well as study abroad, foreign students, and academic courses, the international effort at Ohio University is best described as a decentralized model, with coordination provided by an associate provost for international programs. At this institution international education is the responsibility of *all* academic units.

Guiding the international activities at *Indiana University* are four basic principles: (1) The key to successful international studies is a committed and expert faculty; (2) an incentive system rewards faculty for developing external support for international program activity; (3) disciplinary excellence keeps academic departments as the organizational bedrock of the institution; and (4) the university's responsibility to international studies is best discharged by the auxiliary enterprises that encourage and facilitate the development of the faculty's international interests. As a result, Indiana University has developed seven area studies programs, five of which have been awarded national resource center status by the Department of Education. A combination of a centralized and decentralized approach, this model is quite effective at a large multicampus university.

Texas Southern University, a predominantly black institution in Houston, has tailored its international program to the specific mission of the institution. Through a concentration in African studies, Caribbean studies, and Latin American studies, the institutional commitment of TSU has evolved to include an Office of International Programs, an unusually large international student population, and a large corps of faculty members with international training and experience. A major issue of current concern is the heavy reliance on federal support, not an enviable position in the 1980s. However, TSU does represent a noteworthy approach to international education—developing an institutional commitment inherent in the university's mission, and building upon the strengths of the faculty.

Florida International University, the newest of the institutions included in this book, has made a major commitment to international programs in a very short time. With a strong program emphasis on Latin America, more than a thousand international students, a well-developed program in English as a second language, and an institutionally appropriated budget of more than $250,000 annually, the International Affairs Center (IAC) at FIU is in an excellent position to expand its activities. Florida International represents a model program that has made a conscious decision to focus on one geographic area, but at the same time infuses all departments with this commitment. Cooperative programing among the IAC, the College of Arts and Sciences, and the School of Education has been a key ingredient in successful grant applications to the US Department of Education, in a highly successful program in English as a second language, a Global Awareness Program, and the introduction of major curricular change through addition of new languages and international courses.

The Office of International Studies and Programs at the *University of Nebraska at Omaha* was established in 1974 as a direct result of the institution's commitment to Afghanistan Studies. UNO's international effort represents a model with an area studies focus that began by providing an institutional base for the Afghanistan Studies Association

(ASA). What evolved is the most comprehensive resource center on Afghanistan in the Western Hemisphere. Structural changes made possible the merging of Afghanistan Studies with International Studies and Programs. New components included an undergraduate major, an intensive English language program, exchange programs, and community outreach. The international effort at the University of Nebraska at Omaha is indicative of what hard work, institutional commitment, and dedication to a concept can achieve.

The eight academic institutions discussed vary considerably in size, location, and mission. While the organizational model for each international program differs, as does each focus, all have developed successfully because of a strong institutional commitment that encourages cooperative international efforts across departmental lines. Their success can be attributed also to faculty involvement, diverse funding sources, and creative and imaginative leadership.

CHAPTER 1

The University of North Carolina at Charlotte

EARL L. BACKMAN

International understanding and language proficiency have become essential in an independent world, where each country's survival depends on its ability to understand and cooperate with other nations. Issues of peace, economics, and global harmony hinge on the strengthening of ties among people of diverse cultures.[1]

The guiding principle of the Center for International Studies of the University of North Carolina at Charlotte is: "Strengthening our awareness through the understanding of others." Accordingly, the Center has sought to develop a comprehensive program designed to strengthen international awareness both on and off campus.

The University and the Community

The University of North Carolina at Charlotte (UNCC) campus is located ten miles north of the largest urban center in the Carolinas—Charlotte, a city of more than 300,000 people and the geographic, cultural, and business center of Metrolina, a ten-county area surrounding the university.

7

UNCC currently offers forty-nine major degree options, including eleven at the master's degree level. There are twenty-six academic departments and one nondepartmental program in six colleges, each administered by a dean. The colleges at UNCC are Architecture, Arts and Sciences, Business Administration, Engineering, Human Development and Learning, and Nursing.

UNCC was created in 1965 when the North Carolina General Assembly transformed Charlotte College into a campus of the University of North Carolina. It is one of the newest and fastest-growing universities in the sixteen-campus University of North Carolina system. In 1967, 2,014 students (almost all from the Charlotte area) were enrolled in UNCC's undergraduate programs. By fall 1982, 10,200 undergraduate and graduate students were matriculated at UNCC: 9,300 from North Carolina, 520 from elsewhere in the United States, and 380 from other countries.

Faculty growth has mirrored that of students. In 1967, 116 full-time faculty members were teaching at UNCC; by 1981, the number had grown to 424 full-time and 193 part-time faculty members. Careful recruitment over the last twelve years has brought the institution a predominantly youthful faculty (52 percent are under the age of forty and only 17 percent are older than fifty).

The character of both the university and the Charlotte community has in recent years become increasingly international. The faculty expansion has resulted in a major increase in academic programs, which has been a positive influence on the development of an international studies program. The faculty has itself become more international, as reflected in part by new international courses, hiring of foreign-born faculty members (currently more than twenty), temporary assignments overseas, and new faculty exchange programs. More than eighty faculty members with a strong interest in international studies have been identified, and more than thirty faculty members travel abroad each year, many for international conferences and lecturing. Faculty members with major scholarly interests in international and global issues teach in the areas of anthropology, architecture, business administration, economics, engineering, geography, history, human development and learning, foreign languages, philosophy, political science, religious studies, and sociology.

During the last few years students' parochialism has been reduced as a result of activities sponsored by the Center for International Studies, greater opportunities for travel abroad, and the establishment of two semester abroad programs and new international courses. The UNCC student body is composed primarily of North Carolina residents, mostly from the Charlotte-Mecklenburg area or from within a radius of one hundred miles. They generally come from middle-income families and are often first-generation college students. Most work in addition to going to school. Approximately two-thirds of the students commute and spend little time on campus beyond what is required for course work. The typical student is not well traveled, possesses little knowledge of other cultures and societies, and is primarily concerned with future employment. In part, the center was established to respond to students' international education needs and to increase their international awareness, no matter what their major.

The Charlotte community is a constant support for and active participant in many of the university's international activities. Indeed, a major factor in the sustained development of an international thrust on the UNCC campus has been the ethnic diversity of the Charlotte community. Immigration during the past fifteen to twenty years has led to a foreign-born population in excess of 12,000 people from more than sixty countries. As a local newspaper article said: "Charlotte has grown from an old-time bacon and grits Southern town into a city with spicy international seasonings. . . ."[2]

More than 135 foreign firms in the Charlotte area add to the growing international climate. Some are branch offices of major overseas operations, others are American-owned subsidiaries, while still others are former US businesses that have been purchased by foreign firms. Regardless of their ownership, these businesses employ thousands of area residents, both Americans and citizens of other nations. As a result, the possibilities for linkage between the university and multinational corporations abound. Such linkages have included corporate sponsorship of programs, financial donations, employment opportunities for students, guest lecturers, and participants for university-sponsored activities.

How the International Program Was Established

The UNCC Center for International Studies has taken more than ten years to reach maturity—more than five years of planning, discussion, and review before it came into existence and another five years for it to develop fully.

ORIGIN OF THE PROGRAM

The establishment of the Center for International Studies followed a sequence of events that began in 1966 when D. W. Colvard, the newly appointed chancellor of the University of North Carolina at Charlotte, indicated in his installation address that an emerging institution such as UNCC had a major stake in providing both students and community with an international awareness. For the next several years, the institution concentrated on developing the structure needed to support an interna-

tional program. Faculty members were hired particularly for their
international focus; new courses that included an international perspective
were added; and international education symposia were sponsored.

In 1970, the first concrete step toward establishing an international
program was taken. The vice-chancellor of academic affairs at UNCC
appointed a committee of students, staff members, and faculty members
from nine departments and charged its members with the task of
developing recommendations for an international studies program.
Specifically, the committee was to develop a program to meet the
following objectives:

> to develop the international dimensions of general education in the University
> community; to better prepare students and prospective teachers for lives and
> careers in an increasingly interdependent world through acquisition of
> knowledge and understanding of the people with whom Americans share the
> planet earth; and to prepare future citizens and teachers to deal with cross-
> national problems by increasing their literacy in world affairs.[3]

By 1972, the University of North Carolina at Charlotte had issued its
first statement of institutional goals, and the institution committed itself
formally to contributing to the international understanding and intercultural sensitivity of students, faculty members, administrators, and
community leaders. Specifically, the institution's objectives were as
follows:

1. To develop student, teacher, and community exchange programs
   with specific universities and communities in foreign areas

2. To provide for the communication of a variety of thought on all
   sides of international issues

3. To encourage travel, study, and internships in foreign areas

Meanwhile, the International Studies Committee was continuing its
efforts to make specific recommendations that would help implement the
institution's goals. The committee's philosophy began to take shape and
soon reflected both an interdisciplinary and a comparative approach to
international education. Campuswide meetings were held, three outside
consultants were invited to campus to provide input, subcommittees were
established to study and make specific recommendations on several
program areas, and a final consolidated plan for the development of an
international studies program emerged.

On 1 March 1973 the International Studies Committee submitted its
final report to the vice-chancellor for academic affairs. In its formal
recommendations the committee made this statement:

Our program should afford opportunities for the development of attitudes unencumbered by the limitations of our own social and cultural orientations. The objectives of such study should be a basic understanding of man, his human condition, his potential, his privilege, and his obligation.[4]

The most important recommendations in the report called for establishing an international studies program, including an office and a director; developing a curriculum model that would allow students to have an interdisciplinary concentration in international studies in addition to meeting department requirements for the baccalaureate; expanding overseas opportunities for faculty members and students; and increasing international activities for the entire university and the Charlotte community.

The proposal was meticulously reviewed during the approval process, which took more than a year and a half:

- On 1 February 1974 the program was approved by the University Intercollege Academic Policy and Curriculum Committee with slight modifications.

- On 29 March 1974 the university senate endorsed the program.

- On 9 May 1974 after further review by the UNCC administration, the program was sent to the general administration of the University of North Carolina.

- On 3 October 1974 the vice-chancellor for academic affairs received notification from the general administration that the international studies program proposal had been approved, but no money was being appropriated.

Final authorization came on 25 August 1975 when Chancellor Colvard announced that he was establishing the Program for International Studies at UNCC, fulfilling a long-term commitment. The program was to be staffed initially by a part-time director and a secretary. In his statement, Chancellor Colvard stressed the role of the director:

Success in achieving the objectives of this program, as stated in the "1973 Report by the International Studies Committee," will depend in large part upon the cooperation between the Director of the Program for International Studies and the deans, department chairmen, and faculty. While the Director will coordinate various International Studies activities on and off campus, the successful implementation of programs will require cooperative, joint efforts by all interested parties. It is expected that the Director will work within the existing structure of the University by coordinating activities through the various colleges, departments, the Dean of Students Office, and the Institute for Urban Studies and Community Service. . . . [The director] will report to the provost on all matters relating to International Studies.[5]

PROGRAM HIGHLIGHTS

After more than five years of planning, the Program of International Studies had become a reality. With strong endorsement from the faculty and top administrative leadership, particularly the chancellor, a course was set to expand the international dimension on the campus. During the first year the program established three major thrusts designed to involve the university and the community in the development of an increased international awareness. The three thrusts, which responded to both the 1972 institutional goal statement and the 1973 International Studies Committee report, were as follows: (1) to develop an academic concentration for undergraduates; (2) to sponsor programs designed to heighten international awareness on campus; and (3) to respond to the needs of the business community.

During the first five years, the program grew rapidly, reflecting the institution's high level of commitment to international education.

1975/76

1. Seven campus events sponsored

2. First overseas summer study/travel trip conducted

3. Publication begun of *International Studies Bulletin*

4. Contributions of $8,200 raised from the business community for faculty and program development

5. Total operating budget (including personnel) of $22,500

1976/77

1. Full-time director and secretary appointed

2. Half-time position created for foreign student advisor

3. First grants received—four totaling $90,000

4. Eleven campus and community events sponsored

5. Two overseas summer study/travel trips conducted

6. Thirty-five students concentrating in international studies

7. Office moved out of administrative building to main academic complex

8. Twenty-four faculty members supported in professional development program

9. Contributions of $8,200 raised from local businesses

10. Total operating budget (including personnel) of $126,200

1977/78

1. Commitment to international studies reaffirmed through new mission and goals statement

2. First semester abroad program established

3. Five grants received totaling $122,000

4. Sixteen campus and community events sponsored

5. Five overseas summer study programs conducted

6. Advisement given to 116 foreign students and 60 students concentrating in international studies

7. Five new interdisciplinary courses developed

8. Seventeen lecturers and visiting speakers sponsored

9. Twenty-two faculty members assisted under faculty development program

10. More than $10,000 received from local businesses

11. Total operating budget (including personnel) of $166,000

1978/79

1. Program for International Studies renamed Center for International Studies

2. Three additional professional staff members and two support staff members hired

3. English Language Training Institute developed

4. Three grants received totaling $89,000

5. Advisement given to 200 foreign students and 80 students concentrating in international studies

6. Sixteen campus and community events sponsored

7. Thirteen lecturers and visiting speakers sponsored

8. Twenty faculty members assisted under the faculty development program

9. First faculty exchange program initiated

10. First student exchange program initiated

11. Seven summer travel/study programs conducted

12. Total operating budget (including personnel) of $215,000

1979/80:

1. Additional office space allocated, doubling previous amount

2. Staff size increased to seven professional staff members, six full-time support staff members, and four part-time support staff members

3. Nineteen activities sponsored on and off campus

4. Professional activities by thirty-four faculty members supported

5. Lectures by fourteen off-campus speakers sponsored

6. Eight summer programs overseas and two semester abroad programs (India and Denmark) sponsored.

7. Two faculty exchanges and four student exchange programs coordinated

8. Business contributions received totaling $13,000

9. Three grants received

10. Faculty colloquia series initiated

11. Total operating budget of $400,000 (funds from state, contributions, grants, contracts, and participant fees)

SIGNIFICANT FACTORS AFFECTING PROGRAM DEVELOPMENT

Several factors have been significant in the success of the Center for International Studies, and the most significant elements of success have also become the center's strengths. Although these factors cannot be listed in order of their priority because their roles have varied with each stage of development, they can be enumerated:

1. Major institutional commitment to international education by the institution's highest administrative officers (indicated by resource allocation, mission and goals statement, and program encouragement)

2. Strong support and endorsement by key segments of the UNCC faculty

3. Appointment of a full-time director, with mandate to develop the international program with little administrative interference (freedom to take risks)

4. Development of a dedicated and talented professional and support staff for the center

5. Opportunity to develop community programs, which in turn provide an additional resource base for the center

6. Centralized administration of all aspects of international education programs at UNCC (combined with a commitment not only to service the international educational needs of institutional units but also to increase the number of faculty members and students involved in international education programs)

7. Outside funding from grants, contributions, revenue-generating activities, and contracts

Institutional Commitment to International Education

The University of North Carolina at Charlotte is committed to providing the student body and the surrounding community with significant educational opportunities offering an international perspective—opportunities that recognize the plurality of cultures, the existence of common concerns, and the need for more effective methods of international and intercultural cooperation. Furthermore, it encourages international programs, including specialization in international studies, not only on campus but also in foreign countries.

UNCC's commitment to international studies is reflected both in the institution's goals and organizations, which pertain to its international program, and in the goals and organization of the Center for International Studies.

INSTITUTIONAL MISSION AND GOALS

In its mission statement in the academic catalog, the University of North Carolina at Charlotte "affirms the classical functions of an institution of higher education to preserve, generate, transmit and apply knowledge and understanding, and to foster and support a vital spirit of open inquiry and critical thinking." In addressing this broad mission, the university has

defined six areas of primary concern, and one of the six gives direction to
the operation of the Center for International Studies. As stated in the
Undergraduate Catalog for 1980/81:

> The University recognizes the increasing interdependence of all peoples and
> cultures and the important implications this fact holds for succeeding
> generations. Therefore, the University is committed to provide instructional,
> research and service programs which are designed to advance knowledge and
> foster understanding of intercultural differences, similarities and interdepen-
> dencies.[6]

Thus, UNCC has committed itself to fostering an increased international awareness and has expressed this commitment in the institutional
mission and goals statement.

ADMINISTRATIVE ORGANIZATION

The chancellor of the University of North Carolina at Charlotte is the
institution's chief executive officer. Reporting directly to the chancellor
are five vice-chancellors: for business affairs, student affairs, academic
affairs, research and public service, and development. The Division of
Research and Public Service was created in 1980 to give emphasis and
direction to the institution's research and outreach functions. The Center
for International Studies is located—along with the Urban Institute,
Continuing Education, Public Information and Publications, Grants and
Contracts, Public Radio, and Athletics—in the recently created Division of
Research and Public Service.

The director of the Center for International Studies reports to the vice-
chancellor for research and public service on all matters relating to the
center, for example, personnel, budget, programing, and contracts.
However, given the extensive involvement of the center, direct linkages
also exist with the other vice-chancellors. For example, on matters relating
to academic exchanges, grants for curriculum development, and overseas
programs for academic credit, approval must also be given by the vice-
chancellor for academic affairs. Frequent contact also exists with the vice-
chancellor for business affairs, whose approval is required to set up all
accounts; and the center's expenditures are audited by the Business Office
to insure compliance with state and federal regulations. All direct fund
raising by the center is coordinated with the vice-chancellor for
development.

Because of the chancellor's deep interest and involvement in
international education, the chancellor's office frequently makes direct
requests to the director of the center. Responses to these requests are
communicated directly back to the chancellor, with notification of the

request and the response to the vice-chancellor for research and public service. In this manner, the director of the center is frequently involved directly with the top administrative officials of the institution, but keeps the vice-chancellor for research and public service informed of the interactions.

Within the Division of Research and Public Service several key linkages exist. The most significant are with the director of grants and contracts, the director of continuing education, the director of public information and publicity, and the director of the Urban Institute.

As outside grants and contracts are an important source of revenue for the center, extensive contact exists between the center and the Academic Grants and Contracts Office. Not only does this office send grant leads to the center, but the center submits all contract and grant proposals to this office. The director of grants and contracts must approve the budget and review the narrative of any grant or contract proposal before it is submitted to the other appropriate administrative offices.

Of equal importance is the center's linkage with the Division of Continuing Education, for all the center's programs offered for academic credit must be approved by the appropriate academic department. No academic credit is granted by the Center for International Studies for any of its programs, including the semester-abroad programs, overseas summer programs, and specialized summer institutes held on campus. Instead, credit is awarded by the appropriate academic department and coordinated with the Division of Continuing Education. This arrangement serves to coordinate academic programs held off campus, or organized for an off-campus audience, and to assist the Division of Continuing Education because its budget is partially based on enrollment.

Public Information and Publications is another office that is important to the center's activities. As many activities sponsored by the center are open to a wide audience, publicity is crucial. The Office of Public Information is responsible for press releases and setting up media appearances. In addition, the center occasionally requests that a brochure be developed and designed by the publications staff. However, in most cases brochures are designed by center staff members with assistance in program marketing from the director of public information and publications.

The Urban Institute is important to the center because it has a similar organization and similar relationships with other campus offices, resulting in a certain kinship between the two units. As allies that are often affected in the same way by policy decisions from other administrative offices, they can together carry more weight in the decision-making process. In addition, joint research efforts focusing on urban concerns and global issues are currently being studied by the director of the Center for International Studies and the director of the Urban Institute.

Finally, college deans and department chairpersons provide important linkages with the center because they must approve (1) curriculum development projects, (2) release time for faculty involvement in center activities, (3) overseas programs for academic credit, and (4) faculty and student exchange programs. In return, the Center for International Studies often cosponsors lectures and department activities of an international nature. Requests for financial support for faculty research activities are channeled through departments and colleges to the center. Therefore, the center and deans and chairpersons all profit when the linkage is positive. The center fosters successful linkages by communicating center activities to other administrators and involving deans and department chairpersons in decisions that affect faculty members and curricula.

Thus the Center for International Studies is strategically placed within the Division of Research and Public Service, and the director of the center has considerable contact with all other key offices on campus, including the Office of the Chancellor.

GOALS AND OBJECTIVES OF THE CENTER FOR INTERNATIONAL STUDIES

The Center for International Studies at the University of North Carolina at Charlotte seeks to achieve the institutional goals and strengthen the international component of UNCC's educational programs by following these principles:

1. Assure a high place for international programs in the determination of institutional priorities

2. Encourage increasing UNCC activity in the international intellectual community by promoting the participation of faculty members and students in overseas educational programs

3. Continue support of an advisory committee composed of concerned and competent faculty members to advise on the development and operation of the Center for International Studies

4. Encourage faculty members to reexamine periodically the courses they teach, and to introduce, where appropriate, materials that will add and maintain an international dimension to the courses

5. Expand interinstitutional cooperation with foreign education institutions

6. Offer to the community programs and activities that are designed to enhance international understanding

7. Encourage the College of Human Development and Learning to include in its teacher training programs more courses that are concerned with world society, international issues, and third-world cultures

8. Encourage the enrollment of foreign students and maintain an international student program as an integral part of the educational process

To implement these principles, the Center for International Studies has set forth the following four program goals and corresponding objectives for achieving the goals:

I. To strengthen the international dimension on the UNCC campus
   A. Strengthen the academic concentration in international studies
      1. Work with departments to develop more international courses, particularly interdisciplinary courses
      2. Publicize the existence of the area of concentration and inform departments before advising that option exists
   B. Diversify the foreign student population
   C. Sponsor symposia and seminars of an international nature for students, faculty members, and staff members
   D. Provide opportunities for continuous intercultural dialogue
      1. Sponsor cultural events (festivals, displays, dinners, etc.)
      2. Develop workshops for intercultural understanding
      3. Establish an international house for foreign students and American students to live together
      4. Develop the means by which foreign students have the opportunity to be used as resource persons
   E. Develop a comprehensive faculty development program
      1. Provide funds annually to support overseas travel of faculty members, travel to present papers on an international topic, release time to develop an international course
      2. Continue monthly faculty colloquia series
      3. Assist faculty members with international travel plans
      4. Emphasize the Fulbright program to a greater degree; hold meetings with academic departments
      5. Encourage and assist departments desiring to establish a faculty exchange program
   F. Expand study-abroad programs sponsored by UNCC
      1. Increase participation in current programs
      2. Publicize resources of travel center
      3. Develop a student scholarship fund for travel/study opportunities

    4. Explore funding and financial assistance for students needing additional support

    5. Involve more faculty members in the overseas program

  G. Expand both faculty and student exchange programs

  H. Support international programing of student groups (e.g., International Club, Model United Nations, etc.)

  I. Cosponsor international programs with other departments on campus (e.g., guest speakers, cultural events, student activities, etc.)

  J. Publicize international programs and activities with brochures and newsletters

II. To strengthen services to foreign students

  A. Develop a handbook for foreign students

  B. Coordinate programs using the full resources of the institution and the community to facilitate the academic progress and personal development of foreign students

  C. Maintain the quality of students and work to attract students of a high academic caliber

  D. Expand the effectiveness of orientation programs

  E. Work with academic departments and faculty members in responding to issues that concern foreign students

  F. Provide space and location for foreign students to interact with each other and with American students

  G. Expand the effectiveness of the English Language Training Institute to:

    1. Better prepare students to enter UNCC

    2. Assist students in developing better study skills

    3. Screen students not prepared for university studies

    4. Assist in the recruitment of students to insure a diversified, international student body

    5. Provide internships to graduate students in the Department of English to reduce the burden of teaching special English Courses

III. To strengthen the international dimension in the community and the state

  A. Sponsor a public forum series on international topics of particular concern to the community

  B. Sponsor the Great Decisions Program, a lecture and discussion series on foreign policy issues, on a statewide basis

  C. Develop an international resource bank—both for and on international persons and services

  D. Begin a short-term visitor program that will bring international visitors to the university and the community

    E. Respond more fully to the international education needs of specific clienteles (e.g., international businesses, local school systems, etc.)

    F. Offer travel/study programs that are open to community members as well as faculty members and students

IV. To support and participate in cooperative programs beyond the university

    A. Participate in consortia efforts on international education programs (e.g., Charlotte Educational Consortium, Council on International Education)

    B. Cooperate with national associations committed to international education (e.g., National Association for Foreign Student Affairs, American Council on Education, American Association on State Colleges and Universities, etc.)

    C. Contract with international groups to assist them in programing (e.g., North Carolina World Trade Club, International Trade Center, Friendship Force, Metrolina Trade Club, etc.)

ORGANIZATION OF THE CENTER FOR INTERNATIONAL STUDIES

The organizational structure of the center is derived from the four major program goals. A major problem was how best to divide responsibilities among the staff members in order to take advantage of their skills and interests, while still attempting to accomplish the program's many objectives and remaining flexible enough to respond to new programing requests and grant ideas. The responsibilities and interrelationships of the professional staff members employed in the center are shown in figure 1.1.

The director, in addition to supervising and approving the activities of the other professional staff members, has several remaining major responsibilities. Of these, the most important, time consuming, and difficult is maintaining a constant flow of financial resources into the organization. Because three-quarters of all funds for the center come from outside the institution, the director's time is heavily committed to activities involving fund raising, grant writing, contract development, and the development of revenue-generating programs. In addition, the director's responsibilities include advising all students concentrating in international studies, developing exchange programs with foreign higher education institutions, maintaining an active faculty development program, and assisting in curriculum development as it relates to international studies.

Supporting the activities of the director is a secretary who serves as both administrative assistant and supervisor of all support staff members.

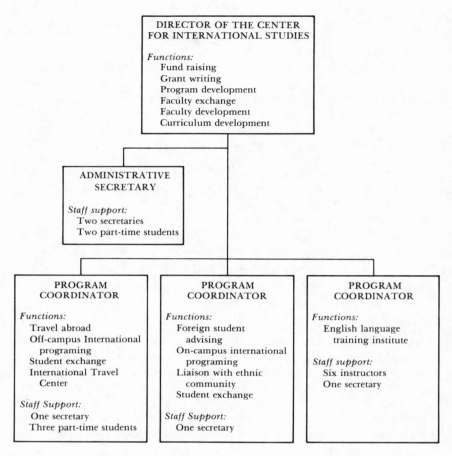

FIGURE 1.1.   Organizational chart for the Center for International Studies.

The major responsibilities of the director's administrative secretary include dispersing the work load, monitoring the status of all active programs, supervising personnel, managing the office, and making logistical arrangements for all programs. Two additional secretaries assist in meeting the responsibilities for the director and the administrative assistant. One serves as receptionist and primary typist for the director and maintains the filing system; the other maintains all financial records, disperses all funds, and handles most conference registrations.

The remaining functions of the center are divided between three program coordinators, who have a range of responsibilities. One of the coordinators serves as the travel-abroad advisor, working with interested students, monitoring the budget of overseas programs, coordinating two semester programs and from three to five summer programs each year, and handling all publicity related to these programs. In addition, this staff member supervises the International Travel Center, a major institutional resource of information on travel, study abroad, and international education. This person also works closely with the foreign student advisor on student exchanges by handling the details of American students going abroad. The other major area of responsibility for this position is programing for community groups, including seminars, institutes, workshops, symposia, and exchanges. Staff support for these responsibilities include one full-time secretary and three part-time students.

Foreign student advising constitutes the major responsibility of the second program coordinator. Specifically, this staff member is charged with issuing appropriate immigration documents, foreign student orientation, student counseling, maintaining all records on the international student body, and advising on the admission of new foreign students. This individual also has other key tasks such as serving as liaison with the ethnic communities in Charlotte, working with foreign students affiliated with exchange efforts, developing and administering program activities sponsored by the center for on-campus groups, and serving as advisor to the International Club.

The remaining professional staff member is the coordinator of the English Language Training Institute (ELTI). Specifically, the tasks of this position include recruiting and publicity, program development, curriculum development, hiring of instructors, and all administrative details related to ELTI. This staff member works closely with the foreign student advisor in preparing foreign students for matriculation into UNCC. In addition, this individual is responsible for ELTI staff development, coordinating summer institutes designed for specific foreign groups who need either additional language training or training to teach English to non-English speakers, and marketing the ELTI program in specific parts of the world. Six instructors and one full-time secretary assist in carrying out these responsibilities.

In summary, the University of North Carolina at Charlotte has made a major commitment to international education as illustrated through its mission and goals, the creation of the Center for International Studies, and the center's guiding principles, goals, objective, and organization. These components, when combined with a faculty that is committed to international education, an administration that gives strong and active support, and outstanding community resources, have led to a highly centralized approach to international education.

Program Description

In carrying out its responsibilities as the primary coordinating administrative unit for international activities at UNCC, the Center for International

Studies has established linkages with scores of offices, groups, and organizations on campus, in the community, around the state, across the country, and overseas. The range and diversity of the center's activities reflect the many ways the center attempts to meet the needs of all its clienteles.

PROGRAM COMPONENTS

The center has established ten major program areas for meeting the international educational needs of the university and the community.

Academic Concentration in International Studies. The device of an academic concentration allows undergraduate students to pursue an interdisciplinary study of foreign cultures while they fulfill the requirements for a major in an approved degree program. The international studies program permits students to choose from a wide array of subjects and encourages course work in modern foreign languages, humanities, social sciences, and international economics and business.

A program of study fulfilling the international studies option may be organized by topic, such as world population, poverty, violence, or the future of war or of peace; by geographic area, such as the Soviet Union, Western Europe, Africa, Asia, or Latin America; or by historical period, such as ancient, medieval, or modern.

Students seeking a concentration in international studies must also fulfill general degree requirements and requirements for a selected major. Students in all majors are eligible to participate in the international studies concentration. The international studies program requires participants to complete successfully a minimum of eight courses selected from a list of approved international courses in at least three departments outside their major. Students plan their program with department advisors and the director of the Center for International Studies. Transcripts of students who satisfactorily complete the program bear the description, "Concentration in International Studies."

Foreign Student Services. UNCC encourages the admission of foreign students as part of its commitment to international education. Aside from the obvious reason of making educational opportunities open to all who can benefit, a major justification for admitting foreign students is that their presence on campus contributes significantly to the educational experience of American students. Contact between American and foreign students often results in cross-cultural communication and an increasing awareness of the world beyond the boundaries of state and nation. However, the university must provide the services that will assist the foreign student in realizing academic, personal, and social goals.

UNCC's commitment to increasing the foreign student population on campus is reflected in three ways: (1) a growth in numbers as indicated by a 1975 foreign student population of 35 and a 1982 population of 380; (2) establishment of the English Language Training Institute; and (3) development of the student services office within the Center for International Studies. This office provides services that are designed to respond to a diverse foreign student population with special needs in areas such as immigration, language, and cultural understanding. Its main focus is the needs of UNCC academic students and English Language Training Institute students who have student visas, but its services are also available to any foreign student, including refugees and students who do not have student visas. Major programs include the following:

1. Orientation before and after arrival

2. Individual counseling and advice on academic, personal, and career questions

3. Liaison with campus and community services related to student needs: health, financial aid, student activities, housing

4. Academic liaison

5. Immigration

6. Special programs such as host families and community involvement activities

Study Abroad and Student Exchange Programs. The President's Commission on Foreign Language and International Studies called for institutions of higher education to establish study abroad programs for American students and to develop student exchange programs. These objectives have been, and continue to be, a major focus of the Center for International Studies, and students at UNCC therefore have the opportunity to participate in the following:

1. Semester or academic-year programs in Copenhagen, Denmark, in the areas of architecture, international business, and general studies

2. Fall Semester in India offered in cooperation with Davidson College

3. Holiday programs to the Caribbean offered during semester breaks

4. Summer study programs offered around the world in a variety of disciplines

5. Semester or summer programs offered by one of the other member institutions of the University of North Carolina

6. Approved programs sponsored by institutions outside North Carolina

Another opportunity for overseas study is participation in a student exchange program. Current options include the Nursing Exchange, a three-week group exchange with Great Britain; the College and University Partnership Program (CUPP), a group exchange with Japan; and the International Student Exchange Program (ISEP), a worldwide exchange designed to fit the interests of individual participants.

International Travel Center. This resource center is operated for students, faculty members, staff members, and the Charlotte community. Center staff members are available for advising, and books, pamphlets, and maps may be borrowed for individual use. Travel Center holdings include information on study abroad, financial aid, work abroad, international travel, and sources of funding in international education. It also carries general reading on international topics, international journals, and filmstrips on international topics. The center is an official issuing agent for International Student Identity Cards and Youth Hostel Cards.

Campus Programing. Annual and one-time events are sponsored both independently and in cooperation with other departments and agencies:

1. Annual International Festival, a one-day event featuring display booths that accent various aspects of the many ethnic communities of Charlotte, including ethnic foods and dances and an international buffet dinner

2. International Film Festival, a week of theme-related films representing various nationalities

3. International Club, a primarily campus-oriented organization sponsoring a variety of international activities

4. Foreign student vacation/study programs and summer institutes, programs planned in cooperation with international agencies in order to provide foreign visitors with a variety of academic, cultural, and social experiences

5. Programs addressing both foreign and American student concerns: e.g., lecturers, Model United Nations, food day

6. Faculty Colloquia, a series of guest lecturers and receptions on a variety of international topics

7. International Dinners, a series of dinners sponsored by the International Club and focusing on ethnic cuisines

English Language Training Institute. This program of intensive English language instruction is for foreign students who are eligible for UNCC admission but need to improve their language and study skills.

Classes are taught by faculty members trained in language teaching and experienced in working with foreign students.

The curriculum is divided into three levels of proficiency—advanced, intermediate, and basic—and is designed for a systematic progression in reading, aural comprehension, and oral and written expression. The program is based on a fifteen-week (one semester) schedule meeting four days a week for five hours a day. Laboratory work is an integral part of the program.

A special program, the "Advanced 50" Program, is designed for exceptionally able students. It permits limited academic work along with advanced English language courses. Students must have already passed one full semester in ELTI to be considered for Advanced 50.

The English Language Training Institute conducts other language training programs including summer institutes of specially designed programs for student and teacher groups and limited-English programs such as conversational English for summer short-term foreign visitors.

Public Service Programs. The center seeks to initiate and respond to the international education needs and interests of the community. Programs designed for an off-campus clientele include the following:

1. Community Forum, an annual fall symposium on international topics of current interest

2. Great Decisions, an annual two-month series of lectures and discussions on eight key policy issues

3. International Business Workshops, programs focusing on specific aspects of international trade, such as letters of credit, custom regulations, international marketing, documentation, and foreign trade zone

4. Friendship Force, an annual community exchange between citizens of Charlotte and a foreign city

5. Community-based programs having an international focus, including the Host Family Program for foreign students, the Bilingual Education Program in the Charlotte-Mecklenburg schools, Sister Cities International, and the International Information Center

6. Summer Institutes for local social studies teachers, three- to four-week summer programs designed to facilitate the teaching of third-world cultures at the elementary and secondary level

7. Services for international information and program development

Although many activities are designed for both the university and the community (for example, the International Festival, the International Film

Festival, the Summer Travel Programs, and the Great Decisions Program), other activities are aimed at a specific off-campus clientele (for example, the International Business Seminars and the Institutes for Social Studies Teachers). In addition, the center's commitment to fostering an increased international awareness in the community is reflected by staff participation in the following: the International Committee of the YWCA, the International Trade Task Force of the Charlotte Chamber of Commerce, the Charlotte Sister Cities program, the Bilingual Education Program, the Organization of Charlotte's Ethnic Communities, and so forth. One outgrowth has been increased support by international business firms and a strong liaison with the local media.

Curriculum Development. The Center for International Studies strongly advocates the development of courses that (1) provide students with an increased sensitivity to cross-cultural similarities and differences, (2) examine key global issues and the implications facing mankind if these concerns are not addressed, (3) describe the importance of international events and issues to the United States and its people, and (4) integrate the use of foreign languages in understanding other peoples.

As part of this commitment, the center allocates a modest amount of money each year to increase the international aspects of undergraduate education. Emphasis is placed on assisting faculty members in developing an international dimension for an existing course, adding a new international course, or teaching an interdisciplinary course that is either international or contains an international component. Support rendered by the center usually takes place in one of the following ways: (1) support during the summer to develop or revise a course, (2) support for researching overseas to gain necessary information needed in a course, (3) release time during a semester, or (4) support for a visiting scholar, a faculty member from a foreign higher education institution. Grants continue to provide the major sources of funding for these activities.

Faculty Exchanges. Faculty members at UNCC are encouraged to work with the center staff in exploring and applying for a wide range of international exchange opportunities, including the Senior Fulbright Program, reciprocal departmental exchanges (for example, the exchange program between the Department of Psychology at UNCC and Sterling University in Scotland), and exchanges based on agreements between UNCC and a foreign institution of higher learning (for example, exchanges between UNCC and the University of Veracruz, Mexico, and between UNCC and National Kaoshiung Teacher's College, Republic of China).

Faculty members are assisted in a variety of ways by the center's staff. First, interested faculty members are informed about existing opportunities. Second, the center handles a substantial number of the logistical arrangements that relate to foreign travel. Thirdly, center staff members are often called on by departments to assist in establishing exchange agreements with foreign institutions. Fourth, a portion of faculty travel costs is shared by the center. (The actual amount varies with the total expenditure.) Finally, visiting faculty members are assisted with housing, visas, travel arrangements, and so forth.

In this manner, the center serves to facilitate faculty exchanges, which are an essential ingredient in "internationalizing" the campus. There is a special need to continue encouraging both young faculty members and older faculty members at UNCC to develop expertise in international matters. By continuing to develop exchange opportunities, making faculty members aware of the exchange possibilities, and recognizing the value of international activities in the faculty reward system, UNCC will benefit substantially.

Faculty Development. The faculty development program of the Center for International Studies supports not only curriculum development and faculty exchanges but many faculty requests for financial assistance in traveling to international conferences and for support of expenses related to research projects overseas. From twenty to thirty faculty members are assisted annually by the center for one of these reasons.

Another form of faculty development is the center's faculty colloquia series. Various international issues, research projects, or overseas trips are discussed in a faculty forum. In addition to presentations by UNCC faculty members, visiting lecturers often participate in the colloquia series.

Faculty development is a key ingredient in strengthening UNCC's international dimension. Funds for this activity are currently not drawn from state appropriations. Future expansion in the international faculty development program will necessitate additional funding, some of which must be appropriated by the state.

FACULTY INVOLVEMENT IN THE PROGRAM

Although the Center for International Studies coordinates UNCC's international activities, it has no faculty of its own and must use faculty members from the institution's academic departments. Good relationships between the center and the departments are not only beneficial but essential.

Faculty involvement with the center and its sponsored activities can take place in a variety of ways. First, faculty members attend events, forums, seminars, and conferences as both participants and resource persons. When they serve as resource persons they are usually well compensated, a circumstance that increases the pool of faculty members the center can draw on.

Second, the International Studies Advisory Committee, composed of faculty members interested in international education, is of key importance to center programing. Its primary purpose is to provide direction, gather support for events, and staff specific ad hoc committees to work on a particular event or grant proposal.

Third, faculty members are often involved in the center's faculty development program or a curriculum development project. Fourth, sometimes a faculty member must be borrowed for a semester or a year to work on a long-range project, an occurrence likely to happen even more often in the future. For instance, a faculty member in the Department of Political Science was released from teaching responsibilities for one semester to assist in the coordination of the North Carolina Great Decisions Program, a lecture and discussion series for the community. Faculty members also sometimes serve as project directors. Primary leadership for the summer abroad programs is derived from faculty members released from on-campus teaching responsibilities.

Finally, faculty members serve the center's goals by publicizing certain activities and recruiting for programs such as the English Language Training Institute. When faculty members are overseas, they are often called upon to visit specific offices and institutions in order to leave written material on the institution and its programs. Some of UNCC's best foreign students have been recruited in this manner.

COMMUNITY LINKAGES

UNCC's Center for International Studies is closely linked with many off-campus constituencies. Figure 1.2 identifies the constituencies both on and off campus for UNCC's international education activities.

In the local community, the center has made an effort to reach out to groups requesting programs and activities. Specifically, the business community and local school systems have been the target of a number of programs. Several times a year one- and two-day seminars are held for businesses engaged in international trade and finance. Topics include letters of credit, documentation, foreign trade zone, international marketing, custom regulations, and other matters. Local school teachers participate in sponsored summer programs designed to provide information on the teaching of non-Western cultures. In addition, most of the local school districts also participate in the center's Great Decisions Program, an eight-week program presenting information on foreign policy issues facing the United States.

Another, rather diverse, constituency served by the center is the ethnic communities of Charlotte. The foreign student advisor works with these groups and assists them in adjusting to a new culture. These groups assist the center by participating in events like the international festival and by providing translators.

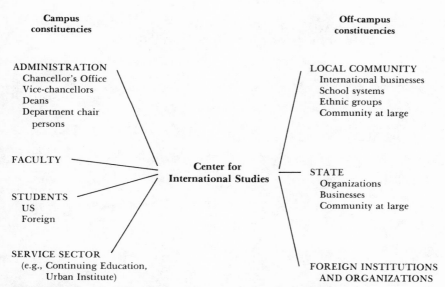

FIGURE 1.2. Constituencies of the Center for International Studies.

Through brochures, newspaper articles, radio announcements, and television appearances, a wide variety of activities are promoted for a broad community audience. Annual events include the UNCC International Festival, the Public Forum on International Issues, the Great Decisions Program, the International Film Festival, the Spring Conference on International Issues, summer travel programs, among others. New activities are added each year; recent examples include a photographic exhibit and a newspaper series on the People's Republic of China. Some local events are cosponsored by the center and *The Charlotte Observer* or a business group such as the Metrolina World Trade Club or First Union National Bank. Cosponsorship of activities has resulted in increased participation and publicity.

At the state level, the center participates actively in the North Carolina World Trade Organization, the Council for International Programs of the University of North Carolina, and the National Association for Foreign Student Affairs. In addition, the center coordinates the Great Decisions Program statewide through thirteen regional coordinators, each affiliated with an institution of higher education. Certain business programs are also marketed on a statewide basis. Semester abroad programs and summer travel programs are promoted at all colleges and universities in North Carolina, as well as in surrounding states.

Linkages with foreign institutions and organizations are of the greatest interest to the faculty. Examples include faculty exchange programs, student exchange programs, overseas research opportunities, and the

TABLE 1.1. Revenues and Expenditures of the Center for International Studies

1976/77 Revenue Sources:

1. State (includes two positions)	$ 31,800.00
2. Grants	$ 38,049.50
3. Business contributions	$ 8,375.00
4. Participant fees (Travel Abroad, Business Seminars)	$ 2,400.00
Total	$ 80,624.50

1980/81 Revenue Sources:

1. State (includes three positions)	$ 64,320.00
2. Grants	$ 99,167.00
3. Contracts	$ 44,900.00
4. Contributions	
5. Participant fees	$ 12,480.00
(Travel Abroad, Business Seminars, Great Decisions, ELTI)	$207,870.00
Total	$428,737.00

1980/81 Expenditures:

1. Personnel salaries	$187,320.00
2. Fringe benefits	$ 19,397.00
3. Travel (staff)	$ 12,000.00
4. Duplicating, supplies, telephone, postage, equipment, etc.	$ 13,478.00
5. Faculty development	$ 32,500.00
6. Programs (honoraria, travel, participant travel costs, tuition, etc.)	$164,050.00
Total	$428,745.00

Fulbright program. These linkages are crucial if UNCC is to make its commitment to international education viable and worthwhile. The 1980s will find faculty members more in need of tangible support for international education activities, including recognition through the faculty reward system.

Funding

To gain perspective on the center's funding patterns, revenue distributions are presented by two different academic years, 1976/77 (the first year with a full-time director) and 1980/81 (the most recent year for which data are available).

The budget comparison between 1976/77 and 1980/81 (table 1.1) reveals two useful findings. First, it dramatically illustrates the tremendous growth in revenues. Secondly, it shows that the major increase has been in participant fees. However, this finding is somewhat deceptive, because the revenue is used largely to cover the expenditures of the programs that generated the revenue. (An exception is revenue from business seminars, which generate funds that can be allocated to cover expenses from other programs.)

State-appropriated funds are the most constant source of income and least subject to change. They are, however, only 15 percent of the center's total budget. Grants from both the federal government and private foundations make a greater contribution to the total budget but are far less secure and are likely to vary from year to year. Thus, a funding strategy should reduce dependence on grants for operating expenses. Steps to take include obtaining increased state appropriations and negotiating long-term contracts with organizations and institutions.

Although still the smallest percentage of the total budget, the contributions from business firms are highly important to the center's operation because these funds can be allocated at the discretion of the center's director. Faculty development projects are the major expenditures to which these dollars are applied.

Expenditures are the other side of the budget coin. The distribution of expenditures for the 1980/81 academic year yields a more complete picture.

As might be expected, personnel salaries and fringe benefits are the largest share of the budget, covering three positions funded by the state—the director, a coordinator, and a secretary—and two coordinators, six instructors, five secretaries, and seven part-time student assistants funded out of program revenue. Program expenses account for the second largest portion of expenditures, used primarily for tuition repayments to UNCC and travel expenses for participants in travel abroad programs. Most of the faculty development costs are honoraria, release-time reimbursement, and travel. Of the basic office expenses, duplication and telephone are the largest.

The degree of control over expenditures and the budgeting process is almost as important as budget size. Budgeting flexibility varies depending on the source of the revenue. For instance, state-appropriated funds, grant monies, and resources from contracts are tightly audited to guarantee that expenditures are for items for which funds have been appropriated. Revenue from these three categories is spent only by authorization of the director of the center. A member of the support staff checks each expenditure to insure that the necessary funds are present. (The center has approximately twenty major accounts, each with six to twenty-five different line items; in accounts for state funds, grants, and contracts, expenditures for a line item cannot exceed the amount budgeted.) The Business Office also monitors these accounts.

Most accounts are program accounts, set up to handle receipts and expenditures from specific programs such as the English Language Training Institute. However, there is greater flexibility in program accounts than in accounts for state-appropriated funds or grant or contract monies. Each year the director sets up a budget for each program account, estimating revenue and distributing the budget over the line items. This budget, however, can at best be only an estimate. During the academic year, expenditures can exceed the amount budgeted for a specific line item. However, total receipts in the account must always be equal to or greater than expenditures for all line items combined. If the account goes into the red during a specific month, the Business Office notifies the director and requests a transfer of funds to balance the account. Although the center director authorizes all expenditures out of program accounts, a staff member within the center charged with handling accounts carefully examines all program accounts monthly to insure that sufficient receipts are available to cover outstanding expenditures.

The third category of revenue, financial contributions, are the most flexible. These monies are deposited into the UNCC Foundation and are available for use by the director of the center. Again, only the center's director is authorized to expend these receipts, and all expenditures must be fully documented.

In summary, the following are key aspects of the center's budget:

1. Revenue is generated from a variety of sources

2. "Soft money" characterizes most of the budget

3. Personnel and programs represent the two greatest categories of expenditures

4. The center's director authorizes expenditures from all budgets (although certain major expenditures may require the approval of one of the vice-chancellors).

Program Strengths and Weaknesses

The institutional model that has been developed at UNCC has strengths that warrant its implementation at other institutions of higher education. However, to assess its usefulness as a model for other universities and colleges, both its strengths and its weaknesses should be examined.

Strengths:

1. Major institutional commitment to international education—by the institution's highest administrative officers and in the mission statement

2. State-funded office with a full-time director authorized to develop institutional programs to strengthen the international dimension on campus

3. Highly centralized administration of international education programs combined with the desire and commitment not only to service the international education needs of institutional units, but also to increase the number of faculty members and students involved in international education activities.

4. A staff with the skills and abilities to exercise professional leadership in the community, state, region, and nation

5. A professional and support staff with requisite complementary skills and abilities, the dedication to carry out goals of the center, and the willingness to work well together

6. Strong commitment to international programming in the community, an activity that reduces both the psychological and physical barriers separating UNCC from the Charlotte residents

7. A budget derived from diversified sources, lessening the impact should one source fail to produce anticipated revenue

8. A diversified constituency, increasing the base of support for sponsored activities

9. A strong faculty development program, leading to strong support by faculty members in many academic departments

10. A center unattached to the academic colleges, thus capable of drawing on academic resources from all colleges and not subject to the constraints of a single college dean

11. A director who reports to top university administrative officials and thus has access to key decision makers

12. Development of community programs that affect all regions of North Carolina

13. Major commitment to facilitating matriculation of foreign students

14. Use of the business community for both resources and programing

15. Use of faculty resources in all phases of programing

16. Strong commitment on the part of the center and departments to develop institutional exchanges

17. Strong beginning at providing UNCC students with an overseas experience

Weaknesses and Threats:

1. Lack of visibility for available services and programs among all sectors of the campus

2. Too heavy a reliance on revenues other than state-appropriated funds; constant search for new dollars needed to maintain programs

3. Lack of state-allocated position for foreign student services

4. Lack of clearly stated support for an increase in funding for international education by the general administration of the University of North Carolina

5. Failure of most students, and to a lesser extent the faculty, to see the need for an increased international awareness (reflected in the curriculum, in the allocation of resources, and in campus programing)

6. A faculty reward system that fails to recognize adequately the advantages of faculty overseas experience

7. The need to revise university overseas travel regulations so that they properly reflect the necessity of participation in the international scholarly community

8. Too few courses in the curriculum with an international dimension

9. Insufficient funding to respond adequately to faculty development needs

10. Location of the center outside the college structure—no natural base of strength from any one college (particularly at budget allocation time) and a tendency for animosities to develop if center resources appear (to an outsider) to be too large

The Center for International Studies at the University of North Carolina at Charlotte has evolved over time to respond to the international education needs of the campus and community. Its strengths have enabled the center to make a major contribution to "internationalizing" the institution. Much remains to be done during the decade of the 1980s; success will depend on continuing to counter weaknesses and threats to the center.

Strategies for the 1980s

The need for a citizenry with an international awareness will grow during the 1980s. Today's students—tomorrow's decisionmakers—must become familiar with terms such as "global problems," "interdependence," "resource distribution," and "north–south." Students and communities must be presented with programs, activities, courses, workshops, institutes, and lectures that increase the level of international awareness to a much higher degree than is currently present.

The staff of the Center for International Studies has addressed this need and defined the issues to which major attention will be given during the 1980s:

1. Selective recruitment of high-quality foreign students, both graduate and undergraduate, particularly from parts of the world not well represented at UNCC (e.g., Latin America, East Asia, and Southeast Asia); faculty traveling, research, and teaching in these areas to be the primary technique for increasing the number and quality of foreign students

2. Continued refinement of the English Language Training Institute, which should serve as a major vehicle for orienting foreign students to American culture and the university, while serving to screen students not prepared to handle a university academic program

3. Expanding overseas opportunities for UNCC undergraduate students by taking full advantage of the International Student Exchange Program and directly confronting the single largest obstacle—finances—by creating internships, developing scholarships, and using financial aid to its limit

4. Increasing the number of courses taught at UNCC that contain an international dimension by obtaining the funds for the faculty at UNCC to participate in overseas research and teaching. (The goal is for all students in the 1980s who obtain an undergraduate degree from UNCC after four years of study to have international experience—courses, activities, or overseas study/travel.)

5. Developing far more extensive faculty exchange opportunities over the next few years, bringing foreign scholars to UNCC, providing opportunities for UNCC faculty to gain an international experience, and initiating collaborative research

6. Establishing an entrance requirement of two years' study of a foreign language in middle school or high school; granting provisional status to students entering without fulfilling such a requirement, on condition that they complete second-year college-level proficiency in a foreign language

7. Providing more support for international faculty development by seeking additional funding from the local business community

8. Assisting in the development of a faculty reward system that does not penalize a faculty member for undertaking an overseas assignment but instead qualitatively evaluates such experiences and provides recognition and rewards for international education activities

9. Seeking more diversified sources of funding for the center because continued programing in the 1980s will depend on successful funding patterns; more assistance from the state budget a major objective

10. Becoming more attuned than ever before to trends in higher education such as lifelong learning, continuing education and community-based programing—concepts that will be increasingly important as the community requires university outreach.

Additional funding for international education activities will be necessary, as the center attempts to move in these directions, responding to new pressures, recent trends, and institutional parochialism. Federal and private grants will continue to be important by providing seed money, initiating new projects, and funding specific research projects. However, money from these sources will probably not increase above the 1980/81 level. Therefore, grant funds and federal government monies cannot provide the solution to funding problems.

North Carolina can—and should—do more by way of support for university efforts in international education. Certainly the center will push for more state-funded staff positions, especially in the foreign student services office. As the institution grows, the state operating budget will slowly be enlarged. However, budget allocations are not likely to keep pace with inflation. So although UNCC will probably commit more state funds to support international education activities in the 1980s, growth will almost certainly not match requirements. The center will have to look elsewhere; additional funding will have to come from the two remaining sources, contributions from the business community and participant fees. A major corporate sponsors program would aim to obtain from the local business community $50,000 to $100,000 per year for support of faculty development, curriculum development, and faculty exchanges. Given the international focus found in the Charlotte business community, this goal is realistic.

Participant fees represent the other major source of new funding. Summer institutes to train teachers of English as a second language, business seminars, and overseas contracts for the training of trainers (or engineers or computer programers) are just some of the programs that will be explored during the 1980s. Revenue generated will be used to strengthen the international dimension both on and off campus and to provide additional opportunities for faculty and student exchanges.

The decade of the 1980s will surely bring a continued commitment on the part of the UNCC administration for international education activities. Creativity, innovation, and risk-taking will be rewarded, because the payoff will be a stronger international dimension and the funding needed to sustain the momentum.

Specifically, the major goals of UNCC's Center for International Studies have been and will continue to be (1) strengthening the international dimension on campus, (2) strengthening the international dimension in the community, (3) strengthening the program and services to foreign students, and (4) continuing to support and participate in cooperative programs beyond the university.

Continued success in achieving these objectives will depend on, among other things, (1) institutional commitment from the top administrative officers; (2) support from the faculty, department chairpersons, and deans; (3) additional funding both institutional and noninstitutional; and (4) a dedicated, highly qualified staff of professionals committed to building an international studies program designed to meet the goals and mission of the university.

> Nothing less is at issue than the nation's security. At a time when the resurgent forces of nationalism and of ethnic and linguistic consciousness so directly affect global realities, the United States requires far more reliable capacities to communicate with its allies, analyze the behavior of potential adversaries, and earn the trust and the sympathies of the uncommitted. Yet, there is a widening gap between these needs and the American competence to understand and deal successfully with other peoples in a world in flux.[7]

The Center for International Studies at the University of North Carolina at Charlotte is dedicated to decreasing this gap, both on and off campus.

Notes

1. "Toward Education with a Global Perspective," *Report of the National Assembly on Foreign Language and International Studies* (Association of American Colleges), 30 October–1 November 1980, Wingspread Conference Center, Racine, WI.
2. "Charlotte, N.C.—Melting Pot, U.S.A.?" *The Charlotte Observer*, September 1975.
3. Memo from the Vice Chancellor for Academic Affairs to the International Studies Advisory Committee, September 1970.
4. Final Report of the International Studies Advisory Committee to the Vice Chancellor for Academic Affairs, March 1973.
5. *Notes from the Chancellor's Office* 9, no. 16 (25 August 1975).

6. UNCC Undergraduate Catalog 1980–81, p. 2.
7. *Strength Through Wisdom: A Critique of U.S. Capability,* Report to the President from The President's Commission on Foreign Language and International Studies (Washington: US Government Printing Office, 1979), p. 2.

CHAPTER 2

The University of Massachusetts at Amherst

BARBARA B. BURN AND
MARYÉLISE SUFFERN LAMET

The international activities of the University of Massachusetts at Amherst date back more than a century. In 1876 William Clark, president of Massachusetts Agricultural College (which would become the University of Massachusetts at Amherst, or UMass.–Amherst), went to Hokkaido, Japan, to assist in the establishment of what was to become the University of Hokkaido. Nearly one hundred years later, the president of Hokkaido made a return visit to UMass.–Amherst to explore what relationship the two institutions might have in the future. A summer study program at Hokkaido for UMass.–Amherst students and a steady flow of Hokkaido students spending an exchange year in Amherst resulted from the renewal of international cooperation that Clark had begun just thirteen years after "Mass Aggie" was established. During the intervening century Massachusetts Agricultural College grew to be a major research university, and its international programs expanded to involve U.Mass.–Amherst in diverse activities in at least twenty-five countries throughout the world, with students coming to the university from ninety countries.

The University and the Community

The University of Massachusetts at Amherst is the major state university in Massachusetts, providing undergraduate and graduate education of the highest quality at a cost that can be met by most Massachusetts citizens. It is located in the western part of the state in the town of Amherst, where education is the main industry.

Incorporated in 1863 as Massachusetts Agricultural College, the future University of Massachusetts at Amherst for many years primarily fulfilled the need for agricultural education in the state. During the 1920s a growing interest on the part of alumni and students in a broader curriculum led to a campaign to change the name to Massachusetts State College. This name change was accomplished in 1931, but it was not until after World War II that the increase in applicants led to a real redefinition of the purpose and scope of public higher education in Massachusetts. The pressing need to educate Massachusetts's many returning servicemen, who through the GI Bill hoped to obtain a college degree, caused the state legislature to expand the campus at Amherst. Enrollment jumped from 760 in 1931 to 2,407 in 1947, when Massachusetts State College officially became the University of Massachusetts. Soon thereafter the School of Engineering, the School of Business Administration, and the College of Arts and Sciences were established to provide the broader curriculum demanded by the growing student body. A strong emphasis on agricultural education continued in the College of Agriculture, since renamed the College of Food and Natural Resources. By 1960 there were more than 6,000 students and 366 faculty members; and in 1970 20,462 students and 1,134 faculty members occupied a quickly expanding campus. By this time the University of Massachusetts at Amherst was joined by the harbor campus in Boston and the Medical School in Worcester.

Today UMass.–Amherst is the foremost public research university in Massachusetts. In fall 1980 there were 24,737 students (19,454 undergraduates and 5,283 graduates enrolled in eighty departments and 121 programs and served by 1,480 faculty members). The university is divided into the College of Arts and Sciences (which has three faculties: Humanities and Fine Arts, Natural Sciences and Mathematics, and Social and Behavioral Sciences); the professional schools of Business Administration, Education, Engineering, Food and Natural Resources, Health Sciences, and Physical Education; and the Graduate School.

Nearly one-half of the students live on campus. The great majority of students come from Massachusetts (20,000), with an additional 4,000 from elsewhere in the US and 700 from other countries. A recent change in the maximum percentage of out-of-state admissions from 5 percent to 15 percent and an increase in foreign student admissions for fall 1982 to 950 promise to add to the diversity of the student body.

The University of Massachusetts at Amherst joins Amherst College, Hampshire College, Mount Holyoke College, and Smith College in Five Colleges, Inc., one of the oldest and most successful educational consortia in the country. Though situated in the rural Pioneer Valley of the Connecticut River, the institutions of Five Colleges, Inc., have created a cosmopolitan center of teaching, research, and cultural activities. The consortium was formally established in 1965, growing out of a long tradition of collaboration and sharing of resources among the institutions of higher education in the Pioneer Valley. Cooperative arrangements span the institution's academic, social, and cultural activities. Each year more than 5,000 students take courses on campuses other than their own. (Student cross-registration for courses is practical because of the largest free bus service in the country operated by the Pioneer Valley Transit Authority.) Cooperative structures include the Five College Astronomy Department, one of the largest and most advanced in the country, the Five College East Asian Language Program, and the Black Studies Program. Collaborative activities like these provide a rich and attractive resource for education, the arts, and international studies for students, faculty members, and the larger community of Western Massachusetts.

How the International Program Was Established

The immediate impetus for creating the International Programs Office at the University of Massachusetts at Amherst came from the increase in foreign students, growing from 56 in 1960/61 to 341 in 1967/68, and the initiation of several study abroad programs. In short, a clientele of UMass. students was requiring more centralized assistance as they came to Amherst from overseas or as they sought to enroll in study abroad programs sponsored by UMass. and other institutions.

Before the International Programs Office was established in 1969, the university had successfully met immediate needs as they arose when activities were on a small scale. Thus, in the 1960s committees of the Faculty Senate were established to address foreign student and study abroad issues: the Foreign Student Committee and the Committee on Scholarships, Financial Aid, Placement, and Study Abroad. Until September 1964, the function of foreign student advisor was handled on a part-time basis by various faculty members in rotation. Because accepting foreign students places certain responsibilities by law on any university (immigration requirements, tax and insurance regulations, and certifications as to enrollment and currency exchange), the inadequacies of part-time faculty attention to these needs became apparent, and the administrative position of foreign student advisor was created in 1964.

Lacking the legal requirements of services found in the foreign student sector, study abroad had to wait until the International Programs Office was created in 1969 to receive urgently needed staff support. In 1966/67, 225 UMass.-Amherst students went abroad for study, research, work, or service. Clearly, there was a student clientele who would be well served by the central collection of information on study abroad and international fellowship opportunities. In addition, program directors needed one place to turn to for assistance in running their programs.

Therefore in 1967 university president John Lederle asked Barbara B. Burn, whose background included international education work with foundations, UNESCO, and the US Department of State, to prepare a report on the international programs of the University of Massachusetts at Amherst.

The first section of her report, completed in 1968, addressed the pressing question of how the university could more effectively handle a variety of foreign student problems. These urgent issues included:

- The need for a coherent university policy on services for foreign students

- The need for more adequate and systematic approaches to evaluating foreign students' academic credentials, English proficiency, and financial resources

- The geographic imbalance in the university's foreign student population in 1968

- The need for more adequate assistance for foreign students in initial reception and orientation, housing, meals, tuition scholarships, emergency financial aid, remedial English training, integration into the campus and Amherst communities, and counseling

Dr. Burn concluded: "The university should establish a new Office of International Affairs in which the Foreign Student Office will be located and which will provide it with needed support and guidance, including continuity of qualified secretarial assistance, an adequate publications acquisition and travel budget, and a closer relationship to the university's overall functioning."

The second and much longer section of the report addressed the less pressing but more wide-ranging question of how the university could best carry out and expand its diverse international education commitments. Summer programs in Oxford and Bologna had completed three successful years, and new summer programs in Madrid and Japan were being undertaken. Some of the problems encountered by directors of the two latter endeavors underlined the need for an office to coordinate planning and to serve as a source of information about accreditation, budget planning, funding, student recruitment, and transportation arrangements for directors. There was a need for similar centralized support and assistance for academic-year programs.

There was also a great need for an office that could coordinate information on programs that existed elsewhere and were affordable by UMass.–Amherst students. The importance of evaluating these offerings, as well as the importance of merely organizing flyers and posters in files, demanded a professional staff person familiar with standards in the field.

Some departments had already become involved in other areas of international education programs. The College of Agriculture (renamed the College of Food and Natural Resources in 1972) cooperated with AID and the US Department of Agriculture in providing foreign trainees with academic study, field observation, and on-the-job experience in agriculture. These short-term training programs contributed to the establishment of the Center for International Agricultural Studies (CIAS) in 1967, which was to coordinate the international programs of the College of Agriculture, including new interdepartmental programs in international agriculture, both undergraduate and graduate.

The historic relationship of the Massachusetts Agricultural College with the University of Hokkaido was revitalized from 1958 to 1962 when the College of Agriculture sent staff members to Japan to strengthen teaching and research at Hokkaido through an AID contract. Some sixty Japanese also came to UMass.–Amherst for training. Another AID contract, running from 1963 to 1970, involved the College of Agriculture in assisting the Government of Malawi in organizing, expanding, and improving the Agricultural Extension Service in Malawi and strengthening agricultural education in general.

Agriculture was not the only area that had been active in international activities. Since 1963 members of the School of Education had been involved in an AID contract to provide technical aid and assistance in the establishment of the Comprehensive Secondary School for Girls in Uganda. For about ten years the School of Business Administration had organized, in cooperation with the Experiment in International Living, a six-week program in business for from thirty to fifty young executives from Europe. The University of Massachusetts also collaborated with the Council on International Educational Exchange to bring about thirty-five young Japanese teachers to Amherst to study English language and American culture. These and many other programs proved useful in enabling American students to have contact with people from other cultures and in contributing to international understanding. A coordinating office could support the development of further programs and facilitate the sharing of information on setting up such programs.

Dr. Burn's report also touched on ways in which the Five College Consortium could cooperate to add to the effectiveness of the institutions' international education programs, and it described UMass.-Amherst's participation in a New England Coordinating Council for International Studies. The report discussed the need to inventory the international experience of university staff members, to list the university's course offerings related to international affairs, and to summarize the university's international programs. Another need Dr. Burn mentioned was improved coordination of the increasing number of foreign visitors to the university.

The Burn report of 1968 concluded by proposing that the University of Massachusetts at Amherst establish an Office of International Affairs. The responsibilities this office might undertake were outlined as follows:

1. Provide direction and support to the Foreign Student Office, which would be transferred to the Office of International Affairs

2. Assist with evaluating the academic credentials of foreign student applicants at the graduate and undergraduate levels

3. Develop relations with organizations involved with foreign students coming to the United States to encourage applicants from countries that now have little or no representation at the University of Massachusetts, so that the foreign student population will be more diversified

4. Collect, evaluate, and disseminate information on overseas opportunities for faculty members and students

5. Provide administrative support to existing study abroad programs as requested by their directors and assist with the initiation of new programs

6. Cooperate with the directors of short-term training programs for foreign nationals in program development and administration

7. Assist with the university's overseas contracts, including cultivating relations with the contracting agencies, mobilizing the resources of the university in implementing the contracts, and helping to ensure that proposed new contracts are studied from the point of view of universitywide interests

8. Provide appropriate assistance in the development of the Center for International Agricultural Studies

9. Coordinate the university's interest in cooperative international programs within Five Colleges, Inc., among the State Universities of New England, and with other such groups

10. Assist the Office of Institutional Studies in preparing an inventory of faculty international experience, a summary of the university's international programs, and a list of university courses related to international affairs

11. Coordinate information on the programs for foreign visitors to the university and possibly to the other members of Five Colleges, Inc., on a reciprocal basis

12. Collect and disseminate within the university information on prospects for funding international programs and maintain relations with organizations that support such programs, including government agencies and foundations

13. Assist with the preparation of guidelines on the university's international programs and the statement of commitment to them in the Long Range Plan for the university.

14. Undertake additional responsibilities for the university's international programs as might be requested by the university administration

Detailed recommendations were also made on budgetary needs, staffing requirements, location within the administration, and physical location on campus of the proposed Office on International Affairs.

The report was submitted to the president of the university and after consideration by various bodies was approved for implementation. In particular, the university agreed to the notion of a single coordinating office to monitor various kinds of international programs and ensure fiscal responsibility and the highest quality in program administration.

In January 1969 the International Programs Office officially came into being at UMass.-Amherst. The basic thrust of the March 1968 Burn report was accepted. A full-time director and secretary and a half-time community relations coordinator were hired, and the foreign student advisor also became part of the new office staff.

The speed with which these recommendations were enacted reflected the basic strength of the university's international programs and the support for them—from the president's office, from the many faculty members participating in existing programs, from students interested in overseas study, and from students coming to UMass.-Amherst from other countries.

Institutional Commitment to International Education

The establishment of the International Programs Office (IPO) in 1969 confirmed the commitment of the University of Massachusetts at Amherst

to expand its international education activities. The university's commitment is further illustrated by the stated mission, goals, and objectives of the
International Programs Office, its place in the university's administrative
organization, and the organization of the office itself.

MISSION, GOALS, AND OBJECTIVES OF THE INTERNATIONAL PROGRAMS OFFICE

In May 1973 the University of Massachusetts at Amherst cosponsored a
conference with the International Council for Educational Development
on the international role of the university in the 1970s. Both the president of
the university and the chancellor of the Amherst campus were actively
involved in the conference. It attracted persons from industry, labor,
government, foundations, and institutions of higher education. A wide
consensus developed on the following propositions, which in many ways
may be considered to form a statement of the mission of UMass.-Amherst
in international programs for the 1970s:

- The university should relate more closely to the public and involve
  itself more in domestic problems as it strengthens and redefines
  international programs.

- The international studies program of American universities should
  be firmly based on collaboration with colleagues in other geographic
  areas. Exchange of scholars should be increased.

- There should be increased cooperation between American colleges
  and universities as they develop and strengthen their international
  studies programs.

- Interdisciplinary cooperation is critical to the effectiveness of international programs.

- There is a need to supplement and reinforce traditional teaching
  and learning approaches through cross-cultural experiences.

Because the activities of the International Programs Office evolved and
expanded during the 1970s, this broad statement of mission could be made
more specific when IPO was asked to formulate a statement of its mission,
goals, and objectives as part of its status report in the "Planning for the
1980s" process undertaken by then university chancellor Henry Koffler.
Broken into the areas of teaching and learning, research, and service,
the IPO mission may be defined as follows:

In teaching and learning:

1. Strengthening international and area studies, including foreign languages and courses on major world issues such as food and resource depletion

2. Infusing an international perspective in courses in all disciplines

3. Supporting and enlarging study abroad opportunities and opportunities to learn about the cultures and peoples of other countries through enhanced curricular and extracurricular contact with foreign students on campus

4. Expanding international faculty exchanges both to bring to campus more foreign faculty members, who provide international content and perspectives in their teaching, and to send more UMass. faculty members abroad so that on their return they can do the same

5. Assuring the availability of a quality English as a Second Language (ESL) program for the expanding foreign student and scholar population

6. Helping to make UMass. curricula more relevant to the educational goals of foreign students

In research:

1. Encouraging faculty research (individual research or joint research projects with foreign researchers) in international and area studies, in foreign languages, and on international issues

2. Assisting faculty members in finding institutional and external funding for research projects

3. Encouraging faculty members in other countries to pursue their sabbatical or other research at UMass.–Amherst.

4. Helping to assure that graduate and other research projects undertaken by foreign students are relevant to their professional goals in their home countries

5. Encouraging and undertaking research and publication on international education exchanges and on comparative higher education

In service:

1. Facilitating and organizing conferences, symposia, and other meetings on international issues and on other cultures and countries for the community beyond the campus

2. Facilitating the use of international studies materials, foreign students, and other visitors from abroad as a resource in the curricular and extracurricular programs of schools in western Massachusetts and in the programs of local civic, social, and ethnic organizations

3. Working with local and regional media to encourage programs on international issues and foreign cultures

4. Participating in community, regional, national, and international associations and organizations that seek to strengthen foreign language learning and international studies and education

5. Encouraging and organizing the participation of UMass. faculty members and staff members in teaching and consulting abroad, especially in third-world nations

6. Consulting with national and foreign government agencies and non-government organizations in the field of international education

The goals of the International Programs Office during the coming decade-therefore include:

1. To increase foreign student enrollments at UMass.–Amherst from the current 600 to 1,500 students, broadly distributed by countries of origin, and to lower the barriers to achieving this goal, such as out-of-state quotas

2. To encourage overseas study by UMass. students and increase study abroad opportunities so that at least one-fifth of all students have this opportunity during their college careers

3. To expand opportunities for study abroad in the non-Western world so that the majority of students studying overseas go to non-Western countries

4. To increase reciprocal faculty exchanges from the current level of about ten per year to fifty, with priority given to developing and non-Western nations.

5. To help strengthen international and area studies, including foreign languages, so that at least one-third of graduating seniors, including those in professional schools, achieve a usable foreign language proficiency and forty percent have taken at least one course on another country, world region, or international issue

6. To revise the faculty reward system so that faculty members who teach or otherwise work abroad or make significant contributions to on-campus international or area studies programs are accorded full recognition for the activity in promotions and other benefits

7. To cooperate with other units on campus, with the Five College Consortium, and with other higher education institutions in the state and firmly establish an active, sustained program of symposia, conferences, and workshops to strengthen international education in higher education throughout Massachusetts

8. To develop (as part of IPO) a high-quality program of English as a Second Language or English as a Foreign Language (ESL/EFL) to meet the needs of foreign students who wish to matriculate at UMass.–Amherst or another institution of higher education in the US, but who lack English proficiency

In the next one to five years, the International Programs Office plans to pursue these goals to the degree possible within its financial resources. Realization of these goals will be neither begun at an appointed time nor suddenly achieved; it will be the result of continued effort on all fronts toward growth in international endeavors, accomplished in the midst of sustaining ongoing activities and fulfilling present responsibilities. Specific objectives for from five to ten years from now include:

- Working with Continuing Education to strengthen internationally oriented and foreign language courses in their offerings

- Revitalizing a statewide network to coordinate international concerns and opportunities at institutions of higher education in Massachusetts

- Establishing a strong study abroad alumni network through publications, conferences, reunions, personal contacts, and development efforts

ADMINISTRATIVE ORGANIZATION

There are three vice-chancellors at the University of Massachusetts at Amherst: the vice-chancellor for academic affairs and provost, the vice-chancellor for student affairs, and the vice-chancellor for administration and finance. The 1968 Burn report had recommended that the proposed Office of International Affairs report to the vice-chancellor for academic affairs and provost. When the International Programs Office was created, it was first placed under the academic vice-chancellor and then was integrated within the Division of Special Programs, reporting to the associate provost for special programs.

After nearly ten years, IPO was reassigned to the Provost's Office and as of 1981/82 reports directly to the provost in all basic matters of administration such as personnel and budget. IPO's placement within the Provost's Office, rather than in one of the colleges or the Office of Student

Affairs is appropriate because IPO serves the faculty and students of all the schools and colleges through activities such as foreign student services and student and faculty exchanges. IPO also works with the Faculty Senate's Foreign and International Studies Council and its several committees, including the Committee of Overseas Programs and Exchange to obtain approval for all exchange programs.

Meeting the needs of foreign students involves significant interaction with the following campus offices: graduate and undergraduate registrars, bursar, academic advising, housing (both dormitory and family) and heads of residence halls, food service, health services and mental health, student employment, Recognized Student Organization Office, Campus Center, graduate and undergraduate student senates, summer counseling, campus ministry, campus police, Provost's Office, and Personnel Office. The Foreign Student Office works actively with the university's admissions office as well as with graduate program directors in all departments.

IPO's study abroad programs require significant interaction with the departments and committees most involved with these programs: French (Angers and Dijon programs), German (Freiburg Program and Linköping exchange), English (Oxford Summer Seminar), Spanish and Portuguese (Salamanca and Lisbon programs), Fine Arts (Studio Art exchanges in Great Britain), Asian Studies (Summer Intensive English Program for Japanese Teachers; Tunghai University exchange; Taiwan; Peking Normal and Fudan Universities; Foreign Languages Institute and Foreign Languages Press exchanges in the People's Republic of China; and Sophia University exchange, Japan), Interpreters Program (Dolmetscherschule Interpreters' exchange, Zurich), Afro-American Studies (Lagos University exchange), Anthropology (Field Studies in Cultural Anthropology program), Latin American Area Studies (Argentina exchange program), School of Education (practice teaching exchange programs in England), Hokkaido Committee (Hokkaido summer program and student and other exchanges), Chemistry (chemistry student exchange with the University of East Anglia), and Physical Education (programs in Australia and New Zealand).

The student exchanges with institutions of higher education in the UK involve significant interaction with a variety of departments because participating students are in a wide range of disciplines. Student exchange and study abroad programs also involve significant interaction with the Registrar's Office, Honors Program, Financial Aid, Bursar's Office, Records Office, Accounting Office, Veterans' Affairs, Transfer Affairs, CASIAC (College of Arts and Sciences Information and Advising Center), Internships, and Graduate Records and Admission. This interaction is to assure that participating UMass. students obtain appropriate counseling and approval before going abroad, receive the financial aid to which they are entitled, obtain credit for academic work done abroad, and receive preregistration and housing materials for their return to UMass.

Other offices with which IPO interacts significantly include Publications (preparation of flyers and brochures for study abroad programs and foreign student information), the undergraduate Fulbright Advisor (to recruit outstanding candidates for the Rhodes Scholars Program, Marshall Scholars Program, and other distinguished scholarships abroad), some other former special programs (including Bachelors Degree with Individual Concentration, University Without Walls, and Inquiry), the Faculty Senate (Foreign and International Studies Council and Committee on Overseas Programs and Exchanges), and the Office of Planning and Budget (which oversees the state-funded budget, fee-based budgets, and trust funds, for example).

IPO is located in the Whitmore Administration Building, a location that provides convenient access to the many offices in the building—such as the Chancellor's Office, the Provost's Office, the Office of Budget and Planning, Personnel, Student Affairs, Financial Aid, Housing, Undergraduate Admissions, Transfer Affairs, Bursar, Registrar, and Duplicating.

ORGANIZATION OF THE INTERNATIONAL PROGRAMS OFFICE

The functions of the International Programs Office can be broadly divided into two areas: service to foreign students and coordination of international exchange. The organizational structure of the office reflects this broad division, with the Foreign Student Office and its staff as one major section within the International Programs Office and the rest of the IPO staff members working primarily on student and faculty exchanges and program development. The two parts of the office interact constantly.

A key characteristic of IPO's organization is the absence of a rigid hierarchy. For example, all staff members, from secretaries to director, take turns serving as chairperson and taking minutes at the weekly staff meeting. Figure 2.1 outlines the basic organization of IPO.

Particular areas of concern to the director include:

- Overall administration of international programs including budgets, staffing, general functioning, and long-range planning

- Liaison with institutions of higher education, professional associations, and government agencies

- Research and evaluation to strengthen international programs at UMass., across the nation, and (in collaboration with individuals, organizations, and international agencies) in other countries

The director is closely assisted by the assistant director and the coordinator of budget. Both these persons are part-time staff members.

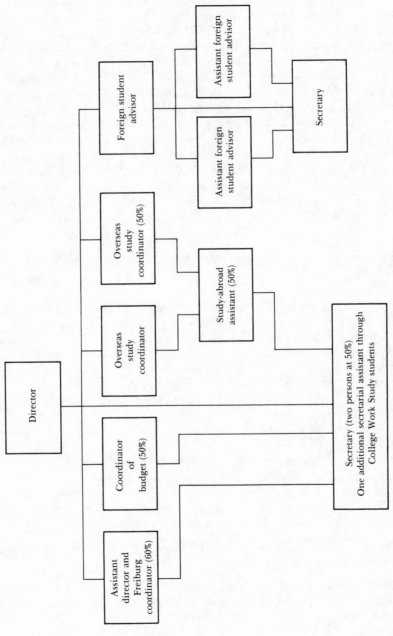

FIGURE 2.1 Organizational chart for the International Programs Office.

With the director, they are responsible for budget and personnel matters. Because IPO funding comes from a combination of state and trust fund (fee-based) sources, the complexity of the financial organization is great, requiring background knowledge of the university and creativity to keep all funds appropriately balanced. The assistant director is responsible for personnel and staffing and for all facets of the administration of the Freiburg Program. The coordinator of budget handles general budgetary questions, fiscal aspects of most programs, and liaison with directors of summer programs and the Semester Program in Angers, France.

The overseas study coordinators (one full-time staff member and one half-time staff member) are responsible for coordinating study abroad information and administration. A husband-and-wife team, they handle UMass. student exchanges and organize the dissemination of information about study abroad programs sponsored by other institutions. Their responsibilities thus include counseling on study abroad, work overseas, and scholarship opportunities abroad as well as supervision of exchange budgets, administrative correspondence, preparation of publicity, organization of meetings and seminars, liaison with faculty members, program development, and supervision of the study abroad assistant (a half-time staff member). The full-time overseas study coordinator also acts on behalf of the director when she is away from the office.

The other major area of IPO activities is handled by the Foreign Student Office. The foreign student advisor supervises two assistants and a secretary in serving the nearly 800 foreign students at UMass.–Amherst. This staff is responsible for issuing appropriate government documents to foreign students, record keeping, and liaison with Admissions and the Graduate School, the academic departments, Housing, and Bursar's Office, and other university offices. One of the foreign student advisor's assistants is responsible for liaison on exchange matters with the overseas study coordinators and the IPO director; the other is responsible for managing aspects of the rapidly developing UMass. exchanges with the People's Republic of China. One of the assistant foreign student advisors is also in charge of monitoring community relations with the foreign student population and developing outreach programs with Amherst and the surrounding area; the other edits the *Foreign Student Newsletter* and is a contributing editor for the newsletter of the National Association for Foreign Student Affairs. All Foreign Student Office staff members are constantly involved in student counseling, with the secretary providing the first contact and line of support for students coming into the office.

The support staff structure of IPO is fragmented and hard pressed. In addition to the secretary in the Foreign Student Office, the IPO support staff consists of one half-time secretary who handles front desk reception and serves as coordinator of travel information, and a full-time staff member who serves half-time as a secretary at the front desk and half-time as the study abroad assistant. The primary responsibilities of the study abroad assistant include keeping records on the more than 250 students overseas each school year, corresponding with them while they are abroad, and working with them when they return to transfer the academic credit they earned abroad. The office handles from 400 to 500 inquiries on study abroad each year, and a thousand students or more use IPO study abroad services each year. The hard-pressed support staff is aided by students on College Work Study when such help is available.

The high levels of program activity mean that what IPO lacks in staff must be made up in dedication and enthusiasm. IPO has a deliberate policy of training new staff members and helping to launch them into other programs or jobs that build on their IPO experience. A continuing staff renewal is a consequence and aim of IPO's approach to professional growth and opportunity.

Program Description

The International Programs Office is authorized by the University of Massachusetts Board of Trustees to encourage, strengthen, and expand undertakings in the following areas:

- Cross-cultural and international education activities through faculty and student exchanges between UMass. and foreign universities
- On-campus curricular and extracurricular programs for both American and foreign students
- Overseas study, research, and work opportunities for faculty members and students
- Expansion and diversification of foreign student enrollments and visiting foreign faculty members

IPO is the main office to which these responsibilities are delegated at UMass.-Amherst, and it is also responsible for liaison with other campus units undertaking international education activities.

PROGRAM COMPONENTS

The activities and programs of the International Programs Office at UMass-Amherst may be broken down into eight areas.

 I. *Foreign student services.* The population of foreign students at UMass.-Amherst will number between 950 and 1,000 students from about ninety countries in 1982/83. This diverse community enriches the Amherst campus by creating an environment for cross-cultural exchange and the expansion of international consciousness on campus. Foreign students also require some special services not needed by the domestic student body. The current foreign student advisor and his assistants, in cooperation with the rest of the IPO staff, work to meet the twin goals of serving the particular needs of foreign students and encouraging cross-cultural sharing. Specific aspects of the Foreign Student Office programs include:

A. Assisting foreign students as appropriate in matters of visa, passport, social security, and income tax procedures; housing; tuition waivers; scholarships; graduate assistantships; employment regulations; and health insurance and medical coverage

B. Providing essential services to outside agencies sponsoring foreign students, e.g., GTE Sylvania, Calcusearch, African American Institute, Institute of International Education, AID, Latin American Scholarship Program of American Universities, etc.

C. Presenting orientation programs for incoming foreign students

D. Providing personal, financial, and academic counseling for foreign students

E. Providing referral services to other offices on campus, and liaison on behalf of foreign students

F. Publishing the *Foreign Student Newsletter* (seven to eight times per year), information pamphlets and guides for new foreign students and visiting foreign faculty members, a guide for hosts of visiting foreign faculty members, and brochures about the Host Family and Round-the-World Women Programs

G. Serving as liaison with the community on foreign student matters and providing special programs to increase international awareness in the community.

II. *Overseas study and student exchange programs.* IPO at UMass.-Amherst has been a pioneer in developing reciprocal exchanges around the world. The approach has been to use informal contacts, by the director of IPO and faculty members traveling abroad, to develop exchange links with foreign institutions. UMass. is also playing an important role in the development of the International Student Exchange Program (currently based at Georgetown University), with IPO's director serving as the chair on its advisory board.

UMass. exchange relationships now number twenty-eight. They offer opportunities in many fields, usually with small numbers of students going to any one exchange institution, though some programs take larger groups of students abroad. During each of the past five years, about 250 students went abroad to study. They studied more than sixty subjects in at least thirty-seven countries. In addition, at least 200 students take part in UMass. study abroad programs each summer.

During any given year, at least a thousand students inquire about, participate in, and return from UMass. study abroad programs. The services extended to these students include:

A. Establishing, maintaining, and expanding study abroad programs and exchanges
B. Administering and managing the funds for study abroad programs and exchanges
C. Presenting orientation programs for students embarking on study abroad programs
D. Providing personal, financial, and academic counseling for students inquiring about or returning from study abroad
E. Providing a referral service to other offices on campus and liaison with them on behalf of students
F. Maintaining an extensive library of information on study, work, and travel abroad
G. Preparing written recommendations on request for students' placement files and for graduate and professional schools
H. Publishing the following: a brochure on all UMass. study abroad programs; flyers; *International Programs Bulletin* (a newsletter that comes out five times a year); *Guidelines for Students Accepted into Programs of Study Abroad;* and handbooks for students going to Britain and Freiburg

The overseas study coordinators are undertaking a follow-up survey of all UMass. study abroad alumni. They hope to formulate some concrete conclusions about the long-range impact of study abroad as well as develop a study abroad alumni network to generate support for study abroad scholarships.

III. *Work and travel advising.* IPO has a reference library for study, internships, work, travel, and financial assistance abroad. The office issues the International Student Identity Card to UMass. and other Five College students. One staff member keeps abreast of major developments in the travel industry and serves as a travel consultant. In addition, the overseas study coordinators are contributing editors to *Transitions,* a periodical resource guide to work, travel, and study abroad.

IV. *Overseas fellowship and scholarship services.* IPO maintains a library of information on overseas funding opportunities for students and faculty members.

The director of IPO is campus coordinator for the Senior Fulbright Programs and maintains regular contact with agencies and organizations in Washington and elsewhere that fund international education projects. The overseas study coordinators serve as coordinators for the Rhodes Scholars Program, Marshall Scholars Program, Rotary International, and other award competitions—publicizing them, screening applicants, and assisting in the application process. They also work closely with the faculty member who serves as the campus Fulbright student coordinator.

V. *Campus international awareness programs.* To make the university community more aware of the international dimension, IPO sponsors several activities:

   A. International Week, seven days of special programs, films, international affairs meetings, speakers, etc., culminating in the International Fair (food, displays, and entertainment) attended by more than a thousand persons.

   B. International Students' Association, a student organization with about 150 members that meets regularly, sponsors dances and films, and supports African, Chinese, Near-Eastern, and Palestinian student groups

   C. Five College International Careers Conference, a conference sponsored in 1977 and repeated in 1980, featuring notable professionals with international careers who discussed opportunities and gave advice about appropriate preparation for international careers

   D. Study Abroad Fair, an annual daylong event in the Campus Center featuring students returned from overseas who preside at booths representing all parts of the world.

   E. Study Abroad Seminar Series, a series of from eight to ten meetings and seminars during the fall on study abroad in specific countries or particular programs

VI. *Community outreach.* Beyond the university, IPO seeks to involve foreign students in the local community so that they can learn about everyday American life and in turn enrich the basically rural communities in the Amherst area. Activities sponsored include: the Host Family Program, the Loan Closet, Friendship Circles, Round-the-World-Women's Programs, Foreign Speakers Bureau, English tutoring, and Local Schools Enrichment Programs (which send foreign students into the schools to make presentations on their home countries). The Amherst Town Committee on Foreign Students provides leadership, ideas, and staffing for these endeavors and is an outstanding example of volunteer commitment.

VII. *Faculty programs.* Faculty interest and support were central to the establishment of IPO in 1969. There has continued a strong cooperative relationship since then between the IPO staff and many university faculty members—they assist in program development, and they direct programs, serve on committees, and interview candidates for overseas programs and scholarships. In turn, IPO provides assistance to faculty members in working out overseas research and sabbatical plans, and it sponsors from seven to ten regular faculty exchanges with institutions abroad.

Faculty exchanges provide an important means to enrich the university's offerings in an era of fiscal restraint, expand faculty members' spheres of contacts, and increase the international consciousness of the academic community. IPO has therefore established exchange links, with the aid and support of faculty members, and seeks to remove obstacles (faculty members' lack of funding sources and strategies, department hesitancy, retirement plan and salary problems) that might deter faculty members from participating in these exchanges.

VIII. *Working to increase the international dimension in all programs.* IPO acts as the university's watchdog to see that international awareness and the international dimension in academic programs are maximized despite current fiscal limitations. For example, the director of IPO has pressed for continuation, with reevaluation, of the foreign language requirement. IPO staff members participate in universitywide discussions of issues such as student motivation and retention and the liberal arts curriculum, particularly focusing on how these issues relate to international affairs. Further, IPO staff members work with departments to encourage student participation in overseas education opportunities and to urge them to take advantage of foreign students as resources—for example, in area studies.

CIRCLES OF INTERACTION

Figure 2.2 presents the major clienteles of the International Programs Office within the university—offices and groups with which IPO has formed linkages of service and cooperation. A few of these linkages deserve further comment.

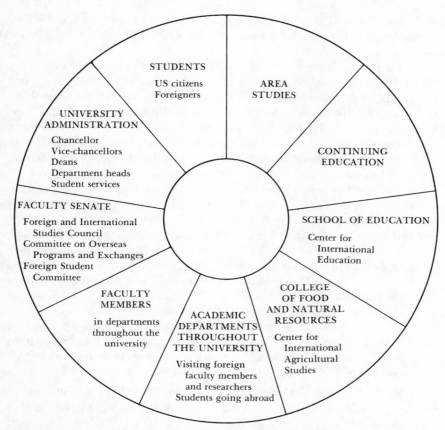

FIGURE 2.2.   Institutional constituencies of the International Programs Office.

1. *Area Studies.* IPO enjoys a close relationship with the International Area Studies Programs whose director (a faculty member) now reports to the coordinating dean of the College of Arts and Sciences but formerly reported to the associate provost for special programs, as did IPO. The Area Studies administrative assistant (a graduate teaching assistant) functions out of IPO. Area Studies majors are encouraged to take advantage of appropriate study abroad opportunities.

2. *Center for International Agricultural Studies, College of Food and Natural Resources.* IPO works closely with the director and the coordinating committee. Recently IPO's director chaired a task force that developed a Board for International Food and Agricultural Development (BIFAD) proposal to expand the university's role in international agricultural development.

3. *Continuing Education.* IPO works with the Continuing Education Summer Session staff on credit for summer overseas programs. In

addition, both IPO and Continuing Education are committed to strengthening foreign language and international studies in citizen education.

4. *Center for International Education (CIE)*. IPO supports and assists the CIE wherever possible in its active overseas education and development assistance programs. Over the years, CIE has been involved in nonformal education assistance in Uganda, Ecuador, Ghana, Thailand, Guatemala, and Indonesia. Incoming foreign visitors and trainees in these programs use the services of the Foreign Student Office. The overseas study coordinators assist students going on CIE teaching exchanges in the UK and Ecuador with administrative arrangements.

5. *Foreign Language Departments*. There is constant close cooperation with these departments on joint study abroad programs and on providing language majors with information on study abroad programs at other institutions. IPO is a major advocate for foreign language study on campus.

Beyond the UMass.–Amherst campus, IPO has many linkages (see figure 2.3). The public service role is reflected in several of these linkages, particularly where IPO involvements extend to foreign students' contacts with the community and where the IPO staff becomes involved in community and professional organizations.

Figure 2.3 shows four rings, separate categories of IPO's interaction outside the institution: within Massachusetts, within New England, within the United States, and in foreign countries. Some of the interrelationships deserve further comment.

1. *Universitywide linkages*. IPO works closely with the foreign student adviser at UMass.–Boston, sharing information, consulting on foreign student matters, and coordinating certain aspects of UMass. study abroad programs such as student recruitment and selection. IPO has also worked with the President's Office at UMass–Boston on several specific exchange programs and on agreements that require trustee approval.

2. *Five Colleges, Inc.* The Foreign Student Office is in frequent communication with the other members of Five Colleges, Inc., sharing its expertise and advising on foreign student and scholar concerns. IPO represents UMass. on the Five College Committee on International Programs. IPO serves as an information and counseling resource on overseas study to students from the other institutions and includes them in UMass. study abroad programs. IPO also advises faculty members at the other schools on research abroad and international faculty exchanges. IPO's director is on the Advisory Committee of the Mount Holyoke College International Internships Program.

3. *Linkages within Massachusetts*. IPO involvements at the state level include:

• Internal Revenue Service, Springfield: income tax assistance for foreign students and faculty members

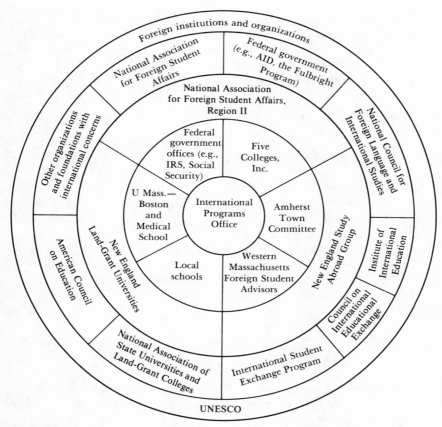

FIGURE 2.3. Off-campus circles of interaction for the International Programs Office.

- Social Security Administration, Holyoke: cooperation in getting social security numbers for foreign students and scholars
- Immigration and Naturalization Service, Boston: visas, extensions of stay, change of status, etc., for foreign students and scholars
- Primary and secondary schools: foreign students' participation in presentations on their countries
- Other higher education institutions (e.g., Harvard, Brandeis, Boston University): consultation on foreign student and study abroad matters; collaboration on workshops and other programs
- Foreign student advisors at colleges, universities, and secondary schools in western Massachusetts: the UMass. Foreign Student Office obtains information on foreign students from the Immigration and Naturalization Service, analyzes it, and disseminates it.

4. *Linkages within the United States.* IPO interacts on a national scale with:

- National Association for Foreign Student Affairs (NAFSA): IPO's director has been on the National Board and was 1981/82 president-elect, 1982/83 president; IPO's overseas study and coordinators have served as coordinators of study abroad affairs in the New England region; IPO's foreign student advisor and assistant foreign student advisor are active in NAFSA regional affairs; IPO's budget officer was supported for professional consultation at Ohio State and Michigan State.

- Council on International Educational Exchange (CIEE): IPO handles CIEE international ID cards; IPO's director is a member of the Executive Board; and IPO participates in CIEE's annual grant and cooperative credit-granting programs.

- National Council for Foreign Language and International Studies: IPO's director is on the Panel of Senior Advisors and the Task Force on Kindergarten Through Collegiate Education.

- National Association of State Universities and Land-Grant Colleges: IPO's director is on the International Affairs Committee.

- Council for the International Exchange of Scholars (CIES): IPO is the campus representative for Senior Fulbrights and handles programing for CIES-sponsored (and many other) foreign visitors for brief sojourns on campus.

- International Student Exchange Program: IPO's director chairs the Advisory Board.

- Institute of International Education (IIE): IPO's Foreign Student Office serves as collaborator and liaison on admission, etc., of IIE-sponsored foreign students such as Fulbright, Ford Foundation, South African Education Program, ITT, etc.

- African Graduate Fellowship Program, Latin American Scholarship Program of American Universities, Pan-American Union, Agency for International Development, World Health Organization, Amideast, Rockefeller Foundation: IPO's Foreign Student Office serves as liaison on foreign student admissions and services.

- American Council on Education: IPO's director is on the Commission of International Educational Relations.

5. *Overseas linkages.* The overseas involvements of IPO are intrinsic to its mission. Student and faculty exchanges of course create particularly strong contacts. Cooperation overseas also involves UMass–Amherst in research projects, curriculum discussions, and development assistance.

Funding

When the International Programs Office was established in 1969, it initially received a state allocation of $40,000 and had three and one-half staff persons. In the twelve years since then the overall budget—including the state allocation, fee-based revenues, grants, and contracts—has increased many times, and the staff has grown to the full-time equivalent of nine positions.

IPO fiscal needs are made up of three major components: the expenses of running the office, the program expenses (in almost all cases entirely fee-based), and grants and contracts. In an ideal situation, state allocations would entirely cover office expenses, because the university has made a basic commitment to provide international programs and their attendant services to students and faculty members. Each overseas study program would generate (through fees) the majority of funds needed to operate, but state allocations might lower student fees when costs were too high for the average student. Grants and contracts would be self-financing and would provide for a diversification of activities or special projects not otherwise possible.

How does IPO's actual situation measure up to this ideal? The state allocation does cover most basic office expenses. In FY 1981, only 3.6 percent of the total payments to persons were drawn from nonstate funds (that is, soft money), whereas that figure was 18 percent in FY 1977. Although additional support staff members are needed, the state's acceptance of its commitment to international education is heartening. Soft money is more crucial to IPO's operation in the areas of office supplies, telephone, and postage, for which state support covers about half the current expenses. Similarly, travel is an area where nonstate funds are essential because no state support is available.

Most program expenses are for summer and academic-year programs and exchanges. These programs are almost entirely self-financing, and their revenues account for most of the overall budget growth in recent years. Whereas the state allocation to IPO was 26 percent of the budget in FY 1977, it was only 19 percent in FY 1981. The fee-based revenues used to run programs and exchanges doubled during these years. Although state support would be desirable to lower the rising costs of these opportunities to students, it is not likely in an era of drastic budget cuts in higher education. Therefore, other avenues are being pursued to provide study abroad scholarship support, such as alumni support.

Grants and contracts have in recent years contributed an average of $60,000 per year to the overall budget. They have enabled IPO to carry out research on the impact of study abroad on students who participate in exchanges, and they have brought groups of foreign students to UMass.- Amherst. This source of support is a continually changing one, and growth is being encouraged in this area.

A look at expenditures further clarifies IPO's funding and finances. Program expenditures drawn from program fees is by far the largest item, making up 77 percent of the total budget. Next comes salaries (22 percent) and finally, amazingly low at 1 percent, are material office expenses and travel (not related to the actual running of specific programs).

During its first twelve years, the International Programs Office has grown dramatically. Yet its fiscal growth has come primarily from fee-based programing and outside funding sources, that is, grants and contracts. Although state funds provide needed stability to support staff salaries, virtually all programs are otherwise self-supporting.

Program Strengths and Weaknesses

A listing of the strengths and weaknesses of UMass.–Amherst's approach to international programs may help in assessing the extent to which the approach might be appropriate for another institution.

Strengths:

1. Well-established major research university in an attractive setting with Five College links is attractive to foreign students and foreign institutions for exchanges.

2. Solid support for international education goals exists within the administration and faculty.

3. Long tradition of international involvements predates IPO; thus IPO is the product of natural, organic development of international programing within the university structure.

4. Strong support and involvement exists among the faculty; internationally recognized research faculty members provide many contacts worldwide.

5. Positive relationships between IPO and other university administrative units allow smooth operation and support.

6. IPO reports to key academic administrative officers, a fact that results in university-wide recognition not tied to any one college or school.

7. Large portfolio of overseas opportunities sponsored by UMass. and a flexible policy on student participation in programs sponsored by other institutions enables students to go virtually anywhere in the world to study.

8. Vitality, skills, and diversity exist among staff; part-time flexibility helps to prevent burnout despite heavy work load. Excellent communication exists among staff members.

9. Most basic funds for the operation of the office are provided by the state.

10. IPO is centrally located in the main administration building; useful open space within the office itself serves as a reception area and meeting place.

Weaknesses:

1. International affairs programs on campus are not sufficiently centralized; IPO needs to be more able to catalyze activities.

2. There is no International House or Center.

3. More nonstate sources of income are needed to support staffing needs and scholarships for study abroad and for foreign students, to expand grants and contracts, to increase contacts with businesses, and to insulate the office from dangers of state budget cuts.

4. Alumni must be mobilized to support international education activities (American study abroad participants and foreign students).

5. The support staff is not adequate, and part-time staff members need to be better coordinated to provide continuity of services.

6. The faculty reward structure fails to recognize—and sometimes even impedes—faculty members' overseas activities.

7. A larger percentage of the student body should be sent abroad at some time during their university career.

8. Quarters are cramped; space is less than adequate for counseling, interviewing, holding small group meetings, and consulting the IPO library.

9. There is no English as a Second Language program.

Suggestions for Other Institutions

The development of the International Programs Office at the University of Massachusetts at Amherst since it was set up in 1969 is a prime example of incremental growth. It began not as a major unit, generously staffed and funded, but as a small office for monitoring, facilitating, and disseminating information about study abroad—an office into which the existing Foreign Student Office was integrated. As IPO found more ways to respond to student, faculty, and administration interests in international programs, its activities and staffing grew, and with them, the university's commitment grew and its international involvement expanded.

Drawing on the experience of the International Programs Office at UMass.-Amherst, the following guidelines may be helpful in developing an active and effective international component at other institutions.

1. *Use the resources in your own backyard.* Most important of these resources are faculty members with overseas contacts whose initiatives can be crucial to developing programs and recruiting foreign students. Also of assistance can be foreign visitors to the campus such as researchers and lecturers. Each one can lead to an international opportunity.

2. *Use all opportunities for international travel by staff members.* Make the most of each trip to increase knowledge of new areas of the world and establish new contacts.

3. *Maintain close relations with all academic departments.* Call on departments for assistance. Advise them in developing international programs, and send them foreign visitors.

4. *Maintain close working relationships with administrative units.* Examples include admissions, housing, and financial aid.

5. *Recruit staff members with international experience and foreign language knowledge whenever possible.* They will maximize the information base in the office. Offer opportunities for advancement and greater responsibilities. Encourage staff development in international education, even when it may lead to staff turnover, because turnover will often stimulate activity.

6. *Use the regional, national, and international networks for international education information and advice.* Examples include the National Association for Foreign Students Affairs, the Institute of International Education, and the Council on International Educational Exchange.

7. *Stay in touch with the literature on international education.* Through research and publication, the staff can be at the forefront of developments in the field and gain national and international exposure that will be helpful in program development.

The International Programs Office has functioned on the premise that many international education resources are available cost-free within a university—principally the time, interest, and international connections of faculty members and the flow of visitors from other countries coming to campus. Programs and relationships with institutions abroad can be developed if these resources are tapped, and in particular, if ways are found for them to reenforce each other. The most effective means is an international education office that has a variety of programs and activities, wide contacts within the university and beyond, and a place in the institution's structure that affirms the centrality of international education to the institution.

CHAPTER 3

Western Kentucky University

RAYMOND L. CRAVENS

The University and the Community

A comprehensive university with an enrollment of over 13,000 students, Western Kentucky University (also known as WKU and, locally, as Western) in Bowling Green, Kentucky, has strong academic traditions of emphasis on international and cross-cultural studies and world affairs. The foundations of this tradition were laid by a number of founding faculty members who had a world perspective and reflected this in the content of their courses. Today the university is among the leaders of institutions of its type and size in the breadth and reputation of its international programs.

Support and encouragement from the Board of Regents and the administration, active cooperation and participation by the faculty, credibility and experience achieved through successful international technical assistance and educational projects, and recognition gained from linkages with national, state, and international organizations have contributed to the standing and reputation of Western Kentucky's international programs.

How the International Program Was Established

The twenty-year period from 1960 to 1980 saw unparalleled growth in enrollment, number of faculty, and physical campus development. During these two decades, four presidents, two academic vice-presidents, and a number of deans and directors shared a common interest and appreciation for the value of international education in the diversifying academic setting of a developing university.

In 1960 there were 3,599 students enrolled at Western Kentucky State College, as the institution was then called, pursuing multipurpose but limited academic programs offered by 131 faculty members. Traditionally, strong programs in history and political science, geography, foreign languages, economics and sociology, and folk studies treated international subjects and emphasized the development of world awareness and the appreciation of global issues in regular course offerings. Occasional lecturers would make presentations augmenting the curricular emphases of departments and individual faculty members. A small cadre of about twelve international students provided limited interpersonal contact with foreign cultures.

During the early 1960s campus interest in international affairs and foreign cultures had been heightened by the inauguration of the Rhodes–Helm Lecture Series. Beginning in 1962, speakers such as General Carlos Romulo of the Philippines, writer Pearl Buck, and other prominent internationalists were brought to the campus under the auspices of this lecture series. From 1960 to 1966, a remarkable increase of student enrollment to 8,703 and an accompanying growth in the number of faculty members to 373 combined to make a significant expansion of academic offerings possible. Moreover, a number of faculty members with specialties in world area studies and several with specialized training in intercultural studies, international relations, and languages, including several people with degrees from universities abroad, were added to the institution's faculty. Developing these faculty resources made possible the coalescing of common interests in international education and provided the base for the expanded programs and activities that occurred after the college obtained university status in 1966.

After achieving university status in 1966, Western Kentucky was to offer enhanced academic program offerings. The university president, who was appointed to serve on the International Programs Committee of the American Association of State Colleges and Universities, and the vice-president for academic affairs encouraged formal attention to international education. Several of the newly appointed college deans, department heads, and academic directors were also sympathetic to expanded international programs.

Administrative emphasis for international programs was heightened in 1973 by the creation of the Office of Coordinator of International Education; this office was to coordinate existing international academic programs, foreign students, and organize and promote programs of study abroad. The first coordinator served from 1973 to 1977 and during this period established strong foundations for future growth of international education programs.

In January 1977 the chairman of the Board of Regents appointed an ad hoc Committee on International Education. This committee received, approved, and recommended to the full board a policy statement about international education programs, and in May 1977 the board approved a new position at the university, dean of public service and international programs, to which the vice-president for academic affairs was named. The adoption of this policy statement and the creation of a separate office and administrator gave important impetus to international programs.

Institutional Commitment to International Education

MISSION AND GOALS

The university statement of purpose sets forth general aspirations to "promote . . . liberal education" and to foster "democratic citizenship"; and the international programs aspire to promote the "international dimension" in the curriculum, meaningful contacts with international students, and international exchange and projects. The Office of International Programs and Projects seeks to provide a focal point of "international stimulus for the community, region, and state."

Although WKU is a comprehensive university, some categorize it as a regional institution. Since the mid-1970s, the Kentucky Council on Higher Education has sought to refine the state "system" of higher education by defining the role and scope of the universities and community colleges. WKU has had to address the provincial concern of some citizens and, surprisingly, some faculty, that an emphasis on international programs might somehow be inappropriate for a "regional school" like Western.

Because of this situation and climate, a clarification of Western's role in international programs was sought, and in 1977 the Board of Regents gave strong support to international education by adopting a statement that recognized the importance of educating students to "live and work in an increasingly interdependent world." The university was given a specific charge to develop new international education programs that would expand student involvement and faculty development.

International program development has been directed toward achieving these objectives. The question of the appropriate kinds of programs for a university like Western may still be on the minds of some individuals, but since 1977 the direction for these program initiatives has been clear. The policy adopted by the board is stated as follows:

> Western Kentucky University has given emphasis to strengthening the international and inter-cultural dimensions of its programs and activities . . .

primarily to provide students from Western's service area and beyond with the opportunity to acquire an education that will better prepare them to live and work in an increasingly interdependent world. In addition, these international resources have been shared with area schools, community groups, and citizens through the University's role as a regional education center.

Western has strengthened its international education program through (1) the development of curricula with the international content including general education, career preparation, and pre- and in-service teacher training; (2) adding to library and teaching resources; (3) sponsoring lectures, performances, and seminars with international content; (4) providing study-abroad opportunities for students; (5) establishing interinstitutional linkages with universities in other nations; and (6) encouraging the development of faculty and student interest and expertise in the international dimension of their field of study through international travel and cooperative and exchange programs. Western has established Asian and Latin American Studies Programs and has an unusually strong program in the latter area.

The University anticipates a continued role as a provider of selected programs and activities in international education with future expansion in the area taking place as warranted by the needs of the region and the state. Special emphasis will be placed on strengthening existing programs and developing new programs in international education which will expand opportunities for student involvement and faculty development.

The Board of Regents has continued its interest in international education activities and has recently reconstituted and continued its Committee on International Education. The support from the Board of Regents and from persons at high levels of university administration has provided indispensable encouragement and stimulation to international education program development.

ADMINISTRATIVE ORGANIZATION

The Office of International Programs and Projects is directed by Dr. John Petersen, Assistant Vice President for Academic Affairs, who is responsible for leading and coordinating all university international programs and projects. Under this officer are the director of the Center for Latin American Studies; a program coordinator who oversees full-time the Office of International Programs and Projects; an international student advisor; and coordinators of British study programs, student teaching abroad, other study abroad programs, and advisors for the Fulbright student and faculty exchange programs. All of these directors and coordinators are also full-time faculty members. One half-time university secretary and three half-time secretaries for the Latin American Studies Center, the International Student Affairs Office, and the British Study Programs, plus student secretarial help, constitute the support staff.

Full-time faculty members coordinate the study abroad programs, which include the British Study Programs, WKU in France Program, and a program of summer study in Europe in cooperation with Murray State University. These coordinators and the two Fulbright advisors contribute their services without teaching load adjustment.

Program Description

Area Studies. In the 1968/69 school year, faculty members from the Departments of Foreign Languages, Teacher Education, Economics, Geography, Government, History, and Psychology were appointed to a Latin American Studies Committee, which began to develop an interdisciplinary program and other special emphases in Latin American Studies. In 1969 a certification program for students pursuing an emphasis in Latin American Studies was begun, and in 1971 a minor in Latin American Studies was approved by the Academic Council and the Board of Regents. In the Spring of 1974 the Latin American Studies Committee began publishing *Intercambio,* a pamphlet–journal containing articles by Latin American scholars and information about Latin American studies and activities at the university.

In 1976 the Latin American Studies Center was established. In that same year the center was designated as a Latin American Language and Area Studies Center by the US Office of Education and was awarded a grant to operate its programs. Federal funding ended in 1981, but the center's programs have continued with institutional support. These activities have included presentations on strengthening and expanding the Latin American Studies Program at the undergraduate level; sponsorship of conferences, lectures, and special programs including musical presentations and art exhibitions; outreach programs to share the resources of the center with organizations and individuals in the university community; and a summer institute for teachers focusing on curriculum materials for approaches to teaching about Latin America.

In 1974 faculty members from several departments with an interest in Asian studies formed a committee and subsequently developed and received approval for an academic minor in Asian Studies. In addition to providing this academic minor to students, the committee sponsors special speakers and programs each semester plus an annual Asian fair for the general student body.

International Dimensions Project. By the early 1970s, the expansion of international education funding categories by the US Department of Education provided opportunities for outside funding of the international programs on college campuses. The first successful funded project at Western Kentucky University began in 1973 with the approval of a two-year grant. It was entitled "Strengthening International Dimensions," and it proceeded under the direction of Dr. John Petersen, a government professor. The purpose of this project was to infuse international dimensions into general education course offerings across a number of disciplines. Faculty members from various disciplines participated in special workshops and curriculum planning sessions through which the course content of their general education offerings was modified or enhanced to include an international dimension. The net effect of this program was to broaden the support on campus for international education as well as to enlarge the impact of the curriculum emphasis in this area.

Study Abroad Programs. Study abroad programs have also been encouraged by the university. One of the first to be developed was a summer quarter term in Mexico in cooperation with the University of the Americas in Mexico City. Under the sponsorship of the Spanish language faculty, this program began in 1964 and continued until the Mexican university structure and character were changed. Western faculty and students were nevertheless able to gain significant international experience during the summer term in Mexico program. Other study abroad programs were conducted on an ad hoc or occasional basis during this time period.

In 1972 the Department of Speech and Theatre inaugurated a London theatre tour for the December–January interim between semesters. This program provides opportunities for students and theatre patrons to spend two weeks in London during the height of the theatre season. This program has been continued each year since its inception.

Significantly more opportunities to study abroad for a full year occurred in 1972 when the university signed an agreement with the University Paul Valéry in Montpellier, France, under which students from Western may attend that institution for one semester or a full academic year. Since its beginning, this program has provided a valuable outlet for those students who want to study in France while developing their fluency in the French language. For the 1981/82 school year ten students took advantage of this unique opportunity.

Other study abroad programs have been offered on a special or ad hoc basis. For example, May term programs in Mexico and in Guatemala were offered in 1973 and a second Central American study tour was conducted in 1975. Another unique program was a special geographical field expedition to Colombia, South America, conducted in the summer of 1974.

In an effort to expand student and faculty participation, a program consisting of summer term in England and Scotland began in 1979. This has now been established as an ongoing study abroad program. Four departments have sponsored programs in which a total of over 235 students and sixteen faculty members have participated. A unique feature of these programs is the provision of home stays with selected English and Scottish families. Lectures by British professors and visits to historic sites are also included.

In 1976 a program of student teaching abroad was inaugurated by the College of Education. The program continues to provide useful experience to a few students each year who conduct student teaching in such diverse locations as Great Britain, Belgium, and Costa Rica.

Western Kentucky works with other institutions to expand study abroad opportunities. WKU cooperates with Murray State University and Eastern Kentucky University in offering summer study programs in Austria, Spain, and France. These programs offer students the chance for experience with the language and culture in the European setting. A faculty advisor from the Department of Foreign Languages and Intercultural Studies coordinates Western's participation. WKU participated in a summer study program in Spain sponsored by the University of Villanova in the mid-1970s, and WKU participated as well in the American Association for Colleges and Universities study center abroad program during the 1970s, and sent a few students to study as the AASCU centers.

During the last ten years, seven Western students have been awarded Fulbright scholarships to study abroad in Germany, Brazil, United Kingdom, Algeria, and France. In the fall of 1982, a cooperative center for study in Britain was established to coordinate and facilitate study abroad in Britain among five Kentucky Universities (Eastern, Northern, Morehead, Murray, and Western).

Foreign Students. The university's international student program had steadily expanded and developed during the 1970s. In the 1970s the university, in consultation with the National Association for Foreign Student Affairs, adopted new guidelines and procedures for admission and counseling of international students. Before 1977, the international student advisor had functioned in that role in addition to carrying a heavy teaching assignment. In 1978 a full-time international student advisor was appointed. The international student program, including supplementary activities such as a host family program, is now firmly established and is a sound operation. In 1981/82, 289 international students from forty-five countries enrolled at the university.

The university has participated in the Latin American Scholars Program of American Universities (LASPAU), under which promising graduate students are brought to study at United States universities. Western has hosted students from Peru, Bolivia, Trinidad–Tobago, Panama, Costa Rica, Venezuela, Belize, Brazil, and Chile.

Faculty Exchanges. Five Western faculty members have been awarded Fulbright lectureships to universities abroad in Pakistan, India, Nigeria, Korea, Turkey, and Colombia. Two Fulbright professors have been assigned to the university, one from Pakistan for one semester and one from Chile for one academic year. In 1980 an administrative intern from a Nigerian university spent several months on the campus, as have other special foreign visitors in recent years. Teachers from the province of Buenos Aires, Argentina, have spent semester-long periods in special school observation, education research, and seminars on the campus for the last three years.

Four faculty members have held visiting professorships at universities abroad in Chile, Iran, Austria, Egypt, and Ethiopia. With sponsorship by the United States Information Agency, two WKU faculty have lectured in Central America (1973), in South America (1976), and in Germany (1980).

International Projects. In 1971 the university was provided the opportunity to engage in its first technical assistance project in conjunction with the Universidad Nacional de Trujillo, Peru. Under the terms of this project, faculty members from the science and engineering areas at Western assisted counterparts at the Peruvian university in selecting laboratory equipment for a new science campus being developed through a loan to the government of Peru by the Inter-American Development Bank. Faculty members from Western traveled to Peru for consultation, and faculty members from the National University came to the Western campus to work on selecting and ordering the equipment. One unique aspect of this project was the adoption of a procedure through which the equipment for the Peruvian university was ordered under the provisions of the Kentucky state purchasing regulations. The competitive bidding and price contracting procedures resulted in major savings for the National University.

The Inter-American Development Bank deemed the WKU assistance to be outstanding and subsequently recommended Western to other Latin American universities trying to develop similar facilities. Coinciding with the opening of other technical assistance opportunities, in 1973 the university hired its first director of international projects. During the period from 1972 to 1979, technical assistance projects were conducted with the Universidad Austral de Chile, Valdivia, Chile; Universidad Industrial de Santander, Bucaramanga, Colombia; Universidad Los Andes, Merida, Venezuela; and Universidad Nacional Leon, Nicaragua.

WKU has subsequently been recognized by the Board for International Food and Agricultural Development (BIFAD) for participation in food and agriculture-related international projects. In fact, WKU is one of the few non-land-grant universities that have achieved eligibility for BIFAD project participation. To prepare for continued involvement in technical assistance projects, the university is pursuing a grant from the Agency for International Development to augment its faculty capabilities and readiness for international project involvement.

In addition to the Latin American projects, in 1971 two professors in Western's Department of Sociology, Anthropology, and Social Work conducted an extensive survey research project designed to investigate the personal and social impact of the newly emerging Icelandic national television system. Funded by the National Science Foundation, the research took advantage of the unique geographical diffusion of Icelandic TV, which made possible rare comparison of television viewers and nonviewers. Undergraduate and graduate students employed by the project in both countries learned much about the complexities of cross-cultural research. The project findings generated numerous journal articles and papers that were presented at professional meetings at state, regional, and national levels.

The major technical assistance activities have provided unique opportunities for WKU faculty to work with counterparts at foreign universities, especially in Latin America. The relationships that have developed have led to faculty exchanges, and some foreign faculty members come to WKU to pursue graduate degrees. Although the technical assistance projects tend to be ad hoc, the long-range academic relationships that can grow out of such projects constitute a valid rationale for continuing university involvement.

Kentucky Council for International Education. In 1973 the Council of Academic Vice-Presidents of the Kentucky state-supported institutions of higher education appointed the vice-president for academic affairs at Western to head a committee of institutional representatives to explore ways of improving interinstitutional cooperation in international education. This committee, which came to be known as the Kentucky Committee on International Education, was reconstituted in 1976 as the Kentucky Council for International Education (KCIE). From 1973 to 1981 the organization was headquartered at Western Kentucky University. In the fall of 1981, the headquarters were transferred to the University of Louisville. The new president is director of the International Center at the University of Louisville. KCIE now includes fifteen colleges and universities from both the public and the private sector in Kentucky, the State Department of Education, and the International Division of the Kentucky Department of Commerce.

KCIE has assisted many international education activities with implications for the universities and colleges in Kentucky. Lecturers and resources have been shared. A communications network has been established, and annual international education conferences were held in 1980 and 1981. Study abroad programs have been coordinated and publicized in an attempt to increase the opportunities available to all Kentucky students for study abroad. A television series developed by the International Center of the University of Louisville has been cosponsored by the KCIE. During the last two years, four funded projects have been sponsored by KCIE. One of these projects, funded by the Kentucky Humanities Council, enabled institutions to train and to take out into surrounding communities a small team of international students who presented public programs to various organizations on the general theme,

"Humanity's Concern Around the World." These presentations were augmented by a humanities professor who lectured to the same organizations in preparation for the visit by the international students. Over 7,000 Kentuckians in thirty-two Kentucky cities heard these presentations.

A second project sponsored by the KCIE was a US Department of Education-funded Group Project Abroad curriculum development project in Guatemala and Costa Rica conducted during the summer of 1980. Nineteen Kentucky college, elementary, and secondary teachers spent six weeks in Central America working to develop curriculum materials for use in Kentucky classrooms.

A third project funded by the US Department of Education under title VI, section 603, called Citizen Education for Cultural Understanding, provided a resource utilization model in twelve districts across Kentucky in 1981. Twelve teams of teachers, led by the district member of the Kentucky Education Association's Instruction and Professional Development Committee along with one representative from a KCIE college or university, conducted an inventory of community resources for global education, and led community forums on global issues with the participation of local resource individuals, teachers, and students from the schools.

A KCIE faculty and curriculum development group project to Egypt, funded by the US Office of International Programs, US Department of Education, was conducted in the summer of 1982, with Western Kentucky University as the contracting agent. This project provided to university, middle school, and secondary school teachers from Kentucky a chance to develop a mediated curriculum unit on modern Egypt for use in Kentucky schools. The Kentucky State Department of Education and the Kentucky Education Association provided vital support in the selection of group project participants and in the implementation of the curriculum objectives.

These examples of the efficacy of a statewide organization and network for joint action and projects in international education have solidified support for the KCIE among the state's colleges and universities. The advantages of participation in these statewide programs and the sharing of resources have been gained without the establishment of a KCIE staff. KCIE operates solely on the basis of annual dues paid by the member institutions and through the volunteer work of the appointed institutional representatives.

LINKAGES

Western Kentucky University maintains membership in the American Association of State Colleges and Universities, the American Council on

Education, the American Association of Colleges for Teacher Education, the Kentucky Council for International Education, the Consortium for International Studies Education, the International Studies Association, and the National Association for Foreign Student Affairs. These organizations have active international programs in which Western often participates.

WKU also maintains contact with the Agency for International Development and the Inter-American Development Bank regarding international projects for which Western may serve as a consultant. Also, from time to time, the International Communication Agency requests that the university host an important foreign visitor.

Western's Office of International Programs and Projects cooperates actively with the local community chapter of Sister Cities International, which has organized exchanges and projects with Ecuador, Kentucky's "sister country," and with Santo Domingo de los Colorados, Ecuador, Bowling Green's sister city. The office also cooperates with and provides assistance to community organizations with an international focus such as civic clubs, the newly formed International Friendship Council for hosting foreign students, and other groups.

At the state level, the university assists the International Division of the Kentucky Department of Commerce in visits of foreign business and industrial leaders. At the community level, the university responds to frequent requests to host foreign visitors, providing translation and other services.

Relationships with foreign universities are maintained on formal and informal bases. In Latin American, a formal agreement of cooperation exists with the Universidad Austral de Chile, Valdivia, Chile, and cooperation on student exchanges and curriculum planning has occurred regularly with the Corporacion International para el Desarallo Educativo, Bogatá, Colombia. There are other linkages with foreign universities related to student and faculty exchanges and study abroad programs.

On-campus conferences on international themes and the university committee structure provide links among faculty from numerous disciplines. A favorable climate for cooperation among departments and colleges has made possible the successful interdisciplinary area studies programs.

FUNDING

The 1981/82 institutional budget for the Office of International Programs and Projects totaled $48,584. This total does not include the pro rata share of faculty and administrators who spend a portion of their time on the programs of the office. That figure would amount to a substantial additional contribution.

One project totaling \$201,000 over a five-year period ended in August 1981, and another totaling \$85,000 was completed in September 1981. Currently, a \$65,000 grant for the Group Project to Egypt is being coordinated through the Office of International Programs and Projects. Fund-raising projects, including the sale of a Latin American cookbook to raise funds for a scholarship for international students, provide small but significant funds from outside the university budget.

The Study Abroad programs are operated through an agency fund set up from program fee receipts (program fees are added to each participant's cost). Most of the direct program costs are reimbursed to the university from these agency funds.

Strengths and Weaknesses

International programs at Western Kentucky University have progressed because of several factors:

- commitment of a core of faculty members from several academic disciplines

- encouragement from the university administration and the Board of Regents

- stimulation from international program grants received from the US Department of Education

- expansion of faculty international experience through technical assistance contracts and exchange programs

- increase in resources and opportunities for faculty and students through interinstitutional cooperation, especially through the Kentucky Council for International Education.

As these various activities illustrate, there is a broad range of international programs at Western. As the availability, the number of participants, and the program's standing have grown, support for continuing and expanding international programs has increased. Many of the programs were successful because faculty members contributed their services generously in addition to their full-time teaching responsibilities. Voluntary faculty participation is a necessary ingredient to success in an institution that gives primacy to teaching.

However, there are weaknesses inherent in the structure and the support for these programs. While the Office of International Programs and Projects gains status from its administrative assignment directly under the Office of the Vice President for Academic Affairs, it must depend on academic departments for faculty resources. This means that resources are generally available only after all teaching responsibilities have been assessed or if the department is able to replace a faculty member with a part-time instructor. International program activities tend to have a secondary status among the priorities of departments and colleges.

Further exacerbating this situation is the fact that faculty activities in the international program or project area may not be considered relevant or important when the annual departmental assessment of the faculty member's performance is done. Because many international programs or projects are interdisciplinary, department heads or deans may not consider successful programs of this kind to be positive contributions to their department's reputation or standing. Furthermore, some deans or department heads tend to discount the importance of these activities because research or publication, particularly in the faculty member's specialty, may not result. This fact tends to discourage faculty members from participating in activities for which they may receive little or no credit in salary or promotion.

Another problem is the lack of sufficient "seed" money to get new programs and new international contacts established. Unfortunately, the emphasis on international programs in the late 1970s coincided with a time of continuation, or actual reduction, of existing budgets. Thus, new programs had to compete with existing programs which had well established "line items" in the budget. Consequently, international programs that have not been funded from outside sources have been starved budgetarily. Remarkably, these programs have mounted some unusually fine events and activities; and while international programs have been affected by recent budget cuts, commitment to this program has been reinforced.

Strategies for the 1980s

In spite of problems such as repeated state budget cuts and retrenchment at the federal level, international programs at Western Kentucky can anticipate new challenges and opportunities during the 1980s. Of primary importance will be a renewal of efforts to enhance international education in the entire university curriculum. The College of Business Administration and the College of Education have expressed new interest in international and cross-cultural content for their majors. Realization of the career potential in international commerce, banking, diplomacy, and many other fields should provide additional incentive for language and international studies as crucial ingredients in new curriculum designs.

Another educational challenge lies with the growing cadre of international students at the university. Offering a well-planned and appropriate degree program for these students, and providing more opportunities for their interaction with other students, should be important university goals. New approaches in this area can have significant curricular impact and can strengthen the international education emphasis of the institution.

Active pursuit of outside funding, including appropriate technical assistance projects abroad, can provide a funding base for the staff and operations—a base that is unlikely to be available through the regular budget. Providing credit and recognition for faculty members who devote time to these projects will be a critical factor.

The 1980s have brought a growing realization among Kentuckians of the reality of global interdependence. The curriculum and programs of Western Kentucky University will need to cultivate and respond to this new citizen awareness. With a sound foundation of resources and experience in international programs and projects, Western Kentucky is prepared to continue its leadership in international education.

CHAPTER 4

Ohio University

EDWARD BAUM

DURING THE PAST TWO DECADES Ohio University has built a strong reputation as Ohio's "international" university. Evidence of the university's broad commitment to international education can be seen in the extent of its international programs and activities, a breadth that includes a bachelor's degree program in business administration in Malaysia, the largest percentage of foreign students on campus of any university in Ohio (10 percent), and international activities undertaken by virtually every major academic unit on campus. Although many of these activities and programs are decentralized throughout the campus, a prime focus for international education efforts is the Center for International Studies.

The University and the Community

Ohio University was founded in 1804 as the first institution of higher education in the Northwest Territory. Since then the university has grown into a major state institution, one of four primarily residential state universities in Ohio located in the four corners of the state. (The others are Miami University in southwestern Ohio, Bowling Green State University in northwestern Ohio, and Kent State University in northeastern Ohio.)

Most of the growth of Ohio University's main campus in Athens took place in the two decades following the Korean War, with enrollment rising to more than 19,000 students by 1971. A drastic decline of enrollment, due to a number of factors, brought enrollment down to a little over 12,000 in 1975. Current enrollment on the main campus is approximately 14,000, about 2,000 of whom are graduate students. Five regional campuses and academic centers in southeastern Ohio enroll an additional 5,500 students.

The university is located in Athens, approximately seventy-five miles southeast of Columbus. It is a small city; the university predominates in much of the economic, social, and cultural life of the community. The total population of Athens, including all the students living on campus and in the town, is approximately 20,000. As a result, the campus is largely residential, with half the students living in university dormitories and apartments and the other half finding private housing close by.

The academic programs of the university are greatly varied. Bachelor's degrees are offered in more than 150 areas; master's degrees in 46; and doctorates in 20. There are eleven degree-granting academic units, including ten colleges—ranging from the more traditional colleges such as the College of Arts and Sciences and the College of Business Administration to the relatively new College of Osteopathic Medicine and the College of Health and Human Services—and the Center for International Studies, although its faculty and most of its courses are located in the colleges.

Institutional Commitment to International Education

Ohio University's international education efforts have grown, both consciously and unconsciously, over the past eighty-eight years, from the graduation of the first foreign student from Japan in 1895 to today's enrollment of more than 1,500 foreign students from eighty countries. However, the university's commitment goes beyond the number of students from other countries. The commitment includes international educational development activities, faculty and student exchange programs, and curriculum content, and it is formally included in the university's goals. The university's commitment is also reflected in the placement of the Center for International Studies within the administrative organization of the university as well as in the goals and organization of the center. Yet despite the existence of the center, many of the university's international education activities remain decentralized and pervade the entire university.

UNIVERSITY INTERNATIONAL EDUCATION PROGRAMS

Ohio University has been involved in several successful education development projects in cooperation with the US Agency for International Development (AID) and its predecessor, the International Cooperation Administration. In 1958, the College of Education began to provide assistance to the federal government of Nigeria for educational programs for teachers in western Nigeria, concentrating first on the Olunloyo College of Education in Ibadan and later on the Advanced Teachers

College, Ondo. This activity was followed by contracts to assist in the development of the Advanced Teachers College, Kano (northern Nigeria), vocational education (eastern Nigeria), and in-service training (northern Nigeria). In Southeast Asia, Ohio University worked for six years with the Ministry of Education of the then Republic of Viet Nam to improve secondary education. Recently an agreement was signed to provide education assistance in the improvement of primary education in Botswana in cooperation with the government of Botswana and the University College in Gaberone, its capital.

Beyond AID programs, the university has provided education services around the world, including a cooperative program in business administration with the MARA Institute of Technology in Malaysia, and English language training in Saudi Arabia. The College of Communication is currently provided training in radio and television for managers and engineers from broadcasting systems in Nigeria and Libya. Staff development is provided for faculty members from a number of foreign institutions under a special scholarship program established by the university, including the University College of Botswana and several Malaysian universities, and through the Fulbright Commission in Ecuador.

Student and faculty exchange programs have been established with the Chubu Institute of Technology in Japan in the areas of engineering, physics, and chemistry, with Feng Chia University in Taiwan, and with the University of Kuwait. Recently a student exchange agreement was signed with Trondheim University in Norway. Formal study abroad programs are run in Mexico, Austria, France, England, Italy, and, on occasion, Quebec.

As a result of cooperative agreements, more than one hundred Ohio University faculty members have direct education development experience overseas, primarily in Africa and Southeast Asia. This number does not include faculty members with international experience from programs such as the Fulbright–Hays program and the Rockefeller Fellowships.

Ohio University also provides an excellent program of intensive English instruction. Founded in 1968, the Ohio Program of Intensive English (OPIE) was the first such program in Ohio. Its primary purpose is to provide high-quality English language training enabling foreign students to undertake academic study at American universities. Another purpose is to familiarize foreign students with the educational methods and approaches of American colleges and universities.

Many courses with an international perspective are taught at Ohio University, particularly in the social sciences and the arts. The university has two focal points for much of this curricular effort. First, the Center for International Studies has worked to expand international offerings particularly on Africa, Latin America, and the Southeast Asia. Through both graduate and undergraduate programs, students may concentrate their study on an international topic that affects the three regions or on a single world area. Second, the university has adopted a set of general education requirements for all graduates of Ohio University that includes a component in Third World studies.

INSTITUTIONAL GOALS

The special commitment of Ohio University to international education can be seen in the university's educational plan for 1977/87, which was adopted by the Ohio University Board of Trustees on 1 October 1977. President Charles J. Ping summed up the plan in his convocation address of 30 September 1977, entitled "Search for Community." The commitments noted in the address are drawn from the goal statements identified by the plan and may be summarized as follows:

1. Commitment to the idea of the university and to being a residential college community
2. Commitment to quality and to the making of judgments
3. Commitment to intellectual community, to the interaction and integration of knowledge
4. Commitment to international community, to education for interdependence
5. Commitment to lifelong learning, to the creation of a broad community of learners
6. Commitment to educational justice, to being a just and socially responsive community

Thus, international education at Ohio University is predicated on the belief that the well educated citizen must be aware of the importance of international interdependence. President Ping noted that Ohio University's commitment to international community builds on a substantial foundation of foreign students, resources and programs in international education, and faculty and student exchanges—to include curriculum content, research design and emphasis, library collection, training of practicing professionals, and the delivery of professional services.

ADMINISTRATIVE ORGANIZATION

The head of the university is the president, and the chief academic officer is the provost. There are vice-presidents for student affairs, university relations, and operations, who report to the provost in matters of planning, budgeting, and administrative coordination and to the president on other matters. The director of the Center for International Studies is also the associate provost for international programs.

GOALS OF THE CENTER FOR INTERNATIONAL STUDIES

In its statement of goals, the Center for International Studies has accepted as its prime mission the encouragement and advancement of international education at Ohio University, with special emphasis on the Third World. Specifically, it seeks to:

1. Enable undergraduate and graduate students to concentrate on international affairs in their programs of study

2. Provide a focus for special study of certain world areas: Africa, Southeast Asia, and Latin America

3. Encourage the development of international programs and activities by every academic unit at Ohio University

4. Support the development of courses and programs with an international dimension by all academic units

5. Serve as a nexus for information on the university's international endeavors

6. Serve as a resource center for international education in southeastern Ohio and throughout the state

7. Work with others in the field to support and develop international education in Ohio

8. Provide a special "international voice" on campus when appropriate

ORGANIZATION OF THE CENTER FOR INTERNATIONAL STUDIES

An examination of the organizational chart for the Center for International Studies (figure 4.1) reveals four major program divisions, although there is a large amount of overlap among them. Because the director of the center is an associate provost, he has two major responsibilities in addition to his responsibility for the center: assisting both the president and the provost in reviewing the total range of the university's international activities and providing staff assistance to the provost.

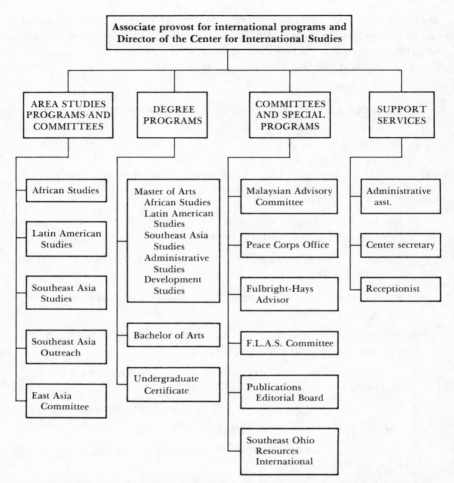

FIGURE 4.1.   Organizational chart for the Center for International Studies.

The center staff for 1980/81 consisted of five full-time staff members (associate provost, an administrative assistant, a secretary, a receptionist, and the director of Southeast Asian Outreach), five part-time staff members (three area studies directors, the Peace Corps coordinator, and the Southeast Ohio Resources International director), and fifteen graduate associates, five of whom are teaching associates for African and Southeast Asian Languages. Also associated with the center are the chairs of special committees (such as the Malaysian Advisory Committee) and the many faculty members and staff members who are involved in the various programs.

**T A B L E 4 . 1. Selected International Education
Activities and Responsible Units**

Activity	Responsible unit or units
1. Study abroad programs	
a. Languages (Mexico, Austria, France)	Modern Languages Department
b. Fine arts (England, Italy)	Comparative Arts Department
c. Press capitals	School of Journalism
2. Foreign students	
a. Undergraduate admissions	Admissions
b. Graduate admissions	Graduate Committees of the various departments and schools
c. On-campus services	Office of International Student and Faculty Services
d. Community volunteers	Athens Friends of International Studies (a community organization)
e. Intensive English	OPIE (Ohio Program of Intensive English) in the College of Arts and Sciences
3. Faculty and student exchanges	
a. Malaysia	College of Business Administration
b. Botswana	College of Education and African Studies Center
c. Japan	College of Engineering
d. Ecuador	Center for International Studies
e. Taiwan	College of Business Administration, Library, College of Arts and Sciences
f. Kuwait	Institute for Mathematics and Medicine
g. Saudi Arabia	Continuing Education and Lifelong Learning
h. Norway	Office of Ombudsman
4. Study abroad information	
a. Other universitys' programs	Center for International Studies
b. Fulbright programs	Fulbright Advisor

RESPONSIBILITIES FOR INTERNATIONAL EDUCATION

The major responsibilities of the Center for International Studies focus on the area studies programs and related degree programs. Ohio University, of course, also supports many international education activities that are normally found in any large university. However, the international dimension of education (both graduate and undergraduate) is widely spread throughout the various units of the university (see table 4.1). The decentralized nature of many international programs, although posing somewhat of a problem of coordination and flow of information, serves to strengthen the commitment of the various academic units to international education.

How the Center for International Studies Was Established

Because of the university's growing involvement in educational programs in Africa and Southeast Asia in the late 1950s and early 1960s, providing the opportunity for international study at Ohio University was only a matter of time. The predecessor to the current center, also called the Center for International Studies, was established in 1964 by university President Vernon R. Alden. The establishment of this center, which involved little or no consultation with departments or deans, was part of Alden's commitment to excellence at Ohio University. In 1966, due to several personnel changes, the center became part of the College of Arts and Sciences and remained there for the next three years.

Because of the growing complexity of the university's international activities and programs, in 1969 the vice-president and dean of faculties decided to centralize them in a new Center for International Studies. The new center included the area study programs and the master's degree programs of its predecessor, study abroad programs, the foreign student office, and AID contracts that had been administered by the College of Education.

On the one hand this centralization provided greater coordination for the university's international activities, but on the other hand, it severed some of the important ties between these programs and the colleges and departments that had staffed them. Many of the departments and scholars involved in the activities lost some of their interest when the activities were no longer seen as "theirs," and centralizing the activities was in fact found to be a weaker arrangement because it eroded faculty support. Declining enrollments and financial stringencies were additional reasons for a certain amount of decentralization in the 1970s. The study abroad programs were returned to their parent colleges and departments in 1973, and in 1980 the Office of International Student and Faculty Services was returned to the Dean of Students Office.

The development of the center's special focus on the Third World is worth noting. Under the guidance of the first center's director, a planning committee on African studies was established in the fall of 1964. As a result of its activities, an African studies grant was received for the 1965/66 academic year from the US Office of Education for library resources, student assistance, and travel. The first academic program in international/ intercultural studies was a master's degree program in foreign affairs, with concentrations in African studies and Southeast Asia studies in 1967. In the late 1960s, a committee on Latin American studies was formed. The work of this committee culminated in the establishment of a formal Latin American studies program in 1971. Thus Ohio University was committed to three area study programs: African, Latin American, and Southeast Asian.

Although much of the focus of academic programs during the late 1960s and early 1970s was on the master's degree program, renamed the Master of Arts in International Affairs, undergraduate course work and programs of study were also established. A certificate program was established for students wishing to focus on Africa, Latin America, or Asia, but the Bachelor of Arts in International Studies was not created until 1976. Today, one of the recently reestablished general education requirements is that a student must take a cluster of courses chosen from several main program areas, one of which is Third World cultures.

Program Description

The Center for International Studies focuses on area studies programs and related degree programs. Because the center must rely on faculty members in the colleges, coordination with departments is a major role. Indeed, faculty involvement and the issue of centralization versus decentralization are primary considerations when evaluating the program's strengths and weaknesses.

PROGRAM COMPONENTS

There are five main areas of program activities and functions at the Center for International Studies.

1. Area studies programs. The three area studies programs focus attention on Africa, Southeast Asia, and Latin America. The directors of each of these programs coordinate classes and special events; encourage lectures, seminars, and cultural presentations; and supervise degree programs in their areas.

The African Studies Program began in 1965 as a National Defense Education Act (NDEA) title VI Language and Area Center. This funding, albeit on a modest scale, provided the foundation for library acquisition, curriculum development, and language instruction on which the program has been built. Language instruction is currently offered in Arabic, Hausa, and Swahili. Each quarter, approximately ten to twelve core African studies courses are taught, with an additional ten to fifteen related courses (a core course is one in which over half of the contest focuses on the region). In cooperation with the other area studies programs, the African

Studies Program sponsors the Africa Series in Papers in International Studies, a well-received, small monograph publishing effort.

The Southeast Asian Studies Program was established in 1967. The first five years of the program were supported completely out of university operating funds. Since 1973, the center has received additional support from NDEA title VI funds. These funds have been used primarily for library acquisition, faculty support, and outreach activities. As a result of the additional support, the Southeast Asia collection of the university library is one of the top such collections in the United States. Recognition of the university's special role in Malaysia came with the establishment of the Tun Abdul Razak Chair in Southeast Asian Studies, funded jointly by Ohio University and the government of Malaysia. Beginning in 1981, the program became the host for three years of the Indonesian Summer Studies Institute, which provides intensive language instruction in Indonesian for both undergraduate and graduate students.

The Latin American Studies Program has just completed its tenth year as a formal program at Ohio University. The program draws heavily on the resources and strengths of the Spanish section of the Modern Language Department. Indeed, much of the undergraduate student interest in the program stems from the study abroad programs whereby an undergraduate student may complete four quarters of language instruction in one quarter through the intensive study of Spanish in Mexico. The director and faculty of the program have established close ties with institutions in Brazil, Ecuador, and Argentina and have worked with the Organization of American States for a special scholarship program for which Ohio University provides tuition scholarships for graduate study and OAS covers living expenses.

2. Academic programs. There are degree and certificate programs at both the graduate and undergraduate levels. The Master of Arts in International Affairs (MAIA) is a multidisciplinary program that can be completed in one year. It provides for five areas of concentration: administrative studies, African studies, development studies, Latin American studies, and Southeast Asian studies. Students in the area studies concentrations are supervised by the appropriate area studies director, while the associate provost and his administrative assistant work with the other students. The MAIA degree requires students to enroll in a minimum of forty-seven quarter hours of work in at least three departments or disciplines. A minimum level of foreign language competency is also required. Most students take a final oral comprehensive examination, although a few opt for writing a master's thesis. Enrollment in the graduate program has been stable for the past three years, averaging 130 in the fall quarter. These students are evenly divided between Americans and foreign students. Of the Americans, a sizeable portion are returned Peace

Corps volunteers, thanks to a special tuition scholarship program initiated and funded by Ohio University.

The Bachelor of Arts in International Studies is administered jointly by the center and the College of Arts and Sciences. With a regular enrollment of about twenty-four majors, it provides a multidisciplinary approach to the study of major world regions: Africa, Latin America, Eastern Europe, Western Europe, and Southeast Asia. In addition to university and college requirements, the student must complete fifty-two quarter hours, sixteen of them focusing on relations among nations and comparative cultures and thirty-six concentrating on a world region. At least two years of a relevant language are required, and a third year is encouraged.

The certificate programs function as a type of minor. A student is granted this certificate after completing six courses on a world region, and the appropriate notation is entered on the student's academic record.

3. Coordination role. A main activity of the center is coordination of activities to provide high-quality education not only for students enrolled in center programs but also for other students. Area studies directors work with department chairs and school directors to reduce class conflict and provide lecturers, seminars, and presentations that will enhance classroom activities. With virtually no courses of its own (other than the introductory freshman-level area studies courses in Africa, Asia, and Latin America) and no center faculty (that is, faculty members who are paid by and work for the center), this coordination role is of key importance.

4. Special programs. There are several special programs and activities, including a Peace Corps Office (funded by a Peace Corps strategy contract), the Malaysian Advisory Committee, the Fulbright–Hayes Advisor, the Foreign Language and Area Studies Fellowships Committee, and a Publications Editorial Board. The Publications Board supervises the publication of the Papers in International Studies (with three subseries: African Studies, Latin American Studies, and Southeast Asian Studies) by the Ohio University Press and the center.

5. Overseas agreements. As of the end of the 1980/81 academic year, Ohio University had entered into twenty-six agreements involving research, contracts, exchanges, or staff development with foreign institutions. Virtually all these agreements are under the direction of other academic units in the university. The associate provost, in his role as staff officer for the provost and president, is expected to be involved in the initial approval of the agreements and kept informed on developments; and under plans put into effect in 1981/82, agreements will have to be routed through his office.

These agreements range in size and scope from the offering of Ohio University degrees overseas in cooperation with foreign institutions (a Bachelor of Business Administration in Malaysia) to an AID contract for primary education development in Botswana that provides for five Ohio University faculty members to go to Botswana and officials of the Ministry of Education and of the University College of Botswana to come to Athens for additional training. Smaller agreements simply provide tuition scholarships for staff members of other institutions or countries.

FACULTY INVOLVEMENT

More than one hundred faculty members are associated with the various activities of the Center for International Studies. Many of these are affiliated with the area studies programs, each of which has a core faculty of about a dozen with an additional dozen or so having some degree of involvement. This involvement includes serving on master's degree examination committees, acting as advisors, participating in curriculum development, teaching courses of an international nature, and serving on various committees related to international education. In almost every case faculty members participate because of their commitment to the area studies programs and the academic programs of the center. They receive no direct remuneration.

Funding

The budget for the Center for International Studies in 1980/81 was slightly under $600,000 (see table 4.2). Of this amount, $100,000 was from federal grants (an NDEA title VI Center for Southeast Asian Studies and a Peace Corps strategy contract), and the remainder was from Ohio university operating funds. A large portion of Ohio University funds are for graduate

TABLE 4.2.   **1980/81 Budget for the Center for International Studies**

	Grants	University	Total
Payroll and benefits	$55,758	$252,754	$308,512
Honoraria	500	750	1,250
Supplies	1,441	2,329	3,770
Travel	6,150	1,969	8,119
Information and communication	3,116	8,660	11,776
Rental and repair		2,112	2,112
Scholarships		228,696	228,696
Indirect overhead	7,337		7,337
Library acquisitions	24,751		24,751
Equipment and miscellaneous		3,247	3,247
Totals	$99,053	$500,517	$599,570

student support, largely for tuition scholarships for students enrolled in the master's degree program.

The budget is relatively stable from year to year, with additions being made to cover salary raises and additional program directions that have been approved through the Ohio University planning process. Within this budget, the chief budget officer (the associate provost) is free to allocate funds among the major units within the center in accordance with the center's goals and objectives. However, changes in allocation that increase staff or faculty must be approved by the provost.

Program Strengths and Weaknesses

This discussion of program strengths and weaknesses must start by making explicit certain underlying assumptions about the program and the university.

First, there is no ideal type of university structure. The ideal is the one that works given the institution's history, staff, goals and objectives, and resources. Although different structures have their advocates, the product approach has not yet been demonstrated to be more or less effective than the functional approach nor has a matrix organization been demonstrated to add or subtract anything. However, given the historic development of colleges and universities, the functional approach of disciplinary departments (such as history and sociology) organized into more or less traditional colleges (such as arts and sciences and education) and presided over by an academic vice-president will probably continue to be the norm. Although a few schools have experimented with other types of organization, such as the University of Wisconsin at Green Bay with a product approach (departments and colleges with an issue or topic focus) or the University of Santa Cruz with a matrix approach, the common organizational type remains functionally oriented.

Second, the disciplinary department will continue to be the main unit on campus. It will provide appointment, tenure, advancement, and salary increases (where based on merit)—judged largely by faculty members' department colleagues.

Third, multidisciplinary efforts—such as international studies, women's studies, Afro-American studies, and environmental studies—must reach out and draw on the departments and colleges. Although in the short run the dedication of a few staff members (and their hard work) may provide success for programs that are at odds with the academic departments, in the long run the programs are doomed unless the staff members develop a symbiotic relationship with the departments.

Fourth, international education is, and must be seen to be, the responsibility of all academic units, not just those that are given a specifically international label.

Given these assumptions, the major strengths and weaknesses (which are, in reality, opposite sides of the same coin) may be noted in three areas: faculty involvement and reward, centralization versus decentralization, and funding.

As long as a faculty member's major rewards are provided by the person's department and college, and multidisciplinary program will succeed only insofar as it shows how its success contributes to the department or appeals to the personal or professional interests of the faculty member. A major weakness of Ohio University's approach to international studies is that some departments discourage faculty members from participating in "extradepartmental" activities.

On the other hand, suggestions that the Center for International Studies develop its own faculty have fallen on barren ground, for two major reasons. First, the center must maintain close ties with the departments, ties that are possible largely through the association of department faculty members with the center's programs and activities. A center faculty would only increase isolation of the center from the rest of the university. Second, a center faculty offering courses that overlap with those of the departments and schools would make the center a competitor for scarce funds and resources, thus even further reducing cooperation.

The question of centralization versus decentralization covers similar ground. The effect of the attempt in the late sixties to concentrate many of the international activities of the university in a single office was to cut them off from the departments that provided much of their strength. This centralization worked for a while, but when resources become scarce in the 1970s, departments were less then willing to continue to contribute to activities they perceived to be not directly under their jurisdiction. As a result, during the mid- and late seventies there was a progressive decentralization, with the final step being the transfer of the Office of International Student and Faculty Services to the Office of the Vice-President and Dean of Studies in 1980.

Greater decentralization has meant the loss of a sense of continuity and overall purpose. Deans and school directors have pursued their own international education activities without exchange of information or coordination. At times the president and provost have found out about commitments after the relevant documents were signed, not before.

To restore some continuity and coordination, the position of assistant provost for international studies was elevated on 1 July 1981 to that of associate provost for international programs. This person remains director of the Center for International Studies but also oversees the development of international programs, projects, and activities on behalf of the president and the provost. The associate provost for international programs has thus become the center of information about the international activities and commitments of the university. Because of the newness of this shift, how it will operate in practice remains to be seen. Perhaps it will provide a middle position in the pendulum swing between decentralization and centralization.

Finally, there is the question of funding. Centers (or programs or institutes) of international studies are generally recent additions to the university setting. They have not yet gained recognition as part of the academic foundation. Indeed, many persons outside international education programs consider them simply nice frills that may be jettisoned in hard times to protect the basic disciplines. In a particularly precarious position are centers that depend on outside funding. Such centers must build a solid foundation of university operating funds for bringing in students or servicing readily identifiable student needs.

Strategies for the 1980s

Under the Ohio University planning process, each academic unit must review its short-term and long-term strategies yearly and update them when appropriate. Defining strategies is particularly important, given enrollment projection that forecasts a 20 percent decline in Ohio University's enrollment during the next decade. For the six-year period up to 1986, the Planning Committee of the Center for International Studies has identified ten program emphases:

1. To maintain current levels of activities in area studies programs (African, Latin American, Southeast Asia) and strengthen them further, through more courses in sociology/anthropology, the performing arts, foreign languages, and economics and through an expanded cultural affairs and speakers program

2. To strengthen cross-cultural thematic studies (international development and administration) in cooperation with other programs

3. To maintain a strong master's degree program, with an average annual enrollment of 125–150

4. To cooperate with other graduate programs in developing integrated and articulated programs of study, including dual-degree and doctoral programs

5. To strengthen the undergraduate programs by developing an international studies minor; by providing certificate options for Western Europe studies, Eastern Europe studies, and peace studies; and by offering courses in Third World studies and a third tier of multidisciplinary courses

6. To improve counseling through increased faculty participation at both the graduate and undergraduate levels

7. To promote international education throughout southeastern Ohio by providing a focal point for speakers and outreach activities

8. To expand faculty, staff, and student development opportunities through cooperation with foreign institutions and associations

9. To encourage research through expanding the publications program to fourteen titles per year

10. To provide information on international education opportunities for students, particularly study abroad programs

Although the foundation of support for pursuing program objectives must, and will, come from university sources, the margin of excellence in international education will depend, in part, on the ability of the center in particular and the university as a whole to obtain outside funding. Grant proposals have recently been submitted to the Department of Education, the National Endowment for the Humanities, and the Ohio Program in the Humanities. Outside funding is what will make the difference, providing the extra assistance that is vital if program objectives are to be achieved.

Ohio University's Center for International Studies is only one approach to structuring international studies programs on a university campus. What has been described is a partially centralized center with several academic programs and a university with broadly spread international education activities. Because of this juxtaposition of centralization and decentralization, the mechanism exists for attracting students, involving faculty members, and adding an important dimension to the curricular and cocurricular activities of the university.

Other institutions must decide for themselves whether this approach is appropriate for them, but the experience of Ohio University (and several others with similar centers) is evidence that it *can* work, that it can moreover provide effective academic programs of study, and that it can strengthen the international dimension of a college and university.

Appendix

The following objectives were approved by the International Studies Program Planning Unit for the current three-year planning cycle (1980/81, 1981/82, 1982/83):

I. Support international academic programs where there is student interest, scholarship, creative accomplishment, and social need.

A. Support and strengthen area studies programs (e.g., African studies, Latin American studies, Southeast Asian studies).
   1. Improve remuneration to area directors through released time and summer support equivalent to half-time during the academic year and during the summer.
   2. Add courses in the social sciences, humanities, and fine arts related to Africa, Latin America, and Southeast Asia either by retraining current faculty members or by adding new faculty members, particularly in the areas of Latin American Art, African sociology, ethnomusicology, and the performing arts (including dance and drama).
   3. Strengthen foreign language offerings at Ohio University (particularly in the non-European languages), by providing instruction in Dutch, Portuguese, Arabic, Chinese, and African languages.
   4. Strengthen library acquisitions and services by adding another bibliographer in Alden Library, with specializations in Latin America and Africa, and increasing the acquisition budget for retrospective purchases.
   5. Offer undergraduate international area studies courses yearly and develop advanced undergraduate area studies courses.
   6. Establish and offer graduate seminars in area studies.
   7. Promote communications among the area studies faculties through establishment of faculty–graduate student colloquia.

B. Support and strengthen cross-area thematic studies (e.g., development studies and international administrative studies).
   1. Provide a balanced offering of courses or concentrations in the social sciences, humanities, and professional areas through the retraining of current faculty members, particularly in the areas of development administration; international communications; food, nutrition, and development; international health administration; and comparative Third World literature.
   2. Cooperate in the development of the Master of Administration, particularly the option in international administration.
   3. Cooperate in the development of an international option within the Master of Science in Environmental Sciences program.
   4. Submit a proposal for a Center for Development Studies.

C. Improve curriculum integration and cooperation with departments.

      1. Develop dual masters degree programs in international studies combined with linguistics, international business, education, health administration, and communications.

II. Attract quality students, both American and foreign.

    A. Maintain an enrollment of approximately thirty to thirty-five students in each program option within the Master of Arts in International Affairs (Africa, Latin America, Southeast Asia, Development, and International Administration).

    B. Obtain scholarship and graduate associateship funds commensurate with these enrollment levels, namely:

      1. Maintain the special residential scholarship program for foreign students and returned Peace Corps volunteers and regular scholarship funds.

      2. Increase graduate associate stipend funds by 10 percent per year to restore the funds removed from the program by budget cuts during the past five years.

    C. Obtain an enrollment of fifty students in the Bachelor of Arts in International Studies program.

    D. Promote the name of Ohio University among international education constituencies—particularly in institutions of higher education, the Peace Corps, and international agencies—through continuous contact and quality publications.

III. Support staff development, including teaching, research, and creativity.

    A. Expand research opportunities.

      1. Identify and regularly publish information about research grant opportunities.

      2. Obtain support from outside agencies for faculty travel abroad for research purposes.

      3. Publish a minimum of twelve papers yearly in the Papers in International Studies series to provide a research outlet.

      4. Provide modest funds for travel to professional meetings for faculty members and staff members.

    B. Provide opportunities for faculty members to develop and improve area expertise.

      1. Obtain support from the Department of Education for faculty preparation and new courses in international development and health.

      2. Develop and strengthen relations with institutions of higher education to provide faculty exchange opportunities.

      3. Encourage faculty and staff participation in study abroad programs.

IV. Improve academic counseling for students in graduate and undergraduate academic programs in international studies.

A. Improve the advising system through quarterly advising sessions for students with program directors.

B. Provide international studies degree program advisors with information on each student assigned to them.

C. Develop, through cooperation with the Placement Office, a permanent file on international career opportunities.

D. Maintain and expand the Peace Corps Office to provide information to all interested students.

E. Assist students interested in further study at Ohio University with appropriate information.

V. Provide an attractive learning environment for students.

A. Expand international studies library acquisitions and services.

B. Promote the exchange of information and communication among international studies students through support of the International Forum.

C. Provide a central location for information on study abroad programs and opportunities (including Ohio University Study Abroad programs, Fulbright programs, and other programs).

D. Support artistic and cultural events (visits, lectures, presentations, films, social activities) that provide an international dimension to Ohio University.

E. Provide outlets for quality graduate research through the Publications Office.

VI. Expand opportunities for international education throughout southeastern Ohio.

A. Provide opportunities for adult education and lifelong learning.

1. Restructure outreach courses to make shorter, more intensive, and more focused workshops and minicourses available.

2. Develop telecommunications courses on Asia and Latin America along the lines of the existing Modern Africa television course.

3. Develop seminars, workshops, and speakers programs, in cooperation with colleges and universities in the region.

B. Provide assistance in outreach activities to teachers and schools.

1. Develop curriculum materials for use in primary and secondary schools.

2. Provide opportunities for school visitation by foreign students and faculty.

3. Serve as a resource center in international education for all levels of education.

C. Support cooperative efforts and expansion of international education.

1. Work with the International Education Association of Ohio Colleges and Universities on international studies seminars and workshops.
2. Cooperate with the African Studies Association, the Consortium of Latin American Studies Program, the Association for Asian Studies, the Consortium for International Studies Education, the Institute of International Education, and similar organizations, in the development of international education.

CHAPTER 5

Indiana University

John V. Lombardi

INDIANA UNIVERSITY HAS FROM ITS EARLIEST DAYS recognized its obligation to become involved in global concerns. During the 1950s and especially during the 1960s, the university began to assume a full range of international education responsibilities and to develop the philosophy of international education that guides its programs today.

Institutional Commitment to International Education

A succession of presidents, deans, and other academic officers, each with a particular outlook and philosophy of education, have shared an understanding of the university's obligation to international studies: that any university must place a high priority on the international dimension of higher education, that it must define its focus in global terms, and that it must infuse its programs and studies with the universalist outlook symbolized by its name. To articulate these goals is easy, but to achieve them is difficult. With the leadership of presidents, academic officers, and especially the faculty, Indiana University has developed a series of structures and operating procedures designed to achieve a universality of studies.

BASIC PRINCIPLES

To an outside observer, Indiana University's wide range of programs, institutes, deanships, and other international education offices often appears chaotic and unstructured. But the appearance is misleading, for Indiana University has created its international programs and activities in accordance with a set of basic principles.

1. *Support and encourage faculty interests in international studies.* The basis for this principle is that the key to successful international studies lies with a committed and expert faculty. Rather than inventing faculty interests and then attempting to find faculty members to cooperate, the university looks for faculty members with strong interests and abilities and then helps them create the programs that will develop those interests. One consequence of this approach is that the university supports an unusually wide range of faculty interests in a broad sweep of disciplines and covering many geographic areas. Few topics or areas are regarded as forbidden or preferred.

2. *Provide incentives.* This principle operated most visibly in the developmental days of Indiana University's international programs. If faculty members find and develop external support for an international program activity, the university then assumes that the activity is valuable and useful and proceeds to build support for it into the ongoing university budget in order to sustain this faculty interest. As a result, a substantial, regular university resource base for international studies has been created.

3. *Support the development of faculty strength in international studies within established academic departments.* This principle is not meant to deny the creation of specialized interdepartmental programs or institutes but to guarantee that faculty members recruited and hired to participate in an expanding international program will have a strong disciplinary base and a substantial disciplinary reputation to bring to international studies. Thus, when a Latin American specialist or an African expert is hired, the critical evaluation of academic quality occurs in the department of history, or anthropology, or political science, or wherever the area studies specialist claims a disciplinary home. This principle of disciplinary excellence has been one of the most difficult to sustain in the short run, but clearly one of the most beneficial in the long run. External support for international studies from foundations, state governments, and the federal government is a variable commodity, but the university always defends its major disciplinary departments. In hard times, faculty members with an international specialization within a discipline are likely to receive the support of their discipline for territorial reasons unrelated to maintaining international studies. Similarly, faculty members in international fields who have been hired, tenured, and promoted by their disciplinary colleagues have an academic legitimacy difficult to achieve outside this structure.

4. *Organize and support auxiliary enterprises whose purpose is to encourage and facilitate faculty international interests.* This principle has meant that area studies programs at Indiana University are well

developed. Of the seven area studies programs, five have been awarded national resource center status by the Department of Education, all seven receive fellowship support from the federal government, and all have institutional structures supported by the university. But most of them do not have a faculty of their own. The university's area studies programs, some of which date back to the 1950s or before, came of age in the 1960s as major national centers thanks to the stimulus of several large Ford Foundation grants for the promotion of international studies. The money subsidized faculty positions in major departments, purchased extensive additions to the library and the library support staff, encouraged the training of graduate students, and supported faculty research, travel, and development. In spending this money, the university arranged to tie the "soft" foundation money into university budget money. When the soft foundation money ran out in the late sixties and early seventies, most international activities that had been supported by the grants continued to function with appropriated university funds. Of course, some faculty members and administrators saw no reason for the university to maintain international education activites, and others wanted to eliminate the support structure for international studies in favor of other activities. However, most university battles occur over maintaining faculty strength in disciplinary departments, and therefore much of the controversy that might have been directed at international studies became muted, because international studies were also in most cases disciplinary studies. The faculty members who studied African anthropology or Latin American history were, after all, entirely and thoroughly disciplinary in training, in career pattern, and in academic location. An attack on the African area studies faculty members turned out to be an attack on traditional disciplines such as anthropology, history, and political science. A retrenchment campaign focused on international studies proved dificult to sustain.

ADMINISTRATIVE ORGANIZATION

In the late 1960s and early 1970s, the university began a general effort to reorganize and restructure the institution. What had been the main campus at Bloomington with subsidiary centers throughout the state became a university system focused on Bloomington and Indianapolis with relatively autonomous campuses in six other locations throughout the state.

This system, with its structured administrative hierarchy and its mandate to operate as an integrated university system, resulted in some changes in the organization of international studies. More coordination of the university's international activities was needed, if only because they had become so complex and varied. The coordinating agency that was devised is the Office of International Programs, headed by a dean who reports to the president of the university.

This new unit, created in 1975, combined a set of universitywide resources: the overseas study programs, open to faculty and students on all campuses; the foreign student office, which also serves all campuses; and other systemwide international activities such as faculty and student exchanges and small grant programs. The dean for international programs also oversees a clearinghouse for the international concerns of departments, schools, and campuses throughout the system. Although the seven area studies programs report to the College of Arts and Sciences (their historical home), the directors of these programs work closely with the dean of international programs to develop activities and pursue the university's international education interests.

In addition to activities that occur under the supervision of the dean of international programs, international studies and programs at Indiana University are carried out primarily by two other groups. One important block of activities takes place within the College of Arts and Sciences on the Bloomington campus, and the other group of programs occurs under the supervision of multicampus schools such as the Schools of Business, Education, Public and Environmental Affairs, and Continuing Studies.

An important determinant of the character of Indiana University's international programs has been the absence of a college of agriculture or engineering. These two specialties, frequently heavily involved in international projects at other universities, have no significant influence on Indiana University's international work. Instead, the dominant force in developing international studies at Indiana University has been the faculty of the arts and sciences disciplines, especially the humanities and the social sciences. The professional schools of Business, Education, Music, Medicine, Nursing and Public and Environmental Affairs have also shown considerable interest in and support for international education activities. For example, the Schools of Business and Public and Environmental Affairs have recently expanded their international commitment in several areas and initiated exchanges, training, and research programs abroad. Similarly, the School of Education has long supported a department of comparative and international education and provided faculty members for research and development work abroad. Nevertheless, without a college of agriculture, the university's approach to international studies and international development work has been substantially different than that of universities of comparable size with agricultural colleges.

Office of International Programs

The Office of International Programs is the general coordinating agency for the university's international activities and has direct responsibility for supervising two other offices, the Office of International Services and the Office of Overseas Study. It also manages several programs directly. Some of these programs are operated on behalf of the Office of the President, such as the President's Council on International Programs. Others involve small grant funds supporting a variety of research and development tasks. The Office also manages many exchange relationships with foreign universities.

OFFICE OF INTERNATIONAL SERVICES

The Office of International Services has primary responsibility for advising and providing student services for the foreign students in the Indiana University system—about 2,600 students from more than 110 countries. Although the Indianapolis campus maintains its own foreign student advisor, the associate dean for international services is the university's representative for foreign student concerns.

The office holds a reception and orientation program for entering foreign students to acquaint them with the resources and structure of the university and to assist them in locating academic services throughout the Bloomington campus where almost three-quarters of the foreign students are enrolled. International Services also provides a general counseling service for foreign students experiencing financial, personal, and academic difficulties. The office is often concerned with technical, paralegal, and documentation services for foreign students and serves as the university's liaison with the Immigration and Naturalization Service. In the admissions process, the office is responsible for financial certification, improved liaison with departments and schools, improving the quality and selection of foreign students, and a general concern with the size and geographic and academic diversity of the foreign student population. The office also maintains close contacts with various referral agencies and institutions handling foreign students in the United States. International Services manages the International House, a center for foreign student programs and other international program activities.

OFFICE OF OVERSEAS STUDY

The Office of Overseas Study manages overseas educational programs that draw students from all schools and campuses of Indiana University. There are eight one-year programs, four summer programs, and one one-month program; and there are also five special programs administered for university students and three programs for qualified high school students.

About 300 students are involved in the university-level program, and about ninety participate in the high school programs. Currently, study abroad courses are supported in France, Germany, Spain, Italy, Israel, England, China, The Netherlands, Peru, and Mexico. Some of these programs are managed through consortium arrangements with other American institutions of higher education, thereby sharing costs and pooling students. The office also cooperates with university departments and schools that have programs for overseas study, including the School of Health, Physical Education, and Recreation, the School of Business, and the School of Education.

The associate dean for overseas study is the university's primary representative for overseas study. He heads the Committee on Overseas Study, which advises on policies for overseas study courses and approves programs designed to offer students university credit for study abroad. Each overseas program administered by the office has a faculty committee to supervise, guide, and develop its activities. The university's overseas study activities rely heavily on strong faculty support for recruiting students and managing the programs.

OTHER ACTIVITIES

President's Council on International Programs. Composed of representatives from all campuses of Indiana University, the President's Council on International Programs (PCIP) is the university's principal advisory committee on international policy. In addition to meeting annually to discuss the university's international activities, PCIP administers a modest research and development grant. The awards are made in a variety of categories, but the bulk of the fund supports research in international affairs. Because the average grant is between $400 and $500, PCIP traditionally gives preference to (1) projects that require only modest assistance to come to fruition, (2) projects with outstanding potential for external funding, and (3) activities that make an important contribution to international program development at one of the university's campuses.

In addition, the fund sponsors participation in the Scholar–Diplomat Seminars offered by the US Department of State, and on occasion, it sponsors international conference travel. The President's Council on International Programs also gives modest support to important international conferences that contribute to the development of programs at Indiana University.

Overseas Conference Fund. Supported by an annual grant from the Indiana University Foundation, this program contributes towards the international travel costs of faculty members attending conferences overseas. The Overseas Conference Fund helps about eighty faculty members each year, although the size of the grants compared with the actual travel costs continues to decline. The average grant in 1980/81 was about $300.

These grants have often made possible faculty members' attending important international meetings, and both the university and the faculty members gain considerably by this experience. The Overseas Conference Fund Committee requires that faculty members be engaged in a substantial and visible activity at the conference. The reports from faculty members about their experiences at the conferences and the research and publication results demonstrate the productivity of this fund.

International faculty exchange.　Indiana University supports a variety of international faculty exchanges. These activities provide opportunities for university faculty members to teach and research abroad while enriching the university with the perspectives and knowledge of faculty members from other cultures. Indiana University's current major exchange programs include:

• Tenri University, Tenri, Japan. The exchange agreement with Tenri provides for Indiana University to send a professor to Japan every other year. The agreement further provides for the exchange of one graduate student each year.

• Hamburg University, Hamburg, West Germany. Under this agreement, each university sends a professor to the other university in alternating years. In addition, there is a short-term research exchange program in which each university nominates two professors to spend four weeks engaged in research activity on the campus of the partner institution.

• Strasbourg University, Strasbourg, France. This program provides for each university to exchange one faculty member with the other each year.

• Warsaw University, Warsaw, Poland. The exchange between Warsaw University and Indiana University is partially supported by a grant from the International Communications Agency. The terms of the exchange provide for each university to exchange two professors with the other every year and for both professors to teach in the appropriate academic departments and carry out administrative duties in the respective study centers. Each university has agreed to establish a cultural and academic center: American Studies in Warsaw and Polish Studies in Indiana. The agreement also provides for the exchange of graduate students.

• Shandong University, Shandong, China. This agreement provides for the exchange of faculty members and students on a short-term basis. There are no restrictions on field.

• Nankai University, Nankai, China. Nankai and Indiana have agreed to exchange faculty members and students. The students generally will be exchanged for academic-year terms and the faculty members for short-term research visits.

The university also has several other agreements in various stages of development.

International Visitors Exchange Program. The International Visitors Exchange (IVE) is a small fund that originated with a Ford Foundation grant to Indiana University for the development of international studies. Now financed with state funds, the IVE program supports speakers whose contributions form an important part of Indiana University international studies center activity. Applications for this program must come from one of the seven international studies programs based on the Bloomington campus or from the international studies coordinator on the other campuses of the university. In most cases, applicants must have cooperating sponsorship of other departments, schools or campuses. Grants average about $200 per visitor. This program has been most productive, providing the margin of support necessary to implement a number of imaginative lecture series and conferences.

Overseas Exchange Fellowship Program. For students attending Indiana University under an exchange agreement, the Overseas Exchange Fellowship Program provides fellowship assistance. The amounts and terms of the assistance vary depending on the reciprocal arrangement between Indiana University and the foreign institution. In 1980/81, this program provided assistance to forty-two students.

HEA title VI centers and fellowships in international studies. Indiana University will have federal support for five Higher Education Amendment (HEA) title VI national resource centers in 1981/82: African Studies Center, Center for East Asian Languages and Cultures, Slavic Language and Area Center, Center for Inner Asia, and West European Studies Center. The Office of International Programs serves as a coordinating and cooperating office for the area studies programs that prepare proposals for the HEA title VI competition. In addition, two other programs, Latin American Studies and Near Eastern Studies, receive allocations of Foreign Language and Area Studies Fellowship funds.

Consortium arrangements. On behalf of the university, the Office of International Programs manages three major consortium activities. The Midwest Universities Consortium for International Activities (MUCIA), founded in 1964, administers several grants and contracts in the international development field. Originally funded by a Ford Foundation grant, MUCIA currently exists on grants and contracts primarily from the US Agency for International Development (USAID). Although Indiana University was a founding member of MUCIA and participated actively in it during its first decade, the recent emphasis of this agency on development funding for agricultural extension activities and similar programs has meant less Indiana University participation.

Indiana University also belongs to the Indiana Consortium of International Programs (ICIP), a group of Indiana colleges and universities that sponsor programs and projects on developing international studies. In addition, the consortium members share information about overseas study programs and special international activities at each participating institution. In 1980/81, five Indiana University campuses participated in ICIP programs.

The university has been a member of the Universities Field Staff International (UFSI), formerly the American Universities Field Staff, since 1956. This consortium of colleges and universities maintains a staff of associates abroad who report periodically in writing and in person on developments in major world areas. In recent years the organization has expanded its activities into other areas such as teaching, media work, and consulting. The UFSI program is active on all campuses of the university, and a number of Indiana University faculty members have participated in UFSI projects.

Small Projects.   Several other projects are also managed by the Office of International Programs. The *Directory of International Studies Faculty and Staff,* which is maintained in the office and updated every other year, lists some 600 faculty members and staff members with international expertise or experience on the campuses of the university. An international alumni newsletter published from two to three times a year and sent to about 350 foreign alumni has been developed by the office in collaboration with the Indiana University Foundation.

A research group, the Women in Development Committee, is sponsored through a grant to MUCIA from USAID and was formed to help create a network of persons concerned with women in international development and to generate substantive research proposals.

Area Studies Programs

Administered within the College of Arts and Sciences, area studies programs are the primary focus of international studies at the university. Because they have a mandate to be interdisciplinary collections of scholars and students from all parts of the university, these programs tend to have constituencies much wider than the College of Arts and Sciences. For a variety of historical reasons, there is no uniformity in program organization or design, although there are some common patterns.

Some of the area studies programs are interdisciplinary units that do not have tenure-track faculty positions located in the program budget, but instead draw faculty members from departments, schools, and campuses across the university. Some of the programs in this category are among the most successful in the university. African Studies, Latin American Studies,

Middle Eastern Studies, and the Russian–East European Institute belong to this category.

Two programs are virtually coterminous with academic departments. The Department of East Asian Languages and Literatures is a relatively recent creation that expanded the East Asian Language unit to include the joint appointment of faculty members in other humanities fields and the social sciences. That department also serves as an area studies center, and with its designation as a national resource center, it has begun to develop stronger ties with schools and campuses beyond its departmental confines. The Department of Uralic and Altaic Studies is a language department that also houses the Inner Asian program. Its faculty, too, is multidisciplinary.

The West European Studies Program represents the final variation. This program is principally constructed as a holding corporation for the university's exceptional resources in West European studies, but at the same time it has department status within the College of Arts and Sciences because it has several half-positions budgeted and tenured within the department.

AFRICAN STUDIES

This program has renowned language and linguistics programs offering instruction in twenty-eight African languages; it has produced almost forty African language manuals under contract with the Peace Corps or the Office of Education. It has one of the strongest programs in African humanities in the United States with faculty members in enthnomusicology, fine arts, folklore, literature, and religion. It has disciplinary strength in history, political science, and economic and social development, with regional specializations in West Africa, East Africa and the Horn, and Southern Africa. The program has been a federally funded national resource center for many years.

LATIN AMERICAN STUDIES

During its twenty years of existence, the Latin American Studies Programs has grown steadily in faculty, curriculum, students, resources, and community programs. Some seventy-six faculty members provide a distinguished record of research and publication. The curriculum spans virtually every discipline within the humanities and social sciences as well as most of the professional schools. The program is strong in the Latin American languages including Isthmus Zapotec, Nahuatl, Quechua, Haitian Creole, as well as Spanish and Portuguese. It has outstanding resources in the library, the Latin American Music Center, the Museum, and the Archives of Traditional Music. This program has received Foreign Language and Area Studies Fellowship support for many years.

RUSSIAN AND EAST EUROPEAN INSTITUTE

This program is the oldest area studies program at Indiana University. Since its creation, its primary objective has been to develop a broad interdisciplinary curriculum offering advanced language and area training on the Soviet Union and the nations of Eastern Europe. About fifty full-time faculty members specialize in some aspect of Russian and East European studies. The program has recently expanded into the areas of journalism, government, and business and has increasingly emphasized undergraduate language and area studies training. This program has been a federally funded national resource center for many years.

MIDDLE EASTERN STUDIES

Although this program was created recently, the university's interest in Middle Eastern studies is well established. Course offerings in this area are spread among diverse academic units throughout the university, including Classical Studies, Religious Studies, Classical Archaeology, Fine Arts, Medieval Studies, History, Political Science, Geography, Anthropology, Sociology, Folklore, and Uralic and Altaic Studies. The program draws heavily on the language and culture offerings of the Department of Near Eastern Languages and Literatures, including Arabic, Hebrew, and Persian. The Middle Eastern Studies Program receives Foreign Language and Area Studies Fellowship support.

WEST EUROPEAN STUDIES

This genuinely interdisciplinary program focuses on contemporary Western Europe. It has aimed to promote faculty and student research and training. It has joint faculty appointments in the departments of Germanic Languages, History, and Political Science. The program, created in the mid-1960s, has an unusually broad base of faculty support in all departments and schools of the university. Associated foreign language programs are extensive, including a program in Catalan. West European Studies is a federally funded national resource center.

EAST ASIAN LANGUAGES AND CULTURES CENTER

Based in the Department of East Asian Languages and Cultures, this program covers a broad span of disciplines in the humanities and social sciences. The department offers some seventy-five courses in Chinese (Mandarin and Cantonese) and Japanese language and literature, in addition to thirty courses on the cultures of China, Japan, and Korea. The program has special strengths in comparative literature and draws support from the offerings of the Department of Uralic and Altaic Studies in Mongolian language and culture. The center has also begun to develop strong ties with the professional schools, especially the School of Business. This program is a federally funded national resource center.

INNER ASIAN STUDIES

This program, based in the Department of Uralic and Altaic Studies, draws on a long history of university interest in the languages and cultures of Inner Asia. From an original emphasis on linguistic studies, the program has been broadened to include the study of all aspects of the cultures and societies of Inner Asia. The program supports courses dealing with Hungarian, Finnish, Inner Asian, Ottoman, Turkic, Mongol, and Tibetan history, civilization, and literature. It also offers courses on the non-Slavic aspects of the Russian and Soviet past and present. The program supports the teaching of modern languages within this world area, specifically, Finnish, Estonian, Hungarian, Turkish, Azeri, Uzbek, Tatar, Kazakh, Chuvash, Tuvin, Yakut, Khalkha, Mongol, and Tibetan. This program has been a federally funded national resource center for many years.

OTHER INTERNATIONAL EDUCATION PROGRAMS

In addition to the programs of the Office of International Programs and the area studies programs, there are international education programs administered through special university units: The International Development Institute, the Polish Studies Center, and the Center for Global Studies.

INTERNATIONAL DEVELOPMENT INSTITUTE

The basic mission of the International Development Institute (IDI) is to help improve the design and implementation of practical development activities. IDI's approach to achieving this mission is to draw information from theory and practice and disseminate it to carefully selected users.

Sponsored by grants from various sources, IDI has developed expertise on international development. Among its activities are materials production, including textbooks used in training and other forms of instruction, design studies of various means–ends relationships, design notes presenting specific lessons from development experiences, and training modules that combine audio, visual, and printed materials in self-instructional packages.

In addition, IDI conducts two-week analytical skills workshops three or four times a year. Designed for persons engaged in problem analysis and program or project design, these workshops cover systems analysis, organizational and managerial analysis, economic and financial analysis, and other principles and methods for dealing with development problems. Participants are AID staff members and host-country personnel involved in practical planning, analysis, and implementation. In conducting workshops in Afghanistan, Kenya, Panama, the Philippines, and Thailand, as well as in the United States, the Institute has made innovative use of audio-visual and computer technology. It has demonstrated that intellectually powerful materials can be fitted to practical uses in ways that do not dilute quality.

IDI also administers a variety of other projects related to development. For example, the Venezuelan Migration Project is an interdisciplinary research group at Indiana University interested in a wide range of issues related to migration. Under another project, a prospectus is being developed for a program called Abstracts on the Integration of Latin America, designed to provide a comprehensive guide to scholarly articles and books about the social, political, economic, and cultural aspects of Latin American integration. The first step in this process, completed in 1981, was a feasibility study sponsored by the Fundación Bicentenario de Simón Bolívar (Caracas, Venezuela).

POLISH STUDIES CENTER

The Polish Studies Center handles the exchange program between Indiana University and Warsaw University. Its counterpart, the American Studies Center, was established at Warsaw University during the 1975/76 academic year and formally opened in October 1976. The Polish Studies Center was established during the 1976/77 academic year and formally opened in November 1977.

Under the terms of the agreement, two professors and two graduate students or research associates are sent by each university to the other each year. The senior professor in each instance serves as associate director

of the center and teaches. The junior professor is mostly involved in
teaching.

In cooperation with the Office of International Programs, the Polish
Studies Center assists all Indiana University professors and students going
to Poland. In the area of community relations, the center is in close contact
with the Polish Cultural Society of Indiana, which is centered in
Indianapolis. The center's monthly newsletter is sent all over the United
States and to Poland.

The Polish Studies Center also sponsors an active program of cultural
and academic events. These programs are cosponsored by the Office of
International Programs, the Russian and East European Institute, and by
appropriate departments and programs in the university.

Under the terms of the Indiana–Warsaw agreement, the two
universities alternate hosting an international conference each year. The
topic of the 1981/82 conference at Indiana University was the Polish
Renaissance.

CENTER FOR GLOBAL STUDIES

The Indiana University Center for Global Studies has three main
objectives. First, the center works to strengthen undergraduate instruction
in global studies on all eight Indiana University campuses. The means for
accomplishing this objective include drawing attention to the importance
of global studies; mobilizing talent and resources behind global studies;
encouraging the infusion of global perspectives into existing core courses;
helping to establish new courses; facilitating cross-disciplinary cooperation
among faculty members who share an interest in global studies; acquiring
new library resources to support global studies; and acquiring fugitive
materials such as syllabi and bibliographies that further global studies.

Second, the center is interested in developing graduate education in
global studies at the master's degree level in the professional schools of
Business, Education, and Public and Environmental Affairs.

Third, the center provides services to the state and region on behalf of
global studies. The center has provided services to schools that are trying
to strengthen international studies instruction.

A major activity of the center has been the Project on Indiana in the
World Economy, which seeks to improve and expand ties between the
university and the local community of each of the regional campuses of
Indiana University so that public awareness and understanding of
international economic issues may be expanded. The project involves
academics, businessmen, and community leaders in the collection and
exchange of information. The project has sponsored conferences designed
to create greater public awareness of the impact of international trade,

investment, and politics on the quality of life in Indiana and the nation. This project is sponsored by the center with the support of a grant from the Metropolitan Life Insurance Company and the International Communications Agency.

The Future of International Studies

Given its strong institutional commitment to excellence in international studies and the wide base of faculty support, Indiana University expects to continue the development of its international programs with vigor and enthusiasm in the next decades. Although the prospects for expanded foundation and government assistance for international studies are somewhat reduced compared with the extravagant days of the 1960s and the early 1970s, the university's resource base has achieved the critical mass needed to continue development on its own.

Nonetheless, the difficulties of maintaining and continuing international program development should not be minimized. With the prospect of declining enrollments and declining state budgets for higher education, faculty members and administrators interested in international studies have no grounds for complacency and will have to be sure that programs in this area are of high academic quality, command strong faculty support, and have aggressive representation throughout the institution.

These programs will not survive merely on the belief that international concerns deserve attention but they will prosper if the faculty members and the students who participate are of the highest quality the institution has to offer.

CHAPTER 6

Texas Southern University

JOSEPH JONES, JR.

TEXAS SOUTHERN UNIVERSITY IS A PREDOMINANTLY BLACK, state-supported university in Houston, Texas, a center of international activity. Under an act approved by the state legislature, the university focuses on urban programing. Because urbanization is a worldwide trend, students are trained to solve urban problems wherever they occur, and the university's international education programs and activities are therefore linked to its urban mission. The Office of International Programs, described here, administers and coordinates international studies programs and intercultural enrichment activities (foreign student services are handled by a separate office). Its community outreach activities are another link to the university's special commitment to the community.

The University and the Community

Texas Southern University was established in 1947. Originally designated the Texas State University for Negroes, its name was changed in 1950 to Texas Southern University. The student population has increased from an initial enrollment of 2,303 to a current enrollment of 8,500. This student population, although still predominantly black and from Texas, includes many nonblacks and foreign students from more than fifty-five countries.

Texas Southern University provides degree programs at the baccalaureate, master's, and doctoral levels in eight schools and one college. Degrees are conferred in arts and sciences, teacher education, business, technology, public affairs, communications, pharmacy, and law. Currently forty-six major degree programs are offered at the bachelor's degree level, twenty-three at the master's degree level, and four at the doctoral level. In 1973, the university was designated as a special-purpose institution for urban programing, and many of its programs are designed to prepare students for service to the urban community at home and abroad.

The academic program at the university is supported by a strong library that contains more than half a million volumes. Special collections are the International Collection, the Heartman Collection on Negro Life and Culture, and the Barbara Jordan Collection; the African archives contain an exceptionally fine collection of African artifacts. The university's diverse programs are further enriched and supported by branch libraries and learning resource centers in the School of Education and in the Thurgood Marshall School of Law.

The university's urban mission is complemented by its location in Houston, a city of approximately 1.5 million. Because of its preeminent position as a regional center for energy resources and energy development, it has been called "the Energy Capital of the World," "the International City," and "the City of the Future." These titles have been justly earned owing to the city's rapid growth in energy-related industries and businesses, oil capital, and activities generated by the export–import market. Houston ranks as one of the leading ports handling foreign freight and serves as a regional center for many multinational corporations, trade missions, and consulates. As a gateway city, Houston attracts persons from the American republics, Europe, and the oil-rich countries in Asia, the Middle East, and Africa. Many visitors come to transact business or attend the university; others come for medical services or personal pleasure and recreation. Those who come for higher education can matriculate in any one of five senior colleges and universities, most of which offer degrees through the doctoral level. Graduates of Texas Southern University and other higher education institutions in the city often secure positions in Houston and surrounding communities.

Texas Southern University has a multiethnic and multicultural faculty of about four hundred full-time and eighty part-time faculty members. Approximately 60 percent of the faculty members hold a doctorate; more than 25 percent have been abroad and have had some international academic experiences. The resident faculty is augmented by visiting lecturers from foreign countries, many of whom are on assignment in Houston or come to the university through university-sponsored, federally-supported visiting professorships.

The student body consists of approximately two-thirds American and one-third foreign students. Most of the American students are residents of Texas, from low-income families in the inner city. Few have been abroad, but most have had contacts with persons from other countries either in the classroom or at work, through the foreign students at the University, the large Mexican-American community in Houston, and the influx of foreigners into the city of Houston. Cultural contacts on campus and international travel are increasingly reducing student parochialism. The Office of International Programs contributes through the Intercultural Film Series, overseas study projects, International Career Day programs, and course offerings in international studies.

The leaders of Texas Southern University have throughout its history evidenced an interest in international affairs and a special concern for the downtrodden of the world. No doubt this interest derived from the mission of the university, which was established to provide higher education for the black people of Texas, and also from the leaders' own experiences. The first president was a former United States Ambassador to the Republic of Liberia, and the second served as the United States representative to the United Nations. Subsequent presidents, including the present one, served in positions of leadership in international affairs in the federal government or elsewhere.

The campus environment over the years has thus been favorable for nurturing international activities and study programs, and out of it has come a broad compendium of courses in area studies and foreign languages. The character of the university's international thrust has been determined in no small way by the recruitment of faculty members whose training and interests have complemented those of the university's leadership. As a result, at no time since the university was established could the campus environment be classified as strictly traditional. The early development of a global perspective has been accelerated in recent years with the influx of large numbers of foreign students and faculty members, coupled with the university's location in a city that is increasingly internationally oriented.

How the International Studies Program Was Established

The development of a strong program of international studies was part of the early planning and development of the university and resulted because of the continuing interest, concern, and support at the university's highest administrative levels.

ORIGIN OF THE PROGRAM

The earliest international studies initiative was the establishment in 1965 of the Houston Inter-University African Studies Program, undertaken jointly by Texas Southern University, Rice University, the University of Houston, and the University of St. Thomas. Through this consortium, courses in African studies were developed at the participating universities, and many of the courses became part of Texas Southern University's ongoing curriculum.

Other area study courses dealing with Asia, Latin America, and Europe evolved as the curriculum grew, and a variety of international projects and activities were initiated. The most notable and significant projects affected faculty and curriculum development, and they broadened students' view of career opportunities, an important outcome because most students at the university are minorities who come from low-income families and have a provincial outlook.

Among the major international projects involving students were the Teacher Corps/Peace Corps Project and the Peace Corps Internship Project. Covering a span of almost ten years, these projects were designed to attract minority students to graduate studies and included a tour of at least two years in the Peace Corps. The programs enabled participating students to combine a domestic teaching internship with graduate study and an assignment in the Peace Corps with study at a foreign university. While meeting the goals of the Teacher Corps and the Peace Corps, the programs afforded participants the opportunity to complete a graduate degree and obtain some teaching experience at home and abroad. Subsequently, some participants joined international agencies as staff members, fulfilling one of the aims of the projects, that is, to encourage minorities to pursue international careers.

International activities at Texas Southern University continued to accelerate during the 1970s with seminars, conferences, colloquia, and study-abroad projects for students and faculty members. In 1972, a grant from the Bureau of Educational and Cultural Affairs of the United States Department of State enabled the university to initiate an annual Fulbright–Hays seminar in cooperation with a consortium of four participating Texas colleges and universities. The programs of the consortium included faculty study abroad, visiting foreign lecturers, and participating Fulbright-Hays students from abroad. The visiting Fulbright–Hays scholars provided opportunities for dialogue between Texas Southern students and students from other countries.

Other projects that affected the development of international studies at the university included: (1) a project to train Haitian civil service personnel, (2) several training programs for foreign students supported by the United States Agency for International Development, (3) initiatives for linkages with new universities in Africa, and (4) a trade mission to Nigeria of persons from the university and the business community.

International studies at the university were given further impetus in 1978, when the Office of International Programs was established to develop and coordinate international programs on campus. The Office of International Student Services had already been established in 1973 to coordinate services and programs for foreign students, whose numbers significantly increased during the mid-seventies. The presence of these students imparted an international flavor to the student body. At first, holding a discussion with a student from Nigeria, Ghana, or Iran was a novelty; now, it is a likely occurrence.

With the formal commitment to a more broadly based program of international studies, funding proposals were submitted to federal and private agencies. Out of these proposals came funds for faculty development workshops, curriculum development activities, and library resources to support international studies at the university. The Center for International Studies was established in 1980 to develop and strengthen programs in international business and technology and to initiate outreach support to the business community. A grant for study abroad was secured for faculty members who were developing modules in international and intercultural studies for inclusion in general education curricula. A minor concentration in international studies was approved for undergraduate students (mostly in the liberal arts), and plans were made to include area study concentrations in the curricula of other university programs.

In late 1980, the new university president, Leonard H.O. Spearman, issued a formal statement of support for continuing development of international studies curricula at the university. His support of international studies was further demonstrated in a proposal to reorganize the academic administration so that international studies would be a component of the Graduate School.

PROGRAM HIGHLIGHTS

Important milestones in the development of international studies at Texas Southern University include the following:

1965   Establishment of the Houston Inter-University African Studies Program
1967   Texas Southern University African Studies Program initiated
1971   Launching of the Teacher Corps/Peace Corps Project
1971   Beginning of the Peace Crops Internship Project
1972   Establishment of the International Program Council
1972   Summer study project in West Africa
1973   Initiation of the Texas Consortium Program
1974   Fulbright–Hays Conference started
1975   Initiation of the Model United Nations Conference
1977   Linkage exploration with Nigerian universities
1978   Global campus concept enunciated by administration
1978   Establishment of the Office of International Programs
1979   Caribbean/American Exchange Project

1979   Haiti/Texas Southern University agreement
1979   International Studies Center established
1979   Undergraduate International Curriculum Studies Committee approved
1979   Trade mission to Nigeria
1980   Summer study project in Haiti
1980   Initiation of conference series on international trade and finance
1981   Minor concentration in international studies approved
1981   Initiation of the Intercultural Film Series
1981   Summer study project in Barbados
1981   Summer study project in Haiti and the Dominican Republic
1981   Proposal prepared for an interdisciplinary master's degree program in international studies
1981   Linkage Agreement approved with Kookmin University in Korea
1982   Linkage Agreement approved with Universidad National Pedro Henrique Wena

Institutional Commitment to International Studies

Texas Southern University is an urban university situated in a fast-growing center of international activity. Its mission grew out of the societal needs of its local constituency, which are based on the diverse dimensions of Houston's economy and social life. As a result, international education became intrinsic to the university's urban mission.

INSTITUTION MISSION AND GOALS

The university's urban commitment was officially mandated in 1973 by the Texas state legislature, which designated Texas Southern University as a special-purpose university for urban programing. The following statement defines the university's mission:

> The purpose of the urban university is to provide an institutional focus upon a spectrum of problems as they exist and affect in microcosm the human products in the urban community. Such a university would vigorously pursue the cultural, social, political, and economic elements of change unique to urbanized society in its teaching, research, and programmatic undertakings and would address itself to a citizen-centered philosophy of public service. The complex issues of urban living do not occur in linear fashion. At one and the same time the urban resident is confronted with problems of health, transportation, employment, and education. Broadly but succinctly stated, the purpose is to bring strategies for remediation of the problems of the urban community through institutions of higher education in manner befitting the extent and the nature of problems as they exist.

To accommodate this role, the objectives of the university were codified with the following express purposes:

1. To provide educational experiences that enable a multiethnic, multicultural student body to gain increased opportunities in the world of work.

2. To establish multipurpose centers for the improvement of communication among cultural groups through languages, art, music, dance, drama, crafts, and other activities that serve to transmit the intrinsic values of selected cultural groups.

In 1977, to define the university's position on international education, the university administration enunciated the goal of developing a "global campus." University academic, service, and research goals would be focused on the achievement of the urban mission, but the urban concept was expanded to encompass urban problems that might be of an international nature. Because urbanization was viewed as worldwide and irreversible, students would be trained to use their knowledge to solve urban problems wherever they occurred. The following statement summarized the nature of the university administration's commitment to the global campus:

> The projection of Texas Southern as "global" in one sense in its definition of its clientele community is best understood as an institutional recognition of the need for its students and its other clienteles to include other nations and other peoples within the purview of their concepts of human understanding. Parochialism, regionalism, and nationalism are clearly giving place in world affairs to internationalism and transnationalism, and the Texas Southern University graduate who has not come to terms with at least a recognition of this fact is in many ways underprepared for tomorrow's reality. Though Texas Southern has involved itself quite extensively in overseas programming and now engages in exchanges of various kinds in a variety of world locations . . . the focus of its "global" activities is the . . . conviction that the University must be alert, receptive, and responsive to unprecedented challenges and opportunities in the area of international, multicultural education and service.

GOALS AND OBJECTIVES OF THE OFFICE OF INTERNATIONAL PROGRAMS

The Office of International Programs at Texas Southern University has been charged with directing, coordinating, and developing international education on the campus. (Foreign student services are provided through the Office of Student Services.) During the past few years, the major thrusts of the International Programs Office have therefore involved the following activities:

1. Working with various academic departments to develop international studies degree programs

2. Facilitating the revision of courses to update international education content

3. Initiating and supporting faculty and student study abroad projects

4. Designing projects to support faculty and student development

5. Providing community outreach activities

6. Supporting intercultural activities and international projects that enhance faculty and student understanding of diverse cultures and peoples

These activities are in keeping with the goals of the Office of International Programs, which are:

1. To expand international studies at the university in a manner consistent with the mission of the institution

2. To support the academic departments in projects that strengthen international and intercultural studies

3. To provide broader perceptions of intercultural and international relations to students, faculty members, and community constituents

4. To increase student perceptions of career options through training in international studies

5. To provide outreach programs and services to the university's community clientele

Specific objectives include:

I. Increase the international content of appropriate university courses.
  A. Help in the development of new courses and revised courses that support the university's international program development.
  B. Support international course content with appropriate learning resources.
II. Support faculty development to increase the international knowledge and intercultural understanding of faculty members.
  A. Support faculty study abroad.
  B. Support inquiry and disseminate information about cultural diversity.
  C. Provide workshops that enhance faculty members' international and intercultural knowledge.

III. Help students develop broader understanding of global interdependence and cultural interrelationships.
   A. Enable students to gain experiences abroad.
   B. Complement basic international instruction in the classroom with a broad program of extraclass enrichment activities.
   C. Facilitate student understanding of career opportunities in the international sector.
IV. Provide for community understanding of international interdependence and cultural diversity.
   A. Support the participation, when appropriate, of community members in campus international activities.
   B. Provide information for business persons engaged in international trade and investments.
   C. Provide forums for the exchange of information and dialogue between community members and persons from abroad.
V. Engage in international cooperative arrangements consistent with the mission of the university and the goals of the Office of International Programs.
   A. Cooperate with consortium institutions in Texas to further international studies on the campuses of member colleges and universities.
   B. Participate in national organizations that are committed to goals that complement the goals of the Office of International Programs.
   C. Engage in cooperative linkages with foreign institutions and international agencies to further international understanding.

ADMINISTRATIVE ORGANIZATION

Management of international programs on campus is a function of the Office of International Programs, located within the Graduate School. The administration of services to foreign students is carried out by a separate office. The major responsibility of the Office of International Programs is to develop, administer, and coordinate international programs that affect the university's curriculum. Proposals for projects, development of new international studies courses and degree programs, and activities pertaining to international programs are coordinated by the director of the Office of International Programs.

Figure 6.1 shows the functional relationships between the director and other administrative offices. The figure shows that the director of international programs reports directly to the vice-president for academic affairs. The director has four basic responsibilities:

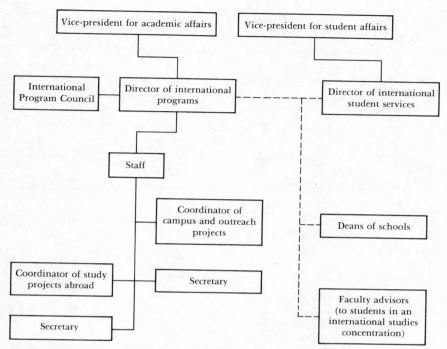

FIGURE 6.1. Scheme of the administration of international programs.

1. Developing and implementing international programs and projects
2. Preparing grant proposals
3. Managing the budget
4. Supervising and coordinating international studies with appropriate academic, administrative, and fiscal offices

Advisory services to the director are furnished by the International Program Council, which is interdisciplinary and consists of representatives from the college and the eight schools and from appropriate administrative offices. Project directors for various international programs report to the director of international programs. A secretary and two administrative assistants constitute the support staff for the Office of International Programs.

Project coordinators are responsible for ongoing activities such as budget control, recommending staff, budgeting and requisitioning, and preparing performance and fiscal reports.

Academic advisors are drawn from all schools of the university. They advise students about course requirements for the concentration in international studies and guide students in selecting courses that will complement their major and satisfy their career goals.

The Office of International Programs has important functional linkages with the Grants and Contracts Office, which is responsible for control and accountability of all federal grants. Close liaison is maintained with Grants and Contracts in requisitioning grant funds and preparing reports.

A close working relationship is maintained with the academic schools and the College of Arts and Sciences. Discussions are frequently held with the deans and department heads concerning new program development and projects and degree programs that are needed in international studies. Significant contacts are carried on continuously between academic departments and the Office of International Programs in developing and implementing outreach conferences, in advising students pursuing a minor concentration in international studies, and in coordinating projects that involve teaching cross-cultural information.

Further linkages exist between the Office of International Programs and the Office of University Development, which arranges media coverage for many of the conferences and other projects of the Office of International Programs. Some support for fund raising is also facilitated by the Office of University Development, but most fund raising is initiated by the director of international programs.

Program Description

The Office of International Programs develops, administers, and coordinates three major types of programs, *academic* (the minor concentration in international studies and study abroad), *community outreach*, and *intercultural enrichment*. The major support for international program activities has come from federal sources.

PROGRAM COMPONENTS

Minor concentration in international studies. The purpose of this academic program is to provide an opportunity for undergraduate students to pursue a minor program of study that will (1) strengthen their knowledge of the world and of the interdependency of peoples, (2) enhance their knowledge of a foreign language, and (3) complement the student's major.

Objectives of the program are these:

1. To increase the student's basic knowledge of the world community.

2. To provide for an in-depth understanding of the historic, political, economic, and social conditions of specific geographic areas.

3. To develop students' foreign language skills.

4. To increase students' career options as well as their attractiveness to international firms and government agencies for employment.

The program is designed to complement the student's major. The student will acquire specialist skills through the major, and the use of these skills either in a foreign country or the US will be enhanced by the minor in international studies.

The program consists of twenty-four semester hours in three clusters: six semester hours in foreign languages (French or Spanish); six in fine arts (art, history, and music); and twelve in social sciences (history, business, political science, geography, economics, communications, and sociology). Within each cluster there is a variety of courses from which the student may choose. There are three major tracks—Africa, Latin America, and the Caribbean—and the student selects courses pertaining to one of these tracks. Should the African track be chosen, the foreign language will be French, and the fine arts and social science courses will have Africa as their subject matter. If the Latin American track is chosen, the foreign language will be Spanish, and the fine arts and social science courses will have Latin America as their subject matter. Because of the multicultural nature of the Caribbean, the student can elect to study this area either under the Latin American track or the African track. The major foreign languages of the Caribbean are French and Spanish, and the student can opt for either of these languages to fulfill the foreign language requirement. The French-speaking areas of the Caribbean are studied in the Afro-French culture and civilization courses, and the Spanish-speaking areas are studied in the Latin American culture and civilization courses.

Study abroad. Most study abroad projects are partially supported by federal grants. Pursuing studies that could not appropriately be conducted in the United States, university faculty members and students have during the past six years engaged in study projects in the West Indies, Europe, Africa, and the Middle East.

Community outreach. Since its inception Texas Southern University has had a strong interest and involvement in the Houston community. Many of its international programs have therefore been designed to provide services to the community such as conferences on trade and finance, seminars on international issues, and consulting services to local businesses.

Interinstitutional activities. For several years, Texas Southern University has served as the host institution for the Texas Consortium for International Studies. The consortium sponsors a series of international and intercultural programs on five college and university campuses in

Texas. Each institution has its own series of on-campus programs, and several activities are sponsored by the consortium. Yearly activities include the Fulbright–Hays Conference, which involves visiting Fulbright–Hays scholars; International Career Day programs; Foreign Scholars in Residence; International Festivals; and seminars on international topics of current interest.

On-campus activities. Another way of fostering intercultural studies is through the Intercultural Film Series, films depicting interesting aspects of the life and culture of a particular people. Faculty lectures, art exhibits, and faculty participation in international study workshops further support international program development at the university.

Funding

Financial support for international and intercultural studies is derived from state, federal, and private sources. Since 1973, a state-supported account has been set aside for intercultural studies. Funds in this account provide partial support for personnel, travel, supplies, and communications. Most of the funds for curriculum and faculty development, library books, conferences, and travel are provided through federal support. During the past two years, federal support has accounted for approximately 50 percent of budgeted funds. However, university in-kind contributions have far exceeded grant funds from federal sources. Some financial support has also been derived from the corporate sector for specific types of international projects.

In 1979/80 and 1980/81, the budgets of the Office of International Programs were as follows:

	1979/80	1980/81
State support	$ 15,000	$ 15,000
Federal support	$115,000	$147,000
Private	$ 6,500	$ 6,500
Total	$136,500	$158,500

The figures for state support do not include university in-kind contributions of personnel, facilities, supplies, travel, and communications.

Obviously, federal sources have provided the major support for international program activities. The tenuousness of this condition is evident from the federal government's history of funding such programs. "Soft" money makes program planning difficult because funds for staff support will probably not be forthcoming on a continuing basis. Further, private-sector support is not likely to be more reliable or continuous.

Therefore, an institution that is committed to the development of a stable program of international studies must commit enough funds to assure that the basic resources needed to carry on programs will be available when soft money is not.

Program expenditures from all sources were mostly for personnel resources. However, a significant amount of the budget provided support for purchasing library books and periodicals. These expenditures were vital to strengthening the minor concentration in international studies and will augment the proposed graduate program in international studies.

Program Strengths and Weaknesses

The Texas Southern University model for international program development has evolved over a period of fifteen years. Early attempts were largely confined to separate departments, and only in 1973 was a concerted effort made to effect the campuswide coordination of international studies. This centralization in the Office of International Programs provided leadership, direction, and a greater sense of institutional support than was previously evident.

There are many advantages to Texas Southern University's approach:

1. An institutional commitment to the support of international studies is a part of the university's mission.

2. There is administrative support for international studies initiatives.

3. A large corps of faculty members have had international training and experience.

4. There are foreign students from more than fifty-five countries.

5. The university is located in a metropolitan city that is a regional center for several large multinational corporations and a hub of international activity.

6. The salary of the director of the Office of International Programs is paid from state funds.

7. The staff of the office is competent and strongly committed to intercultural and international programs and is augmented by a significant number of faculty members who are interested in international projects and programs.

8. A large segment of the university's community clientele is interested in the various international programs and activities sponsored on campus.

9. The location of the Office of International Programs in the Graduate School provides for contacts with all academic departments and facilities making programmatic initiatives institutionwide.

10. There are major workshops and other activities for faculty development that produce strong support from the faculty for curriculum development in international studies.

11. Other universities in the area are interested in interuniversity projects.

12. Texas Southern University has worked with other institutions in Texas to develop and expand international programs at those schools, a venture that has increased the visibility of Texas Southern University's own international programs.

13. The director of international programs reports directly to the vice-president for academic affairs.

14. Budget resources from several sources have provided for a more diversified approach to program development.

15. The minor concentration in international studies at Texas Southern University will increase student awareness, international training, and employment options.

16. The administration is commited to developing a major in international studies and an area-specific center for international studies.

The approach has certain deficiencies that adversely affect the progress of international studies at Texas Southern University and that are common in international studies programs at other institutions:

1. Adequate funds are lacking to support continuous, systematic planning. Funds derived largely from federal or private sources cannot be relied on if the international studies program is to become an integral part of the institution's curriculum.

2. To articulate international program objectives to the public at large and to many segments of the university community is often difficult. Therefore, frequent activities that require funds must be carried on to maintain program visibility.

3. Adequate staff support is needed to relieve the director, who must often write grant proposals, help implement programs, travel, and develop new initiatives for program development.

4. In a university that has a large population of low-income students, setting up study abroad projects and finding funds to support them

is often difficult. Most low-income students must work while attending school and therefore have neither the funds nor the time to participate in study abroad.

5. There is a need to generate greater support for international program development from the private sector. Such support would help to counter the inconsistency in federal support, and it would specifically contribute to training students for service in the corporate sector.

Strategies for the 1980s

In the years ahead, the international program will emphasize enhancing opportunities for faculty development and increasing the number of faculty members with international training and experiences abroad. Enhanced faculty development would result in curriculum changes— setting up international studies programs and infusing international studies into other programs of study. Through faculty and curriculum development, more students trained in international studies should be graduated, students who will have greater career options for service abroad in government agencies and private firms and organizations.

Texas Southern University is especially committed to serving as a resource for the community and plans to expand its outreach programs and services. To address the interests of the university and the community in specific geographic regions, the university hopes to establish a center for international studies. Such a center will enhance the development of human resources, library resources, and other forms of support for persons who are interested in a region for research, business, or other activities. Greater community involvement will probably lead to increased financial support from the private sector.

Other efforts will include:

- Increasing the emphasis placed on intercultural enrichment activities in order to expand the awareness of faculty members and students about cultural diversity and the interdependency of peoples

- Creating more opportunities for students to study and work abroad, to gain a better knowledge of foreign languages, to gain entry into foreign service careers, and to engage in activities with students from other cultures

- Increasing the involvement of faculty members in study abroad programs, curriculum development workshops, and activities that foster a commitment to expanding international studies on campus

- Augmenting the state-supported component of the budget so that a more systematic plan for continuing program initiatives can be developed

Texas Southern University's international programs have greatly developed during the past fifteen years. The challenges ahead can best be met if programs are assured the basic resources needed for them to continue, resources that will in large measure have to come from state-allocated university funds. To do less invites an uncertain existence for significant program initiatives.

CHAPTER 7

Florida International University

THOMAS A. BRESLIN

The University and the Community

Florida International University, a division of the State University System of Florida, holds a charter from the state that sets three goals: the education of students, service to the community, and greater international understanding. The charter mandates the university to become a major international education center with a primary emphasis on creating greater mutual understanding among the nations of the Americas and the rest of the world.

Situated in Miami, the university opened its doors in 1972. By 1982, it comprised six schools: Arts and Sciences, Education, Business, Hospitality Management, Technology, and Public Affairs and Services. A seventh school, Nursing, was ready to start operation. The university's operating budget for 1981/82 was $42 million, and it had grown into a two-campus institution with 1,326 employees, including 475 faculty members.

By December 1981 the university enrolled 11,885 students, 7,554 of whom were full-time students. There were 867 foreign students in degree programs; another 251 were studying in the English as a Second Language Certificate Program. These students were, by percentage of enrollment (7.3 percent), the largest group of foreign students at any public university in Florida. Between 1976 and 1981 their number increased from 242 to 865, but between 1981 and 1982 foreign student enrollment stalled at 867. Three-fourths of the students were males and they represented seventy-seven countries.

By early 1982, the university had ninety bachelor's degree programs, forty master's degree programs, and one doctoral program. It was operating self-supporting programs in a dozen countries and Puerto Rico and had exchange agreements with several foreign institutions of higher education. Efforts to develop on-campus degree programs and university-sponsored publications with an international orientation had thus been successful. The university also developed the Interamerican University Council for Economic and Social Development (CUIDES) and was deeply involved in organizing special, federally funded programs for Cuban and Haitian refugees.

These last programs are the most recent in a series of responses to the arrival of Latin American and Caribbean refugees who have made Miami the de facto capital city of the Caribbean Basin. The energy of these refugees, beginning with the Cubans who fled from the Castro regime in the early 1960s, transformed Miami from a sleepy retirement city and torpid tourist haven into a bustling commercial city with an insatiable demand for bilingual service workers, technicians, and business people.

In the wake of the Cubans and other exiles, millions of tourists from the Caribbean and Latin America came to Miami for extended shopping sprees. Many invested in real estate. The city's merchants and bankers responded by orienting themselves more and more to the south; the airlines decided to impose higher rates on excess baggage. The boom took its toll of the local social fabric; indeed, it rewove the pattern altogether. Incoming Cubans displaced local blacks from the service sector. They then displaced local white English-speaking persons from the small business and industry sector; and recently they have made strong inroads into banking and finance. The black community was further desolated by competition from Cuban and Haitian laborers who arrived in 1980. The frustration of native blacks led to the rioting that destroyed the Liberty City area of Miami. Demographic realities did not favor the blacks—by 1980, Hispanics already constituted half of Miami's population and a third of the population of surrounding Dade County. In both absolute and relative terms, Hispanics were growing in number. That growth spread throughout Dade County and north into the Fort Lauderdale–Broward County area. Hispanic political clout was growing while black political influence was waning.

Florida International University was established mainly because of the influx of Cuban refugees during the 1960s and the attendant rise in Miami's economy. Cubans wanted affordable higher education beyond that provided by Miami–Dade Community College. As the area's contribution to the state revenues soared farther and farther beyond that of other areas, the lack of a public university in the state's largest metropolitan area became less and less defensible. Indeed, Miami was the nation's last large metropolitan area without a public four-year college or university. Reluctantly, the state legislature authorized the establishment of Florida International University as a four-year institution; however, under intense political pressure from Miami–Dade Community College, the University of Miami (a private institution), and older public universities far to the north, the politicians provided funding only for an upper division and an attenuated graduate program.

From its opening in 1972, the growth of the university has reflected the boom and then semistagnation of the local economy. Pent-up demand and a strong economy accounted for the largest opening day enrollment in US history—five thousand students. Growth continued unabated into the late 1970s but as the economy cooled in the 1980s, enrollment growth fell behind projections.

Enrollments closely reflect the ethnic composition of the area's population. Hispanic students account for about 35 percent of the student body; blacks, about 10 percent; Asians, American Indians, Africans, and other minorities, about 4 percent. Slightly over half of the students are female. The average student is about twenty-eight and is as likely to attend classes at night as in the daytime. Thus, the typical student is a minority female who is older than the typical American undergraduate student.

In September 1981 a special lower division program for talented high school graduates was initiated but it did not have an impact on the student body as a whole. Because it is limited to a few thousand students, the program's impact will be more qualitative than quantitative; nonetheless, the additional enrollment and funding will be welcome, especially in the hard-pressed College of Arts and Sciences, which will be responsible for most of the lower division instruction.

University administrators anticipate that the economy will continue to weaken in the years ahead and, barring new waves of wealthy or middle-class Latin American and Caribbean refugees, enrollment will grow slowly. Growth in foreign student enrollment—or even maintenance of current enrollment—will be a function of the enrollment of Middle Eastern students. Their educational prospects will be somewhat less affected by decline in the global economy (including the price of oil) than will the educational prospects of, for example, Nigerian or Venezuelan youth.

In the face of such gloomy economic prospects, the university administration recently found a private developer who will build dormitories on campus and thus make it easier for nonlocal students to enroll—a pressing need, owing to a serious shortage of reasonably priced rental housing in Miami for some time. Additional attractions will be the new School of Nursing, the upgrading of the School of Technology to a School of Engineering, and the expansion of the computer science program in the College of Arts and Sciences. The administration also hopes to maintain the momentum of its international program development and widen the impact of that programing on other educational institutions in Florida.

Institutional Commitments to International Education

The key administrative component in the design, development, and coordination of almost all the university's international activities has been the university's Center for International Affairs, later renamed the International Affairs Center (IAC). The center, brainchild of the university's founding president and his academic vice-president, opened in April 1972. The first dean of international affairs and the vice-president, after extensive consultation with outside experts and faculty members, set out three main functions for the center: provision of counsel and assistance for study abroad endeavors; assistance in using faculty resources and money to support things international; surveillance of international developments in academe. The main emphasis was on the brokerage function.

FUNDING

The availability of adequate state funding was a critical factor in the operation of the International Affairs Center. In 1981/82, the university budgeted for the center $156,653 in salary money, $5,500 for consultants and temporary and student labor, and $27,000 for expenses such as travel, office supplies, and communications. In addition, the university allotted to the center special funds known as Quality Improvement Program (QIP) funds provided by the state to help each of the nine public universities achieve national recognition for a select few programs. In 1981/82 QIP funding for the center amounted to $65,164 for salaries, $14,000 for temporary help, and $8,000 for expenses. QIP funding was used primarily to develop the CUIDES concept into a substantial program. Management of international contracts and grants provided another $10,000–$12,000 to the center for program development and support. State-provided expense funds were particularly useful for program development and support of faculty research activity. Management fees enabled the center to acquire much needed word-processing and improved telecommunications equipment.

Also critical to the expansion of international programing was the support of the Florida International University (FIU) Foundation, Inc., which until 1981 contributed $5,000 annually to the IAC. The Foundation's International Committee has managed the Foundation's relations with

IAC and has assisted the center is raising funds. Privately raised funds fell into two categories: those given for the support of specific programs, most notably in Mexico, Panama, and Honduras; and those that could be used for general purposes of representation abroad and hospitality on campus.

ADMINISTRATIVE ORGANIZATION

The Office of Student Affairs has a Department of International Student Services with four professionals. There is also an International Student Admissions Division in the Admissions Office employing two full-time staff members. International student participation in student government is perennially strong. Foreign students are usually full-time students while students from the local area tend to be part-time because of commitments to jobs and family. The fact that foreign students are more visible tends to strengthen their influence in campus life and also to intensify contact with Student Affairs personnel. One of the two major campus events (if not the major event) is International Week in early March. Overall responsibility for these activities has perforce given the administration and work of the Office of Student Affairs an international dimension that complements that of the Office of Academic Affairs.

The Office of Academic Affairs has encouraged the various academic units to engage both in international education and training and research activity and, where appropriate, to add an international dimension to their curriculum and employ foreign faculty. Through the deans of the various schools it has monitored the academic quality of these efforts and authorized the expenditure of funds to achieve these ends. The Office of Academic Affairs provides for the orderly development and implementation of these activities through IAC.

Certain internationally oriented activities at the university—the MBA program in Venezuela, the International Banking and Finance Program, the publication of the award-winning *Caribbean Review,* the *International Journal for Housing Science and its Applications,* and the *Interamerican Review of Psychology*—fall outside the purview of IAC, though the center has provided partial support for the *Interamerican Review of Psychology* durings its sojourn at the university. Also outside the purview of IAC are international student affairs other than those involving groups of students at the university on a contractual basis.

The institutional mission for IAC emerged only after the advent of the university's second president, Harold B. Crosby, who stabilized the young institution and favored its international dimension. He made IAC a division of his office and brought in as dean K. William Leffland, a seasoned developer and director of international programs. Crosby made the dean a member of the Council of Academic Deans. He also modestly increased the center's budget and assisted Leffland in making contacts with the local corporate community, particularly with multinationals that had their Caribbean or Latin American offices in Miami. Finally, he saw to it that IAC received from FIU a modest annual grant of seed money.

With Crosby's blessing, the new dean worked with the vice-president for academic affairs, himself a former acting dean of international affairs, to formulate a clear-cut institutional mission for the center in the form of a new universitywide policy on the center's role as promoter, developer, and coordinator of international education, training and research programs, and activities offered at the university or conducted abroad under its auspices. According to this policy, any faculty member or administrator contemplating international activity must clear it with IAC before developing and initiating the activity. IAC reserves for itself the right to develop programs of its own through the various academic units, subject to the approval of the respective deans. The vice-president for academic affairs serves as arbiter in case of disagreement. Under this policy, IAC has the right to sign off on all travel outside the continential United States.

Recurrent discussions about moving the center out of the President's Office and back into Academic Affairs came to a head in spring 1982. Given the enduring close relationship between IAC and Academic Affairs and the need of IAC to work closely with the academic deans and the dean of University Outreach, the university administration transferred IAC into the Office of Academic Affairs. The president, however, retained CUIDES in his Office. IAC would continue its role as developer, a bent encouraged by the president, who has discouraged any idea that the center should have its own academic programing.

After Leffland became dean in early 1977 he immediately began to create an aura of legitimacy for IAC. Support from the President's Office and Office of Academic Affairs were critical to his efforts. IAC began to build substantial working relationships with each academic unit. The dean focused his energies on the School of Public Affairs and Services and the School of Business and Organizational Sciences; the associate dean, on the College of Arts and Sciences, the School of Technology, and the School of Education; the coordinator, on the School of Business and the School of Hospitality Management.

Through substantive relationships with the academic units, IAC sought to involve every academic department in international education, research, and training. Because state regulations decree that all international programing be self-supporting, IAC concentrated on developing long-term contract and grant programs, particularly those with a multiplier effect. A program of interinstitutional cooperation initiated with the College of the Bahamas (COB), whereby the university provided COB with three bachelor's degree programs in technology, met the first criterion. A two-part program with the Mexican Ministry of Finance satisfied both criteria. The first part was a seminar program in tax administration involving the School of Business; the second part was a master's degree in public administration offered by the School of Public Affairs and Services. The work with the Mexican government was self-supporting and opened government and institutional doors abroad and foundation doors at home.

GOALS OF THE INTERNATIONAL AFFAIRS CENTER

After developing or assisting in the development of a number of international activities, IAC staff laid out a series of five- and ten-year internationally oriented goals and objectives designed to institutionalize international education, training, and research throughout the entire university. In summary, the goals were as follows:

- Increased foreign student population (10–20 percent of full-time equivalent)
- One International Institute of Excellence per school
- Graduate degree programs with international components
- An endowment for international education, research, and training
- International academic and professional contracts in each school
- Foreign student housing
- International faculty with excellent reputations and credentials
- Strong international library
- An affordable program for international students
- High quality publications
- Consulting services in disciplines of expertise
- Increased enrollment in English as a Second Language (ESL)
- A strong international career placement program
- Creation of an International House
- More internationally related faculty research opportunities

GROWTH OF THE INTERNATIONAL AFFAIRS CENTER

The nucleus of the center was a four-person team of dean, associate dean, coordinator, and a staff (later administrative) assistant. In 1979/80 QIP funding allowed the addition of a research professor who was to develop umbrella programs that would involve several units of the university in common activities, preferably activities shared with other institutions. Two such activities were a Joint Environmental Enhancement and Protection Program for the Caribbean (JEEP) and the CUIDES concept.

In 1980/81, the center added coordinators—one full-time and one part-time—and assigned them to various units on a part-time basis to assist programs. This method was more effective than borrowing professors from the academic units on a temporary basis to work with their own units. Funding for the additional coordinator positions comes from QIP monies. Without the QIP-funded positions, expansion of the university's international programing would have ceased in 1979 or 1980 because the core staff could not take on more activities.

To achieve closer coordination of activities and an image of greater legitimacy, IAC formed a faculty advisory committee drawn from the various units. It failed to link IAC effectively to the other units, felt itself to be a rubber stamp, and died. Later, under pressure from President Crosby's successor, Gregory B. Wolfe, IAC formed a Policy Advisory Council composed of administrators and faculty members from several units. The vice-president for academic affairs is a member of this council, as is the director of the college's federally funded undergraduate Latin American/Caribbean Studies Center (LACC). No students are members of the council.

IAC took one other step to link its operations with those of the academic units. It encouraged each dean to appoint a faculty member as coordinator of international programs and activities in his or her school. Not every dean did so, nor was every faculty coordinator responsive to international interests other than his or her own. This aspect of the center's organizational efforts has been the weakest and least productive to date.

Program Description

The strongest demand for assistance with internationalizing the curriculum has come from the College of Arts and Sciences and the School of Education. The strongest demand for university programing abroad has come from agencies and institutions interested in the areas of advanced management, public and private, and graduate education. The services of the university's School of Hospitality Management have also been in demand in the Caribbean.

Academic program development has greatly benefited from federal funds granted to underwrite the Latin American/Caribbean Studies Center, the Global Awareness Program, the International Human Rights Education Program, and the master's degree program in international studies. IAC played a strong developmental role in each of these activities. Program development in the Caribbean and Latin America has benefited from the IAC dean's long-standing connections with Mexican officials and from Miami's position as the leading US airport for Latin and Caribbean traffic. In addition to easy access, proximity to the area has greatly reduced transportation and other program costs.

Occasionally, as in Mexico, new materials for the professional seminars, credit courses, and degree programs offered abroad need to be developed, tailored to local circumstances, and translated for local use. Sometimes a local counterpart must be used as coinstructor; language has been a barrier in the Spanish-speaking institutions where the university has not had Spanish-speaking faculty available to teach. In cases where translation of materials and lectures has been necessary, translation and simultaneous interpretation have been left to the sponsor. In the case of credit programs, management of academic records is handled through the Department of Off-Campus Courses of University Outreach.

Often, the university must insist on the assignment of a local counterpart to coordinate program matters abroad. This necessity has obviated many problems. Other problems have also occurred: currency restrictions, slowness of local banks to clear drafts on foreign banks, foreign withholding taxes, lack of Spanish language teaching materials, poor local telephone service, and tardiness of professors in meeting precourse deadlines for submission of materials to be translated.

As of 1 January 1982, the university had completed, or was still engaged in, contract and grants programs of different sorts in various countries. The following list summarizes these programs.

Bahamas:	Three bachelor's programs in technology; real estate seminar
Haiti:	NSF-funded geological mapping of the southern peninsula
Aruba:	Development of the Aruba School of Hotel Trades
Curaçao:	Professional seminars in business administration for the Netherlands Antilles University; teacher exchange
Venezuela:	MBA programs for the University de Oriente; Joint professional seminars with Universidad Simón Bolivar
Panama:	Cooperative MBA program with University Santa Maria la Antigua
Mexico:	Tax administration seminar program and MPA program for Ministry of Finance; professional seminars for federal district government
Honduras:	In-service training for American school teachers; small business development seminar program for Honduran government

Peru:	In-service training program for American school teachers, Lima; seminar program for the Graduate School of Business Administration (ESAN)
Uruguay:	In-service training program for American school teachers, Montevideo
Brazil:	Consultations and visiting examinations for British Brazilian course; joint seminar program with Foreign Trade Foundation
Iran:	M. Ed. program for government-sponsored students
Saudi Arabia:	Certificate program in Industrial Safety and Fire Science for Ministry of Interior
Kuwait:	ESL and various bachelor's and master's degree programs for Ministry of Education-sponsored students

In addition to the above, the Center organized summer study abroad programs to be delivered with and through the faculties of Laval University, Canada; Cambridge University, England; Universidad Autonoma de Guadalajara, Mexico; and Universidad de San Pedro Sula, Honduras.

The rapid multiplication of overseas programs, particularly in the organizational sciences, was not altogether satisfactory because these diverse programs were not conducive to broad funding. Consequently, shortly after Leffland became dean, he attempted to bring the university to the forefront of efforts to develop a North–South counterpart to the East–West Center (EWC) in Honolulu. He hoped to attract support from Congressman Dante Fascell, congressional sponsor of a proposed North–South Center and the congressman in whose district the university is located. Fascell showed the dean a General Accounting office East–West Center report that criticized EWC's dependence on the University of Hawaii and its lack of active support from foreign institutions. Leffland then enlisted the moral support of the University of Miami, Fascell's alma mater, and the support of the Universidad Simón Bolivar of Caracas with which the university had some joint professional programing. To help the university, Leffland also brought in a Chilean consultant who was advising the Organization of American States (OAS) on transfer of technology.

The Chilean consultant, Jaime Lavados Montes, laid a broad foundation for what was to follow. He organized a faculty seminar on the status of science and technology in Latin America that drew faculty from several schools. He assisted with the organization of an international conference at the university on integration of science and technology with development in the Caribbean and Latin America. Cosponsoring the conference were the University of the West Indies and the University of Guyana. Lavados also assisted IAC in developing a North–South Center model that was to go through many subsequent versions.

The IAC next went to the OAS and successfully proposed that OAS fund the participation of Latin American and Caribbean university rectors in an international conference (in Miami) to discuss a new model for North–South interuniversity cooperation. IAC coordinated the seminar in November 1980 and a follow-up meeting in February 1981 at the Universdad Autonoma de Guadalajara in Mexico. Participating in the seminar were the rectors of a dozen Latin American and Caribbean universities as well as representatives of twelve North American universities such as UCLA, Georgetown, and the University of Texas at Austin. Out of the first international seminar came an agreement to develop a plan for a new institution that would find and funnel new money into Latin and Caribbean universities. The university was appointed to serve as secretariat and, through IAC, developed a general proposal for the new organization. At the follow-up Guadalajara meeting, this proposal was accepted as the basis for a constitution subsequently presented to the founding assembly of the new organization in March 1982 at the OAS headquarters in Washington. The founding assembly confirmed President Wolfe as the leader of the Interamerican University Council for Economic and Social Development (CUIDES) and the university as its temporary secretariat.

While work on the CUIDES master project was proceeding apace, the IAC was developing a broad multidisciplinary program, the Joint Environmental Enhancement Program (JEEP) for the Caribbean Basin. It, too, went through various permutations at the hands of IAC research scholars. Its presently established goal is to develop collaborative programs involving the university with Caribbean institutions in environmental science, social science, and technology.

To balance the development of contract and grant programs abroad and to fulfill the other part of its institutional mission, IAC decided to encourage units to add an international or comparative element to each of their degree programs. An initial survey in fall 1977 showed that only thirteen of the university's 120 degree programs had an international or comparative requirement. Worse yet, until 1981 the university was an upper-division institution fed by Miami-Dade Community College (MDCC), and IAC inquiries revealed that only one program at MDCC had a required international component, and international or comparative course offerings often had to be canceled for lack of enrollment. It was clear to the IAC staff that adding faculty who could teach international or comparative courses or construct paper programs would not be enough. A clientele had to be developed. The university already had a rather large number of Caribbean and Latin American specialists and was putting ever greater resources into course offerings on that region. Many of these courses were drawing poorly; some were being canceled. Without a larger stream of interested students, Caribbean, Latin American or other international course offerings would quickly fall victim to the state's minimum enrollment requirements and the programs built around the courses would wither.

The center accordingly adopted the long-range strategy of cultivating an interest in international or comparative topics in the local school children. (The Dade County school system is the nation's fourth largest.) Working with Dr. Jan Tucker of the School of Education, who is a member of the Committee on International Education of the National Council on Social Studies, IAC surveyed the county's social studies teachers and found strong interest in comparative and international programing providing that curriculum materials and workshops could be made available. At IAC's urging, Academic Affairs gave Tucker release time in summer 1978 to develop a number of proposals, including an eventually successful one to the US Office of Education for a Global Awareness Program aimed at junior high school social studies teachers. That same office funded another of Tucker's proposals, an International Human Rights Education program for graduate and advanced undergraduate students. Both programs involved IAC and the College of Arts and Sciences with the School of Education.

Tucker's Global Awareness Program benefited from the interest which he developed in the Florida commissioner of education's office. He worked very closely with the Office of the Commissioner to position his program as the pilot for statewide programing of this sort. He and colleagues developed a highly successful pilot program that has been used throughout the state. Moreover, with IAC assistance, he has expanded plans for the program to include community college and university educators around the state. This expanded effort is taking shape and initial response to suggestions for cooperative programming has been very positive. Should the program develop the support that it needs to permeate postsecondary education in Florida, the university will indeed have become Florida's center for international education.

IAC staff believed that more conventional efforts to internationalize the curriculum should be promoted and decided to assist the Caribbean and Latin American specialists of the College of Arts and Sciences to win federal funding for their certificate program in Latin American and Caribbean studies. Accordingly, IAC worked closely with interested faculty members in preparing a successful grant proposal to the Office of Education establishing a title VI undergraduate Latin American–Caribbean studies program at the university. The number of curriculum offerings in the Caribbean and Latin American subjects grew. To attract more attention to the program, IAC assisted the Latin American–Caribbean Center (LACC) in funding an international conference on Latin American theater. IAC also assigned a half-time coordinator to LACC to assist with refunding and other program needs—a particularly critical area because LACC was otherwise dependent for its momentum on federal funding.

Finally, to enhance professional opportunities for the majority of LACC's associated faculty who are in social sciences, IAC has tried to ensure that its Joint Environmental Enhancement and Protection Program for the Caribbean Basin incorporated in each proposal a study of the social impact of the proposed activity.

FACULTY INVOLVEMENT AND LINKAGES

To augment faculty resources and promote faculty development, IAC has encouraged the university community to compete for Fulbright Program grants and to welcome Fulbright visiting scholars. The associate dean, whose work normally deals with faculty members, is the Fulbright faculty adviser. For the past several years the university has either had a faculty member receive an award or has been able to host a Fulbright Scholar. This program has benefited the university and has been supplemented by faculty exchange programs with the University of Guyana and the Universidad Simón Bolívar of Caracas.

Another area in which IAC has taken a continuing interest is the development of the noncredit English as a Second Language (ESL) program. The College of Arts and Sciences and the School of Education, with assistance and support from IAC, has developed a highly successful ESL program that attracts more than 200 students per quarter and generates a large sum of surplus cash. Although the ESL program is tightly integrated into the School of Education's Teaching English to Speakers of Other Languages (TESOL) master's degree program, the college controls ESL. The titular head of the program, the associate dean of the School of Education, has just been reassigned to the associate deanship of the IAC. This shift allows IAC to influence the program, marking a shift toward an earlier pattern according to which IAC would control noncredit intensive language instruction in the university.

IAC successfully lobbied for a foreign language requirement in the new four-year university undergraduate curriculum. IAC has given continuous moral and occasional financial support to Chinese and Japanese language instruction. Without that support, instruction in these languages would have been as sporadic as student interest and instruction in other rarely taught languages such as Arabic. To institutionalize the offerings of Chinese, IAC encouraged the School of Education to develop an informal exchange program with the Beijing Foreign Language Institute (BFLI). Under this agreement, the School of Education accepts BFLI instructors, as well as those from other Chinese institutions, as fellows in TESOL. The fellowships are funded by the ESL program in which the fellows do their apprenticeship. These fellows are then available to teach Chinese on a regular basis. The university also ties itself into a national network of Chinese governmental translators and interpreters, laying a modest but broad foundation for other activities in the future. Through cooperation with the Japan–American Society of South Florida, IAC has also been striving to standardize Japanese language instruction. And at the urging of IAC in late 1981, the School of Education's Multilingual Multicultural program undertook sponsorship of a Saturday Japanese school for those children whose parents wish them to have the experience of schooling in Japanese language and culture.

Another area in which IAC has helped tremendously is study abroad programing. Under pressure from the state Board of Regents to provide more study abroad opportunities for Floridians, IAC in 1980 developed a brief summer program at Cambridge University, England, and two study abroad courses in China. These programs complemented courses in Mayan civilization offered in Mexico and Guatemala by the Department of Sociology/Anthropology. Negotiations are under way with Universidad de San Pedro Sula to establish on a long-term basis a joint archeological field school in the Sula Valley. All such programing by state regulation must be enrollment-generated and thus is subject to fluctuation. IAC works with the Division of International Student Services and the respective academic units to attract sufficient numbers of students.

Establishing a residential study center abroad seems even more difficult than attracting sufficient enrollment for study abroad courses. For economic reasons, the State University System's (SUS) London and Florence Centers have declined over the past several years. The SUS has no year-round center in Latin America and, while the idea of an SUS residential study center in Latin America has merit, there is no evidence that student interest would be sufficient to support even a modest center. Indeed, the typical FIU student is twenty-eight, female, employed, and probably not likely to leave Miami for more than a few weeks at a time. Active solicitation and extensive advertising have attracted few, if any students from other SUS institutions into FIU study abroad courses. The depressed economy will tighten the market and put greater strains on university resources. Consequently, rather than invest heavily in a residential study center in Latin America, IAC decided to develop agreements with Latin American universities whereby those institutions would accept Florida students on the same basis as local residents. Thus in summer 1982, the university offered its students the opportunity to study Spanish language and culture at the Universidad Autonoma de Gudalajara in Mexico. For those students who prefer to study French, the university arranged access to Laval University's intensive summer French program.

Research is another area in which IAC has been active. IAC assists faculty from the various academic units with research projects that have an international dimension. Some of the projects may yield revenues that would support international programing.

Faculty involvement with IAC has been strongest in research and contract instruction abroad. From the beginning, IAC policy was to distribute the benefits of program participation as widely as possible in order to generate faculty support for itself and international education, research, and training. As noted above, an early attempt to gather faculty support by forming a faculty advisory council was unsuccessful. Professional opportunity, not prestige, was the key to gaining faculty support.

Strengths and Weakness

The strengths of the International Affairs Center have been: Florida's mandate to the university to promote international understanding among the nations of the world, especially the Americas; the consequent university commitment of state funds to the center; the lack of an academic program tying the center to any one set of academic activities; access from the President's Office to all units of the university; modest success in raising private sector funds; success in generating self-sustaining projects; success in developing CUIDES; administrative continuity in the person of the staff assistant; the dynamism of the current dean and the dedication of the core staff.

The weaknesses of the center, ironically, are its very strengths: the possibility of a cutback in state funding as the Florida economy falters; lack of the academic legitimacy that comes from offering one or more degree programs and consequent sniping from area studies faculty and administrators; dependence on the personal commitment of any given president to international education; the instability associated with short- and medium-term programing abroad and the possibility that CUIDES might swallow the center without returning anything substantial to the university; and finally, dependence on the dynamism of the center's core personnel for its momentum.

Strategies for the 1980s

Hard times lie ahead. The issue for the eighties and nineties will be survival; that is, first avoiding nuclear war and then avoiding economic and social disintegration. To be attractive and meaningful, international studies programs will have to incorporate courses on peacemaking and disarmament as well as global economic issues. Program directors will have to make strenuous efforts to see that their programs are tied to programs in business administration and teacher training. Foreign language program directors would do well to remember that in hard times many students will seek escape or respite in literature, including literature in translation, and they might want to tailor their offerings accordingly. Program directors might also remember that as times grow harder, more students will have to devote more time to earning a living and consequently program scheduling should be flexible enough to accommodate their needs.

Certain activities will shrivel away during the next decade. Teacher exchange programs and study abroad programs will probably become less numerous. International research will increasingly be conducted closer to home, if at all, unless it is tied to military or short-term commercial or industrial purposes. Domestic and international outreach programs may have to grouped together to achieve maximum cost-effectiveness. Insofar as the success of international education over the next dozen or more years is tied to exploitation of local opportunities, flexibility and ingenuity will be key characteristics of successful programs.

CHAPTER 8

The University of Nebraska at Omaha

Thomas E. Gouttierre

"To earn a living and live a cultured life not as two processes but as one. . . ." This phrase, the motto of the University of Nebraska at Omaha (UNO), can be found in university publications and on a bronze tablet in the main entrance of the original building on campus. It is not likely that the individuals who some decades ago inextricably united the phrase with the institution had any overriding international focus in mind. But, in light of current levels of commitment at UNO to internationalize education, the motto has taken on new meaning.

The University and the Community

The University of Nebraska at Omaha is situated on a seventy-three-acre campus in the geographical center of Omaha. Surrounded by parks and residential areas, it is located in one of Omaha's most attractive and coveted neighborhoods.

The University of Nebraska at Omaha shares a history common to many urban universities. It was founded in 1908 as the University of Omaha, as a private nonsectarian college. However, by the 1960s, the financial base of the University of Omaha was unable to keep pace with the needs of the community which it served. In 1968, after much negotiation and political maneuvering, the Nebraska legislature and the citizens of Omaha voted to

151

merge Omaha University with the University of Nebraska System—that is, the University of Nebraska at Lincoln (UNL) and the University of Nebraska Medical Center (UNMC), located in Omaha. Omaha University was renamed the University of Nebraska at Omaha (UNO).

Although it became part of the University of Nebraska System, UNO is linked as much as ever with Omaha and the surrounding metropolitan area; its mission is distinctly urban. The university provides a full range of instruction, research, cultural enrichment, and public service programs.

UNO serves more than 15,000 students through its day and evening classes. All students commute; there are no dormitories, nor are there likely to be any in the future. One of the conditions under which UNO became part of the University of Nebraska System was that the Omaha campus would not offer competition with the residential Lincoln campus.

The profile of a recent entering class offers an interesting analysis of the kind of student who attends UNO. More than 95 percent of the students were Nebraskans, 2.2 percent were Iowans (primarily from Council Bluffs, which is directly across the Missouri River from Omaha), and the remainder (2.2 percent) were from other states and foreign countries.

THE OMAHA METROPOLITAN COMMUNITY

Omaha, the most populous city in Nebraska, is located on the west bank of the Missouri River, directly across from Council Bluffs, Iowa. Preliminary 1980 census figures place the population of the metropolitan area at 570,399 and of the city of Omaha at 314,600. Significant numbers of Polish-Americans, Czech-Americans, Italian-Americans, German-Americans, and Irish-Americans live in the area. Nonwhites make up approximately 8 percent of the surrounding population and 11 percent of Omaha's population.

Today, Omaha is a major midwestern center of commerce and industry. It is the nation's second largest food-processing center and the fourth largest rail center. The Omaha livestock market is the nation's third largest in receipts. Thirty-seven insurance companies, including Mutual of Omaha, the world's largest in health and accident insurance coverage, have their home offices in Omaha. The headquarters of the nation's Strategic Air Command (SAC) are located south of the city at Offutt Air Force Base, where approximately 14,000 military and civilian personnel are stationed. In 1975, more than 570 manufacturing firms were operating in Omaha.

UNO'S ROLE IN NEBRASKA

The UNO has benefited greatly since it joined the University of Nebraska System. Development and expansion that would not have been possible without the merger have transformed the academic and physical conditions of the campus. However, opinion has not changed as dramatically and rapidly as has size. The people of Nebraska, and even many Omahans, still generally regard the University of Nebraska at Lincoln (UNL) as *the* University of Nebraska, and UNO as "Omaha U." These opinions are buttressed by the historical relationship of the Lincoln campus with Nebraska citizens, the association of the land-grant UNL campus with the state's agribusiness economic base, and a statewide preoccupation with the Lincoln football team.

UNO shares the same Board of Regents with the other campuses of the University of Nebraska System. The programs on all three campuses of the University of Nebraska System are initiated and implemented under authority and guidelines established by the Board of Regents and delegated through the office of the president of the system to the campus chancellors.

The relationship of UNO to Omaha and UNL to the state has been confirmed by the board's decision. Extension programs from the UNO campus for Nebraskans outside of the Omaha area must be administered through the UNL campus. Similarly, programs from UNL designed for Nebraskans within the Omaha area are administered through UNO's College of Continuing Studies.

UNO's survival and development were made possible by the merger. Accordingly, UNO has had to define its mission within the confines of its role in the University of Nebraska System.

Historical Development of International Studies and Programs at UNO: Phase I

In 1972, when UNO began to develop an international perspective, it lacked most of those resources commonly associated with international programs on university campuses. There were no area studies programs and only a handful of faculty and students with international experience or demonstrated interest. UNO did not possess programs in agriculture or extensive graduate-level programs to attract the notice of the sponsors of foreign assistance programs.

To a prospective foreign participant in 1972, UNO might have appeared to be an institutional reflection of H.L. Mencken's statement that "if English was good enough for Jesus Christ, then it's good enough for me." UNO had no dormitories, no intensive English classes, and no foreign student advisor. It is little wonder that of 13,000 students in the fall semester of 1972, only 24 were foreign.

What the university did possess were several faculty members eager for leadership and direction in internationalizing education, a new chancellor who was committed to internationalizing education at UNO, and a young faculty member with an idea.

The young faculty member was Christian L. Jung, a dynamic and engaging person. His father, Christian W. Jung, was a member of the International Education Department at Indiana University. From 1966 until 1970, the elder Jung served as project director of a US State Department contract at Kabul University (KU) in Afghanistan. For two of those years, the younger Jung joined his family in Afghanistan, pursuing research on his doctoral dissertation and teaching at the American International School of Kabul. Upon his return to the US, he joined the Department of Geography/Geology at UNO as an assistant professor. His idea? To link UNO to Afghanistan through the development of a studies and research program.

Jung was a member of a newly formed association of North American scholars interested in the study of Afghanistan. Since its inception in 1971, this group had been seeking a campus that would agree to serve as the institutional base for their Afghanistan Studies Association (ASA). Their motivation was to have a single location serve as a repository for the collection of materials essential to the study of Afghanistan and as a center for interaction of scholars of Afghanistan Studies. Many institutions were contacted, but none was interested in making a commitment.

The lack of interest displayed by other universities gave Jung an opportunity to pursue what had been in the back of his mind all along. He suggested to his other ASA colleagues that they approach UNO, and they agreed with the idea.

The collective decision of the ASA to approach UNO roughly coincided with the arrival of a new chancellor on that campus. An individual committed to internationalizing education, Ronald W. Roskens recognized early that UNO was lacking in that dimension. Soon after the chancellor's arrival, Jung conferred with him.

Eventually, Chancellor Roskens became convinced that, since no other institution was willing to affiliate itself to the ASA and Afghanistan, UNO had an opportunity to develop a unique international program. He also recognized that such a commitment would open up the possibility of grant and research opportunities UNO had never previously enjoyed. In the fall of 1972, the ASA announced that it had an institutional base at UNO.

Chancellor Roskens supported the development of an Afghanistan Studies and Research Program (ASRP) at UNO by allocating university resources to the project. At this stage no outside resources were used. Jung, who was released temporarily from one-half of his teaching duties, concentrated on two basic objectives: to lock the ASRP into active participation on the UNO campus and to pursue outside assistance and participation. Jung persuaded many colleagues at UNO to become involved in the ASRP in a variety of ways. Most importantly for the long term, he developed a close working relationship with the assistant dean of the College of Arts and Sciences, sharing ideas, dreams, and plans.

Jung and others in the ASA informed the administration and Afghan colleagues at Kabul University of the founding of the ASRP at UNO. He approached various US government agencies and private foundations, seeking updated information on various contracts and grants pertaining to Afghanistan. He focused on educational exchanges through Fulbright and other programs, on participant programs through the State Department's Agency for International Development (AID), and on a major AID-funded contract for the development of higher education at Kabul University. Chancellor Roskens assisted and encouraged Jung by providing funds for several trips to Washington for Jung and the assistant dean, and a trip to Afghanistan for Jung.

By the summer of 1973, UNO began to realize some results from Jung's tireless efforts and its own commitments. The Fulbright program in Afghanistan agreed to participate in and partially support an annual exchange of faculty and students between UNO and KU, one of each from each institution. A number of Afghan students arrived at UNO under AID sponsorship. UNO obtained its first internationally related contract, also funded by AID, to train Afghan government personnel in management. (This contract extended UNO campus involvement into the Department of Public Administration and the College of Business Administration). Jung prepared and submitted a proposal for the major AID contract for the development of KU and spent August in Kabul and Washington promoting UNO as the appropriate recipient. Unfortunately and tragically, as UNO began the fall semester of 1973, the young architect of the university's first venture into international affairs died suddenly and unexpectedly of a rare blood disease.

In a spirit of dedication to the memory of Chris Jung, UNO faculty and administrators strengthened their commitment and rededicated themselves to developing the university's linkage with Afghanistan. The assistant dean with whom Jung had shared his plans took over the administration of the ASRP. When AID announced new guidelines and requested resubmission of proposals on the KU contract, he prepared a new and even more competitive proposal. He also served as the head of a team assigned by Chancellor Roskens with the task of identifying a full-time director to succeed Jung.

In the spring of 1974, UNO announced that the executive director of the Fulbright Foundation in Afghanistan would assume the directorship of the ASRP in August of that year. Shortly thereafter, perhaps as an expression of support for UNO's reaffirmation of its commitment to the Afghanistan program, a number of new projects and grants were awarded to the university. One windfall was the major ($1.8 million) AID contract with KU. Another was the presentation to UNO of the major privately owned library on Afghanistan.

The Afghanistan Studies and Research Program is today the UNO Center for Afghanistan Studies (CAS)—the most comprehensive resource center on that country in the Western Hemisphere. It has the largest university library collection on Afghanistan. Before the Soviet invasion and occupation of Afghanistan in December 1979, the Center had received more than $2 million in grants and contracts. Nearly fifty of UNO's faculty and staff gained international experience in Afghanistan. Over 150 Afghan faculty and students had taught, studied, and conducted research on their own country while at UNO.

Since the Soviet occupation, the importance of the CAS as a research center has increased significantly. Because of the increased international attention focused on Afghanistan by its recent tragic history and because of the wealth of personnel and other resources at the center, UNO has gained much national and international recognition. Most importantly for UNO, the Center for Afghanistan Studies has provided the university with an enlightening window on the world.

Historical Development of International Studies and Programs at UNO: Phase II

After arriving at UNO in August of 1974, the new director of the center also assumed (at Chancellor Roskens's request) the additional position and responsibilities of interim dean of international studies and programs. Chancellor Roskens charged the interim dean and director with expanding UNO's international dimensions and with developing strong linkages with the Omaha community. While he was committed to maintaining the CAS as the primary component of UNO's international development, Chancellor Roskens indicated that additional components were essential to extending the process of internationalizing the university.

This new structure in the development of international studies at UNO was evidence that Chancellor Roskens wanted a centralized approach. All internationally related activities, except for advising nonsponsored foreign students, were to be centered in the Office of International Studies and Programs (IS&P).

Within two years of the creation of IS&P at UNO, Chancellor Roskens left the campus to become president of the combined campuses of the University of Nebraska. He continues his commitment to internationalizing education, initiating, stimulating, and encouraging programs that involve each of the campuses collectively or individually.

Delbert D. Weber succeeded Ronald Roskens at UNO in the fall of 1977. Within his first year as chancellor, UNO's Afghanistan program received a severe programmatic setback because of a pro-Soviet coup in Kabul. While the major, AID-funded contract ended on schedule in December 1977, this political crisis effectively stopped the development of new grants and contracts. This event notwithstanding, Chancellor Weber has proved to be as committed to internationalizing UNO as his predecessor was.

Shortly after his arrival, international programs were reorganized within the UNO administrative structure. IS&P and CAS were formally combined and the title of interim dean was eliminated. The director of IS&P had the choice of locating the combined unit within the Office of Academic Affairs or the College of Arts and Sciences. He chose the College of Arts and Sciences, because the program was becoming more academic (in particular, a new international studies major had been established), and because the center had always been a part of the college. In 1982, IS&P relocated within the Office of the Vice-Chancellor for Academic Affairs. The current administrative arrangement affords IS&P a broader departmental base and enhances its ability to serve faculty and students campuswide.

Both Chancellor Weber and the vice-chancellor have assumed what might be described as an institutional proprietary interest in IS&P. The support of all these individuals has been most crucial in preserving the integrity of the IS&P budget and IS&P's central role on the campus during periods when budget cutting has affected other units.

The Office of International Studies and Programs at UNO

ORGANIZATIONAL STRUCTURE

The IS&P director is the primary supervisor for all IS&P professional staff. In addition, he serves as the academic advisor for all UNO students majoring in international studies. He has, in the past, taught as many as eight hours per semester (currently, he is averaging three hours per semester). Much of the director's time is spent on program development and supervision, with special emphasis on budgetary matters.

The support staff are essentially divided into two units; one deals with the broad range of activities housed within IS&P, including the Center for Afghanistan Studies, and the other deals primarily with the intensive English language program. In the former are two research associates, a full-time secretary, a part-time study abroad advisor, and two work/study students. In the latter are two coordinators, a foreign student advisor, a number of intensive language instructors (varying from six to nine depending on enrollments), a full-time secretary, and a work/study student.

The two coordinators of the intensive English language program (ILUNO) report to the director. One manages all the academic aspects of the program; the other handles the admissions, budgetary, and operational details of the program. The instructors report to the academic coordinator and are employed on a .75 full-time equivalency or a .375 full-time equivalency, depending on the number of courses they teach per term.

Program Description

As indicated earlier, the Office of International Studies and Programs at UNO serves as a central location for the coordination and administration of the various international activities at UNO. The following paragraphs present details on each of the components.

PROGRAM COMPONENTS

1. *Center for Afghanistan Studies.* This unit maintains its unique role among American universities through an active program of research and outreach activities. Its members are consultants to US government agencies and other organizations, and are busy making presentations, nationally and internationally, because of the current interest in the tragic events in Afghanistan. The center continues as the institutional base of the ASA, and efforts continue to ensure the comprehensive development of the center's library collections.

2. *International Studies Major.* This interdisciplinary major is a degree program within the College of Arts and Sciences. The IS&P director serves as the administrator of the program and, as such, reports to the dean of the college. One of the director's first activities was to send a questionnaire to all faculty to determine the extent of faculty interest in international studies at UNO. The director asked some of the respondents to serve on an ad hoc International Studies Program Committee to advise him on the development of international studies at UNO. Among the first recommendations of this committee was to develop a concentration in international studies under the interdisciplinary degree provision of the College of Arts and Sciences. A program was developed and approved by all of the relevant campus academic units in the spring of 1975. Concurrently, a proposal, which sought funds to develop two introductory core courses for the new major, was developed and submitted to the then US Office of Education. These were the only new courses developed for the International Studies (IS) concentration, which essentially was a repackaging of more than fifty

courses of international import already available at UNO in geography, foreign languages, history, political science, economics, and sociology.

In June of 1975, UNO was notified that its proposal would be funded for two years. Because the courses were successful and interest developed in the international studies concentration, UNO sought and obtained approval in 1977 from the Board of Regents for an International Studies major within the College of Arts and Sciences. The course of study remains interdisciplinary. Students must meet the basic requirements of the college and satisfy a foreign language proficiency requirement. Students may major in general international studies, area studies specialization, or an international management and business specialty. Nearly 90 percent of all IS majors have chosen the management and business specialization.

3. *International Studies Faculty.* The International Studies major has no specific faculty of its own, except for the IS&P director. With the formal approval of the IS major, a structure was developed for establishing a cadre of international studies faculty drawn from the faculty members at UNO who teach courses with international content or who had otherwise demonstrated sustained interest in and commitment to international studies.

Faculty members who want to be designated IS faculty submit their credentials to the director who, in turn, distributes copies to members of the International Studies Program Committee (ISPC). The ISPC reviews the credentials and makes recommendations to the director; then the director reviews the credentials and recommendations and makes a recommendation to the dean of the appropriate college. The dean reviews the material and makes a recommendation to the vice-chancellor for academic affairs, who makes the final decision on appointment or nonappointment.

The ISPC has six members and is elected from and by the IS faculty. Its members serve staggered terms of three years each. The committee's official role extends only to matters relating specifically to the IS major and IS faculty designation. Participation in the International Studies major and IS core courses, which are team-taught, has given IS faculty members the chance to develop new areas of interest and specialization. These courses provide an introduction to the Third World for UNO's students and for many faculty members who have had to diversify their academic interests in preparing for their own participation in these courses.

4. *Classroom Instruction.* Although only the director enjoys faculty status among the staff of IS&P, ten courses in four different disciplines are offered owing to the qualifications of CAS research associates. These courses are the only ones that offer UNO's students classroom exposure to the Middle East. Course enrollments have been increasing steadily as interest in the Middle East has been expanding.

5. *Intensive Language Program.* UNO's Intensive Language Program (ILUNO) was established in the summer of 1977 to provide intensive English training to international students. When international programs at UNO began, the university had a very low international student enrollment, and one of the primary reasons was the lack of intensive English study opportunities.

The lack of dormitory housing was a major obstacle to establishing the intensive English program. Investors were contacted and persuaded to purchase a motel near the campus and to convert it to a private dormitory. This development, coupled with other arrangements, has provided the necessary living quarters for international students.

ILUNO schedules six eight-week sessions each year. During each session, courses are offered at six levels of proficiency. Students spend twenty-five hours per week in classroom, laboratory, and cross-cultural instruction. Since its beginning, ILUNO has attracted over 2,000 students from forty nations to the UNO campus. Enrollment per session averages nearly 100 students. Typically, 40 percent of ILUNO's graduates continue their education at UNO.

6. *Shizuoka University Linkage.* UNO has established a sister-university relationship with the university in Omaha's sister city, Shizuoka, Japan. The combined approach of cities and universities has made this linkage UNO's most rapidly developing international program. Lessons learned from the Kabul University experience have been incorporated into this program's development.

This linkage has emphasized the development of faculty and student exchanges. Each summer twenty students from Shizuoka University (SU) come to study English and American culture and history and to study and tour Nebraska. Up to five students from SU have come to UNO each year to study intensive English and/or take regular classes. Some are sponsored by the prestigious Mombusho (Ministry of Education) scholarship program; the others have received tuition scholarships through the ILUNO program.

The linkage with SU currently offers UNO its only yearlong annual student scholarship. Each year, through the Mombusho scholarship program, SU provides a comprehensive scholarship, covering all travel, academic, and maintenance costs for a student from UNO to study Japanese language, history, and culture. SU has recently announced additional scholarships that will cover tuition and fee remissions for UNO students to study intensive Japanese in Shizuoka. Exchanges involving faculty have been short-term to date. Four faculty from UNO have spent up to three months at SU and eight Shizuokans have visited UNO. Outside funding sources are being approached to permit more exchanges for longer periods.

7. *Midlands Consortium for Japanese Studies.* Perhaps the most

interesting aspect of the Omaha-Shizuoka/UNO-SU relationship is the development of a Midlands Consortium for Japanese Studies involving UNO and Creighton University in Omaha. This consortium has been established to capitalize academically on the considerable programmatic resources related to Japan that each possesses (Creighton has a sister Jesuit university, Sophia, in Tokyo). This combined approach is more likely to win grants than single institution efforts. The consortium's objective is to promote faculty exchanges involving all four universities to make possible the study of Japanese language and related courses on the Omaha campuses, and English and related courses at the Japanese universities. IS&P serves as the UNO administrative unit for this program.

8. *China Exchange Program.* This exchange program was initiated by President Roskens in his role as the head of the University of Nebraska System. Drawing upon his experience with the Afghanistan program at UNO, President Roskens has worked with appropriate personnel on all three campuses of the University of Nebraska to initiate linkages with eight universities in the People's Republic of China. The stated objective of this program is to enable the University of Nebraska to take advantage of the opportunities made possible by improved relations between the US and China.

IS&P serves as the UNO campus administrative link in this program. Procedures for facilitating the exchange of faculty have been developed along the lines of UNO faculty development leaves. Through the 1981/82 academic year, ten UNO faculty have been fully or partially supported in short-term programs in China. The first faculty member in an extended program arrived in Canton in December 1981. Several other similar programs for UNO faculty are projected for the coming academic year. More than thirty academicians from various institutions of higher learning in China have come to UNO for short-term programing. Five others have been at UNO for periods up to six weeks and have participated in various courses and workshops.

9. *Conferences.* IS faculty at UNO have developed several national conferences focusing on international themes. Two of these, the Third World Studies Conference and the European Studies Conference, are annual events that bring hundreds of participants to Omaha. The former, in particular, has focused much international and national attention on UNO. Both are financially self-supporting. A committee of IS faculty members administers the European Studies Conference, which was held for the seventh consecutive year in the fall of 1982. The Third World Studies Conference is conducted jointly by IS&P and the Department of Black Studies. It convened for the fifth time in the fall of 1982.

Each year students interested in international affairs at UNO conduct an Annual UNO Model United Nations General Assembly for area high school students. In 1980 UNO combined with colleagues from the

University of Alabama to sponsor in Omaha a joint conference on Americans Abroad Programing.

10. *Faculty Exchanges.* IS&P staff work with UNO faculty to explore ways through which they may gain international exchange experience. Since IS&P began in 1974, over seventy UNO faculty have participated in such exchanges. Most of these have been through contract programs like those linking UNO with Afghanistan. Others have gained international experience through one of the following ongoing approaches:

• *Fulbright Program.* The IS&P director serves as UNO's Fulbright advisor. Before 1974, there were no Fulbright grants awarded to either faculty or students from UNO. Since that time twelve faculty members have participated in Fulbright grants.

• *International Faculty Exchange Program.* Under this program and with university support, UNO faculty are able to spend one or two semesters abroad. Under arrangements that must be approved by each faculty member's department and college, faculty are permitted to retain full salary for one semester or half salary for a full academic year while on international exchange programs. Teaching loads are assumed by one's departmental colleagues. This is a new program and has been used only with the Shizuoka University and China Exchange programs to date.

11. *Professional Memberships.* IS&P maintains institutional membership in several professional associations and with a number of educational exchange organizations. Such memberships provide UNO access to a wide range of contacts and professional services. Included are the International Studies Association (ISA), Institute of International Education (IIE), American-Mideast Educational and Training Services (Amideast), International Program Consultants (IPC), National Association for Foreign Student Affairs (NAFSA), etc. IS&P is in regular contact with foreign educational missions, such as the Malaysian Students Department, the Saudi Arabian Educational Mission, and the Fundación Gran Mariscal de Ayacucho.

12. *International Student Advising.* IS&P is the point of initial contact for most of UNO's international students. All ILUNO and sponsored students are advised through IS&P auspices. Nonsponsored international students are advised within the Division of Educational and Student Services. A committee involving all those who have responsibility for advising international students permits the coordination of advising activities campuswide.

13. *Other International Linkages.* Other linkages have been initiated to connect UNO with countries indicated in previous paragraphs. To date, these linkages have not produced extensive involvement. Yet exchanges have been realized with Nepal (Sano Thimi Education Institute), Nigeria (Ministry of Manpower), Sudan (University of Khartoum), Bangladesh

(Dacca University), Pakistan (Peshawar University), and a number of other countries.

14. *Study Abroad Programs.* Probably the least developed area within UNO's international programs, study abroad is not expected to develop significantly because of the nature of the UNO student body. Yet there are some bright spots. The exchange with Shizuoka University holds promise for increasing opportunities for student exchanges. The UNO Ambassador Program, which is funded through a combination of university and private resources, permits one student annually the opportunity to participate in a summer program under the auspices of the Experiment in International Living (EIL). Also, a few UNO students participate in a between-semesters Flights and Study Tours Program in conjunction with the University of Nebraska–Lincoln campus.

CAMPUS LINKAGES

Primary campus linkages, apart from those related to organizational alignment, are derived from the contact and support that IS&P obtains and provides. Faculty linkages are maintained primarily through the various committees and programs involving IS faculty. Among these are committees established by the IS&P director to advise him on various programs like the Shizuoka University Exchange and the China Exchanges. Additionally, the chancellor appoints a University Committee on International Programs (UCIP) which advises him on developing international programs at UNO. Its members include faculty, staff, and students. The IS&P director serves ex officio.

Student linkages are maintained through advising foreign students and students majoring in International Studies. In addition, members of the IS faculty serve as the faculty advisors to the International Students Organization, the International Relations Organization, and Pi Gamma Mu, the social studies honorary society.

Most of the other important linkages are with units within UNO that serve the university community in general. As examples, the grants development and grants accounting offices are exceedingly crucial to the development and management of IS&P programs. Another unit actively involved with IS&P is university relations. The high local, national, and international profile of IS&P (due primarily to the Center for Afghanistan Studies, ILUNO, and the Third World Studies Conference) is nurtured and supported by the public relations resources this office provides.

IS&P's conference activities depend on close working relations with the College of Continuing Studies' Conference Center and the Department of Black Studies, a cosponsor of the Third World Studies Conference. Likewise, the need to coordinate international student advising activities campuswide necessitates open lines of communication between IS&P and the appropriate personnel in the Division of Educational and Student Services.

INTERCAMPUS LINKAGES

The three campuses of the University of Nebraska are located within fifty miles of one another: two are in Omaha—UNO and the University of Nebraska Medical Center (UNMC); and one—the University of Nebraska at Lincoln (UNL)—is located in the state capital, just an hour's interstate drive away. With such proximity, the need and opportunity for cooperation is a consideration in almost every educational endeavor.

Those involved in the international programs on the various campuses claim that cooperation has been most effective in their area. Several committees have been established by the president's office to coordinate international programing in general and specific universitywide approaches, like the China Exchanges Program. Such cooperation and coordination promote information sharing and the use of faculty from other campuses in grants and contracts managed by one of the three. Universitywide committees also deal with various area studies programs, for example, Latin American Studies, Western European Studies, and Eastern European Studies.

COMMUNITY LINKAGES (OUTREACH)

One of the director's primary responsibilities has been to develop and maintain close ties with various sectors of the Omaha community. Such linkages, both personal and institutional, have enhanced local international awareness and created a high profile for IS&P within the community. IS&P's outreach into the Omaha community has focused on several target areas—local public and parochial school systems, the business and professional community, and community organizations.

Contacts with the local school systems have been designed to offer the international dimensions of the university as resources both for area teachers and their students. IS&P staff and IS faculty have conducted workshops and seminars on global awareness at teacher convocations and in-service training programs.

Interaction with the local business and professional community is fostered primarily through IS&P staff participation in a number of local service and professional clubs and organizations. The director serves as a member of the Board of Directors of Rotary, as a member of the executive committee of the Omaha Committee on Foreign Relations (an affiliate of the Council on Foreign Relations), as chairman of the International Affairs Committee of Omaha; and he is past president of the Omaha Sister City Association. The last-mentioned affiliation has served to enhance greatly the sister-university relationship with Shizuoka University.

IS&P is introduced to the community at large through a variety of means. Members from the IS&P staff and the IS faculty are invited regularly to appear on local radio and television shows as foreign affairs resource personnel and are often interviewed by the press on the various international crises of the day. The public is invited to attend public events on current international issues sponsored by the IS&P on campus. A significant number of Omahans expand their international horizons through the various Host Family programs affiliated with IS&P activities. Other local residents regularly attend the annual International Student Banquet. The director maintains links with other segments of the Omaha community by requesting a number of prominent local citizens to serve on his IS&P Community Advisory Council. Recently, due in large measure to the tragedy in Afghanistan, the Center for Afghanistan Studies staff have been active in support of the substantial Afghan refugee community—over 300 refugees as of January 1983.

Funding

Since its inception, IS&P has maintained a varied pattern for funding. Only in the past several years has this pattern stabilized. In this case, stabilization is not necessarily a positive development, inasmuch as past fluctuations were the result of major grants or contracts. As an example, the contract that the Center for Afghanistan Studies held with AID for the project with Kabul University was the largest single contract ever obtained by UNO. After it ended in December 1977, the budget for IS&P (including CAS) changed in a major way. Because of these major fluctuations, a comparative study of the varying budget periods would not serve any real purpose.

In recent years, the combined budgets for IS&P have settled into a consistent pattern even though variations in amounts still occurred. The consistency has enabled IS&P to initiate long-term program planning. As with most international studies programs, IS&P is heavily dependent on "soft funds" or those not provided by the state budget. However, even in this period of nationwide cutbacks in educational programs, IS&P's state-appropriated funds represent the most constant source of revenue. The largest source of revenue is from participant fees (almost wholly from ILUNO tuition). Grants and contracts still constitute an important source of revenue even though they are not as significant as they were five or six years ago.

TABLE 8.1.   IS&P Revenue and Expenditures for 1981/82

REVENUE

Source	Amount	Percentage of Total Budget
State	77,263.00	21
Grants and contracts	52,428.00	15
Participant fees	230,000.00	63
Contributions	4,250.00	01
Total	363,941.00	100

EXPENDITURES

Salaries	214,391.00	
Fringe benefits	42,858.00	
Operational	28,632.00	
Program	48,060.00	
Other	30,000.00	
Total	363,941.00	

A breakdown of revenue and expenditures for the 1981/82 program year is presented below in table 8.1. Only the figure representing the amount of participant fees is likely to change. (Even that figure is based on statistics covering three-quarters of the program year and any variance would be minimal.)

The ILUNO program, after several years of development, has stabilized and is now developing a fund balance. That figure is represented under the heading "Other" in the expenditure section of the budget. The total fund balance projected for 1982/83 is $30,000. It is included under expenditures as an amount to be held in reserve against the uncertainties of enrollment in intensive language programs. Similar positive balances in subsequent budget periods above and beyond the amount held in reserve will be used in future program development.

The expenditure represented under the heading "Salaries" includes those for the director, two coordinators, one international student advisor, two secretaries, one student worker, two work/study students, and nine intensive language instructors. Of these, only two are state-funded positions—the director and one secretary. The two CAS research associates are funded out of the "Program" line.

Strengths and Weaknesses

The model provided by the development of international studies and programs at UNO has several unique, though not exclusive, features. One is the university's relationship with its urban-based constituency. Another is the lack of association for UNO with Nebraskans outside the Omaha area. But the feature most unique to UNO is the degree to which the development of international studies and programs was predicated on establishing linkage with Afghanistan. Subsequent program developments also followed the pattern of establishing linkages (such as the Shizuoka University program and the China Exchanges). It would be erroneous to assume that there would have been no development of international education at UNO without these linkages. Yet, given the void preceding the Afghanistan linkage, one can assume that UNO would not have matured internationally to the point that it has today without the Afghanistan connection. The UNO model is often cited as an example by US governmental agencies and by university associations to other institutions seeking to internationalize their campuses.

STRENGTHS

The primary strengths of the UNO model are the focus and foundation provided by the Afghanistan linkage, and the university administration's commitment to internationalizing education. The first of these engendered an institutional proprietary interest that overcame even the death of its initiator. Such a focus stimulated a number of people to band together for a common purpose rather than taking a scattered approach. Because other universities, agencies, or associations had little interest in Afghanistan at the time, there was little competition for the resources that were the program's building blocks. Obtaining some of these resources led to the establishment of an institutional base (the Center for Afghanistan Studies) upon which other internationally oriented initiatives were conceived and constructed.

UNO's other primary strength has been the commitment of administrative officers, particularly the two chancellors involved, to the concept of internationalizing education. Their commitment led to essential fiscal and administrative support at crucial junctures. The most significant aspect of administrative support was the decision to develop international studies and programs at UNO through a centralized approach.

Other factors also must be counted among the strengths of the UNO approach: the strong linkages shared by UNO and sectors of the Omaha community; the diverse revenue sources; and the decision to link international program development with international studies development.

WEAKNESSES

The weaknesses in the UNO approach became evident with the passage of time. Most could not have been anticipated because of the risk factor that had to be accepted in making the decision to internationalize. Others are inherent with international studies and programs everywhere.

The most salient weakness is the vulnerability that single-country programing ensures. The Russian occupation of Afghanistan effectively terminated all programmatic relationships UNO enjoyed with that country. Though UNO continues to be active regarding Afghanistan, there is no question that this abrupt termination disrupted the many plans and mutual projects initiated under this program. Fortunately, UNO had already substantially diversified its approach by the time the occupation occurred.

The other weaknesses are largely due to the unpleasant fiscal conditions many universities are experiencing at this time. State legislatures generally do not consider international studies and programs the most essential components of a university. Competition for diminishing resources converts even sympathetic faculty to neoparochialism. Also, the lack of a reward system within the promotion and tenure process at UNO that adequately recognizes the importance and the contributions of international service (committees, exchanges, travel, conferences) to the university has substantially hindered development.

One other significant weakness at UNO has been the failure to incorporate all international student advising within IS&P. This one deviation from a highly centralized approach unfortunately dissipates the resource that this function brings to a university. Steps have been taken to coordinate international student advising activities through committee work; however, redundancy and confusion have been the products of this disjointed approach.

Strategy for the 1980s

In constructing strategy for a period as extended as a decade, one is tempted to think in broad philosophical terms. However, a realistic appraisal of the conditions that international studies and programs are likely to encounter across the country would suggest a more mundane strategy—a strategy for survival. Such a strategy need not preclude development and even expansion. In fact, both would seem to enhance prospects for survival.

IS&P should pursue these essential activities in the 1980s:

1. Seek programmatic involvement to complement activities related to Afghanistan. While the center's involvement in this area is not likely to diminish in the near future, initiatives like that with Shizuoka University will ensure continued faculty and student involvement.

2. Seek ways to strengthen and improve ILUNO. As the major source of funding revenue for IS&P, attention focused on this unit would help it to play a central role in the future IS&P development.

3. Seek to expand opportunity for faculty exchanges under the Shizuoka and China programs. The structure already exists in both of these programs. Further refinement and creativity should produce desired results.

4. Seek to find funding to support faculty international development. Since the termination of the KU contract, this area has received little attention, owing to lack of resources. A potential store of such resources could be the developing fund balance from ILUNO.

5. Press for a faculty evaluation process that rewards rather than penalizes individuals for participating in overseas projects. This effort would have to involve the vice-chancellor for academic affairs, the Council of Academic Deans, and the college faculty advisory committees.

6. Expand efforts to link IS&P and local elementary and secondary school systems by conducting summer workshops on international themes.

7. Seek to link IS&P with the agribusiness corporations in Omaha. The 1980s will see increased worldwide food shortages. Nebraska's role in seeking to solve these problems will be substantial. IS&P has the resources of the Third World Studies Conference around which to develop such ties.

8. Pursue every possible approach to find new sources of funding. Efforts have already been initiated to obtain development assistance contracts and to seek support from local business corporations.

Much of what has been suggested already exists in some measure within the current activities of IS&P. Yet it is not unreasonable to hope that, by seeking to improve those resources already at hand, new opportunities will follow.

UNO has clearly demonstrated in the past decade that it believes international experience is a vital component in encouraging its students "to earn a living and live a cultured life." The challenge for UNO in the 1980s is to maintain and develop this commitment under increasingly complex circumstances.

PART II

Private Colleges and Universities

THIS SECTION OF THE BOOK is represented by institutions that, according to the Carnegie Commission's classification, fall into two categories—comprehensive and liberal arts. However, all six case studies differ from those in part 1 in that they are supported by non-state-appropriated funds. Chapters 9, 10, and 11 present three distinct models of an international program at a traditional liberal arts college. Chapter 12 describes an international program at a college which is part of a larger private university. The remaining chapters focus upon two recently developed international programs at comprehensive institutions.

As Humphrey Tonkin and Jane Edwards (1981) so accurately point out, generalizations about liberal arts colleges and their respective degree and level of commitment to international education are extremely difficult to make. Few studies similar to the surveys conducted by Gray (1977) and Harari (1981) of institutions belonging to the American Association of State Colleges and Universities or Shannon's (1978) study of two-year institutions have been made of the more than seven hundred liberal arts colleges. However, these institutions have several characteristics that help develop a total institutional commitment to internationalizing the campus.

First, by virtue of their small size, an impact can be made on curriculum much more easily than is possible at larger universities. Faculty members usually have much broader interests, frequently teaching courses that transcend normal departmental boundaries. In fact, at many institutions, departments containing only one discipline do not exist, and thereby a major impediment to the development of international/intercultural courses is removed.

171

Second, the residential campus found at most liberal arts colleges allows for intercultural programing to span not only the academic life but the residential life of a student as well. Creative living situations involving foreign and American students help create an international environment. From this pattern evolves a wide variety of programs that take place on the weekend as well as during the school week, that occur in the residence halls as well as the academic classrooms, and that are experimental as often as formal.

For several reasons, study abroad programs often flourish at these institutions. First, the parents of students attending private institutions have themselves often traveled abroad or are aware of the advantage of such an experience. Therefore, a student entering the institution is more likely to know about study abroad opportunities. Second, many private colleges and universities with religious affiliations often began their international efforts by sending students to work overseas in missionary ministries. This origin allowed for an easy transfer to other overseas study programs. A third factor that has contributed to the development of study abroad programs at private institutions is the cost differential between on-campus and overseas programs. For instance, at state universities, the cost of a semester's tuition, fees, and room and board is normally considerably less than the cost of these items in a semester abroad program. Travel and personal expenses add further costs, ruling out the experience for many. While this differential holds true for some private colleges and universities, still a much higher percentage of students attending these institutions can avail themselves of this opportunity. For many students a semester abroad study program actually costs less than attending the home campus. Higher tuition, a greater percentage of students living away from home, and an increased international awareness on the part of students all contribute to the study abroad success. A fourth characteristic of private colleges and universities that aids in developing an international commitment is a simplified bureaucratic structure. At small colleges there are normally fewer administrative approval levels for new programs, course revisions, and so on. Perhaps the biggest advantages are that international centers are able to define their own mission and are able to appropriate the necessary funds. State institutions are more severely constrained by bureaucracy on the campus—and, more importantly, off the campus. Boards of governors or regents, consolidated university systems, and legislative approvals all hinder innovation, new program thrusts, and activities, which may be viewed as little more than frills. More than one international effort has been delayed or stalled as a result of these barriers.

Finally, the faculty reward system at most liberal arts colleges helps strengthen the international dimension on campus. Excellence in teaching is valued over significant research efforts, leading to a concern for curriculum and, in particular, a curriculum that will prepare students for the world in which they will live. From this emphasis on teaching and curriculum develops a receptivity to teaching global studies, internationalizing courses, and stimulating students to think about the world, mankind, and their relationship to both.

Many private colleges and universities have developed international programs that permeate the entire campus. The six case studies presented in this section exhibit not only the diversity of programing efforts but the impact such efforts can have on the institution.

Warren Wilson College, located in the mountains of North Carolina, received its first impulse from abroad with the arrival of international students from Cuba in the 1920s. Following World War II, another wave of foreign students arrived on campus. This influx initiated a longstanding commitment to provide educational opportunities to students from foreign countries. An institutional goal of 20 percent international enrollment was established for the institution in order to bring the world to the students of Appalachia. There is no formal or informal aspect of the life of the college which is not touched by a complete and total commitment to providing international educational experience for all. With strong support of the Board of Trustees and the president, Warren Wilson's international effort is operated through the Department of Languages and Intercultural Studies and the International Student Services Office.

Across the country, with an enrollment twice that of Warren Wilson, *Linfield College* has a history of religious affiliation in its early years. However, Linfield's international program is representative of many similar institutions that initiated international efforts in the 1970s. By focusing initially on study abroad, the college set out to design programs that would allow every student to receive an international experience, regardless of financial resources. In 1979, 130 years after the founding of Linfield, an Office of International Programs was established to give direction and guidance to study abroad programs, and to insure that such efforts were integrated with the academic course work. Programing efforts now include international students, faculty exchange, and curriculum development. Linfield's experience represents a model of evolution that can be adapted to a variety of institutional frameworks.

Earlham College, long a recipient of international students from around the world, has had a commitment to foreign study since 1956. The program was initiated by Quaker instructors taking students to France for study. Other faculty soon began programs in German- and Spanish-speaking countries. Strong support for language instruction served as the backbone of these efforts. Students can now study in several non-Western countries including those in East Asia, Latin America, and Africa. The institutional commitment to this effort is demonstrated by the fact that 7.5 percent of current students study off campus each year, and over two-thirds of all graduates participate in at least one off-campus learning experience. Through the foreign study programs a curricular emphasis on Peace and Global Studies and East Asian Studies has evolved. Earlham's program illustrates what can be done with cooperation, resourcefulness, ingenuity, and commitment.

The international focus at *Utica College*, one of Syracuse University's twenty colleges, represents a model that can be used by several types of institutions. The college had an undergraduate international studies major in the early 1970s, then decided to create a concentration in international business. Using a grant from title VI of the Department of Education, an academic curriculum was established with the cooperation of the business, foreign languages, and liberal arts departments. This effort has increased demands for language programs and it has increased enrollment and interest in international courses.

Situated in Atlanta, Georgia, *Emory University* offers the Emory Program in International Studies (EPIS), instituted in 1979 with grants from the Department of Education. With a major institutional commitment of over $250,000, Emory established a structure to coordinate the many and varied international activities sponsored both on and off campus. EPIS sponsors lectures and programs, funds release time for faculty, supports course development, encourages the development of programs featuring summer study abroad, and sponsors international activities in the community. The international program does not confer degrees but has a substantial effect on the undergraduate education of Emory students.

The final model described in this section is the Foreign Area Studies Program (FASP) of *Pacific Lutheran University*. FASP is a multifocused, multidisciplinary curricular program in international and cross-cultural studies appropriate to a small liberal arts university. This easily replicated program comprises three interrelated segments: (1) Global Perspectives; (2) Regional and Topical Clusters; and (3) Senior Seminar/Semester Abroad. Through the internationalizing of courses and the inclusion of international modules and courses in PLU's various departments, FASP has affected the entire university. The universitywide Advisory Council for International Education and the Office of International Education give leadership and coordination to the entire effort.

Warren Wilson College, Linfield College, Earlham College, Utica College, Emory University, and Pacific Lutheran University are but samplings of successful international efforts at US private colleges and universities. They are by no means the only effective programs, but they do combine necessary ingredients for long-term impact and success. In all cases the institution has made a commitment to support international activities, and this endorsement is reflected in both written policies and administrative decision making.

CHAPTER 9

Warren Wilson College

JEANA DUNN MCKINNEY

"This is . . . a time when extreme parochialism affects many American students in terms of their attitude toward world affairs and their knowledge of the lives and problems of people in other countries. . . . If we want students to understand the reality of the world problems, they will have to understand the reality of the situations in which other students and citizens around the world now find themselves."[1]

Harold Taylor

This concern for international understanding at Warren Wilson College has been the basis of its continuing curriculum and program development in international education for the last fifty years.

The College

Warren Wilson College is a small liberal arts institution in the mountains of western North Carolina. It was supported until recently by the US Board of National Missions of the United Presbyterian Church. Warren Wilson's priorities include a special commitment to low-income students from the Appalachian region; an international community, 12 percent of whose members are from Asia, Africa, South America, the Middle East, and Western Europe; its Work Program, in which all 500 students, regardless of financial need, participate fifteen hours per week to maintain the college; quality liberal arts education that seeks to utilize natural and human resources to their fullest; and a commitment to racial integration, undertaken somewhat earlier than at most southern institutions of higher education.

Because the college started as a farm school for mountain boys in the late 1800s, Work Program involvement has traditionally included landscaping, farming, plumbing, carpentry, food preparation, secretarial services, laboratory and library assistance, maintenance, and cleaning—all the necessary daily tasks. During the last several years work assignments geared more toward human services have been developed as well, such as day care, peer counseling, tutoring, and language instruction. The college has also made a concerted effort to merge the Work Program with the Academic Program so that students receive academic knowledge of a subject as well as on-the-job training.

All students perform some distinct service for others as a graduation requirement. Service projects have included work with the handicapped, serving as a Big Brother or a Big Sister for children at the community center, assisting newly arrived refugees, weatherizing the homes of the elderly or the indigent in nearby Asheville, and teaching native languages not offered by the professional teaching staff.

Striving for equality is another goal of Warren Wilson College. All employees are referred to as staff members with distinctions made only between teaching staff and nonteaching staff. The teaching staff is completely unranked, and continued employment is based primarily on excellence in teaching, which is evaluated regularly. Staff members' salaries are based on amount of experience and vocational or educational background. The student body is represented on every college committee including the Tenure Review Committee.

Every formal and informal aspect of the life of the college has been touched by the college's commitment to providing international education experiences for all. The most distinctive features of the college's international education program are (1) the foreign student program, (2) the international curriculum; and (3) the openness and willingness of the college community and its friends, supporters, and governing bodies to making Warren Wilson truly international in nature. What follows depicts how the members of this small liberal arts community have come to interpret and incorporate internationalism into their everyday living.

How the International Program Was Established

As early as the 1920s, Cuban students were enrolling at Warren Wilson College. These students were primarily from Presbyterian schools established in Cuba by the United Presbyterian Church. What these students encountered was an environment that was predominantly rural, white, and Appalachian.

The onset of World War II forced another wave of foreign students to seek enrollment and refuge at Warren Wilson College. Hans Forell, a young "Christian Jew" fleeing Hitler's Germany, arrived on 10 July 1929, and said he wanted to be a farmer. These facts are recorded: He was assigned to the school's farm. He broke a leg in a tractor accident and couldn't work for some months. He stayed for one year, but found regulated boarding school life in the US something of a shock. After all, in those days strict institutional rules forbade alcoholic beverages, tobacco, dancing, card playing, and so on. Thus Han Forell presents an early case of culture shock. But he also opened a door. If your college could accept one European, it could accept more.[2] Shortly thereafter, the college rescued two young Japanese-American women who had been destined for detention camps in the West.

The conclusion of the war, when many European academic systems were in disarray, saw a large influx of foreign students. Under the auspices of the American Field Service, they came from Finland, Greece, Holland, Belgium, Czechoslovakia, and Germany. Through the established Cuban connections, students from South America began arriving.

The arrival of foreign students seemed to have invoked mixed feelings. In his history of the college, Dean Henry Jensen wrote:

> The Appalachian students were genuinely curious about cultures beyond their experience. Here it was in their midst. Some faculty welcomed them warmly; many of them were superior scholars because they had been carefully selected. Others, especially the work supervisors, often found them a burden because of the language handicaps and lack of manual skills, or simply the native European conceit that a student should only be expected to study, not slop the hogs and stoke the furnace or bake the bread. So, many a faculty meeting heard the argument, "We have too many foreign students." Yet, the dean persisted in pushing for a sizeable overseas contingent, sufficient in size so that it would actually count in the social life of the community. "Foreign students" at most colleges and universities are but a token presence. However, the integration process was accommodated most easily amongst the students themselves. The fact that all the students worked part of a day, placed the American and overseas students in close working contact in situations where job performance and often personal safety depended upon adequate communication and cooperation.

> Of course, headquarters for the Board of National Missions in New York was also aware of what was happening. Not only were students coming from all over the world but from increasingly distant places in the U.S.A. Warren Wilson was beginning to be known north of the Mason–Dixon line. Eventually a ruling was made that 50 percent of the enrollment must be from the South (and it was a generous territory), no more than 25 percent from overseas, and no more than 25 percent from outside the South in the U.S.A. However, the staff at

W.W.C. determined after some experience that about 20 percent from overseas is about right, and not too many from any given country.[3]

Other perceived difficulties were financial in nature. When the college was a school, all foreign students received free tuition in addition to room and board through participation in the Work Program. Once the college was no longer a mission school, the policy of free tuition simply had to be discontinued.

In spite of the problems, the general consensus seemed to be that because most American students at the college could not afford to travel abroad, the presence of foreign students "brought the world to the American student." Again, it is useful to quote Dean Jensen:

> In retrospect, an institution cannot assemble people from such diverse cultures without also reaping some very considerable benefits to the whole college community and the surrounding area where the overseas students frequently make their impact felt as they speak to civic and church groups, exhibit their dances and ceremonies, or act as a leaven to world-wide understanding between people by their very presence. They even provide themselves as spouses for some of the faculty or fellow students from time to time.[4]

Under the direction of Dean Jensen, the college committed itself to the active seeking of foreign students through the American Field Service, the YMCA, American embassies and AID personnel, alumni, and church ties. Such representatives abroad disseminated admissions materials, recommended students, notified students of their admission, and in many cases actually admitted them. Often the representative provided predeparture orientation for the student.

At one point, foreign student enrollment was as high as 32 percent of the total student body, owing to Dean Jensen's efforts. Most staff members—past and present—feel that a 20 percent foreign student population is necessary to carry out the college's international education objectives. Over the years, nevertheless, the enrollment ration of foreign students as well as their actual enrollment decreased because of a variety of factors: a decrease in financial aid, a rapid increase in American students, the change from a two-year to a four-year institution, and the shift to being a more selective college. By 1978, foreign student enrollment had reached an all-time low of slightly less than 10 percent even though the retention rate of foreign students and the total enrollment were at an all-time high. As a result, the college examined the foreign student program and decided to make a comeback by once again actively soliciting foreign students.

Institutional Commitment to International Education

Paralleling the development of the foreign student program was the development of an international curriculum. When the college became a four-year institution in 1965, it added an intercultural requirement to the liberal arts program with the assistance of specialized faculty members from Duke University. Making the curriculum more international continues to be a major thrust.

The foreign student program and the "internationalized" curriculum receive the support of the Board of Trustees, the president and the other administrators, staff members and students, and regular contributors. Until 1979, however, the college operated without a written statement of commitment on international education.

The impetus to articulate a statement on international education grew out of the recognition that former methods for obtaining foreign students were no longer productive, and as a consequence, foreign student enrollment was declining. A written statement was drafted and received unanimous endorsement from the Board of Trustees, the College assembly, the Student Caucus, the administration, and the staff. Furthermore, at the same time, the Board of Trustees and the administrators decided not only to support the foreign student program at its present level, but also to expand the position of the International Student Advisor and create another half-time position to devise a foreign student recruiting plan. Warren Wilson formulated this policy statement:

> It is essential in today's increasingly interdependent world that education in the United States have a strong international dimension. In addition, it becomes increasingly apparent that citizens of all nations need to understand their citizenship in not only local and national contexts, but in terms of global concerns. Indeed, people whose perceptives transcend the borders of their own country and who demonstrate the ability to form good relationships across barriers of class, culture, nationality, race, age, etc., are more likely to recognize and respect the needs and rights of other nations; to realize how their own destiny is ultimately entwined with the fate of all peoples; and to function better in the 21st century.
>
> In this context, Warren Wilson College's responsibility to its students is addressed by providing educational opportunities which recognize the plurality of cultures, the existence of common concerns, and the need for more effective methods of international and intercultural communication and cooperation. The college, therefore, is committed to providing the student body significant educational opportunities with an international/intercultural perspective. The college further encourages international education programs not only on campus, but also in U.S. subcultures and foreign countries.

Program Description

The international education program at Warren Wilson College centers on two primary structures: (1) the Department of Languages and Intercultural Studies and (2) the International Student Services Office. How they are

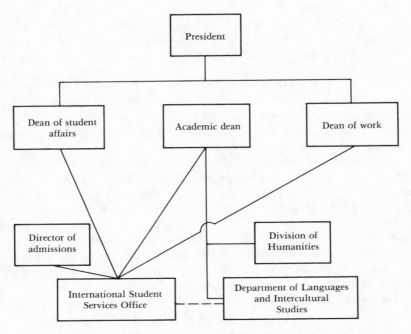

FIGURE 10.1.   Placement of the International Student Services Office and the Department of Languages and Intercultural Studies.

placed in the administrative organization of the college is shown in figure 10.1.

THE DEPARTMENT OF LANGUAGES AND INTERCULTURAL STUDIES

This department oversees the major and minor programs in intercultural studies and the intercultural awareness liberal arts graduation requirement. The department consists of three full-time staff members, one of whom is the chairman, and six adjunct staff members, all of whom have either administrative positions or teaching responsibilities in other departments. Its staff members have been trained in numerous academic disciplines—including foreign languages, literature, history, political science, sociology, anthropology, economics, education, geography, and the fine arts—and they have all had experience either living abroad or traveling extensively. This diversity accounts for the breadth of courses offered by the department and enables the department to have connections throughout the college.

Although the department offers a major, its main functions also include supporting the intercultural and international offerings and activities of other departments; providing students and staff members information and opportunities for travel or study abroad; assisting other departments with intercultural programing or cosponsoring it with them; providing an intercultural resource center for the community; and coordinating the foreign language program. Long-range department planning sessions always consider the interests and professional needs of each department member; consequently, ideas for new programs, course offerings, and activities are constantly being generated and carried out. Also, the department reflects the college's desire to cater to student academic needs by providing many independent study opportunities.

The major or minor in Intercultural Studies. The department recognizes that an undergraduate major or minor concentration in Intercultural Studies is best combined with a major in another field. Counseling a student considering the Intercultural Studies major involves exploring the student's other interests and helping the student establish an integrated course of study. The student discovers, for example, that an Intercultural Studies major supports careers in social work, the ministry, and related fields; that it also supports careers related to transportation services, communications, business and trade, and environmental management; and that it can lead to employment with the government, volunteer agencies, foundations, and associations.

To major in Intercultural Studies, the student must make written application to the chairman of the department by the junior year. The application procedure insures an integrated program because the student must set forth the proposed area of specialization, second major or minor, career aspirations, explanation of how the proposed course of study and experiences will form a cohesive program, and travel and other supplemental experiences.

Most proposed programs for the major are tailor-made to meet the student's interests and needs. Every student, however, must take at least four foundation courses from the following list:

Introduction to Geography

Intercultural Communications

Cultural Anthropology or Education and Anthropology

Global Issues

Economic Development or International Trade or Comparative Economic Systems

International Relations

Selected Topic in International Studies

The student must also include at least twenty-four hours in the concentration. Most students choose an area studies concentration (for example, Hispanic studies, Asian studies, Latin American studies, Chinese studies, Japanese studies, or Indian studies). A few students, however, elect to follow an interdisciplinary approach (for example, international education, international business and trade, US minority groups, international art management).

The Intercultural Studies major is popular with both American and foreign studies. Majoring in Intercultural Studies presupposes that the student has reached a certain level of maturity and responsibility and that the staff is engaging in quality academic advising. All majors are encouraged to involve themselves in the intercultural activities of the college and the community. Although traveling or studying abroad is not a well developed aspect of the college's program, most majors use their own funds to incorporate independent study abroad into their programs.

The Intercultural Awareness liberal arts requirement. Every student is required to satisfy the liberal arts graduation requirement by taking four hours from each of ten core categories, one of which is Intercultural Awareness. At Warren Wilson College, the view is that intercultural awareness is not acquired simply through the accumulation of facts; rather, it is an ongoing process or "way of knowing," with universal principles applicable to the student's future role as mediator and conciliator in a troubled world. Although many Intercultural Awareness courses concentrate on one area of the world, at the end of each course the student is asked to list or give examples of the processes for intercultural awareness learned in the course. A student could graduate without ever having spoken to a foreign student, but that same student could not graduate without having been at least touched by the Intercultural Awareness academic program.

THE FOREIGN STUDENT PROGRAM

During his career at the college, Dean Jensen had personally overseen everything pertaining to foreign students, from preadmissions correspondence to cross-cultural counseling and immigration matters. However, between 1973, the year of his retirement, and 1975, when the college's first foreign student adviser was hired, the needs of foreign students were met in a variety of decentralized ways. The academic dean's executive secretary, because she had served under Dean Jensen, handled immigration and embassy matters; English as a Second Language (ESL) instruction was provided by whoever had the skills or the inclination (double standards regarding English proficiency were tolerated then); and evaluating of credentials and issuing the appropriate government documents were handled by the Admissions Office.

The appointment of the college's first foreign student adviser in 1975 was in part prompted by the receipt of federal funds for strengthening developing institutions. Also, some college officials recognized that a decentralized foreign student program was a rather weak approach to utilizing fully this significant population. Others pointed out that the legal factors involved in international education exchanges were becoming increasingly more complicated and complex and that specialization was required.

The first foreign student adviser, hired as less than a one-third full-time position, felt that her role was to make foreign students feel comfortable and to serve as a party planner. There was no written job description. The foreign student adviser's office was her on-campus home; yet in spite of budgetary privations, that year the students and their adviser organized from international shows sufficient money for a trip to Washington, DC.

Upon the resignation of the first adviser, the second foreign student adviser was hired in 1976 for the same amount of time and salary but was given an office on campus, a small activities budget, and a half-time student worker at the end of the first semester. (At the same time an instructor trained in English as a Second Language was hired half-time.) The second foreign student adviser had the task of developing a job description, which led over a period of five years to the establishment of the International Student Services Office, staffed by a director whose current primary responsibilities are to advise foreign students, arrange foreign student programing, and supervise three student workers. Now, the International Student Services Office has connections with virtually every other college office, division, and department (see figure 10.2).

In addition to foreign student advising, the International Student Services Office has sponsored the following progams:

1. Workshops on topics such as cross-cultural perspective on changing sex roles, social work and welfare practices in South Africa, and women and professionalism.

2. "The Origin of Values: Six Cross-cultural Case Studies," a lecture given by four foreigners and two Americans who had grown up in other countries. The series was designed to introduce comparative methodology to teachers.

3. Speaker's Bureau, through which members of the community or faculty members who wish to introduce the comparative approach to their students or constituency may request foreign students to be guest lecturers.

4. Global Awareness Week, a project that combined International Student Week and Earth Day to produce a week-long program on global environmental problems.

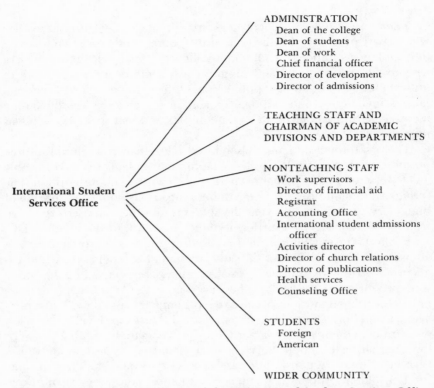

ADMINISTRATION
Dean of the college
Dean of students
Dean of work
Chief financial officer
Director of development
Director of admissions

TEACHING STAFF AND
CHAIRMAN OF ACADEMIC
DIVISIONS AND DEPARTMENTS

NONTEACHING STAFF
Work supervisors
Director of financial aid
Registrar
Accounting Office
International student admissions
    officer
Activities director
Director of church relations
Director of publications
Health services
Counseling Office

International Student
Services Office

STUDENTS
Foreign
American

WIDER COMMUNITY

FIGURE 10.2.   Formal linkages of the International Student Services Office.

5. The Great Decision Program, a one-credit course based on the eight issues discussed annually in a booklet published by the Foreign Policy Association. The format for the presentation of each issue combines the expertise of a foreign student, an American student, a faculty member, and a member of the wider community.

6. "Alternative Futures for the 21st Century," a lecture series.

7. Service projects for foreign students.

Funding for these activities and other program comes primarily from grants. A budget for funding social functions is administered by the International Student Services Office. On occasion, there is some cost sharing with the College Activities Office budget.

Most activities carried out by the International Student Services Office are open to the entire college community. One program that is exclusively for foreign students is a college-supported summer program. For newly arrived foreign students, the eight-week credit course serves to (1) meet the language need of students, (2) orient students to the college as well as to the services and features of the wider community, (3) use cross-cultural communication and understanding as a mechanism for examining the individual's adaptation to a new environment. The course is both academic and experimental, and it includes conferences with each new student.

Foreign students who came to Warren Wilson College from American high schools or American schools abroad are not exempt from enrolling in this course. Indeed, with very few exceptions enrollment at Warren Wilson College requires participation in the summer course. By the beginning of the fall semester, most newly arrived foreign students are acclimated to the rigors of the college's academic and work program and to the local environment and culture. Course evaluations and subsequent conversations with students indicate that the course is probably a significant retention factor.

The foreign student program at Warren Wilson College entails three other areas that deserve mention: the admissions process, foreign student financing, and foreign student recruiting.

Foreign students and the admissions process. During the last six years Warren Wilson College has standardized the admission process for foreign students. The student must submit the application form accompanied by the application fee, financial information, and Test of English as a Foreign Language (TOEFL) score.

The application process and the acceptable standards are probably similar to those of other institutions, with perhaps two major differences. First, instead of writing an essay the foreign applicant is asked to respond to five specific questions:

1. Why have you decided to attend Warren Wilson College?

2. What do you expect to gain from pursuing studies in the United States or at Warren Wilson College?

3. What do you feel you are able to contribute to Warren Wilson College?

4. What are your goals upon finishing the four-year college program at Warren Wilson College?

5. What significant extracurricular activities have you participated in in high school, your community, or church? Identify any work experience you may have had, honors you have earned, and leisure activities.

The response to these questions indicate whether or not the prospective student and the college are well matched.

Second, when a foreign applicant is offered admission based on academic and language proficiency, the International Student Services

Office is notified, and the person receives a series of communications from the college. (All applications that pass the scrutiny of the foreign student admissions officer are placed before the Admissions Committee. The committee determines only if the applicant is academically admissible; financial admissibility and financial aid qualification fall under the jurisdiction of the director of financial aid.) The student may of course choose not to attend Warren Wilson College, but the view is that the more information the person has about the college before enrolling, the greater the chances are of retaining the student once he or she actually arrives.

The student is first sent a congratulatory picture postcard. Then a series of three single-page fact sheets about various significant aspects of the college (such as the work program, the liberal arts philosophy and requirements social life and extracurricular activities) are sent to the student on a staggered schedule so that the student receives information from the college regularly. The student then receives a two-page letter from the foreign student adviser, advising the student about matters such as what clothing and supplies to bring, and further details of life at the college. The final piece of mail a student receives from the college is an aerogram from a currently enrolled foreign student (not necessarily a fellow countryman). Students asked to send these personal letters are given addressed, prestamped aerograms and a few guidelines on what topics should be included in their letters. Newly arrived foreign students report that of the six pieces of correspondence they receive from the International Student Services Office before they arrive, the letter from a student is the most important.

Data collection on the admissions process is another important feature. At the conclusion of the summer course, newly arrived foreign students are asked to evaluate the admissions process. Three years of research reveal that such data collection helps to fine-tune the foreign student program and improve the admissions process. The college has learned, for example, that students continue to be perplexed by financial forms and financial aid contracts. The college has also learned that students from Asia and Africa feel that Warren Wilson College could achieve its commitment to a cultural mix more fully if at the admissions stage it became attentive to differences among tribes, castes, and other ethnic backgrounds within countries. "Too many Brahmans or too many Kikuyus don't create a healthy cultural mix," reflected a perceptive student. "Ethnic Origin (Optional)" therefore seemed an appropriate item to add to the evaluation sheet.

Financial aid for foreign students. As a private college, Warren Wilson has set aside scholarship funds for foreign students who have demonstrated need. Most of these funds accrue as the result of individual benefactors or interest on endowment.

Tuition is presently $3,600 and additional fees come to $350. Under the half-tuition plan, the foreign student receives $1,575 in aid ($975 for fifteen weeks of vacation work at $65 per week and $600 as a Warren Wilson grant). Most international students take advantage of the opportunity to earn half their tuition. The Vacation Work Program is legal according to US immigration regulations, and the college provides a home during vacation periods. Whether the half-tuition plan will remain a reality in light of rising tuition costs is unclear at this time; nevertheless, the college will continue to give significant assistance to foreign students and meanwhile to search for new sources of aid.

Sources of funding from home countries through government channels and private sources are researched by the foreign student adviser. The case of each student needing aid is investigated in an attempt to reduce the costs as much as possible. Because no US government aid is available to foreign students, most of whom are not sponsored by their own governments, additional scholarship funds have been sought from private organizations, private persons, and churches.

Presently, there are several competitive scholarships for which foreign students may apply. They range from half-tuition scholarships to a scholarship for $60.00 per semester for textbooks and supplies. What is unique about these scholarships is that for the first time foreign students may have the experience and take the responsibility of making application. Often a one-to-one relationship between donor and student ensues. As one recipient remarked: "I was pleased to have been selected to receive the scholarship, but over the years the relationship with the donor is what is really important." Of course, if need is a qualification, the foreign student adviser makes the necessary verifications. No doubt these scholarships instill competition among foreign students, but they also serve to reward excellence and ultimately to improve the quality of the foreign student program. Moreover, friends and donors have had the opportunity to learn not only *what* but also *whom* they are assisting.

Financial aid through grants, competitive scholarships, and the Work Program is believed to be a positive retention factor, The search for even more forms of aid will continue as the college strengthens its foreign student program.

Recruiting Foreign Students.   Warren Wilson College has engaged in recruiting foreign students with varying degrees of ardor and success. Present efforts at recruiting are intense due to the college's renewed commitment to the foreign student program. Evidence of the commitment is the creation in 1980 of a half-time position under the director of admissions, charged with devising and executing a foreign student recruiting plan.

Interestingly, there is no job title associated with this responsibility. Because the person is, in fact, the foreign student adviser and because foreign student recruiting is seen as a way to improve the quality of the foreign student program and improve Warren Wilson College as a whole, the title "director of international student services" seems to weld together all jobs for this one individual.

Advising foreign students and devising the plan for recruiting them may appear to be conflicting job assignments. The college is aware of this situation and expects quality and ethical recruiting. Since the college is not desperate to "fill the beds" and is driven only by its fifty-year involvement with international exchange, it can afford to strive for a quality program and recruiting plan.

A variety of recruiting approaches are simultaneously being tried, and data are being collected to determine the effectiveness of each activity. The fact that Warren Wilson College is actively engaged in comprehensive foreign student recruiting is receiving the attention of respected international organizations, associations, and service boards. How successful the recruiting program will be remains to be seen, but if the first year is any indication, the college may once again expect to achieve a foreign population of 20 percent of total enrollment.

ADDITIONAL CHARACTERISTICS

The International Student Services Office and the Department of Languages and Intercultural Studies also engage in cooperative programing. Sample projects during the last five years include:

1. The Self-Instructed Language Program, in which carefully selected foreign students teach their native languages; at the end of each semester their students are examined by an outside evaluator. Courses in Arabic, Swahili, Hindi, Japanese calligraphy, and Chinese are among the language courses the college is able to offer in addition to French, Spanish, German, and Latin in the regular language program.

2. International Week, a time set aside to examine a major issue from a global perspective.

3. Traveling Troupe, a group of foreign students who conduct an itinerary around the Southeast or Northeast in order to share their cultures with interested civic or church-related organizations.

4. Intercultural workshops for area elementary and secondary students and their teachers (day programs for children).

5. Intercultural meals, craft demonstrations, international dancing and music, and international fashion shows.

6. Travel and study abroad advising.

7. Office worker sharing.

8. International Excellence Award, a monetary award presented to one or more seniors who have distinguished themselves in the area of cross-cultural understanding.

The Department of Languages and Intercultural Studies and the International Student Services Office support the need for their staff members to take advantage of professional development opportunities. Active participation in appropriate workshops and conferences is encouraged, as is the acceptance of leadership responsibilities in selected organizations.

In curriculum development, concerted efforts have been made to continue strengthening the intercultural offerings throughout all departments and the four academic divisions. Warren Wilson has for many years been using grants as seed money to increase the number of international courses, provide overseas travel experience for faculty members, and encourage the teaching staff to add an international dimension to their courses. When Warren Wilson began "internationalizing" the curriculum, its library collection was drastically expanded to include materials on all areas of the world. Warren Wilson has continued to enjoy the reputation of having one of the most complete intercultural libraries existing in a college its size.

The programing initiated by the International Student Services Office and the Department of Languages and Intercultural Studies serves to reinforce the formal academic program. For example, with advanced planning teachers often require their students to attend international or intercultural programs relevant to a particular course. Similarly, an attempt is made to schedule certain programs when pertinent courses are being taught. Hunger Awareness Week, for instance, is scheduled during the term in which the Global Issues Course is offered; International Perspectives on the Environment is planned for the term when most environmental courses are taught. This approach to program planning has proved to be the best use of financial and human resources, to ensure an audience, and to maximize staff cooperation and involvement in making the curriculum more international.

Of course, many unplanned cross-cultural experiences occur daily among the college community members. Foreign students are not allowed to room with their countrymen during their first semester; thus they are introduced at once to new languages and cultures. Moreover, many foreign students visit in the homes of their American friends during semester breaks; and students are regularly "mixed up" in classes, extracurricular activities, and in the Work Program.

Program Strengths and Weaknesses

Strengths

1. Major institutional commitment to international education at all levels, including the Board of Trustees, administration, and staff

2. A sizeable number of benefactors who are attracted to the college's international education endeavors

3. A staff with varied interests, goals, and styles (many of whom chose employment at Warren Wilson College expressly because of the international focus and presence of foreign students), which serve to expand the possibilities for international programing at a small college

4. The recruitment of several younger staff members with experience in living abroad (e.g., Peace Corps) to take the role of older, retirement-aged staff members whose international experience and language skills were acquired through missions and similar activities

5. The dedication to continue making the curriculum more international in new and varied ways

6. Support for staff members to attend and participate in professional development activities

7. A significant number of foreign students (12 percent of the student body) from an adequate variety of countries

8. An office for handling services to foreign students, recruiting and retaining foreign students, and coordinating a sizeable amount of international programing

9. Support from the Work Program in the form of assistants for international program activities

10. The graduation requirement that all students must complete at least one Intercultural Awareness course

11. The freedom to experiment with novel programing to meet student needs and interests

12. An international education program that fits within the system of well articulated institutional goals

Weaknesses:

1. Lack of clarity regarding the division of responsibilities and channels of communication and cooperation, with the danger that programs may become too decentralized

2. Lack of a consensus about which foreign students the college is unable to admit and serve, e.g., students of limited financial resources and students who need a large amount of ESL training

3. A staff reward system that fails to recognize adequately the advantages and usefulness of staff overseas experiences

4. Insufficient funding to respond adequately to the international development of staff members

5. Lack of a consensus on a workable policy and program of implementation for study abroad for students

6. Lack of visibility for the international education program in the wider community

The Future of International Education

The survival of a college whose enrollment presently exceeds the number of dormitory spaces is dependent on factors other than the foreign student program. However, international education has well established roots in the history of the Warren Wilson College. When a program is as old as Warren Wilson's international program, optimism about longevity can be afforded. The question is not what aspects of the program will remain, but rather how and in what form they will remain.

Success will lie in the quest for excellence through emphasis on the college community's collective thinking, energies, and talents, and it will rest on the recogntion that change is not only inevitable, but necessary and welcome. Indeed, college staff members are confident that international education will continue in a variety of forms, and many are looking forward to the evolutionary process.

Planned change will have to occur within the confines of the current level of manpower. There are no immediate plans to add more staff members. The present staff will have to devise new ways to balance individual professional needs, the needs of the college, and the needs of a quality international education program. Limited growth will also require a better utilization of students and the wider community, and linkages that never before seemed logical or feasible will take on new meaning.

With this "limits to growth" policy, what areas of international education are appropriate for Warren Wilson College's consideration?

1. Renewed emphasis on study abroad, particularly as part of professional staff development, with a written rationale and statement of commitment. Overseas development and service projects (as opposed to research) are appropriate given the college's emphasis on service to others and the value and dignity of work.

The involvement of students in study abroad will lend reality to their programs.

2. Cooperative programs and ties with other institutions that have well developed study abroad programs for students or staff members

3. The recognition of the importance of learning other languages and the need to discuss including a second language requirement for the bachelor's degree. Staff members should also tend to their own second language needs. Staff members' foreign language proficiencies—regardless of their chosen disciplines—should be incorporated into the curriculum.

4. The development of an international education program that would attract the attention and participation of the wider community, especially nontraditional students or the occasional student

5. Continued emphasis on making the curriculum more international with a focus on developing skills of mediation and reconciliation across cultures and the use of appropriate technology. Curriculum areas currently offered by the college that merit particular regard include environmental studies, social work, and business management.

6. Continued search for funding for scholarships and program support

7. The ability to make adaptations and adjustments based on data already being collected about alumni, currently enrolled students, and staff members.

The international education program at Warren Wilson College permeates all facets of college life, and the college has repeatedly affirmed its commitment to international education. A recent survey of alumni indicates that the international and intercultural component of students' education has as significant an impact as the Work Program. No doubt the wise use of resources and the ability to adapt are what will preserve the international education program as well as propel it, along with other worthwhile programs, into the future.

Notes

1. Harold Taylor, "Strangers in the World Community," *Saturday Review*, July 1973.
2. Henry Jensen, *A History of Warren Wilson College*, 1974.
3. Ibid.
4. Ibid.

CHAPTER 10

Linfield College

JOSEPH V. NAVARI

LINFIELD COLLEGE IS A FOUR-YEAR undergraduate liberal arts institution in Oregon. Its international education programs are based on the principle of integration—an integration of its study abroad programs with its on-campus academic programs.

The College Setting

Linfield College is located in McMinnville, Oregon, a small city near the foothills of the Pacific Coast Range, thirty-eight miles southwest of Portland and about twenty-five miles northwest of Salem. The town grew up as a service center to agriculture when a mill was set up in 1844. Today the city not only services agriculture but also has diversified its economic base with light industrial manufacturing and a broad range of service industries. The community still retains its original rural atmosphere and is surrounded by rich agricultural lands. McMinnville has a population of about 15,000, and like Oregon as a whole, its population is relatively homogeneous. Although the town has grown steadily, it has done so without sudden influxes of people from diverse cultural backgrounds.

The campus covers ninety-two acres with twenty-seven buildings. the student body numbers approximately 1,250 and has been growing steadily during the last six years. The college offers baccalaureate programs in thirty-one fields. There are ninety-one faculty members; seventy-seven are full time. Most hold the Ph.D. or other terminal degree in their field. The faculty is relatively young, and only about 50 percent of the faculty are tenured. The college is headed by a president with appropriate administrative officers for academic affairs, admissions, business and finance (including physical plant), external relations, and student services.

Most of the students who registered for the 1980 fall term were from the Pacific Coast states. Students from Oregon, Washington, California, Hawaii, and Alaska made up 89 percent of the total fall term enrollment; Oregonians alone represent 60 percent. Linfield is therefore a regional institution with largely regional ties and affiliations, and its students are homogeneous in their backgrounds, education, and upbringing. With the exception of the sixty-three students from Hawaii, few of Linfield's American students have much international experience or cross-cultural awareness. Many of them come from small communities in the Pacific Northwest, where opportunities to meet and deal with foreigners are limited.

How the International Program Was Established

By American standards, Linfield College is an old and well-established institution. It was founded in 1849 when a new territory was being settled and McMinnville was but a five-year-old hamlet. Members of the American Baptist Church were prominent in the founding of the college, a link that Linfield continues to this day.

In contrast, the history of Linfield's international programing is quite recent. In the early 1970s the college was involved in several international education efforts, mostly short-term programs to which administrators and faculty members could devote only part of their attention. In 1975 and 1976, however, the leadership of the college changed; in those two years a new president and a vice-president of academic affairs came to Linfield. With their arrival, international programing for Linfield received greater emphasis and a more prominent place in the planning of the college.

BASIC PRINCIPLES

Early in the planning process, a statement of general principles emerged:

> The principle behind the international programs at Linfield College is the belief that cross-cultural experiences and learning are an integral part of a liberal arts education. Contact and exposure to a foreign culture lead to a high degree of intellectual and personal sensitivity to the variations in life, culture, and scholarship around the world. International experience, whether at home in the classroom or library, or abroad in a museum or foreign university, promotes observations and analysis, self-awareness and tolerance. . . . When abroad you quickly learn that your perceptions . . . are limited. You learn that prejudice is, in part, a function of perceptions circumscribed by cultural

horizons that are less distant than they need be. As you begin to move into a foreign culture—whether living and traveling in a contemporary one or reading and studying the records of an historical one—new horizons enlarge your range of vision. . . . Through its international programs, Linfield promotes the values of a liberal education which have for so long been taught in its classrooms.

Thus the view at Linfield was that the general goals of a liberal arts education, among them to develop adult maturity and analytical competencies, could be furthered by carefully designed international programs. Indeed, there was a perception that international programs, if properly designed, could promote the same type of liberal learning that was taking place in Linfield's classrooms.

Because the aim of the liberal arts is to provide an awareness of diverse sets of human values, Linfield's vice-president of academic affairs felt that the homogeneity of the student body—which was predominantly regional and without much international experience or cultural awareness—limited the learning process, both in the classroom and in the general life of the college. To develop diverse viewpoints and cultural backgrounds in the student body therefore seemed to be the first priority. Toward this end, a plan to "internationalize" the college was developed between 1977 and 1979. The thrust of the plan was first to develop a study abroad programs that would feed students culturally, and then to return those students to the campus to enrich on-campus life.

STUDY ABROAD PROGRAM MODEL

A study abroad program model, designed primarily for sophomores with one year of language, held out the best hope of achieving Linfield's objective of educating students in a broad array of human values around the world, and then returning them to Linfield to share those values. The model consists of courses specifically designed for the Linfield group. Normally faculty come from a foreign university, but they are hired directly by Linfield as the sponsoring institution.

Core program models can assume several forms. Though they do not benefit from interinstitutional linkages, which normally increase the flow of persons between countries, they do possess significant advantages. The first is academic control, because faculty members are hired directly. By requiring curriculum vitae, reviewing recommendations, and interviewing prospective instructors, program administrators can guarantee a high degree of quality control.

An equally important advantage achieved through the hiring process is control over course content. This control makes possible the integration of study abroad course work with on-campus academic programs and may affect enrollment patterns in courses on the home campus. This degree of control may even produce, if desired, curriculum modifications in on-campus programs such as general education and language and even in noninternational majors such as biology.

The general administrative control over these study abroad programs can be used by the sponsoring institution to meet a broad range of needs:

1. To promote academic enrichment of on-campus courses (closely related to the diversification of the student body)

2. To exert a favorable influence on "sophomore slump" and the general problem of retention

3. To attract students interested in international affairs and cultural diversity

4. To create new patterns of student expectations and fulfillment in the liberal arts college experience

Study abroad improves a student's ability to contribute to and benefit from a college's course work. It may also create a demand for new and more sophisticated course work on the home campus, which would have a beneficial impact on the overall academic quality of the institution. Linfield is pursuing this theory in its study abroad programs.

Based on the foregoing concepts, Linfield specifically designed its four study abroad programs around the following features:

1. The program would be designed primarily for sophomore students who would return to the college for at least two years to share their foreign experience with students and faculty members.

2. Because the program is a means of developing the student body, every Linfield student, regardless of financial resources, should be able to participate. The cost of participation was therefore set at the prevailing sum of tuition, room, insurance, and activity fee (and in some cases board) at Linfield College. Transportation to and from the site is covered in this cost.

3. Course work abroad would be integrated with the college's general education requirement, adding an academic incentive to the financial incentive, thus encouraging students who might be less than cosmopolitan to go abroad. At the same time, course content, controlled through the faculty hiring process, was designed to modify Linfield's general education requirement by making it more international. Courses abroad deal with the host country and are comparative in content.

THE OFFICE OF INTERNATIONAL PROGRAMS

To implement these principles and program characteristics, a new office was created. In July 1979, 130 years after Linfield's founding, the college opened its first Office of International Programs, and a full-time director was hired.

The directorship of the Office of International Programs was placed directly into the academic framework of the college. The director reported to the vice-president of academic affairs and was given faculty status with limited teaching responsibilities. Because the study abroad programs were to be integrated with the college's general education, the director was asked to sit as an ex officio member of the General Education Committee. At the same time, the director held an ex officio position on the International Studies Committee, which exercises broad responsibilities in overseeing the full range of the college's international concerns.

In other less formal ways the director was given status within the structure of the college. Most importantly, the director was granted full powers in negotiating agreements with persons and institutions overseas. As the representative of the college in international matters, the director of the Office of International Programs has from the beginning been allowed to exercise negotiating powers and wide latitude in the use of college resources to implement programs and agreements.

In its first two years of operation, Linfield's Office of International Programs has followed three corollary principles:

1. All international program courses must be academically sound and intrinsically coherent.

2. All international programs, including their course components, must be articulated with on-campus academic work.

3. All international programs must meet the needs of the college in a precise and definable manner.

Program Description

The Office of International Programs oversees three major program areas: study abroad, the American Language Program, and faculty and curriculum development.

STUDY ABROAD PROGRAMS

With a good deal of administrative freedom, the Office of International Programs has established four study abroad programs of the core program type in the last two years. Located in Austria, Costa Rica, France, and Japan, the programs consist of a nonelective curriculum package of four courses, which are fully integrated with the college's general education requirement.

A student can satisfy up to half of the college's general education requirement by participating in one of these four study abroad programs. The twenty-semester-hour package is made up of ten semester hours of language, five semester hours in the humanities, and five semester hours in the social sciences. The two nonlanguage courses are comparative in content and add a significant international dimension to the college's general education requirement. For example, a course is offered in Costa Rica on the comparative history of the Americas, and a course in Paris is an introduction to the French and American societies as reflected in their legal institutions.

Currently, each program enrolls fifteen students for five months of study abroad at approximately the cost of attending Linfield for an equal period. Each program is supervised by an on-site coordinator who may also be a member of the teaching team. Using standard hiring procedures, the Office of International Programs directly hires each member of the program team (coordinator and faculty members).

The funding of these four programs is based on tuition and depends on (and permits) enrollment expansion even though the college is at capacity in relation to its housing space. How does this policy work? Two conditions must be met. First, the per-student cost of the program (for simplicity, room and board costs are not considered program costs) must be less than or equal to tuition. Second, the campus must be at or near capacity.

If these two conditions are met, the difference between the per-student cost of a particular study abroad program and the amount of tuition will actually represent income to the institution; if there is no difference, the sponsoring institution will break even. Of course, if the sponsoring institution charges its students a high tuition, the formula is easy to manage. Similarly, if program costs abroad can be kept minimal, the formula is again easy to manage.

At Linfield, the difference between income (tuition) and expenses (per-student costs)—with campus costs being covered by sufficient numbers of students on campus—is the key to financing the study abroad program. Because Linfield's tuition is more than sufficient to cover program costs (the college does not have to support a library or counseling center abroad), this funding approach creates a budgetary surplus.

THE AMERICAN LANGUAGE PROGRAM

A second phase of Linfield's plan to enrich its community emerged during the academic year 1979/80. To encourage having foreign students in residence at Linfield, a plan was developed in the latter part of 1979 to establish an intensive English as a Second Language (ESL) program for admissible foreign students. Because Linfield does not offer any graduate programs, which ordinarily draw large numbers of foreign students to American universities, Linfield's only option to increase its foreign student population was to establish an ESL program, which would attract foreign students who expected to enter degree programs at American universities after they improved their English to the required level.

The program began using an interinstitutional relationship with Kanto Gakuin University in Yokohama, Japan, which had agreed to act as the local coordinator for Linfield's study abroad program. Linfield agreed to host fifteen of the Japanese students, and subsequently set up especially for them an intensive English program that would also serve other foreign students at Linfield. What is now called the American Language Program is therefore linked not only to the study abroad program in Japan but also to the language needs of currently enrolled foreign students. At the same time, the program is attracting foreign students to the college for English language training. Their presence has already begun the cultural diversification on campus that the college hopes to achieve off campus through the study abroad program.

The value of the linkage between the on-campus and off-campus academic programs cannot be overemphasized. For example, Linfield's American students in Japan influence Japanese students to come to Linfield where they make several American acquaintances. The Japanese at Linfield in turn influence American students to go to Japan on Linfield's study abroad program. Not only were there far more applicants than the fifteen available places for the 1981 fall study abroad program, but Linfield's enrollment patterns and course offerings on campus are also changing as a result.

FACULTY AND CURRICULUM DEVELOPMENT

Faculty and curriculum development are the third element of Linfield's emerging plan to make its community more international. The overriding needs here are money to provide library resources and time away from teaching to rethink current courses and develop new courses.

During the last three years Linfield has been successful in securing grants to fund this crucial third element. A two-year grant from the US Department of Education made possible library acquisitions and several curriculum developments in upper-division courses and the general education program. The same grant established a faculty colloquium on international studies to share ideas and generate enthusiasm.

A second grant, recently awarded by the National Endowment for the Humanities, is making possible important curriculum development in upper-level language courses. This grant is allowing the language faculty to develop a fixed cycle of special-topic courses for upper-division students, some of whom will have participated in one of Linfield's study abroad programs. The unique feature of the fixed-cycle, special-topic course is that it will be available to language and nonlanguage majors alike. The cluster of special-topic courses consists of a three-semester-hour core lecture course taught in English, and two-semester-hour satellite courses taught in the appropriate foreign language.

A recent grant from the Northwest Area Foundation is making possible an important experiment at Linfield in the mobilization of the college's international resources—that is, students and faculty—in an effort to extend international understanding to the campus as a whole. The effort consists of a theoretical and applied component.

The theoretical component is a new Linfield course on social and cultural change. Among the theories of cultural change which this course will discuss is acculturation. Since Linfield's study abroad students will themselves go through this process while abroad, they will take this course before going abroad and will act as discussion leaders in the course after their return from abroad. The purpose of this is to give Linfield's students a solid understanding of what happened to them while they were abroad, so that they will be well prepared to express in public forum their own transformation and development.

The applied component of the effort consists of providing public forums on the Linfield campus in which Linfield's returnees can express to the broader community the international perspective developed by living and studying abroad. The college is furthering its faculty development by providing summer stipends in the amount of $2000 for specific international projects. The stipends are competitive and faculty recipients are required to participate in the public forums mentioned above upon their return to the campus.

ON-CAMPUS INTERNATIONAL ACTIVITIES

The Office of International Programs was given a broad mandate to develop, coordinate, and oversee all international matters at the college. Most of these are specifically planned to bring to the attention of the college as a whole the importance of international perspectives. Utilizing Linfield's American students who have been abroad, its foreign students and its faculty, the college's international program officer is responsible for developing a series of international activities and events designed to promote international understanding. This general mandate covers a broad range of educational activities as listed:

1. Managing all foreign student affairs, such as orientation, academic advising, International Club activities, and immigration matters, and linking these to American students, student clubs, and the wider community.

2. Handling foreign visitors, and utilizing them as resources in on-campus activities

3. Arranging for special speakers and events as part of the college's international plan

4. Overseeing faculty development and grant applications in service to the college's international effort

5. Supervising students who are pursuing an individually planned major in international studies

6. Advising students and faculty members on travel

7. Coordinating the granting of financial aid to foreign students

8. Advising on independent study and work abroad

9. Assisting the registrar and the admissions office in evaluating foreign credentials

10. Serving as Fulbright advisor

11. Coordinating special field tutorials abroad led by Linfield faculty members

An attempt is made to create linkages between various programs and events. For example, a Japanese political scientist who came to Linfield last April to deliver a public lecture on Japanese politics, also participated in the orientation program for members of Linfield College going to Japan.

The Future of International Programs

Faculty and curriculum development is perhaps the greatest challenge facing Linfield's new international program. International expertise can be a legitimate criterion in the selection of new faculty. But with current faculty members, a shortage of money for faculty and curriculum development is the chief obstacle to further international development. Curriculum development requires large blocks of free time during which faculty members can pursue their studies and broaden their perspective by incorporating ideas and information drawn from around the world into their work. The college cannot send a faculty member to Japan with a group of twenty-five students and expect the faculty member to return with enough information to develop a new course or significantly modify an existing one. Experience has shown that this approach is inappropriate for curriculum development.

The future of Linfield's international programs clearly lies with its faculty and how they will respond to the efforts already undertaken. Will the faculty be able, through appropriate planning and support, to match the development of Linfield's students? Grants to provide release time and library acquisitions are crucial here. One way the college hopes to assist its faculty is through a series of affiliations with foreign universities to provide faculty members with academic opportunities abroad. Two such faculty exchange opportunities now exist: affiliations with Kanto Gakuin University in Yokohama, Japan, and with Eberhand-Karls University in Tübingen, Germany.

Linfield is also planning an interdepartmental concentration in international studies. This academic program of fundamental work in language and the social sciences at the college would be tied to foreign universities that can provide specific training in area and topical studies. Not only would the international studies major require academic experience abroad, but the program would also provide mechanisms to link faculty members, students, and the curriculum across international boundaries. This type of program would greatly expand the principle of integration that underlies Linfield's current international programs.

CHAPTER 11

Earlham College

LEWIS M. HOSKINS

EARLHAM COLLEGE HAS A SPECIAL EMPHASIS on international education stemming from a Quaker tradition of concern for peace and international understanding. For many decades the semi-rural and rather isolated campus of one thousand students has welcomed foreign students from Asia, Africa, Europe, and Latin America. Foreign policy and international relations have been the subject of curriculum and extracurricular convocations. Foreign languages have always been important, and for more than twenty-five years opportunity has been provided to students to study language, culture, and politics abroad.

How the International Program Was Established

Earlham's foreign study program began in 1956 when instructors of the French language saw the importance of immersing their students in families and cultures where the French language was spoken. The first group of students in the program was in France for one semester. Emphasizing language and area studies, the France Program was so successful and the learning so greatly facilitated that it has continued since then at least every other year.

Other language faculty members wanted to have the same advantage for their students, and soon programs evolved in Germany and in Spanish-speaking countries. The original pattern was followed, with some modifications. A faculty family took as many as twenty students to spend at least three months—usually six—in a foreign environment where the language would be spoken intensively by both faculty members and students. Home stays were arranged for the students, and excursions supplemented the

203

formal courses that were usually offered by specially hired local professors to fit the atypical calendar.

A nonlanguage program was developed in Scandinavia in 1960 to give students a cross-cultural experience. Again, home stays were arranged, and carefully designed study tours revealed the cultural variety within the three major Scandinavian countries. Because Scandinavian language competence, at least at the beginning level, was soon seen to be a great asset, Danish was added as an option and was strongly recommended.

Before 1960, off-campus opportunities were primarily in Europe and focused on Western civilization, because most American students were a cultural product of that portion of the globe. The sixties brought increasing concern for the non-Western world. Programs were designed to enrich the curriculum in East Asian studies and shortly thereafter in Latin American studies and African studies. The college administration established two closely coordinated offices that report to the academic dean or provost: one for East Asian studies and the other for international programs.

The curriculum expansion required the skills of the instructional staff. Faculty seminars were organized in which staff members from a variety of disciplines participated in a yearlong seminar: first on Japan and China, then India, and then Africa. This professional development helped to expand not only the curricular offerings but also the extracurricular cultural activities on campus.

Under the guidance of an eminent East Asian scholar, Jackson H. Bailey, Earlham developed a specialized interest in Japan, an emphasis enhanced by a tokanoma (Japanese study center), two Japanese gardens, an office on East Asian programs (including an extensive film-lending library), Japanese professors of language and art in residence, and various visitors. The opportunity for students to supplement their on-campus Asian studies with a field immersion was initiated, by means of outside funding, jointly with Antioch College at first and shortly thereafter with a consortium, the Great Lakes Colleges Association (GLCA). Careful cultivation of connections in Japan by historian Jackson Bailey produced an agreement with Waseda University in Tokyo (the largest private university in Japan) whereby it was to develop an international study center. Students from GLCA schools were among the students invited to participate, and Earlham became the "agent college" for administering the Japan Study Program for the consortium.

This program was designed for students who have at least an initial start in the language—some as much as a full year, others just an intensive immersion before departure for Japan. It includes a summer of language study followed by one or more terms studying a variety of disciplines at Waseda's International Division, taught in English by Japanese professors. Language training continues throughout the year. All the students benefit from home stays, both urban and rural, that help immerse them in the culture. They return for their nine or twelve months' experience with remarkably improved language skills and a greatly increased knowledge and appreciation of Japan. Returned students have stirred enthusiasms on their campuses, so that the number of students interested in the programs continues to grow. Faculty members from institutions in the consortium see supervising students in Japan as a rich opportunity for faculty development and professional advancement. The sister consortium, the Associated Colleges of the Midwest, has joined the group of GLCA colleges participating in the program, bringing the total to twenty-five.

Throughout the turbulent years of the sixties and into the seventies, students showed serious concern about acquiring a better understanding of their world, a concern that produced great interest in foreign study opportunities. Through Earlham's own expanded programs study abroad opportunities grew. While making use of the GLCA facilities in Bogotá, Colombia, Earlham also developed its own intensive language program in Mexico. Similarly intensive, or double immersion, courses were developed in Germany at Marburg and in France at Rodez. At several sites Earlham was able to coordinate with local Quakers to add a service dimension such as teaching or to enrich the experiential learning aspects. In Japan, a shorter program was developed in Morioka as an alternative to the longer Japan Program in Tokyo.

A program in London was developed for students who lack second-language competence and for those with special concerns in the United Kingdom. Emphasizing literature, politics, economics, the theater, and Quakerism, it continues to be popular. Field visits to the Lake Country, early Quaker sites, and Shakespeare territory have always been included. A parallel program was developed in Edinburgh, Scotland, but it was eventually withdrawn, and a GLCA program in Aberdeen has somewhat compensated for that loss.

One of the newer offerings emphasizing non-Western countries, or the Third World, has been a program that started in 1977 in Kenya. Students in the first group, led by faculty members with special interest, background, and skills, studied animal societies, ornithology, and ecology. A social science program has also been developed that uses anthropological leadership and skills. The program in Kenya has also been popular, and students report having valuable experiences, particularly when local Quakers, members of East Africa Yearly Meeting of Friends, arrange for them to live in villages with families.

Earlham has also participated in cooperative efforts to develop opportunities for study in China. The college also makes use of programs offered by either members of the consortium or other colleges or universities—programs in other parts of the world, such as the Middle East and South Asia, for the occasional student with special claims to study in an exotic area.

Program Characteristics

Earlham's foreign study program is the primary focus of its international education activities. The college also engages in many community outreach activities, and it offers a substantial curriculum in international affairs.

STUDENT PARTICIPATION

The development of Earlham's foreign study program has been facilitated by strong administrative support and encouragement. This support extends to the recognition that having a certain percentage of the students studying off campus is appropriate, even if, as a result, total tuition income is reduced. A figure of 7.5 percent of current enrollment is approved by the administration for off-campus study each year. More than two-thirds of Earlham's graduates will have one off-campus learning experience, either foreign or domestic.

Students to participate in study abroad programs are carefully chosen by the field supervisors, by the International Programs Office, and by the Off-Campus Study Committee, which is composed of faculty members and students. Each student applies for a specific time and place, submitting a carefully worked out application, and in many cases, interviews are conducted. Usually there are more candidates than can be accommodated. Criteria for selection include the academic relevance and appropriateness of the student's program of study as well as the student's personal qualities, group and leadership abilities, sense of humor, ability to operate in unstructured situations, and general stability. Students are notified of their acceptance at least one term before departure, which permits them to take background courses and participate in a carefully designed orientation program.

The orientation program is primarily the responsibility of the faculty supervisor, but staff members of the International Programs Office provide supplementary, practical information and guidelines, and help organize resources; particularly helpful are those faculty members and students who have returned from the area. The college requires serious participation in the orientation program, and a nonrefundable deposit is collected. Whenever possible, students who will be participating in the study abroad program help plan and design the orientation program and the program itself.

Earlham does not have as many foreign students studying on campus as the college would like. In recent years, lack of scholarship funds has inhibited foreign student enrollment. However, there are several students from Japan and from East Africa, particularly Kenya. Other students come from Latin America, Europe, and of course, Canada. Although the goal is to have foreign students contribute 10 percent of enrollment, they are usually 6 or 7 percent. Foreign students are particularly helpful to the International Programs Office in orientation programs for groups preparing to go abroad. They can also help with language and cultural background studies.

FACULTY PARTICIPATION

Earlham usually sends about eight faculty members with their families abroad each year as supervisors of specific study abroad programs. The leaders are chosen by the academic dean and provost from nominations by the director of the International Programs Office. Factors such as availability, expertise, competence, and interest are weighed.

Faculty supervisors in the foreign study program appreciate the assignment to work with a group of students in a favorite area abroad, regarding it as a valuable opportunity for professional development. They may brush up on their foreign language ability, carry out research, or continue their stay beyond the student program on a special leave or by using a free holiday period. Another aspect of the experience that faculty members find personally satisfying is having their families abroad with a group of young people, all teaching and learning from one another.

Earlham has recognized that study abroad programs are an important part of faculty development, and the college has from time to time provided supplementary funds. However, study abroad programs do lead to faculty overload, particularly during the term before departure, in the selection and orientation process, and during the reentering period. Spouses are inevitably involved in responsibilities but are seldom compensated adequately, unless they can teach or share in the teaching of a formal course.

Each Earlham faculty member leading a group abroad is expected to teach one of the courses and make sure that local instructors are used for other courses. Thus, at least two-thirds of the study abroad courses are offered by foreign nationals, but the Earlham faculty member provides overall supervision and assurance of academic standards.

Faculty supervisors are asked to help students with their reentry problems and to encourage students to make use of their foreign experience in their classes. Faculty members are also encouraged to use their foreign experience as effectively as possible in their own teaching. Earlham has found that the quality of teaching is clearly improved by the language refreshment, updating of information, and professional advancement associated with study abroad programs

The International Programs Office has recently been increasing its activities regarding reentry, working with both returning faculty members and students. The sharing of experiences, problems, and frustrations among returning students and faculty members can itself be educational, and participants are sometimes surprised to find they have reentry problems and other cross-cultural issues in common.

There is no regular faculty exchange program other than that with Japan. But other faculty exchanges, particularly in European languages, are arranged when possible.

LINKAGES ON CAMPUS

Although the International Programs Office (IPO) coordinates foreign visitors' activities, cultural events, and speakers on international topics, it is by no means the only place on campus where such enrichment of campus life is fostered. For example, the Committee on All-College Occasions always makes sure that some of its activities are related to foreign affairs. The IPO makes suggestions to this committee and works closely with them.

The Japan Study Program and the East Asian Studies Program are part of the office complex with IPO, and because the support staffs overlap, coordinating activities is relatively easy. The Peace and Global Studies (PAGS) Program has a separate staff and office, but there is an interrelationship with IPO through overlapping committee members, both faculty members and students. The director of PAGS and the director of IPO are in frequent consultation about common concerns and interests. When a PAGS student wishes to study abroad, IPO can sometimes make arrangements or help make recommendations.

An overarching, ad hoc committee—the International Studies Coordinating Committee—has been created to coordinate campuswide international concerns and set policy. All subsidiary offices and committees are represented on the committee. One function of the committee is to monitor and coordinate federal grants recently received by Earlham. A grant from the US Department of Education augments the staff of the International Programs Office so that orientation programs and reentry efforts can be improved. Grant money from the National Endowment for the Humanities supports faculty development; through this means, social science faculty members are helped to recover foreign language skills, and instructors in foreign languages are helped to extend their teaching methods by adding cultural dimensions to their courses.

FUNDING

Because Earlham charges a relatively high tuition, it can operate off-campus programs successfully by billing its students abroad the same amount they would be paying for tuition, board, and room at Earlham for an equivalent period. From this total, a percentage is retained for campus overhead (costs such as accounting, registrar's office, International Programs Office, and faculty supervisor's salary). The remaining portion—more than three-fourths of the funds—is available for field expenses and student services abroad, including cost of living, academic fees and tuition, excursions, and cultural events. Students must arrange and pay for their own international transportation, which the college facilitates but no longer charters.

Some study abroad programs operate comfortably in the black; others are marginal because of inflationary pressures and variations in the exchange rate. However, as a whole, Earlham has been able to operate these programs over the years without subsidy. Students receiving financial aid can carry it abroad for at least one program; only rarely when students are approved for a second off-campus study program will the financial aid package be available again. Loans can usually be arranged to make up deficiencies. The present tightening of federal funds will handicap the study abroad programs with the increased risk that they will become available primarily for the affluent. Cooperative enterprises or consortium arrangements will offer some response to the inflationary pressures and tighter budgets.

Because international activities at Earlham are scattered throughout the college, they appear in several budgets, and to segregate funds allocated purely to international programs is therefore difficult. For example, IPO has a modest budget for services and programing; the Japan Study Program office also has a budget for field operations supervision, supplemented by a relatively modest on-campus overhead and pro-graming fund; and the Peace and Global Studies Program also has a separate budget, with the costs of the international studies major absorbed by the appropriate academic departments. In all these budgets, the biggest item is personnel costs. In many cases faculty members have joint responsibilities between an academic department and international programming.

COMMUNITY OUTREACH

Community outreach has always been important to Earlham, and the college has served the city, county, and region in several ways. Among the most important have been conducting teachers' institutes and providing materials at conferences, including visual aids, for high school teachers in the area. The state of Indiana requires an international dimension in refresher work, and the Earlham programs help provide it.

An office dealing with public relations provides speakers for the community. Clubs and organizations often turn to IPO or the Japan Study Programs, as well as academic departments, for suggestions of students, foreign students, or faculty members with special expertise. The college often hosts prospective students with international interests or foreign language concerns during events that IPO coordinates with the Admissions Office. Earlham faculty members and some IPO staff members have recently been involved in community discussions on varied issues.

Quaker interests at Earlham work closely with the American Friends Service Committee, both the nearby regional office in Dayton and the national headquarters in Philadelphia. Similar cooperation exists with the Friends United Meeting in Richmond, Indiana. Special concerns include work in Kenya, Japan, China, and Mexico. Earlham has also nominated both undergraduate and graduate students (the latter from the Earlham School of Religion) to the Friends World Committee for Consultation for special assignments at the United Nations or in areas of tension such as Northern Ireland.

Earlham's Lilly Library offers its facilities to the broader community, including materials dealing with foreign affairs and international activities. The Audiovisual Office and the East Asian Film Library are extensively used not only throughout the region but also throughout the country. As part of Earlham's concern for community outreach, it has sponsored public conferences as well as campus symposia and seminars related to international affairs. Sometimes these meetings are specifically sponsored by the Japan Study Program, IPO, the Peach and Global Studies Program, or the African-American Studies Program. Usually, they are short-term, a day or a weekend, and the broader community is invited to attend. A recent example was a two-day conference dealing with study abroad programs, their organization, administration, and evaluation. More than sixty representatives from most colleges and universities in the state attended, and discussion was held on how best to facilitate international education.

CURRICULUM

As a matter of policy, Earlham did not start out to create majors such as the one in Japan studies, because the college espouses the philosophy of a broad general education with a strong international component. The international affairs curriculum is therefore embedded in several departments. Political Science takes a major lead, but other departments have also increased their offerings in recent years to accommodate the peace and global studies major as well as the international studies major.

In the Peace and Global Studies Program, the core of the field of concentration includes courses in anthropology, politics, economics, and philosophy or religion. Other departments offer pertinent courses such as history or the humanities. Students majoring in peace and global studies to some extent tailor their own academic program, together with a field internship, to their individual special interest, language skills, and competences.

Similarly, in the new International Studies Program, there is a solid core of courses in fields such as political science and economics, with supplemental courses from other departments and field experiences for breadth. Neither the International Programs Office nor the Japan Study Program office has wanted to build an empire. Rather, the hope was to infuse a non-Western and international dimension into the curriculum and campus life. Thus, efforts have been made to increase the international dimension in courses and departments throughout the college, including the natural sciences, rather than set up a special international center that has a tightly organized, growing program. The number of faculty members who have been abroad, either with Earlham or other programs, suggests that most disciplines include some comparative international or cross-cultural course work.

Outlook for the 1980s

In more than twenty-five years since Earlham began its foreign study program, evaluators of Earlham's program have found it to be worthwhile. The Admissions Office regards the program as an asset in attracting students; the Registrar's Office suggests that the opportunity for off-campus study lowers attrition and provides a creative change of pace; the Dean of Students Office feels it is a morale booster; and the Office of the Dean or Provost of the College recognizes the value of study abroad programs for faculty development. Enough faculty members have participated and are enthusiastic about the program to make it an accepted and integral part of Earlham College education, and it is generally supported by all portions of the community. But study abroad is primarily endorsed because it makes the Earlham educational program more relevant to tomorrow's interdependent world and sounder for students seeking quality training.

As highlighted by the recent President's Commission on Foreign Languages and International Education, America's challenges in the eighties are for a better understanding of the world and for more young people with genuine skills and concern to move into leadership roles in international affairs. While the graduate schools will produce specialists in language and area studies, the country's undergraduate schools must provide liberal art students with a broad approach to international affairs and responsibilities.

The experience at Earlham College suggests that such an education can be provided even if outside funding from foundations and government is limited. Colleges across the country must work together to find ways to maintain their international programs because they are needed now more than ever. More cooperative enterprises through consortia, joint programs, and international exchanges are needed. Colleges should also provide more opportunities in the non-Western world, away from large and expensive urban complexes. With resourcefulness and ingenuity, programs can be continued even if federal funds and subsidies decline.

Earlham's experience is not unique, but its Quaker ethos carries with it an expectation of international education and service that has produced at Earlham a strong commitment. Earlham's record suggests that comparable liberal arts colleges can develop their own programs and find similar rewards.

CHAPTER 12

Utica College of Syracuse University

RICHARD B. ROSEN

Most business firms, regardless of size and type of operations, will be affected by economic and political developments on the international scene. Most businessmen will, therefore, need an ability to understand and anticipate those effects. Also, the number of American managers stationed abroad will probably not diminish during the coming decade. Several surveys have found, however, that very high percentages of individuals are still becoming presidents of multinational corporations without ever having had any international work experience, and that many managers with international responsibilities had had no international studies while at the university, and no management development programs with international studies with international content, while employed to prepare them for such international responsibilities. (From Business and International Education, *a report submitted by the Task Force on Business and International Education to the Government/ Academic Interface Committee, International Education Project, American Council on Education, 1977, p. 3)*

In order to begin addressing this problem Utica College established within its international studies curriculum an international business concentration. This chapter varies in format and content from other chapters in the book

213

because it focuses on the business concentration. Utica's international program is helping to meet an important need in New York's business community. This program is included to illustrate how widely varied international education programs can be and to show what a significant role they can play in the future of the US economy.

The College and the Community

Utica College is the second largest college within the Syracuse University system, but is the most geographically separated, located fifty miles from the main campus. It is the only college of the university that is independently accredited by the Middle States Association. Utica is also the most autonomous college within the university system, given its physical distance from the main campus and its separate admissions, business, development, and presidental offices.

The college is set in a 185-acre campus in the upper Mohawk Valley of central New York, situated within the urban nexus of Utica–Rome–Herkimer encompassing a population of 300,000. It was founded in 1946 and was first housed in a cluster of old buildings near downtown Utica; then, between 1960 and 1972 a new campus was constructed at the southwest perimeter of the city.

Utica College was started by Syracuse University to serve the returning World War II veterans of the Mohawk Valley. This area had undergone hard times when the textile industries critical to its economy moved to the South. In the upgrading of the local economy during the postwar period, more sophisticated industries settled in, requiring improved higher education facilities. Utica College had two major functions—to meet the needs of the changing economy and to educate a growing professional service class. These conditions determined the basic educational philosophy of Utica College; namely, to be a career-oriented liberal arts institution.

In the last twenty years, coinciding with the building of the new campus, Utica College's student population mix has been progressively altered. Half of the full-time students now come from outside the Mohawk Valley. These students are drawn to the college primarily for its career program opportunities. Thus, in its short thirty-five years of existence, Utica College has grown from a local college to a small magnet institution servicing the Northeast. The college's original mission still remains because it is the only four-year college committed to students from the Mohawk Valley.

Students, Faculty, and Programs

The first students to matriculate at Utica College were the children of the farmers and working-class residents of the Mohawk Valley. Most of the original students were of Italian and Polish-American ancestry and were the first generation of their families to receive a college education. However, the student composition has changed substantially over thirty-five years; presently female students outnumber males and minorities represent 12 percent of the student body.

The student–faculty ratio at Utica College is sixteen to one, permitting close interaction. Although the college emphasizes the instructional side of education, a substantial number of instructors do research and are active in their professions. Because the college has a history of instituting career programs, many faculty members have had positions in the health or business professions. Their backgrounds have aided in the development of an international business curriculum. Faculty members at Utica College are continually involved in curricular enrichment, both in the liberal arts and career programs.

The college offers thirty-five different major and minor programs of study in divisions of Humanities, Behavioral Studies, Business Administration and Journalism, Science and Mathematics, and Allied Health. All students are required to earn thirty credits from a liberal arts and science core. Newer programs at Utica College include computer science, journalism, occupational therapy, gerontology, actuarial management, and international business. Utica College's educational philosophy has earned it a reputation as the "Pioneer College" for its tradition of initiating.

THE URBAN NEXUS: UTICA AND NEW YORK CITY

The greater Utica area is among the more economically depressed sections of New York; its per capita income was below the national norm in 1979. The city of Utica has been hurt by the general economic decline in the Northeast caused by escalating energy costs and the departure of industries to the Sunbelt. In addition, Utica plays the subordinate role of an economic satellite in industrial, banking, communication, and transportation investments. Syracuse has historically generated more business than Utica; for example, although the Syracuse area is only twice the size of Utica, export sales of manufactured goods have been four times greater.

On the positive economic side, Utica possesses a large skilled and dependable work force. Its water resources are outstanding and high-grade transportation routes, particularly in the east–west direction, abound. It is a physically attractive and very livable area, a little over two hundred miles from New York City. Recently, these factors have enticed electronic and computer firms with international markets to locate nearby in upstate New York. Three major New York City banks have just established branches, and other New York City firms are evaluating Utica for sites. The local chambers of commerce, banks, industrial service consortia, the US and New York State Commerce departments have begun to accentuate Utica's participation in foreign trade. Concurrently, more of Utica's small and medium-size businesses are assiduously entering or enlarging their international market sectors. In at least a minor fashion, Utica College's international business program has influenced, perhaps even brought about, these events.

PRELUDE: INTERNATIONAL STUDIES 1970–75

An international studies major was created at Utica College in September 1970. It was intended at that time to serve three functions: to provide an undergraduate, interdisciplinary (social science) background for students interested in careers outside the United States, or in international agencies within the United States; to provide a challenging major with broad subject selection to students of high academic ability; and to form within Utica College an identifiable group of students whose studies would be international in perspective and scholarly in orientation. This beginning was reinforced between 1970 and 1975 by four actions that expanded the international studies *major* into an international studies *program*.

First, overseas study opportunities were made possible through arrangements with a number of universities and colleges that sponsored programs in various parts of the world. For example, Utica College students studied in Italy, France, Holland, England, Spain, Latin America, and East Africa. Utica College became a member of the Council of International Educational Exchange (CIEE) so that Utica College students could study in CIEE social science centers in France and Spain. Arrangements were also made for students to obtain intensive Cantonese or Mandarin language studies at the Chinese University of Hong Kong.

Second, the study of languages was facilitated during the 1970/71 academic year by a small, one-year grant from the US Office of Education that established a "Critical Language" program at the college. The grant was administered by the National Association for Self-Instructional Languages (NASILP). Cross-registration in critical languages between Utica and Hamilton Colleges was established. This program initiated a closed relationship between the colleges and NASILP.

By 1975 Utica College was offering five critical (less commonly taught) languages: Arabic, Hebrew, Chinese (Mandarin), Hindi, and Italian. Utica College students studied Japanese and Greek at Hamilton. By an arrangement with the Department of Languages, any language class with insufficient registration to make presentation possible under the traditional system could be offered through the international studies program. The language program, which is based on a tutor–tape system, permitted a language to be offered with a minimum enrollment of three students.[1]

Levels of language achievement by Utica College students in the critical language program varied. Although formal language instruction was preferable, this program expanded language offerings and reinforced the growth of the nascent international studies major. Quality control in the critical languages was maintained by the external examination requirement built into the program. Students were examined and graded by an outside language instructor at the end of the semester. Credible performances were recorded by students in all languages but Hindi, which was subsequently dropped.

Third, a permanent advisory committee was established for the international studies program. The committee was composed of faculty from several disciplines with expertise in the international field. In addition to advising students, the committee met regularly to review the career needs of students, curriculum standards, and course offerings. The undergraduate curriculum had been tailored by the advisory committee to mesh with the better graduate programs. Utica College majors would proceed to Johns Hopkins University, George Washington University, and Columbia University for graduate studies.

The fourth action, namely, the creation of an international business concentration, was the most crucial to ultimate success.

INTERNATIONAL BUSINESS STUDIES: THE BEGINNINGS

In 1971, while engaged in research at Tokyo University, I had the opportunity to meet with a small number of American businessmen stationed in Japan. Though I was trained as an East Asian historian, it became apparent that the people I met had serious gaps in their knowledge of Japan, which impeded their effectiveness. These were intelligent individuals who were successful in their American-based operations but were obviously floundering in Japan. The seriousness of this problem did not lie solely in their ignorance of Japanese culture but also in their limited understanding of Japanese marketing and distribution systems.

In discussions, these American businessmen all admitted to little, if any, preparation for doing business in Japan. In their day-to-day business operations they relied completely on their Japanese staffs. Additional problems were generated by their families who had, in differing degrees, accommodated poorly to what they perceived as an alien land.

Upon returning to the United States, I began to examine closely the dimensions of this overseas problem. Interested parties arranged meetings for me with senior executives of major American corporations. At each meeting I politely queried whether or not my experience in Japan was atypical. The responses of these executives was relatively uniform; the problem was endemic worldwide. I then spoke with presidents of small and medium-sized companies involved in international trade. These chief executives asked me what higher education could do to remedy the weak posture of American's overseas personnel. During one conversation with a businessman from central New York who has companies and holdings here and abroad, the idea was suggested that Utica College examine the feasibility of developing an international business emphasis in its international program. The idea became a reality when this businessman provided a generous grant for the feasibility study. Then an anthropologist and a historian began slowly building the credibility of having an international business curriculum in a small college.

INTERNATIONAL BUSINESS: CONFERENCE AND WORKSHOP

In the fall of 1974, an international business conference was held at Utica College. The conference was conducted by seven participants from the international business, banking, and commerce communities. The conference's purpose was twofold: to signal the commencement of new program preparation to the college community, and to provide the faculty and administration with an external and professional view about the feasibility of such a program. These panelists, all nonacademicians, were the key to developing the college's international business component.

The panel consisted of three presidents of companies with international divisions, two vice-presidents of multinational firms, and international trade consultants from the New York and federal commerce departments. Invited to the conference were the faculty of the college and a group of student representatives. There were differences among the panelists about language study and about the varying personnel needs of multinational corporations versus smaller companies. However, the panelists enthusiastically agreed that a program should be established at Utica College and that employment prospects for graduates were good to excellent. Recommendations on courses ranging from marketing to cultural studies were offered. The stage was now set to prepare a curriculum.

In 1975, curriculum was designed for a degree that fused international studies and international economic/business courses. The proposed curriculum would credit cross-disciplinary and cross-divisional registrations in the Business Division and the Behavioral Studies Division, in which the international studies program is located. An international business management minor was planned for business students that would require international studies courses and a relevant language. A minor was also planned for international studies students that would give credit for courses in the business and economics division. International studies majors were already required to have at least one language. All students were to be advised by two faculty members, one from each division:

Behavioral Studies and Business. Two degree programs, international business management minors in both the Behavioral Studies Division and Business Division, were proposed.

In the fall of 1975 curricular proposals (summarized in figures 12.1 and 12.2) were presented to the college faculty and administration for discussion.

INTERMEZZO: INTERNATIONAL BUSINESS PROGRAM 1975–1977

Although some of the faculty and administration were infected with enthusiasm for this program, its implementation faced problems. Some of these problems emanated from the proposal itself, and were part of the normal evaluative process and faculty hesitance about new programs. Other problems were external and were the product of change at the college. One problem was unique in that it depended on a successful interdivisional marriage between the business and nonbusiness faculties. Of critical importance was programmatic funding, given the new courses and activities that international business required.

During the period 1975–77 there was a shift in the top administration of the college. Additionally, the faculty established a collective bargaining unit. At this time faculty and staff energies were being diverted from more mundane academic concerns. A few kept interest in the program alive and began submitting grant proposals. Certain faculty and administrators expressed doubts about business faculty members' having any flexibility in their teaching loads to allow for international business courses. Also, there was concern about who would administer the program. However, since many of the business faculty had participated in the workshop, they defended the integrity of the plan.

The new college administration realized the potential of an international business curriculum. Of particular interest was the possibility of developing a more positive relationship with the business community. Several senior faculty, including those in the Science and Humanities divisions, supported the program's adoption. Those in opposition began to appear reactive and unaccommodating. Two events then released the proposed program from its confinement: First, in anticipation of program implementation, two persons with broad international training in economics and marketing joined the faculty; and second, in 1977, the US Office of Education (as it was then called) awarded a title VI international studies grant to Utica College. After all the planning and politicking, the program could now become operational.

During the first year, many new courses were introduced. They included a freshman-level course entitled International Studies World Survey. A team-taught, cross-disciplinary survey of a key world area, this

Major in Business Administration
(Minor in Finance Management, International Business
Management,* Marketing Management, Personnel Management,
or Production Management)

(Bachelor of Science Degree)
Business Administration Division

The purpose of the major is to prepare students for competent and responsible participation in the business and society. To acquire this, a core of general education courses is required of all students; a set of required courses in business and economics; a minor in one of five areas; and twenty-four credit hours of nonbusiness elective. The business core of required courses helps develop an understanding of business principles and structure.

Total credit hours required for degree: 120

Credit
Hours

ACADEMIC OPTIONS 27

Must take Economics 11 and 142 and either Math 109 and 110 or at least one year of traditional mathematics through differential calculus. (International Studies World Survey required.) (For those selecting the minor in International Business Management, six hours of a language are strongly recommended.)

MAJOR COURSE REQUIREMENTS

Accounting 101, 102	Elementary Accounting	6
Business Law 226	Law of Contracts and Sales	3
Business 222	Business Writing	3
Economics 241	Statistics	3
Economics Electives		6
Finance 251	Corporate Finance	6
Marketing 211	Principles and Problems	3
Production Management 272	Production Management	3

MINOR CONCENTRATION

Day students should elect one sequence or minor from among Finance Management, International Business Management, Marketing Management, Personnel Management, or Production Management. The only sequence or minor available to Continuing Education students is Business Management.

INTERNATIONAL BUSINESS MANAGEMENT

International Trade 3
*The Multi-National Corporation
Either: European Economic Community 3
Or: Europe and the Third World 3
One course from the following group: 3
   *Comparative Economic Systems, Economic Development, Comparative Political Systems, International Relations
One course from the following group:
*International Marketing Management, *Foreign Trade Management 3
Upper-level courses relating to International Studies (no more than six hours in any one area):
   Anthropology, Literature, Geography, History, Political Science, Sociology, basic courses in Art and Music, Computer Studies,
Language 12-30
Free Electives 30-42

*Courses starred represent those to be developed.

FIGURE 12.1. Utica College curricular proposal (Major in Business Administration).

Major in International Studies
(Bachelor of Arts Degree)
Behavioral Studies Division

The major in International Studies is designed to provide a cross-disciplinary background for those interested in careers that are concerned with parts of the world beyond the borders of their own country. Its goals are twofold: to give a broad cross-disciplinary background and to permit a secondary focus on the areas of anthropology area studies, international business, and the foreign service, and other fields. A minimum of six hours of a language is required for all majors.

Total credit hours required for degree: 120

Credit
Hours

ACADEMIC OPTIONS 27-36
(The following courses are recommended as supportive to this major: Accounting 101, Anthropology 101, Economics 141, Geography 154, History 202, Literature 205, 206, Music 225, Political Science 101, Psychology/Sociology 211.) International Studies World Survey required.

REQUIRED DISTRIBUTION FOR MAJOR 24
Six hours of upper-level courses relating to International Studies (or basic courses in Art and Music, Computer Studies and Language: Anthropology, Economics, English and Literature, Geography, History, Political Science, Sociology, Business, Science).

MINOR CONCENTRATION 24
Students may focus on one of the following sequences (or, with consultation with advisor, other fields).

Anthropology
Medical Anthropology 3
Area Studies 6
Upper Level Anthropology 15

Area Studies (Multi-Disciplinary)
Area Studies*
Africa, Asia, Europe, Latin America,
Middle East 24

International Education
Business Law 266 3
Corporation Finance 251 3
Marketing 3
International Trade 3
*Multi-National Corporations 3
Either *Comparative Economics 3
Or Economic Development 3
Either *International Marketing 3
Or *Foreign Trade
Either *Europe and the Third World 3
Or European Economic World
Community 3
Free Electives ....

Foreign Service
International Relations 3
International Organizations 3
From the following: 12
Comparative Political Systems
Comparative Economic Systems
International Trade
International Law
Economic Geography
Anthropology
East Asian International
Relations 3
European Economic Community 3
.... 36-45

*A minimum of 9 hours in one area required.
**Courses starred represent those to be developed.

FIGURE 12.2. Utica College curricular proposal (Major in International Studies).

course examines from a historical perspective the relationship of the cultural and political backgrounds of various peoples to international relations. The world survey course proved to be an important academic portal. By focusing on a region of the world other than the United States, and by examining it through the point of view of faculty specializing respectively in Asia, the Soviet Union, the United States, international economics, and international organization, the students were encouraged to explore cultural diversity intensively. Student evaluations of the course revealed significant enthusiasm for the team-taught seminar approach to the course.

Courses developed in the business division because of this new concentration were Foreign Trade Management and International Marketing. Also added was a cross-disciplinary course, the Political Economics of Multinational Corporations. These courses were tailored to fit an undergraduate curriculum.

In the Behavioral Studies division, most of the curricular refinement occurred in area studies. Faculty resources were adequate in African, American, Asian, and European studies. Gaps existed in the key cultural areas of Latin America and the Middle East. In 1980, certain improvements were initiated to correct the two deficient area studies. However, as size and resources dictate, a small college often has gaps in areas of international emphasis. Therefore, using outside academic, business, and government lecturers became an important ingredient in filling Utica College's area gaps.

During the first year, consultants on curriculum and international careers were numerous and diverse; all spoke in classes and symposia for students and faculty. There were consultants from multinational corporations, small exporting firms, major newspapers, state and federal governments, banks, universities, and research institutes. They discussed careers in export management, transnational law, international banking, journalism and marketing, foreign multinational corporations, and state and federal international employment. During its baptismal year, the international business management program at Utica College was saturated with VIPs who commanded the attention of the institution. Most important in this process was the sensitizing of a larger pool of students, faculty, and administrators not only to the new business component, but also to overall international studies.

Concurrent with curriculum development was expansion of library and map resources. The original request for federal funds and matching college support for these resources proved to be inadequate for program requirement. The Office of Education approved rechanneling of grant funds into these areas. Accordingly, Utica College was able to sponsor a workshop in International Traffic Management on 16 September 1978. The eight panelists included the chief traffic or export managers from medium-size companies such as Oneida Limited to large corporations such as General Electric. Also represented on the panel were presidents of shipping companies and personnel agencies. Attending the workshop were faculty from the Behavioral Studies and Business Division, international studies and business students, college administrators, and special guests from the community. The purpose of the workshop was to discuss the feasibility for Utica College to implement an international traffic program. The implementation of such a program under international studies, and as a part of international business, hinged on college resources and employment potential.

The most sensitive question was whether or not such a program would be more appropriately located in a community college. The technical courses in transportation and documentation could be offered in the first two years of college. Faculty and staff analyzed various international transportation program designs from associate degrees to certificates. The consensus was to examine the possibility of a consortia relationship.

In 1979, in conjunction with Key Bank of Central New York, Utica College presented its most technical foreign trade workshop. This workshop, called "Solving Your Export/Import Credit and Collection Problems," was the first to consider import topics. Specific agenda items on credit, documentation, letters of credit, customs, and correspondent bank relationships were presented and discussed in operational terms. The audience reacted favorably to the workshop because, as one of the businessmen stated, the workshop presented hard information, not "war stories." The International Business Program charged the business community a higher fee for this workshop and expected some complaints. However, there were no negative reactions to the higher cost; instead comparisons were made to similar workshops elsewhere that were ten times as costly. The businessmen felt the college had again provided them a valuable service at a nominal cost.

The second year of the International Business Program ended with course enrollments registering solid increases. Perhaps the most important factor accounting for the program's growth was increased student awareness. Publicity about the program through campus periodicals and the workshops were critical. Material on this new offering was sent to all faculty members as an information guide for student advising. A brochure on international studies at Utica College and the international business program was produced and included in student recruitment packets. The program was also highlighted in alumni periodicals. As the program became known, it became the responsibility of the director of international studies to validate its positive image.

THE DIRECTOR

The international studies directorship is unlike any other in the college because it is cross-divisional and includes its own language component. At

minimum, the director should have a smooth working relationship with the
Behavioral Studies and Business divisions, as well as the Humanities
division, which houses the traditional language department. The directorship is located in the Behavioral Studies division and, since its inception, all
of the directors have come from that division. As the director's activities
have expanded to include supervision of business and language programs,
there is flexibility to relocate the directorship to other divisions if deemed
advisable.

An effective director of international studies should have familiarity
with scholarship and academic leadership. The position of director should
also be rotated periodically. In addition, because international studies
require broad college support, there is need for larger faculty involvement
and leadership.

Strategies for the 1980s

Two developments at the beginning of the decade benefited international
studies. An Ethnic Heritage Program was created, enriching the Critical
Language offerings and deepening community relations. Additionally, an
outreach program in Middle East studies was developed with assistance
from Harvard University. This outreach program immediately produced
external support to expand college library resources and brought Middle
East scholars to the campus for seminars.

Critical language offerings in the 1970s ranged between two and four
courses with additional sections in some courses. It appears that with
renewed interest in Japanese, these tutor–tape courses should stabilize at
three or four offerings per semester. To conform to NASILP standards,
classes are kept small. The most difficult task for the director is
maintaining tutor quality, especially when a new language is being
presented. However, this program does allow a small institution like Utica
to broaden its spectrum of available languages.

Close relations with the Humanities division and its language
instructors will be continued. In the late 1970s, as Russian language
enrollment declined in the Humanities division, an agreement was reached
to relocate Russian in the Critical Language Program. The advice and
participation of traditional language faculty members in critical languages
will be sought.

Course development within the International Business Program should
witness less growth than during its inception. The most recent addition to
the curriculum is an elective entitled Business Policy. This course, open
only to seniors, deals with business policy making and administration from
the viewpoint of top management. Case problems in international business
are among the major topics. The course instructor, a specialist in
international marketing, has fashioned it along colloquia and seminar lines.
The class hold weekly luncheon seminars with foreign and American

business executives. These executives also share time with other faculty and students, as well as college administrators and members of the outside business community.

In the planning stage at this time is a short intensive overseas seminar program. Juniors and seniors in the International Business Program would be able to visit overseas firms and attend a series of briefings on marketing, management, public relations, and trade operations. This program would take place during intersession or the summer. Based on cost factors, time allotments, and the number of firms to be involved, the first pilot program would be most suitably centered in one or two countries of Western Europe. At least one more year of planning is required.

CONSORTIA

One of the promising areas of development for Utica College's International Studies Program is in linkage with the local two-year college, Mohawk Valley Community College (M.V.C.C.). M.V.C.C. initiated an international studies program in the Fall 1980. The A.A. degree program prepares students to transfer to a four-year program in business, humanities, or social science with an international orientation. The college also provides training in a European language.

Since 1972 Utica College has had a formal academic transfer policy with M.V.C.C. These two institutions have been operating in a close consortium arrangement during these years. Therefore, developing a more intimate relationship regarding international studies programs would be an important refinement in achieving academic compatibility. The colleges are only four miles apart and are both located in Utica. Large numbers of M.V.C.C. graduates transfer to Utica College to complete their undergraduate studies and faculty and administrators at both schools have always had cordial working relationships.

Planning and coordinating international programs with M.V.C.C. has reached the point of mutual grant submissions. Utica College has begun discussing with the M.V.C.C. administration the feasibility of their designing an International Traffic Management program. Fusing the first two years of technical traffic courses with Utica College's International Business concentration could provide the student with an excellent undergraduate academic base. The emergence of this combination degree program would be the major elaboration of the international business curriculum over the next few years. As a prelude to shaping this program, a pilot course entitled International Business Policy Seminar is being proposed. In an effort to integrate the classroom work pursued in both Utica College and M.V.C.C. programs, this seminar would focus on how various pieces of the international trade puzzle fit together. At this juncture both M.V.C.C. and Utica College are serious about creating bonds.

PROGRAM VITALITY

Although the additions to the college's original international business program already described are exciting, the original core program must remain healthy. The basic curriculum, the workshops, internships, and advisory components are key elements in Utica College's program, which require adequate resources to function. These resources are the director, the faculty, and college and community supports.

In order to perform adequately the director must continue to have a reduced teaching schedule. Faculty sabbaticals, transfers, and leaves present problems both in recruitment and temporary employment. Obtaining quality instructors with the credentials and training to service international study needs at a small college, especially in the fields of economics and business, is a considerable challenge. Utica College is aided in this complicated situation by two factors: the existence of interdivisional search committees for vacancies, and the cooperation of the main campus. Syracuse University has been helpful in providing support faculty when necessary.

Continued financial support by Utica College of its International Studies program through underwriting of the Critical Language Program, expansion of library resources (in particular, trade journals) and support of travel and workshop projects is of utmost importance. Support from the outside community is presently linked to an overall college capital campaign. The business community's perception of the college has been enhanced by the introduction of the International Business Program. The circle of business connections has also been expanded by the program and should prove important by their support of college development.

There is little doubt that American business requires personnel for international operations. If America expects to compete effectively in international commerce, businesses must have a management cadre attuned to foreign cultures and business methods. An undergraduate international business concentration tied to an overall international studies program might be one start in the right direction in preparing such management. The need for trained personnel is evident, but the awareness and commitment of American higher education and the business community are necessary to bridge the gap. Utica College's modest International Business Program finds its operation an exciting challenge.

Note

1. The initial agreement to establish programs of this kind was the Kirkland College, which was absorbed by Hamilton College in the late 1970s.

CHAPTER 13

Emory University

KENNETH W. STEIN

ONE OF EMORY UNIVERSITY'S STATED OBJECTIVES is to expose its students to a culture other than their own. The Emory Center for International Studies (ECIS) helps students open their minds to other peoples and other cultures through special programs and course development. The program also serves many people in addition to students. The development of syllabi and bibliographies help faculty members broaden their courses; and many people in the Atlanta community take part in ECIS programs.

The University and the Community

The Emory Center for International Studies enriches the entire Atlanta community, of which Emory University is an important part. The Emory campus is located ten minutes from downtown Atlanta, a busy metropolis that has witnessed unprecedented growth during the past decade. An increasing number of foreign banks and thirty-five consulates have made their home in Atlanta. Hartsfield Airport, which opened in September 1980, is the busiest international airport in the country, serving seven international airlines. Emory is therefore in an excellent position to share Atlanta's growing international role.

For more than a century, Emory College—which was founded in 1836—has been considered one of the principal private colleges in the Southeast. Originally located in Oxford, Georgia, it was moved in 1915 to a new campus in Atlanta. Today, Emory College is the coeducational undergraduate arts and sciences school of Emory University. The other components of Emory University are the professional schools of business, dentistry, law, medicine, nursing, and theology; the graduate school of arts and sciences; and a two-year college on the original campus at Oxford.

Emory College students choose Emory because of its excellent academic reputation. As of September 1982, Emory College had enrolled approximately 3,100 students, and there were approximately 5,000 more students engaged in study in the eight other schools of Emory University. Each successive incoming class at Emory College has steadily increased in size since 1975, a growth that has necessitated concurrent increases in the number of faculty positions, course offerings, and campus programs. Forty-four percent of the student body comes from Georgia, 22 percent from other southeastern states, and the remaining 34 percent from outside the region and from foreign countries. More than 70 percent of Emory College graduates continue their education—in law, the health care professions, and other kinds of graduate study.

As determined by questionnaires administered to incoming Emory freshmen, students' knowledge about different regions of the world varies widely, and their ability to answer questions correctly is particularly influenced by travel abroad and high school courses on international affairs. From its inception in July 1979, the Emory Program in International Studies (now ECIS) has done much to reduce student parochialism and has increased awareness about global issues among students as well as in the community at large. During the past four years, the large attendance at ECIS events has demonstrated the increased student interest in global affairs.

The faculty of Emory College includes 239 full-time faculty members on regular appointment, ninety-eight percent of whom hold a doctoral degree. More than twenty-five percent of the full-time faculty members in Emory College are directly involved in some aspect of international, global, or area studies as their primary teaching and research commitment. Approximately one-third of the recent additions to the Emory faculty are associated with International Studies and are graduates of the National Defense Education Act (NDEA) Center. More than two-thirds of the fifty faculty members associated with ECIS are tenured. Three of the faculty members associated with the center hold university chairs.

The community resource base in Atlanta has broadly strengthened ECIS programing efforts. Local consulates, the print and electronic media, and other institutions in the city committed to international affairs have repeatedly cooperated with ECIS in coordinating programs. For example, consular officials have aided ECIS in sponsoring cultural programs such as a presentation of Japanese music, a German film festival, and lectures, and an outcome of this type of cooperation has been discussions between ECIS and various consulates during the past two years to establish faculty exchange programs with German, Japanese, and Chinese institutions of higher education. Both the *Atlanta Journal* and the *Atlanta Constitution* regularly send reporters to cover programs sponsored by ECIS, and visiting specialists sponsored by ECIS provide radio and television interviews and give background briefings to the editorial boards of both major newspapers.

Local organizations that have helped sponsor and announce ECIS programs have included Atlanta Church Women United, the International Ladies Garment Workers Union–Southeast Region, the League of Women Voters, the NAACP–Atlanta Branch, the Southern Center for International Studies, Spelman College, the Global Studies Program at the University of Georgia, the Experiment in International Living, the American Friends Service Committee, the Goethe Institute, the Foreign Policy Association, the Center for Disease Control, the Atlanta Historical Society, the World Congress Center, and a dozen other labor, civic, religious, and education organizations and institutions in Atlanta. The Bureau of Public Affairs at the US State Department in Washington, DC frequently assists ECIS in programing lectures, conferences, and symposia.

Institutional Commitment to International Education

Emory's commitment to international education is perhaps best exemplified by its inclusion of knowledge of another culture as one of its stated curriculum objectives and undergraduate requirements. Indeed, the Emory Center for International Studies is a direct outgrowth of that objective and requirement. The program has a full-time staff headed by a faculty director who reports directly to the dean of Emory College.

INSTITUTIONAL OBJECTIVES AND REQUIREMENTS

There is a collective commitment by the administration of Emory University and the faculty of Emory College to continue qualitative academic growth over the next several decades. In October 1976, the Emory College faculty articulated fifteen specific curriculum objectives and undergraduate uniform requirements:

1. The ability to organize and express ideas effectively in English, especially in written form

2. The foundation of the ability to organize and express ideas in a way other than English

3. An understanding of the modes of inquiry that characterize mathematics and the natural sciences

4. An understanding of the modes of inquiry that characterize the social sciences

5. An understanding of the methods of identifying, interpreting, and evaluating ideas that characterize the humanities

6. A historical understanding of Western civilization

7. The capacity to make informed responses to questions of value, moral responsibility, and the ultimate meaning of life

8. The capacity to comprehend, appreciate, and evaluate the creative arts

9. Knowledge of a culture other than one's own

10. An understanding of the self

11. Knowledge of the nature of the contemporary society, especially in the United States

12. Knowledge of the natural world

13. Knowledge of physical health and recreation

14. Knowledge of some depth of a particular academic discipline

15. An awareness of the ways in which the cooperation of different disciplines can contribute to the solution of problems

To fulfill these objectives, a student must complete 128 semester hours of academic work, with one-third of the courses distributed among six specific areas of uniform requirements:

1. Tools of Learning

2. Natural Science and Mathematics

3. Historical Perspective of the Western World

4. Individual and Society

5. Aesthetics and Values

6. Health and Physical Education

Subsequent to the introduction of uniform requirements, foreign language enrollment increased dramatically. In addition, the faculty expressed the need to heighten global awareness when it adopted the undergraduate uniform requirements, and it indicated that increased course offerings and study abroad were two ways to achieve this goal.

The paragraph explaining the ninth objective of the fifteen curriculum objectives of the undergraduate uniform requirements for a liberal arts education at Emory—knowledge of a culture other than one's own—gives the rationale behind the requirement:

> In order to live creatively in a culture, one must not only understand it from within, but have some perspective on it from without. In a world ever more closely interdependent, it is essential that students develop an understanding of peoples and settings different from their own. Such cross-cultural understanding can never be complete, but a realistic objective for an undergraduate education would be that students acquire a knowlege of at least one national or ethnic culture significantly different from their own. Ideally, meeting such an objective would include a period of study on location within the culture; however, it is clearly not feasible at present for the College to require such a period of study, so this objective could be met by sources that focus on an appropriate area.

The faculty concluded this statement by asserting that the international dimension of general education at Emory College had to be strengthened to guard against cultural and national insularity.

The faculty of the 1980s is still concerned that students be prepared to understand the impact of global affairs on their daily lives and that they attain fresh perspectives on their own cultural assumptions. At a college where students primarily define their interests as preprofessional, courses with global, area, or cross-cultural emphases strengthen academic preparation and enable graduates to be better informed in making career decisions.

The Emory Program in International Studies, now ECIS, was established in July 1979 to fulfill the stated objectives of Emory's faculty and administration through the following means:

- Increasing the number of courses offered

- Increasing or revising the international component of existing courses

- Contributing to faculty development

- Encouraging student participation in study abroad programs

- Fostering student awareness about global issues through additional centralized programing

- Enhancing international studies understanding among the general public

How the International Program Was Established

During the last seventeen years, Emory's attention to issues of international concern has grown dramatically. In 1964, Emory College offered only seventeen undergraduate courses in five departments (excluding foreign language courses) that had specific relevance to the global contemporary world. Now Emory College offers ninety-four such courses in ten different departments, including foreign languages. Thirteen new faculty positions that pertain exclusively to global or area studies have been created since 1966, twelve of them in the last five years. The president and the executive vice-president of Emory University and the dean of Emory College are all interested in world and international affairs.

The atmosphere at Emory was thus quite congenial in 1978 when the Department of Health, Education, and Welfare decided to use federal funds to encourage international programs and centers in parts of the country that had not had them before. The Emory Program in International Studies was established in July 1979, when Emory received a NDEA title VI grant of $72,000 for the period 1979–81. In 1981, ECIS was created out of the Emory Program in International Studies. ECIS received a NDEA title VI grant of $202,000 for the period 1981–83.

In the last four years, because of retirements, three new deans have been appointed in the Graduate School, the Business School, and Emory College. Each has enthusiastically committed time and budgetary allotments to the development of ECIS, and each supports ECIS activities.

The commitment to educating Emory students on international and global issues is not merely at the upper level of the administration; the commitment is institutionwide under the leadership of the current president. In an address to the faculty on November 8, 1978, university president James T. Laney stated his conviction that "Emory is destined to be a world class university by the year 2000." A capital funds drive was subsequently authorized to realize that objective. Then in November 1979, in a stunning and unprecedented endorsement of higher education in general, and Emory in particular, the Woodruff Foundation presented Emory with the largest single gift ever made to any university. The president's active and personal involvement in programs sponsored by ECIS reaffirms the entire administration's commitment to the philosophy and goals of the program and is combined with faculty support, interest, and commitment.

PROGRAM GOALS AND OBJECTIVES

The Emory Center for International Studies has the following goals and objectives:

Goals:

1. Course development
2. Increase in faculty positions

3. Programing: lectures, conferences, lunches, symposia, film festivals, and special events

4. Program administration

5. Evaluation of students' knowledge of international studies

Objectives:

1. To expand the undergraduate curriculum and improve the quality of general education at Emory by offering ten new or revised courses in international studies.

2. To increase the number of faculty positions in international studies.

3. To encourage and increase cross-cultural sensitivity among Emory students, faculty members, and staff members.

4. To develop awareness and understanding among Emory's students of the implications of global events on their lives and careers. For most, this perspective may be their only contact with global issues between now and when they complete their professional training in three to six years.

5. To foster a sense of community and the value of international education among Emory faculty members and other faculty members in Atlanta and Georgia who specialize in international studies.

ADMINISTRATIVE ORGANIZATION AND PROGRAM STAFFING

To a large extent, the program's success in achieving these goals depends on the experience, creativity, and drive of its administrators—a faculty director, a full-time program coordinator, and a secretary-assistant.

The director of ECIS reports directly to the dean of Emory College, as if the center were a regular course-offering and degree-conferring department. However, ECIS is not a department. It does not list courses in the catalog nor does it confer a degree. Instead, it functions as an administrative umbrella, and it acts as a catalytic agent for international studies. The dean of Emory College in turn reports to the vice-president for academic affairs.

The faculty director plays the central role in implementing the center's program. He works closely with the faculty, the administration, and the program coordinator to effect the program's success. The director's responsibilities include supervising the smooth introduction of proposed courses into the undergraduate curriculum; regulating the expenditure of funds for all center activities; organizing lecture series, conferences, luncheons, and special events in conjunction with the program coordinator and other faculty members; seeking additional sources of outside funding to augment future program development; establishing contacts with other relevant organizations and institutions in Atlanta and the Southeast; and producing and moderating the center's semimonthly Public Television program on Georgia entitled "World in Review." The director has half-time teaching responsibilities in the History Department so that he can supervise the center properly.

The program coordinator works closely with the faculty director in supervising program activities. This person handles publicity, logistical arrangements, and mailings for all activities; is responsible for evaluating ECIS through questionnaires and other means; and disseminates course bibliographies and syllabi to appropriate faculty members at other postsecondary education institutions in Georgia. Through an international studies newsletter and program brochures, the program coordinator maintains liaison between Emory's faculty members and students and interested community members and schools in Atlanta, Georgia, and the nation.

Supporting the activities of the faculty director and the program coordinator is a secretary who serves as receptionist and typist and maintains the filing system and financial records. The three staff members work together to insure smooth functioning of the program.

Program Description

To date, the Emory Center for International Studies has focused its activities in four major areas: introducing new or revised courses with an emphasis on international, area, or world studies; developing programs aimed at enriching the international awareness of Emory students and community members; evaluating incoming students' knowledge of international studies through a questionnaire; and reaching out to the general public interested in International Affairs. The center relies heavily on faculty participation and linkages with many administrative offices. Funding comes from the institution and federal grants.

COURSE DEVELOPMENT

One of the five goals of the original grant proposal of 1979 was to introduce into the Emory College curriculum twenty-three new or revised courses with an area, world, or international studies emphasis. Eighteen such courses were developed by fifteen faculty members during the summers of 1979 and 1980. More than fifty-seven professors from other postsecondary education institutions, primarily in Georgia, benefited in some manner from this course development project. Almost half of all postsecondary education institutions in the state requested course bibliographies and syllabi.

The courses introduced at Emory were developed in seven departments by faculty members who had the necessary research, archival, and linguistic skills but who required several months of free time to acquaint themselves with the current literature in their particular fields of new course interest. Courses were introduced in the following areas:

1. Economics: Seminar in Business–Society Relationships in Selected Market Countries (Japan, Sweden, France, Brazil, Israel, and West Germany)

2. History: World War II in Europe and After; Imperialism and Dependency in the Third World; Africa Before the Europeans: Dark Continent of Kingdoms of Light; Africa in the Modern World; and Introduction to the Modern Near East, 1798–1977.

3. Political Science: Political Violence, Science, and Technology: The Impact on International Relations; Latin American Politics; Introduction to International Relations; US–Latin-American Relations; and Government and Politics of China

4. Anthropology: Comparative Economic Systems

5. Sociology: The Sociology of Forced Change: The Nazi Conquest of Eastern Europe and Its Aftermath; and Contemporary East Asia: Societies and Institutions

6. Modern Languages: Artistic Forms of Social Protest in Latin America

7. Religion: Seminar in Asian Religion: Religion, Culture, and Politics in South Asia; and Modernization and Traditional Religious Culture

FACULTY PARTICIPATION

The creation of ECIS stimulated departments within both Emory College and the university as a whole to augment their faculty with additional positions, some of which cover international or area studies. Since September 1979, the director of ECIS has steadily worked with the deans of Emory College and the graduate schools and members of the Art

History, Economics, Political Science, History, Philosophy, Religion, and Romance Languages Departments to identify funding incentives for hiring faculty members with international focuses.

The Modern Languages and Classics Department has hired a second Hebraist and a part-time faculty member to teach Arabic; the Economics Department has hired a specialist in African Economics, and the Philosophy Department will soon hire a professor whose specialty is Medieval Arab Logic. In the 1979/80 academic year, the History and Political Science Departments, in keeping with a growing student interest in international studies, requested additional faculty positions for the year. The Political Science Department hired an assistant professor to teach international and Latin American politics, and the History Department hired a specialist in African affairs. Finally, Emory's Graduate School is now led by a nationally recognized Sovietologist who is energetically commited to the Emory Center for International Studies.

Faculty involvement with ECIS and its sponsored activities takes place in numerous other ways as well. Acting both as participants and resources, faculty members attend lectures, conferences, luncheons, symposia, and special events, and their importance to such ECIS programing is crucial. Not only is ECIS dedicated to increasing the number of faculty members who deal with international subjects, but it also helps fund faculty development of new courses that deal with world interests and therefore increase the international emphasis at Emory. ECIS funds are also used to assist faculty who will be giving papers at international conferences.

The fifty faculty members associated with ECIS have strong backgrounds, as evidenced by their publications, positions held in professional organizations, major fellowships received, participation in international conferences, and editorial activity for scholarly publications. Twenty-two of the fifty faculty members have held or are currently holding positions in professional associations and organizations. Since 1979, seventeen faculty members have received major fellowships. They include Andrew W. Mellon Post-Doctoral Fellowships; grants from the National Endowment for the Humanities; Woodrow Wilson Fellowships; Fulbright–Hayes Fellowships; Ford Foundation grants and fellowships; and grants from the National Institute of Mental Health. Twenty-two faculty members have participated in international conferences since 1970, and thirty-four faculty members have been or are currently engaged in editorial activity for scholarly publications.

The faculty members associated with the program have carried out archival research in more than twenty-five countries in Eastern and Western Europe, the Soviet Union, Africa, Latin America, the Middle East, and East Asia. In addition to research in all the modern Western European languages (except the Scandinavian languages), the faculty has engaged in research using more than twenty other languages, including Akadian, Aramaic, Arabic, Catalan, Chinese, Hausa, Hebrew, Hungarian, Japanese,

Korean, Latin, Nepali, Old Occitan, Polish, Russian, Serbo-Croatian, Sherpa, Tibetan, Ugaritic, and Ukranian.

PROGRAMING

To help students appreciate the implications of global events and issues in their lives, a systematic plan to develop student awareness has been planned, implemented, and evaluated. The programs sponsored by ECIS have captured the attention of the entire campus, as shown by heavy attendance at lecture programs, at Russian, Japanese, and German film festivals, and at luncheons, conferences, and special programs.

No other program on the Emory campus focuses specifically on international and global affairs. No other program offers the student body such a wide range of international programing. ECIS has implemented a comprehensive program in international studies, making sure that proposed lectures coincide with new course offerings, that lectures and conferences relate directly with specific faculty and student interests, and that luncheons provide a meaningful interchange of ideas. All programing is coordinated with other Emory College and Emory University activities (such as summer programs in interdisciplinary programs) and coordinated whenever possible with other activities and organizations in the Atlanta metropolitan area.

Only persons with proven expertise are brought to Emory to participate in ECIS programing. During each of the two academic semesters, at least one lecture is scheduled on contemporary events and supplemented with additional lectures of diverse topical content. Each academic year, a one-day conference is held, centered on a contemporary issue. In 1980, the conference was on terrorism; in 1981, energy.

Each academic year, a major special event of college, community, and public interest is organized. In 1979, for example, a debate concentrating on the merits and liabilities of SALT-2 with Admiral Elmo Zumwalt (con) and Mr. William Colby (pro), moderated by Emory University president James T. Laney, was held. The debate was subsequently rebroadcast by National Public Radio in Atlanta.

As another example, in May 1981 ECIS hosted a symposium on the hostage crisis in Iran. The participants were Colonel Charles Scott, a former hostage; Mr. Hamilton Jordan, former White House Chief of Staff for President Jimmy Carter and currently a Resource Fellow at Emory University; and Mr. Henry Precht, an Emory alumnus and former Country Director for Iran at the US State Department. The CBS affiliate in Atlanta taped portions of the symposium for later airing.

ECIS provides to foreign embassies in Washington and foreign consulates in Atlanta an excellent academic setting for scholars, politicians, diplomats, and other professionals seeking an opportunity to make presentations. In 1979/80, more than thirty-one embassies without a representative in Atlanta were contacted in an effort to have qualified speakers from their countries come to Emory. The People's Republic of China responded by sending its ambassador to the United Nations in April 1981. Turkey's ambassador to the United States made a presentation under ECIS sponsorship a year earlier. One reason ECIS is able to sponsor guest speakers who come to Atlanta is that its costs are often shared with Spelman College, the US State Department, and the Southern Center for International Studies.

A unique feature of ECIS is its semimonthly television program, "World in Review," seen on the nine Georgia Public Television Stations. The program uses local and visiting experts to discuss world affairs, global problems, and international political and economic issues. Topics exclusively of international import are discussed, sometimes with a program designated for a particular issue such as world food shortages, US–German relations, succession in the Soviet Union, the Falkland Islands crisis, the labor movement in Poland, and others. More than 40,000 people see this program in Georgia on the first and third Fridays of each month.

The most important forum for presenting ECIS programs is the monthly newsletter, which is sent to more than 1,500 people. Through the newsletter, the general public as well as the campus community is kept abreast of ECIS programing and news. Not only does the newsletter provide a calendar of events, it also contains information about lectures, programs, and other presentations in Atlanta and throughout the South of interest to all who care about international events. The general public is urged to attend all ECIS programs and activities.

Other forms of publicity include flyers that are posted on campus for each event, and telephone calls to interested organizations. A news release on each ECIS event or activity is sent to Emory News Services to be distributed to all local media.

EVALUATION OF STUDENTS' KNOWLEDGE OF INTERNATIONAL STUDIES

One of the tasks of the center is to evaluate students' knowledge about international studies. A student questionnaire was devised to obtain information about students' understanding of international studies. Students' knowledge of various world areas, important persons, foreign language ability and exposure, and travel experience were ascertained. Whereas one student was able to answer all seventy-eight questions correctly, most students displayed a much spottier level of knowledge. Students' ability to answer questions correctly was influenced by foreign travel and high school courses on international affairs.

The students' knowledge about different regions of the world varied widely, with questions on Asia answered correctly more often than those of any other region of the world; 66 percent of the students answered more than half of these questions correctly. The least familiar region was Africa, where only 20 percent of the students answered more than half of the questions correctly. On the whole, students were more acquainted with famous persons than with geography.

The information gleaned from the questionnaire will not only provide a profile of entering freshmen, but more importantly, it will help ECIS develop appropriate programing. Continuous monitoring of students' ability and shortcomings will enable ECIS to recommend the addition of salient features to existing courses and to identify areas where course development and additional programing are needed to create a comprehensive range of subject matter in international studies. As a result of the findings from the first questionnaire, ECIS has suggested to many of its faculty members that they include in their courses a geography exericse, if one is not already present in the syllabus for the course. A similar student questionnaire was administered to the incoming class in September 1982.

CAMPUS LINKAGES

The Emory Center for International Studies has important linkages with several groups on the Emory Campus.

Leading administrators involved in the program's planning and implementation include the president of the university, the vice-president for academic affairs, and the deans of the Graduate School and the School of Business Administration. Financial matters are handled through the Comptroller's Office, and the associate dean of Emory College is responsible for monitoring external grants. Year abroad programs as well as summer abroad programs are monitored and coordinated by the dean of summer school programs in Emory College. ECIS also works with the Information Services Office, the public information branch of the university, which disseminates notices, reports, stories, and announcements of ECIS activities.

ECIS often assists and cosponsors various programs with departments and schools throughout the Emory campus. In turn, various deans have enthusiastically committed time and budgetary allotments to the development of international studies.

Because one goal of ECIS is to introduce new or revised courses with an area, world, or international studies emphasis into Emory College curriculum, the college's curriculum committee is another important linkage. Following development, courses must be submitted to the curriculum committee for acceptance into the general curriculum.

Funding

In July 1979, when the Emory Program in International Studies (EPIS) was established, Emory College was the recipient of $72,000 over a period of two years under a Department of Education grant. In July 1981, the same program, renamed the Emory Center for International Studies (ECIS), received $202,000 over a two-year period, again from the Department of Education. Federal funding is utilized for faculty and administrative salaries, faculty stipends for summer course development, and programing (lectures, conferences, and special programs).

From July 1979 through February 1981 EPIS sponsored more than eighty programs with an attendance of more than 5,500. The dollar amount spent for programing, which is a portion of Emory's contribution to the program, was approximately $4,000. Put differently, EPIS spent an average of $52 per event, excluding publicity and administrative costs, or approximately seventy-five cents per person attending each event.

Another cost-benefit analysis pertains to course development. The bibliographies and syllabi developed for the Emory undergraduate curriculum are funded in part by title VI funds. Eighteen new or revised courses have been designed, and syllabi have been distributed on request to professors at twenty-seven institutions throughout Georgia and elsewhere. The approximately 21,550 students at these institutions are therefore potential beneficiaries of the $27,000 spent to develop these courses. Half of this sum came from Emory's contribution and half from the government grant. In tax dollars alone, only seventy-three cents per student were spent to enrich his or her curriculum with international, world, and area studies courses.

Future Development

From 1979 to the present, EPIS and then ECIS have been unqualified successes. Their diverse efforts to make the Emory environment more international have been favorably received and vigorously supported by Emory students, faculty members, and staff members, as well as citizens from the Atlanta community and around the state. The impact of the program as gauged by the number of participants at ECIS sponsored events is far greater than originally anticipated.

A coordinated effort by competent personnel will, however, be required to maintain student awareness of global interdependence and to familiarize students with the concepts and axioms that will affect their lives. There will be six areas of program activities: course development, lectures, conferences, film series, informal gatherings, and outreach functions such as workshops and television programs.

Emory College provides funding for supplies, dissemination of bibliographies and syllabi, staff travel, partial support for faculty and administrative salaries, and faculty stipends for summer course development. The college's contribution is 70 percent of the estimated cost. In addition, Emory spends $250,000 each year for library acquisitions in international, global, or area studies. Programing will focus on the intricate interrelationships that characterize world problems and issues. In addition, faculty exchange programs may be established with foreign universities.

CHAPTER 14

Pacific Lutheran University

MORDECHAI ROZANSKI

The University and the Community

Pacific Lutheran University (PLU) is located in Tacoma, Washington, forty-five miles south of Seattle. It was founded in 1890, became a private, four-year liberal arts college in 1941, and was chartered as a university with undergraduate and graduate programs in 1960.

The growth in the size and quality of the university has also been reflected in its faculty and student populations. In spring 1981, PLU employed 204 full-time and 65 part-time faculty and enrolled 3,168 undergraduate and 308 graduate students. International and minority students represent about 12 percent of the campus population.

FACULTY

Expansion and selective recruitment have brought PLU a young (of an average age under forty) and increasingly diverse faculty. Some eleven faculty members are foreign-born; twenty-five faculty members (12 percent of the full-time faculty) have recently participated in overseas experiences as scholars, teachers, and study abroad directors; and PLU's international programs have grown in number and quality over the last five years, some fifty faculty have been involved as instructors of new or revised courses or as general program participants on campus and abroad.

STUDENTS

The PLU student body is composed in large part of Pacific Northwest and California residents; about half identify themselves with the Lutheran church. And as a private, residential institution (where 1,720 students live on campus) with costs for tuition, room, and board approaching $6,500 per year, PLU attracts many students from middle-income families. To some extent, these characteristics give the typical PLU student a somewhat narrow cultural and regional perspective. This judgment is shared by the students themselves.

In a 1976/77 survey of over 500 students (conducted as part of an international education needs assessment), PLU students frankly admitted to being somewhat parochial: Few had taken courses about foreign peoples and nations, few had traveled beyond their homes, and only a small number were proficient in foreign languages. However, more than 96 percent of the students sampled decried this state of affairs and strongly endorsed a plan to strengthen the international dimensions of general education at PLU. The plan that was implemented includes new international majors and minors, some 60 new and revised courses, extensive study abroad, and various on- and off-campus international programs. In 1980/81, over 1,400 students enrolled in international courses and more than 4,000 people participated in cocurricular international offerings.

COMMUNITY RESOURCES

Made up of diverse ethnic groups and over 300 foreign-owned or internationally oriented business firms, the local community provides tangible support and stimulus to the university's area studies, cultural studies, and international business programs.

Among PLU's most important ethnic communities have been the Scandinavian and the Asian. Scandinavians have played a special role in the history of PLU; they helped found the university and have sustained it through the years as students, teachers, alumni, financial supporters, and friends. This special relationship has extended beyond Washington state to Scandinavia itself. PLU has instituted exchange programs, has been visited by the King of Norway, by government leaders, and by other important personages. These traditions, relationships, and encounters have all contributed to the thriving Scandinavian Area Studies program (which will be discussed later).

Similarly, and most recently, the growth of the Asian community has fostered programmatic development focusing on China and Japan in PLU's four-year-old Foreign Area Studies Program. The Asian community has become the largest ethnic group in western Washington. Asians have added cultural richness, energy, and economic vitality to the pioneering tradition of the Pacific Northwest. PLU's Minority Affairs Office has established strong relationships with this diverse ethnic community and sponsored several programs including an annual Intercultural Fair.

The burgeoning international business activities of Puget Sound has also provided PLU with a special support for its various international programs—especially its international business programs. International trade has become Washington's primary employer; one of every five jobs involves international trade. This represents over 300,000 jobs, including 60 percent of all jobs in agriculture. In fact, while Washington ranks twenty-second among US states in population, it is first both in total international trade and in per capita international trade. Two-way trade generated over $21 billion in 1980/81. Moreover, this two-way trade has increased an average of 20 percent during the last two years. Foreign investment has also played a major role, infusing the area with $650 million and establishing 212 foreign-controlled firms and over 10,000 jobs. It is little wonder that Washington has become one of the major centers of international trade, particularly with Asia as a special focus of that trade.

The intensity of this international trade activity has fostered international program development at PLU. In curricular terms, it has been a stimulus to the Foreign Area Studies Program's International Trade minor, to the School of Business Administration's new three-year internationalization program, and to the innovative foreign language courses being developed for business and travel use. In cocurricular terms it has been a rich resource providing consultants, speakers, occasional financial support (through workshops and conferences held for the business community) and, most importantly, internship and employment opportunities for PLU's international studies students.

Historical Development of the International Program

The First Stage (to 1970). PLU's international programs evolved in three incremental stages from 1970 to 1980. The first stage began well before 1970 and was marked by sporadic developments. As with most small private universities, PLU was focused on issues of mission, faculty recruitment and enhancement, core curricula, and funding. International education was at best a serendipitous development, emerging incidentally and accidentally as a concomitant of institutional growth and external stimuli.

Principal areas of international development included study abroad programs (the instrument and preserve of the foreign language department) and foreign students (an early PLU acknowledgement of the diversity of the world that also helped balance the budget). These first steps were cautious and small; growth was by accretion rather than by calculation. Curricular development in international studies was limited to the typical offerings of the Departments of History, Political Science, and Foreign Languages, and new courses emerged primarily with new faculty.

The Second Stage (1970-76). While the first stage largely reflected informal initiatives and development, the second stage was marked by several institutional initiatives which created two structural innovations in intercultural and international programs. These two innovations were the Ethnic and Non-Western Studies Program and the Scandinavian Area Studies Major.

Among the two most important factors influencing this second stage were first, the encroachment of national and international events on the campus, and second, a new group of institutional leaders, including a new provost, who responded with sensitivity and political acumen to the emerging pressures of diversity and change.

The early 1970s were somewhat traumatic for PLU. Largely introspective, conservative, and middle-class, the institution had escaped much of the turmoil of the Vietnam and civil rights movements. But this isolation ended in the early 1970s when both Vietnam and the "black activism" movement penetrated PLU as minority enrollment and students' political consciousness rose. The resulting agitation, while comparatively tame, upset the institution's splendid isolation and stimulated faculty and administrative reactions that led to the Ethnic and Non-Western Studies Program.

Established in 1972, this program represented a compromise between minority students' demands for a black studies program and the provost's and faculty's desire for a broader, more generic curriculum serving the entire university. Unfortunately, the Ethnic Studies Program was largely stillborn. Its goals were unclear, if not confusing, and its purpose largely political and palliative. Moreover, its leadership suffered from isolation and an inadequate support system within the curriculum and among a largely homogeneous group of students and faculty. Not surprisingly, when the political crisis waned, so did the program.

The other program to emerge during this second stage was Scandinavian Studies. Its origins were partly influenced by the rising ethnic self-consciousness that minority students had fostered, but more importantly, its origins reflected the sustained traditions and curricular offerings of the university's Scandinavian heritage. In 1975, Scandinavian Area Studies became a multidisciplinary major focusing on language, literature, philosophy, and history. The initiative came from the Humanities Division and the provost strongly supported it.

The Third Stage (1976-81). This stage was marked by a focused and coherent effort to establish and institutionalize a multidisciplinary international studies curricular program. The major impetus for this effort came from the new head of the Social Sciences Division, who believed that PLU needed to expand its curricular and cultural horizons.

BUILDING THE PLU INTERNATIONAL STUDIES PROGRAM.

The Role of Administrators.   The first step was taken in 1976 when the division head won the provost's support for a new Asian position in the History Department. This new position went beyond merely expanding the horizons of the department. The goal was to recruit an energetic and politically astute program-builder who could use this area studies training as a base for the larger effort. The person hired had taught Chinese History at a small private college and thus understood the political dynamics of private institutions. Moreover, he had initiated a interdisciplinary non-Western studies program at his former college. The department chairman gave the new professor both a written mandate to build a non-Western studies program and access to a support structure that included the division's budget, the divisional chair's authority, and a network of sympathetic divisional faculty and administrators.

While the divisional chair's role was pivotal, the provost was also crucial because he sanctioned the divisional mandate and added his political clout. He believed that a comprehensive international studies program involving foreign languages, area studies, and global issues was essential both for citizen education and as an integral part of PLU's liberal arts commitment. Elaborating on this viewpoint later in a published interview, the provost declared, "We have ignored the world to our disadvantage. We do not know and understand well many peoples and cultures around the globe. This condition originated, in part, because of educational failures that included the decline in the study of foreign languages. The result was a lack of awareness of the rest of the world." [1]

This deficiency had to be remedied, and the provost was prepared to support the new international studies effort originating in the social sciences. The importance of such a perspective by the chief academic officer cannot be overemphasized. The provost clearly supported international education for its intrinsic merits, but he also shared an appreciation for the instrumental role that international studies could play in enhancing the university's curriculum and quality. This larger institutional perspective of international studies has been one of the central factors in the rapid development of an international studies program at PLU.

While administrative and other internal support was essential to the program, external factors clearly stimulated events. Thus, when the Asian historian was hired, a grant proposal was submitted to the Fund for the

Improvement of Post-Secondary Education (FIPSE) to underwrite a three-year comprehensive program (which included international studies) to revitalize the social sciences. Awarded in 1976, this grant provided some seed money and an external impetus for the new international studies effort. By providing a federal imprimatur and national legitimacy for the projects involved, it acted as an external lever for internal change.

The Roles of the Faculty and Planning Committee. An international education committee was created that included faculty members from nine disciplines who had an interest or expertise in international education. Attached to the FIPSE-funded new Center for Study of Public Policy, this international education committee was designated the Non-Western and Comparative Area Studies Group.

This faculty committee quickly became the focus of program planning and implementation. There was a clear recognition by all that while the administration's role was central and invaluable, the program would only succeed if the faculty had a vested interest in it and were delegated the responsibility to develop it. This faculty role was important for both programmatic and political reasons because the quality and intensity of faculty support was seen as the key to sustaining internal support and to mobilizing external resources, including grants.

After a series of meetings, the committee initiated an extensive needs assessment and inventory of university resources as the first step of program planning. Once the strengths and weaknesses were assessed and documented, realistic objectives for PLU's specific needs could be formulated.

This institutional inventory also had several secondary benefits. It gave the faculty committee visibility as an active task force soliciting the opinions of faculty peers and of the various departments whose interests were possibly affected (such as Foreign Languages and Political Science, for example). While this process did not quiet fears in all cases, it did tend to encourage a dialogue and to steer the program onto firmer political ground.

The committee's major assessment interests included the quality and quantity of faculty resources in various departments, the strength or weakness of the library, the availability and suitability of curriculum in place, the need for new or revised courses for a thematically or regionally focused minor or major and, finally, the need for cocurricular and outreach elements such as study abroad, forums, cultural events, and workshops for the community. The needs assessment was divided into four categories: curriculum development, program supports, structural supports, and outreach. These categories, in turn, became the basis for a five-year master plan with specific objectives within each of the four categories for each year. The ultimate objective of the plan was a coherent major combining an area studies and a global issues approach. In the short term, however, the objective was a minor which offered choices of area studies or global issues. The minor provided an academic and political focus for faculty and students allowing the Global Studies major to evolve incrementally over a planned period of time. Course revisions or additions would follow according to academic need and political opportunity.

The value of this process of structural organization and "masterplanning" cannot be overemphasized. It gave coherence, developmental logic, and a controlled growth pattern to a emerging program. This method had distinct political advantages. The program evolved from the strengths and in response to the needs and interests of PLU. It prevented the fragmentation of program elements into isolated endeavors and promoted a comprehensive program. This approach also proved helpful in targeting and writing some twenty grant proposals worth over $960,000.

The Master Plan.   The Non-Western and Comparative Area Studies Committee (subsequently renamed the Foreign Area Studies Committee in 1978) issued its recommendations including the previously discussed five-year master plan in final form in January 1977. Foreign languages and international studies, the committee report stated, prepared students with the knowledge, skills, and values essential for understanding and managing the opportunities and problems of citizenship and careers.

Specific objectives of the report included a comprehensive Foreign Area Studies Program (FASP) which would first develop a minor and then a major. Curricular revision would follow the "infusion" strategy where possible. That is, existing courses within participating departments would be revised to incorporate an international dimension.

Reflecting PLU's strengths and interests, four world regions and four global issues would be emphasized. The four regions were Asia, Europe, the Third World (Africa, Latin America, Middle East) and Scandinavia (incorporating PLU's ethnic heritage and Scandinavian Studies Program). The four global issues were modernization and development, global resources and trade, cultures and traditions, and war, revolution, and peace.

The foreign language program was also to be expanded to include non-Western languages and competency-based language skills relating to business and other needs. While the specific curricular objective was an international studies program, the committee strongly supported the internationalization of the general undergraduate curriculum.

The committee also made several cocurricular and structural recommendations. These included library purchases, new and varied study abroad opportunities, foreign research and travel assistance for faculty, outreach to the K–12 grades, ethnic and business communities.

The structural objectives emphasized the need for an organizational framework which included an international education director and office for program building. Reviewing past efforts at PLU, the committee recognized that curricular offerings were fragmented and compartmentalized in an uncoordinated organizational structure, and that this approach had diminished program effectiveness, faculty commitment, student participation, and financial support. The remedy suggested was administrative and programmatic coordination among the various existing international education components. This meant establishing an office and director of International Education who, in turn, would coordinate the newly emerging curricular program with the existing Study Abroad office, with the proposed Intensive English Language Institute and with other departments such as Modern and Classical Languages, the School of Business, and the Scandinavian Studies Program.

The committee believed that a director was essential to the effective implementation, coordination, and use of institutional and external resources which form or complement an international studies program.

It should be noted that this organizational plan was not intended to replicate an absolute centralized program. Centralization was neither politically feasible nor programmatically desirable at a small institution like PLU. The emphasis was on linkage and coordination of the new Foreign Areas Studies Program with existing programs such as Scandinavian Studies and Study Abroad. Therefore, rather than undermine the integrity of existing programs, the director of International Education coordinated and highlighted the individual efforts and helped create an environment conducive to an integrated international studies program. The committee's point was to develop an organizational structure and comprehensive program that was effectively stronger than the mere sum of its parts; that would coordinate and integrate the existing diffused or dispersed program elements.

PROGRAM IMPLEMENTATION

In April 1977, a proposal for a Foreign Area Studies minor was submitted for approval to the Educational Policies Committee. At this point, some opposition surfaced from the chairperson of the Political Science Department, who feared that the minor would undermine student enrollments in his international relations courses. Not having anticipated the rapidity of events or the level of support for the Foreign Area Studies Program, the Political Science chairperson quickly submitted to the Educational Policies Committee a competing international relations minor based exclusively in the Political Science Department. Negotiations followed and resulted in the incorporation of an international relations component in the Foreign Area Studies Program. Cooperation had always been the objective of the Foreign Area Studies Program, therefore this episode strengthened the proposal and encouraged confidence in its flexible plan. On 12 May 1977, the Educational Policies Committee approved the Foreign Area Studies Program and its minor. This move represented university endorsement.

In summary, the subsequent stages of the international studies program's structural growth included the following significant achievements: On 3 April 1980, the director of the new Office of International Education was appointed. The director was given three courses release time (one-half the normal teaching load at PLU), and allowed to engage a full-time administrative assistant, a coordinator for off-campus programs, and several student assistants.

Simultaneously, a new universitywide Council on International Programs was established, chaired by the provost. Council members included all administrators, department chairs, and coordinators involved in international programs. Among its members were the registrar, the dean of graduate studies, and the dean of admissions. Finally, on 16 April 1982 the PLU Faculty Assembly unanimously approved the "complementary" Global Studies major.

This summary, of course, neglects the substantive accomplishments in curriculum, cocurricular activities, grants, community outreach, and national recognition that advanced the five-year plan. Space constraints will permit only highlights of institutional developments.

PROGRAM HIGHLIGHTS

1977/78

1. Eleven courses were "internationalized" to form the Asian and Third World clusters for the FASP minor.

2. Ten students registered for the FASP minor.

3. Nine major cocurricular and outreach events were held, including lectures, an Asian film festival, and a China Trade Conference. Over 1,100 participants attended.

4. Grants from the Center for Study of Public Policy (FIPSE) totaled $5,710.

5. Total operating budget including personnel was $16,000.

1978/79:

1. Fifteen courses were "internationalized," enrolling 465 students.

2. Thirty students elected the FASP minor.

3. The FASP Office was created with a director, an advisory council of faculty and a support staff of a one-half-time secretary, a full-time outreach coordinator for the nearby military base, and several student assistants.

4. External grants totaling more than $50,000 were received, including grant money from the National Endowment for the Humanities.

5. Total operating budget including personnel was over $70,000.

1979/80:

1. Twenty courses from eight departments were "internationalized," creating sixty courses in the FASP program, which enrolled 537 students.

2. Enrollment in the FASP minor increased to 49 students.

3. Four new faculty members were hired (three full-time and one part-time) whose duties, in part, were to assist the program in area specializations (Africa, Asia, Middle East, and Native Americans).

4. An Intensive English Language Institute was created.

5. The thirty-six-member Pacific Northwest International/Intercultural Education Consortium was created with PLU's assistance.

6. Four grants were received totaling over $72,000.

7. Total operating budget including personnel was over $98,000.

1980/81:

1. A new "Global Perspectives" introductory course was developed, and fifteen courses were "internationalized" to be added to twenty existing courses, thus creating the new Scandinavian (Area) and Global Resources and Trade (Issues) clusters, which enrolled 690 students.

2. FASP minor students totaled 59.

3. A new mission and goals statement was issued to accompany the creating of a director and Office of International Education.

4. A universitywide Council on International Programs was established, chaired by the provost.

5. Support staff of the Office of International Education included a three-quarter-time secretary, a one-half-time assistant director, a full-time military programs coordinator, three part-time K–12 outreach coordinators, and two student assistants.

6. International Business Curriculum developed with School of Business, including an international trade minor, international trade internships, and international business workshops.

7. A consortium was established for International Business Education involving six schools of business in Idaho, Oregon, and Washington.

8. PLU was awarded six institutional and consortium grants (Pacific Northwest International/Intercultural Consortium and Consortium for International Business Education) totaling $347,000.

9. Total PLU revenues for on- and off-campus international programs and PLU grants were $269,877.

10. Total PLU operating budget including personnel was $152,173.

1981/82

(Interim Report)

1. The Global Studies "complementary" minor was given university approval one year early.

2. Eighty-two students were enrolled in the FASP minor.

3. A new chair of the Global Studies major was appointed; the founding director of the Office of International Education (Rozanski) was succeeded by Dr. Ann Kelleher.

4. Three grants were awarded, including a three-year grant from the Fund for the Improvement of Post-Secondary Education for a total of $388,000.

SIGNIFICANT FACTORS CONTRIBUTING TO PROGRAM DEVELOPMENT

PLU's international education program has evolved over a ten-year period, reaching a high level of cohesion in the last five years. Although it is still far from complete, it has achieved maturity and significant success and has won wide support and national recognition as an exemplary international education program.[2]

The generic factors in the success of the program have been diverse and somewhat fortuitous; nevertheless, several can be mentioned.

1. The political and budgetary support provided by top administrative officers has been invaluable and irreplaceable. Without this support nothing would have occurred.

2. The participation of key faculty—particularly "master" or "star" teachers—has earned the program considerable departmental and student support.

3. The program benefited from the leadership of an energetic, entrepreneurial, and occasionally politically astute program director, who focused on small victories as a strategy for success. This individual's role was that of catalyst and risk-taker. The director's willingness to take on more work than was necessary or expected in the beginning was crucial to success.

4. Seed money, initially some $2,000 from the institution, acted as a leavening agent for program planning and experimentaton. This seed money allowed interested faculty to develop a pilot effort to prepare for a full-fledged project proposal submitted to the National Endowment for the Humanities.

5. Various external grants unlocked many gates and helped recruit administrators and faculty.

6. A strong academic and organizational focus existed for the program. It led to the selection of specific foreign areas and global issues as curricular concentrations; the creation of a minor and eventually a nonthreatening, noncompeting "complementary" second major in Global Studies; and the revision of existing courses within departments to give faculty and departments a vested interest in the success of the program. Finally, stressing the packaging approach at the beginning—using and revising established courses—avoided the dangers of proliferation and of isolation as an esoteric program.

7. Structurally, the director and Office of International Education were conceived as coordinating instruments providing a focus for on- and off-campus international programs.

8. Externally, supports such as the Pacific Northwest International/Intercultural Education Consortium provided a valuable resource for prodding program development by making PLU's program part of a larger regional movement—even in competition with other institutions—rather than an isolated phenomenon. Other important external supports were national and regional recognition, contacts with federal and private agencies, and authoritative consultants. Finally, a significant outreach effort to business and the K–12 community created important constituency support and helped maintain a momentum of activities.

9. Student support and interest were factors vital to success.

10. Intangibles played their part as well—such as a record of success, good luck, good will, and an excellent staff who were politically astute and assiduous in task performance.

Institutional Commitment to International Education

As is evident in the preceding discussion, PLU has demonstrated a significant universitywide commitment to international education both through work and deed. Four elements manifest this commitment:

I. The establishment on 13 March 1980 of a universitywide Council on International Programs chaired by the provost and comprising top administrators of the university, including the deans of admission, summer, and graduate studies, the registrar, the foreign student advisor, the study abroad coordinator, the coordinator of Scandinavian Studies, and the director of the Office of International Education. Its purpose is to coordinate the flow of information and to advise on major policy issues. Most importantly, it signifies that international programs have been institutionalized as a universitywide—rather than a divisional or departmental—concern.

II. The establishment of the Office and director of International Education on 3 April 1980 as the central focus for international programs at PLU.

III. The 16 April 1982 approval by the university faculty assembly of a multidisciplinary and complementary Global Studies major. This major is unique in that its faculty committee and chair do not report to any one department or division, but rather to the chief academic officer. In other words, the major is a universitywide program.

IV. The declaration of a new mission and goal statement for international programs at PLU.

The goals of PLU's international programs are:

A. A recognition of the complexity and interdependent nature of the world's political, economic, and social systems.

B. An understanding and appreciation of human commonalities and differences.

C. An awareness of how perceptions, values, and priorities differ among various individuals, groups, and cultures.

D. A commitment to the development of skills that will enable individuals to respond creatively to local, national, and international events and to participate effectively at those levels. Among these skills is proficiency in a second language.[3]

ADMINISTRATIVE ORGANIZATION

PLU's president is the institution's chief executive officer. Reporting directly to him is the provost, who is the chief academic officer. The director of the Office of International Education (OIE), the chairperson of the Global Studies (major) Committee, and the universitywide Council on International Programs all report directly to the provost.

OIE's director reports directly to the provost on all matters relating to personnel, budget, programing, and curriculum. However, given the universitywide nature of the office, several other important administrative linkages exist. All grants are coordinated with the vice-president for development and his staff.

All budgetary matters, accounts, revenues, and expenditures are coordinated with the business office under the director of fiscal affairs and the vice-president for finance. The OIE's other significant linkages are with the dean for graduate and summer studies, who is also responsible for continuing education.

In addition to these administrative linkages, OIE also has special academic linkages. Following are the principal areas of academic coordination and linkage.

The Division of Social Science. The Foreign Area Studies Program (FASP) was initiated within this division, and the OIE director has been a tenured member of its history department. The majority of the present Global Studies faculty and courses are from departments in this division. This division has also undertaken the vast majority of course revisions and hirings to assist the growth of the program. The master's degree in International Studies is also based in this division.

The Cooperative Education Program. OIE has initiated a ten-week summer work and study program in Europe. This program is coordinated with the cooperative education program and called International Cooperative Education (ICE).

The Modern and Classical Languages Department. Languages are an essential feature of PLU's international studies program. Proficiency in a second language is required of all students in the Global Studies and Scandinavian Studies majors. Evaluation and testing for proficiency is the responsibility of this department. It is also responsible for self-instructional language offerings and for the development of business or "survival" language courses related to the international business program. Finally, this department coordinates the academic orientation of the International Cooperative Education program—particularly the language training. ICE requires a minimum of one year of language study.

Study Abroad Office. This office predated OIE and continues to provide study abroad information and coordination to PLU students. The office's coordinator works closely with the OIE director and with

Scandinavian Studies to integrate study abroad and curricular programs. PLU offers four varieties of study abroad: semester or yearlong academic programs; short-term study tours in the January interim or in the summer; service-learning programs that involve internships or experiential activities—not related to an academic association abroad; and international cooperative education, which involves ten-week, salaried summer positions in Europe. PLU has, or is developing, semester programs in China, London, Sweden, Spain, Germany, France, and Mexico. Affiliations with several study abroad consortia such as ILACA and Pacific Northwest International/Intercultural Consortium, among others, provide additional opportunities. In 1981, 111 PLU students studied abroad; 26 were part of semester or yearlong programs.

Foreign and Minority Student Office. A separate office for foreign student advising exists as part of the Office of the Vice-President for Student Life. This office advises and provides support services for PLU's foreign students. The International Student's Organization also works closely with this office. OIE coordinates such matters as the Intercultural Fair and foreign student activities with this office.

The Intensive English Language Institute (IELI). This program provides instruction in English as a second language, both for PLU foreign students and participants in nonmatriculating studies. This program was initiated by the OIE director, and OIE continues a close relationship with it. IELI also conducts special short-term certificate programs for groups of professionals or English students and teachers from Japan and elsewhere during the summer. Students graduating from the IELI program are eligible to apply to PLU but are not regular students until admitted by the dean of admissions. IELI also assists the Admissions Office in the evaluation of foreign student applications to PLU.

Scandinavian Area Studies Program (SAS). An independent area studies program, SAS also coordinates with the Scandinavian area cluster in the FASP minor. Its director is a member of the Global Studies Committee and helps coordinate the major's European area cluster. OIE has assisted SAS in grant and program development.

The School of Business. The director of OIE has established a special relationship with the business school and its dean. After three years of discussion, an international business program plan was developed in 1980 to internationalize the core curriculum of the business administration degree. The strategy of the three-stage effort is, first, to introduce international modules dealing with international business knowledge and skills as well as the cultural, historical, and legal environment of international business into the nine introductory business courses; second, to internationalize the functional areas of the business program (management, personnel, finance, accounting, and marketing); and third, to develop an optional joint business and international studies degree including a language element. At present, OIE has developed an International Trade minor for the business school involving international studies courses primarily. OIE's director has also helped organize the Consortium for International Business Education. Finally, the dean of the School of Business serves on the Global Studies Committee.

McChord Air Force Program. OIE has coordinated a undergraduate certificate in international studies for officers at the nearby air force base. Equivalent to a minor, this certificate is part of a undergraduate degree program for these officers. It is directly administered by OIE, and classes are conducted on base. Instructors are either regular departmental or part-time faculty. Credit is awarded by the appropriate departments and the dean of continuing education.

School of Education. OIE has developed and conducted a series of K–12 global education teacher-training programs with the assistance of the School of Education. These are usually graduate-level classes for two or four semester hours' credit. The courses are taught by OIE-affiliated instructors while credit is offered by the School of Education and the Office of Continuing Education. Over one hundred teachers have participated in these credit courses.

The Global Studies Minor and Major. These curricular programs—a development of the Foreign Area Studies minor–have been administered until recently by OIE, which planned and developed them. At present, a multidisciplinary faculty committee for Global Studies has been organized. This committee was chaired by the OIE director, and will now be chaired by one of the faculty coordinators of the area and issues cluster. The Global Studies program receives budgetary and staff assistance for OIE. As a universitywide program, it reports directly to the provost rather than to any one division or department.

ORGANIZATIONAL STRUCTURE OF THE OFFICE OF INTERNATIONAL EDUCATION

The office is organized on a decentralized model with responsibilities being delegated to its full- and part-time staff. Nevertheless, while responsibilities are shared, authority for policy and budgetary decisions rest with the director, who is in turn directly responsible to the provost.

The number of staff has fluctuated according to program activities and funding availability. Generally, however, the following staff have served the office and the director: an assistant director/program coordinator, an administrative manager and grants/budget coordinator, a secretary/receptionist, program coordinators, and student assistants. While these five categories of support staff are central to the effective functioning of the OIE, other support for Study Abroad, program development, and grants come from the several units already discussed in the previous section.

Academic Program Components

PLU has developed a comprehensive, multifocused, and multidisciplinary International Education Program to expand students' understanding of the global condition. In curricular areas, students may select specialized programs among two undergraduate majors, three minors, a master's degree, or single courses from a list of over a hundred courses with an international or intercultural dimension. In cocurricular areas, students and faculty may participate in a series of international forums, lectures, symposia, film festivals, and related activities.

   I. *Majors*
      PLU offers two multidisciplinary international studies majors. The first is Scandinavian Area Studies; the second is Global Studies.
      A. *Scandinavian Area Studies*
         Established in 1975, this major focuses on the languages, culture, and literature of Scandinavia. The major requires the completion of ten courses (forty semester hours), including two years of either Danish, Norwegian, or Swedish language courses, one course in Scandinavian literature, and one course in Scandinavian history. The remaining courses may be selected from a designated list of courses in eight different departments. Students are encouraged to spend one year in Scandinavia.
      B. *Global Studies "Complementary" Major*
         Established in 1982, this major succeeds the Foreign Area Studies Program. It focuses on three world area clusters—Asia, Third World (Africa, Latin America, and the Middle East), and Europe, and four topical clusters—Modernization and Development; Global Resources and Trade; Revolution, War, and Peace; and Society, Cultures, and Traditions. Each cluster is an aggregate of courses from various departments selected or developed to represent a world region or global issue. The goal is knowledge about one world region *and* one global issue. Students may select this major as a complementary or second major only (e.g., History and Global Studies, Political Science and Global Studies, etc.). They select a total of eight courses (thirty-two semester hours), including the introductory Global Perspectives course, three courses from a list focusing on one of the three world regions, three courses from a list focusing on one of the four global issues or

topics, and a concluding seminar/special study course which may be part of an overseas study program). In addition, students must demonstrate proficiency in a foreign language relating to their selected world region.

II. *Minors*

A. *Global Studies*

This five-course minor (totaling twenty semester hours) is the same as the major above. However, it requires only three courses from one world region *or* one global issue cluster, in addition to the introductory and concluding courses.

B. *International Affairs*

This five-course minor (twenty hours) focuses on international relations; its orientation is primarily political science.

C. *International Trade*

Coordinated by the dean of the School of Business and created for economics and business majors, this five-course minor (twenty semester hours) involves international studies rather than international business courses. The goal is to increase business students' understanding of international business. All students must select the Global Perspectives course from the Global Studies major and a concluding International Business Seminar. The remaining three courses must include one world area concentration in addition to courses on International Economics and International Organizations.

III. *Masters in International Studies*

This program is based in the social science division and entails nine courses (thirty-six semester hours). It is fundamentally a parallel of the area and issues approach of the Global Studies major. In addition, methodology and theory courses are required and a thesis as well.

IV. *Cocurricular and Outreach Programs*

The OIE has designed a series of on- and off-campus programs to enhance international education and act as a resource to the surrounding community. Among these programs are:

A. *International Forums*

This is a continuing series of presentations on current international issues.

B. *Symposia*

These have provided an intellectual focus for the world area or global issue clusters developed over the last four years. They have served both as promotional and curriculum development instruments.

C. *International Business and Trade Conferences and Workshops*

These have been cosponsored with the School of Business and

have focused on Asia and other regions as well as on special topics. An example is "Doing Business with China."

D. *Project Advance*

This program has been aimed at high school students who have enrolled in a one-to-two-credit course at PLU (at subsidized rates). Two examples are a series of five lectures on the Global Dimensions of International Trade (tied to the high school national debate topic) and the Great Decisions program. Clearly, the goal has been to recruit students for PLU by increasing their interest in international issues.

E. *Global Education for K–12 Teachers*

The OIE has sponsored conferences and graduate-level courses for K–12 teachers.

These cocurricular and outreach programs are an integral part of international education at PLU. They stimulate significant interest in and support for international studies by students, faculty, and constituencies not regularly involved in these programs. Such outreach builds *esprit de corps* among international studies faculty and helps recruit students and supporters. It also generates jobs, internships, and financial and consultant support.

Funding

PLU's administration recognized the importance of seed money for international studies development by investing some $5,000 during the program's first two years, in addition to small $300 or $500 awards to the faculty planning the program. These funds not only offered economic support but also demonstrated political and institutional support and quickly mushroomed into a full-fledged program returning significant value to the institution.

To put this issue into perspective, the following statistics are offered. In 1976/78, the FASP program had a total budget of $9,710, including grants but excluding personnel costs. Personnel costs are excluded because faculty generally volunteered their time to plan the program and used the funds for consultants, travel, materials, and assessment work. If faculty-time contributions for the FASP director had been included, the budget would have totaled $16,000.

In 1980/81, the last period for which complete figures are available, program and personnel expenditures totalled $139,067.

Salaries	$ 65,532
Fringe benefits	13,106
Program support	47,000
Travel & office support	13,429
Total	$139,067

Revenues, however, for the same period were $269,877.

Grants and contracts	$76,389
Fees for off-campus programs	78,162
Tuition for campus courses	115,326
Total	$269,877

It should be noted that the tuition figures above represent revenue generated by courses specifically developed by the Office of International Education at PLU. Most of these revenues passed directly into the university operating budget. Nevertheless, by 1980/81, the International Studies Program more than held its own and returned $1.77 for every dollar invested. Another important observation is that grants (not contracts) played a crucial funding role because they provided essential discretionary funds. While grants represented only 19 percent of total revenue, they made up 34 percent of expenditures. Finally, the total expenditures for international education represented less than 2 percent of PLU's $12 million academic budget. If grants and contracts are subtracted, that figure becomes .8 percent. Considering the benefits earned by the university, international education has been an excellent investment.

Strengths and Weakness of the PLU Approach

PLU's model for international education is, in many ways, unique to its personality, size, ethos, and political and curricular character. It would be folly to suggest that this model could be replicated elsewhere. However, while the program's character and content are idiosyncratic, its evolutionary process and emphasis on assessment, master planning, and infrastructure building offer a model for other private institutions. Even its weaknesses and problems offer warning to those who may wish to avoid them.

Strengths

1. The unstinting support of president and provost as well as university unit heads was without a doubt the most important factor in the birth and growth of the program. This support was mani-

fested in institutional policy, political clout, budgetary support, and patience.

2. An entrepreneurial, politically adept, and energetic director was given 50 percent release-time to plan and cajole the program along. The office and the support staff helped to develop international education on campus. Moreover, with this office support, the processes of planning and direction were separated from the mundane execution of office tasks, providing PLU with a structure for planning and implementation.

3. Seed money was provided for pilot efforts, assessment, and planning.

4. Faculty sharing similar perspectives played a crucial role in planning, assessing, and implementing program elements.

5. A thorough assessment and inventory process preceded planning; then a five-year master plan, clearly indicating goals and objectives, was established.

6. Program activities focused on curriculum rather than on service or administration. The director remained a faculty member, and the program committee was made up of faculty, who also taught in the program.

7. High-quality publicity, brochures, and community outreach enhanced the image of the program and the office.

8. The multidisciplinary and "complementary" approach of the program encouraged participation rather than competition. Indeed, the process of revising existing departmental courses left internationalized courses within departments, whether the international studies major or minor survived or not.

9. The program emerged from one academic division, but became institutionalized as a universitywide effort. This outcome was the result of effective political and academic alliances built throughout the university.

10. The program was sensitive to the mission and ethos of the university, complementing it rather than challenging it.

11. Students were consulted and involved.

12. External linkages such as consortia were established to assist in program development and in grant generation. Other linages came from extensive outreach efforts to various community groups.

13. Grants were written and received. This factor was very important because the nearly $1 million in institutional and consortial grants gave the OIE budgetary discretion and political leverage.

Weaknesses

In many ways, the strengths of the program can also be its weaknesses.

1. Although top administrators play a central role, when they leave—as the chairperson of the Division of Social Science did—significant political gap is left. In addition, faculty and unit heads can come to resent or envy attention paid to a program outside the normal structure of departmental accountability.

2. A strong, dynamic director may be crucial to establishing a program, but he or she may be a detriment to the process of consolidating a program. Although the same person can direct both tasks, the politics and sensitivities of a small institution, where the stakes are small but each issue large, may be better served by a transition to new leadership dependent on teamwork.

3. On the one hand, there is danger that a decentralized structure may become more cosmetic than real; on the other hand, as centralization by accretion or calculation occurs, turf and policy problems may arise. The greatest danger is for the director to outrace his faculty support network and dictate policy or, even worse, not inform faculty members of his decisions.

4. Institutionalizing the program has the danger of transcending the essential support network of departments and divisions. The result may be a double-edged sword—escape from divisional policies but also isolation.

5. Depending on grants is folly. New sources of revenue must be developed with rewards to faculty as a priority.

The most difficult problem for a successful program is that success if not only ephemeral, but it also engenders jealousy. Good will, grace, and good human relations are indispensable, particularly at a small institution.

Strategy for the 1980s

Institutionally, administrators of international education programs must face several issues. First, international academic and service programs must develop closer relationships. As more institutions develop international studies programs, the tendency will be for faculty in area or international studies to lead the way. These individuals are academically trained to have a curricular focus. However, they will need to be trained to understand organizational systems and the techniques of management because they will be involved in both academic and services sectors.

Second, greater attention must be given to content rather than process in international education. What are the cognitive and affective goals of international programs; what skills are necessary for students as they enter the so-called "Global Century"? This inquiry will require the combined efforts of faculty, administrators, and employers. Ideological training is not enough; students must be prepared to deal creatively and effectively with a changing world—they cannot be dumped in a world of problems and issues that defy resolution. If they are, their reactions will be cyncism and parochialism of greater magnitude than exists now. Ironically, international education, which preaches interdependence, may be turning out students who are opposed to that very concept because of the apparent intractability of the problems it engenders.

A third area of concern is language instruction. Language entrance requirements must be reinstated, as well as language programs that achieve proficiency rather than merely cumulative classroom hours.

A fourth problem is the need to internationalize the professional schools, particularly schools of education and business. If schools of education provided preservice training in foreign languages and international studies more effectively, less in-service training would be needed. Perhaps the unfortunate results that were revealed in the Council on Learning's Education and World View survey could be avoided. In that 1980 test of global literacy, education majors scored lowest among nine disciplines with an embarrassing 38 percent.[4] Similarly, schools of business must respond to the realities of economic interdependence by preparing students with functional international business skills and with a cosmopolitan perspective.

A fifth area of need is to "internationalize" international education. Right now students learn *about* other nations and cultures rather than *from* them—the rest of the world is a passive object of US voyeuristic scrutiny.

One way of remedying this problem is more effective integration of foreign students into classrooms and learning processes. An additional approach is to encourage more experiential study abroad, both for students and faculty. Because of the skyrocketing costs of study abroad, internships and work and study positions may help provide an alternative for students who cannot afford traditional programs.

A sixth and final area of need is programmatic. Global perspectives courses should be a part of the core curriculum. The goal should not be elitist, intended merely to train international studies specialists; instead, it should be to incorporate a global perspective into the education of all students. Such a curricular goal also means that more effort must be given to internationalizing introductory courses in various disciplines and to assisting faculty in research and travel that can help advance that objective. Ultimately, such efforts require creative strategies to raise funds for their support.

Regionally, coalitions must be formed to assist in building international awareness at the very time that many communities may want to retreat from the world's increasing complexity and our nation's loss of preeminence. Efforts must be aimed at community outreach, with institutions taking on the role of resource centers and catalysts of change.

Nationally, international education programs must be supported and organized across divisional lines of elementary, secondary, collegiate, and graduate education. There should be a national commitment to international education and the programs that support its development.

Notes

1. James Peterson, "We Have Ignored the World," *Scene,* December 1980, pp. 2–3.
2. See Council on Learning, *Handbook of Exemplary Programs* (New Rochelle, NY, 1980); also Association of American Colleges, *Forum for Liberal Education* 3, no. 1 (October 1980).
3. These objectives are derived from the Center for Teaching International Relations, University of Denver, 1980.
4. Thomas Barrows, John Clark, and Stephen Klein, "What Students Know About Their World," in *Educating for the World View: Understanding the New Imperatives* (New Rochelle, NY: Council on Learning, 1980), pp. 10–22.

PART III

Community Colleges

In 1978 A SURVEY OF TWO-YEAR COLLEGES reported considerable interest and activity in responding to the interdependent nature of the modern world.[1] More than 300 institutions, out of a total exceeding 1,200, were estimated to have made some sort of commitment to international education. Although there was considerable variation in the nature and strategy of implementing an international program, the study verified a wide range of activities taking place on two-year campuses. Most common were foreign students, exchange programs, study abroad, bilingual programs, English language programs, and technical training.

Enlightened administrative support contributed greatly to the development of international education at many community colleges. Such support, often beginning with the president, enabled institutions to respond positively to the international challenges facing two-year schools. Perhaps the biggest stimulus to international programing was the massive influx of international students. More than 50 percent of foreign students enrolled in undergraduate study are at community, junior, and technical colleges. The need to respond to the educational requirements of this group of students, as well as the increasingly larger refugee influx, led many institutional leaders to develop international programs.

Intensive English language and bilingual programs were established where large numbers of foreign students and refugees enrolled. Technical training programs in engineering technology and allied health were created to meet a need expressed by students from Third World countries. Study abroad programs were established to provide opportunities for US students enrolled in a variety of occupational fields to learn work in a similar setting abroad. Businessmen on local trustee boards and college presidents concerned with increasing local support were quick to see the potential in the development of ties between two-year colleges and international businesses located in the community.

Thus, from the mid-1970s into the early 1980s international education grew significantly at two year-institutions. This expansion was greatly influenced by two additional factors. First, excellent leadership was present not only at the institutional level, but also in consortia and through the American Association of Community and Junior Colleges. Workshops, conferences, and seminars provided leadership training to newly hired administrators. Resources were shared, enabling institutions to avoid the onus of "reinventing the wheel."

Second, and perhaps of equal importance, was the commitment made by the US Office of Education (later the Department of Education) to provide grant funds under the NDEA title VI program. Many two-year institutions would have had difficulty starting an international program if they had not received modest grants from the Group Projects Abroad program, the Foreign Curriculum Consultants program, or the Undergraduate Strengthening Program in International Studies and Foreign Languages. All of these programs provided financial assistance to community colleges (including the three institutions described in this section) making an international/intercultural commitment, which in turn led to revamping of curricula, linkage of international and intercultural projects, curriculum infusion, and building ethnic heritage programing to international studies. These one-and two-year grants, when combined with institutional commitment, allowed community colleges to respond to the international needs of enrolled students and the community.

During the 1980s, two trends are likely to affect the expansion of international studies at community colleges. They are pressures that contradict each other. The continued pressure from Third World countries to train their students, to provide technical training to foreign firms, to respond to increasing refugee enrollment, and to assist in transferring the community college system to other countries creates great opportunities in such occupational fields as allied health, engineering technology, and international business.

However, efforts to respond adequately to these requests are likely to be hindered because of reduced operational budgets. State legislatures and local funding agencies are pressuring community colleges simultaneously to reduce expenditures and to respond to local community educational needs. Among the programs most likely to receive a disproportionate share of budget cuts will be international/intercultural activities. Without grant support from both the public and private sectors, community colleges will find it increasingly difficult to initiate international programs. Unfortunately, this fiscal situation at the state and local levels is mirrored at the Department of Education. Recommended cuts in the funding for undergraduate international programs will have a significant impact on how well community colleges are able to respond to the international challenges of the 1980s.

When general economic conditions inhibit program development, institutions must rely on other methods to obtain the necessary skills and techniques to internationalize the campus. One option is to find out how other institutions have approached this problem. The three case studies presented in this part of the book illustrate the diversity in international programs at two-year institutions. Their respective approaches to international programs offer other institutions successful models that can be emulated (often with minimal funding) by a wide variety of two-year institutions.

Pima Community College, located in Tucson, Arizona, demonstrates a commitment to international education that evolved out of a ten-year program in bilingual education. Beginning with a title VI grant from the Department of Education, PCC modified existing courses by adding an international dimension; developed faculty exchange programs; increased foreign student enrollment; and built the bilingual program by adding additional foreign languages, establishing training programs, and offering workshops and seminars for faculty. The international education effort at Pima is supported by faculty and administrators, endorsed by the Board of Trustees, and closely integrated with a well developed, highly successful bilingual program.

Another approach is illustrated by *Bergen Community College* in Paramus, New Jersey. Built on a foundation of committed faculty and strength in foreign languages, the college is committed to strengthening the international dimension of the entire curriculum. Bergen has responded to its unique setting and resource base by adding concentrations in international marketing and import/export management. Through these concentrations, as well as an International Trade Round Table Association, Bergen's Center for International Studies seeks to meet community business needs, provide training for students, and gain local financial support. The model presented in chapter 16 illustrates how an integrated program evolves; and it presents a college strongly committed to develop practical international business programs.

Chapter 17 describes *Rockland Community College* in Suffern, New York. This college's international program began with study abroad programs for students enrolled in occupationally related study programs. After several successful years of developing overseas programs, Rockland turned its attention to internationalizing the campus and community. The establishment of the Rockland Center for International Studies completed the development of a highly centralized method of administering study abroad efforts. This chapter explains how such a program is administered and how overseas study is related to campus curricula.

These final case studies illustrate three distinct focuses for community college international programs. Pima focuses on bilingual education, Bergen on international business, and Rockland on study abroad. Each institution, using its own strength and outside grant support, has expanded international activities to include faculty development, curriculum development, and programs for foreign students. Although each program has its own distinct set of elements, all have been successful because of strong commitment from top-level administrators, motivated faculty, and excellent leadership from individuals committed to strong international programs.

Notes

1. William G. Shannon, *A Survey of International/Intercultural Education in Two-Year Colleges: 1976* (La Plata, MD: Charles County Community College, 1978).

CHAPTER 15

Pima Community College

G. Elisabet Bailey

Institutional Description

Pima Community College, located in Tucson, Arizona, is a multicampus college district that serves the 532,000 residents of Pima County. The college currently enrolls approximately 21,000 students in credit courses and over 6,000 students in noncredit classes at the four campuses, the Skill Center, or at one of the thirty locations of the noncredit Community Service Program. The full-time student equivalent (FTSE) figure for the district credit classes is between 10,000 and 11,000 FTSE per semester. The college has provided educational services to over 150,000 students since it opened its doors in the fall of 1970. It is estimated that one out of every four Tucsonans has attended classes at Pima Community College (PCC).

The institution, mainly supported by county taxes and state aid, offers approximately 1,000 courses each year in Pima County and, through special arrangements, in neighboring Santa Cruz County, which does not have a community college. These classes are taught by 265 full-time and over 650 associate faculty members.

The idea for the college began in 1965 when Tucson citizens started preliminary discussion and planning for a junior college in Pima County. Two years later an election approved the formation of the Pima County Junior College District. In September 1970, with most of the classes housed in a temporary facility, Pima College offered 260 courses to 3,728 students. From 1970 to 1976 the college experienced an enormous enrollment surge to over 20,000 students. To help ease the overcrowding at the newly completed West Campus, some classes were moved off campus into

271

community facilities during 1971/72; in 1974 the Downtown Campus opened, immediately filling to near capacity, and in 1976 the East Campus opened to serve students on Tucson's far east side.

From 1976 to 1979 the enrollment was still increasing but at a much slower rate. Enrollment declined in 1980/81, partially because a tuition per-credit-hour fee was adopted. In the fall of 1981 enrollment grew by 5 percent over the previous year. The college is expected to have a moderate but continuing enrollment growth pattern over the next five-year period.[1]

The institution has been fully accredited by the North Central Association of Colleges and Secondary Schools since 1975. A six-year accreditation renewal was received in the spring of 1981. In addition to the North Central accreditation, specific college programs are accredited by numerous national occupational and vocational organizations.

STUDENTS

Ninety percent of the students that attend the college are Pima County residents. The out-of-county but in-state enrollment is about 4 percent; out-of-state students make up 3 percent of the student body. The largest number of out-of-state students come from California, followed by Illinois and New York. The college has an admission policy that welcomes foreign students and, as a result, 3 percent of the enrollment is international. More than 580 students, representing sixty-two countries, attend Pima Community College. In the spring semester of 1981 the majority of the foreign student population came from Mexico (175), although a sizable number came from Saudi Arabia (83), Venezuela (65), Iran (48), Libya (27), and Japan (22).

The college attracts people from all income groups. However, about 60 percent of the college's students have family unit incomes lower than the median income for metropolitan Tucson households.[2] A study conducted a few years ago indicates that younger students take courses for career training or college transfer, somewhat older students generally attend to improve job skills or for self-improvement, and middle-aged or older students are more likely to take courses to retrain for a new career.

The average age of the Pima College student is between twenty-eight and twenty-nine. In the spring semester of 1981, 77 percent of the student body was classified as part-time. Eighty percent of all students are attending classes while they also have full- or part-time work or household responsibilities.

In Tucson, as in the nation, more and more women are attending college. Fifty-two percent of the enrollment is now female. Fifty-two percent of all students are continuing their education from the previous semester, 18 percent are returning to Pima after a semester or so away from the college, 17 percent are new to higher education, and 13 percent have transferred from other institutions.

The ethnic makeup of PCC students reflects the unique blend of cultures in Pima County. About 17 percent of the students are Hispanic, four percent are black, 3 percent are American Indian or Alaskan Native, and 2 percent are Asian or Pacific Islander. Seventy-four percent of the students are white. Projections indicate that the student population in the future will continue to be part-time, and will include more women, more minorities, and slightly older persons.[3]

FACULTY

The college faculty also mirrors the broad range of ethnic background found in the community. Twenty-two percent are classified as ethnic minorities, mostly Hispanic. Pima's instructional staff has a low turnover rate; a large portion of the instructors hired in the early 1970s are still teaching at the institution.

The faculty has continued to demonstrate commitment to professional development by earning advanced degrees and participating in the college's professional development program. Fifteen percent of the full-time teachers now have doctorates as compared to 7 percent in 1974; 67 percent currently hold masters as opposed to 56 percent in 1974. The college's professional development program encourages faculty members to take classes for academic credit and to participate in noncredit professionally related activities, such as workshops, seminars, faculty exchanges, and professional development leaves.

THE COMMUNITY

The college serves an area of 9,230 square miles. Only 12 percent of Pima County is privately owned, since most of the territory consists of Indian reservations and state and federally owned lands.

The area is rich in multicultural history. Native Americans settled in the territory as early as AD 800. Since then the flags of Spain, Mexico, and the Confederacy have flown over the territory. Today the area contains a Papago Indian Reservation and four Yaqui Indian settlements. A number of county residents are Navajo and Hopi Indians. Blacks make up about 3 percent of the population, about equal to the percentage of native Americans. There is also a small Oriental population. Twenty-five percent of the county's population is classified as minority; of these, most are Hispanic.

Tucson, a metropolitan city of 450,000, contains about 85 percent of Pima County's population. The city, located in a semiarid valley, is one of

the fastest growing regions in the United States. As Tucson grows, so does
its minority population. For example, in 1979 alone, over 6,000 Hispanics
moved into the Tucson area.

Tucson's economy is based on tourism, service businesses, mining,
ranching, manufacturing, government service, press services, and educational activities. In addition to Pima College, Tucson is also the home of the
University of Arizona, which enrolls well over 30,000 students. Companies
such as IBM, TEC, Inc., and National Semiconductor Corporation have
been attracted to the Tucson area. In addition, Hughes Aircraft, Burr
Brown Research Corporation, and Davis Monthan Air Force Base have
been an integral part of the economy for many years. Many of these
businesses and industries have international activities and/or operations.

PCC Educational Program and Organizational Structure

Pima College provides an undergraduate curriculum of college transfer,
occupational, and special interest courses. Of the credit course offerings,
24 percent of all enrollments are in college transfer, 44 percent are in
occupational programs, and 32 percent are in general programs. The
college offers an associate degree in 130 programs of study. Students can
earn some ninety basic and advanced certificates in various business,
health, public service, art, technical, and trade-related occupational fields.

The West Campus, completed in 1971, is the oldest and largest (9,000
students) of the district campuses. It is located at the foot of the Tucson
Mountains about three miles west of Tucson's central business district. The
campus offers special interest, transfer, and occupational courses.

The Downtown Campus, opened in the fall of 1974, provides students
with a fully comprehensive program of study together with some of the
specialized industrial technology programs. The campus has an enrollment of 6,500.

Opened in 1976, the East Campus offers introductory courses in a wide
range of subject areas, some advanced (sophomore level) college transfer
courses, and selected courses in occupational programs. A new facility for
the East Campus opened in the fall of 1981. Approximately 4,000 students
are enrolled at the campus.

The Community Campus, a "campus without walls," was established
in 1975. The campus provides credit for occupational, college transfer, and
special interest courses. The philosophy of the Community Campus is to
bring college courses to people where they work and live. Currently the
campus offers classes at some seventy locations in the Tucson, Ajo,
Marana, Sells, Green Valley, and Nogales areas. Approximately 5,500
students attend classes at these sites.

The Community Service Program, started in 1975, offers all of the district's noncredit classes and programs. These programs include family life education, women's programs, and senior citizen education programs. About 6,000 students enroll in classes through Community Services.

The Pima Community College Skill Center has been associated with the college since 1973, and in 1979 officially became a part of the college organization. The center is a nonprofit vocational facility that provides training to the physically handicapped and the educationally and economically disadvantaged. Some 250–300 people receive training at the center during peak months.

History of the PCC Bilingual Education and International Studies Program

By virtue of its mixed cultural heritage and its proximity to Mexico, Tucson is a community with an international/intercultural perspective. Because of this perspective, the college has always recognized the need for international/intercultural education.[4]

In the summer of 1970, just before the college opened, a federally funded training institute was developed to prepare college faculty and staff to meet the educational needs of a culturally mixed student population. This institute, held in Guadalajara, Mexico, was conducted again in 1971 and 1972. One of the codirectors of the institute became Pima's first Director of Bilingual Education. Under his leadership the college developed an impressive number of bilingual courses and several certificate and associate degree programs in bilingual education. By 1976 the activities of the Office of Bilingual Education had so broadened in scope that it was retitled the Office of Bilingual Education and International Studies (BEIS) and the director's title was changed to associate dean.

From 1970 to 1979 the BEIS office received four major bilingual grants totaling over $440,000 from the US Office of Education (now the Department of Education). During these years the college also diversified its international/intercultural activities with the help of other segments of the institution. Student Services worked in conjunction with the BEIS Office to promote bilingual and international student activities. The college's director of athletics also worked with the office to foster international activities through athletic exchanges and team–coach exchanges with Mexico. In addition, numerous faculty members from various subject areas, including Spanish and English as a Second Language (ESL), worked with the associate dean of BEIS to develop specific projects and programs with international/intercultural dimensions.

In late fall of 1978, the acting dean for educational services (now retitled vice-president for educational services) stated his desire to strengthen the international program at Pima Community College. The rest of the college supported the idea and when an administrative intern was assigned to the Educational Services Office in the spring of 1979, part of her duties were to develop the international education program.

That spring she helped organize a conference on international education that brought to the college four nationally recognized leaders in international programs. On the basis of the interest expressed by faculty and students at the conference, PCC submitted to the Department of Education a grant proposal for internationalizing the curriculum. This title VI grant project, funded in 1980, was the first grant the college received in international education. Since then Pima has received other grants.

In addition to her duties as project director of this grant, the administrative intern authored, at the request of the vice-president of educational services, a document entitled *International Education at Pima Community College: An Institutional Plan.* This document, approved by the Board of Governors in November 1980, specifies the goals and objectives of international education, including internationalizing the curriculum, providing for faculty and student exchanges, and instituting student study abroad programs. The document, which is discussed in greater detail under *Goals and Objectives for the International Program,* provided the framework for the international program at the college. With this increased emphasis on international activities, the college named a director of international education in 1982.

In summary, the BEIS Office coordinates the offerings of certificate and associate degree programs in bilingual education by providing over 150 bilingual classes per semester, facilitates faculty and student exchanges, develops study abroad programs, and assists faculty in internationalizing the curriculum. The international component of the BEIS Office has been strengthened in the past two years by the creation and adoption of an institutional plan for international education and the procurement of several grants to internationalize the curriculum.

Institutional Commitment to International Education

There is little doubt that the ethnic population of Pima County helped to provide the impetus for international education at Pima College. However, several other factors, both external and internal, also helped spur the development of the international program.

External factors

1. Key community organizations are involved in international activities. The Chamber of Commerce actively promotes international tourism; the Tucson Trade Bureau (TTB) recognizes and presents

TTB awards to foreign dignitaries; organizations like the Cultural Exchange Council and Una Noche Plateada promote cultural exchanges; and Tucson law enforcement agencies have developed cooperative programs with Mexican law enforcement officials.

2. The community is involved in sister city associations including the Tucson–Guadalajara Sister City Committee, the Tucson–Taichung Sister City Committee, and the Tucson–Ciudad Obregon Sister City Committee.

3. Geographically, Tucson is in close proximity to Mexico.

Internal factors

1. Pima's college professional development program has three main components. One program provides monetary incentives to faculty members if they enroll, attend, or participate in professional activities related to college assignments. These activities include academic course work, workshops, and seminars in intercultural/international studies. A second program supports faculty exchanges so faculty can teach or study at other colleges both inside the US and abroad. Finally, the professional development leave program enoourages faculty to study and work in multicultural activities while on leave from the college.

2. A faculty grants program supports faculty members in curriculum development endeavors. Because of the student/faculty makeup of the college many of these projects are intercultural/international.

INVOLVEMENT OF BOARD OF GOVERNORS, ADMINISTRATORS, FACULTY, AND STUDENTS

Pima's international commitment to international education is perhaps best demonstrated by examining some specific activities undertaken by four of the college's organizational levels: the Governing Board, the top administration, the faculty, and the students.

Pima College's Governing Board has approved:

- an admission policy that welcomes foreign students and affirms that "their presence adds to the multicultural diversity which is a part of all aspects of the college"[5]

- a professional development and faculty grants program described in the previous section

- employment of a full-time international student counselor

- employment of an international student admissions specialist
- creation of a Minorities Affairs Office
- retitling of the Office of Bilingual Education to the Office of Bilingual Education and International Studies
- a master plan document for 1980–85 reaffirms Pima's commitment to international education and states that the faculty will be assisted in internationalizing the curriculum

The president, the vice-presidents, and the executive deans have provided administrative support and funding for the following internationally focused programs and activities:

- an extensive training program in foreign languages. Students may study French, German, Spanish, Papago, or Swahili. Four semesters of study are offered in all languages with the exception of Papago and Swahili, which offer a one-year program. The Spanish department alone offers a total of nineteen courses to native and nonnative speakers. A foreign language auditorial laboratory is available to all foreign language students as well as ESL students.
- a bilingual program offering more than 150 courses.
- an extensive history program that includes numerous courses on Africa and Mexico.
- an English as a Second Language (ESL) program.
- a library with a total collection of over 300,000 books and audiovisual materials. The collection is particularly strong in the area of ethnic studies and Latin American history. In addtion, the library features six special collections. Two of these, Spanish Language and Faculty Professional Development, have been extremely valuable to faculty interested in internationalizing the college curriculum.

In addition, top administration has supported the following activities of the BEIS Office:

- an educational and cultural exchange effort in 1976 between the United States and Germany
- an international/bilingual/multicultural conference hosted by Pima College and cosponsored by the Overseas Liaison Committee of the American Council on Education and by El Congreso Nacional de Asuntos Colegiales (CONAC) and attended by educators from Africa, Asia, Latin America, and Europe

- a 1979 conference sponsored by Pima College and CONAC, which brought together nationally recognized leaders in international education from American community colleges

- an annual four-day Bilingual-Multicultural Symposium

- grants in bilingual and international education that have been supported by varying amounts of college matching funds

PCC faculty members have supported international education by the following activities:

- incorporating international studies and intercultural materials in existing and new courses and programs (a brochure published by the Office of Bilingual Education and International Studies lists over 140 courses that have an international/intercultural dimension).

- attending numerous conferences, workshops, and seminars on international/intercultural topics.

- participating in a grant project to internationalize the curriculum.

- studying and traveling abroad each year as part of their personal and professional development.

- participating as directors and instructors in study abroad programs for students. (Study abroad programs have been conducted in Mexico City and Ciudad Obregon.)

Students on all campuses have involved themselves in the following international/intercultural activities:

- formulating numerous student clubs. Some of these include the Arab Student Organization, the Black Student Alliance, the French Club, the International Club, M.E.Ch.A. (Movimiento Estudiantil Chicano de Aztlan), and the Native American Student Association.

- establishing and participating in the following activities: International week, Black Culture Week, Semana de la Raza, and Indian Culture Week; and the Bailes Folklóricos dance group; and the University of Arizona/Pima Community College Artists Series (in which many of the performing artists are from foreign countries). In addition, Pima Students help sponsor Tucson Meet Yourself, an annual city international/multicultural festival, with the Cultural Exchange Council.

- enrolling in 150 bilingual courses (enrollment of 2,000 for 1980/81).

- publishing *Llueve Tlaloc*, a student bilingual literary magazine.

In summary, all levels of the college have supported and are involved in international/intercultural activities.

MISSION OF INTERNATIONAL AND INTERCULTURAL EDUCATION

As stated earlier, Pima College has recognized the need for international/intercultural education since its inception. The BEIS Office was established to develop and provide bilingual/intercultural/international education to students at Pima Community College.

On November 19, 1980, the Board of Governors approved "International Education at Pima Community College: An Institutional Plan." That plan states that the goal of international education at the college is twofold: to provide students with basic information that allows them to function better within their own culture and to foster understanding of other cultures. The document provides the following rationale for international education.

1. Tucsonans will increasingly need an international education to understand and cope with local and national contemporary problems. Many of the fundamental problems of the Tucson Community, e.g., energy, inflation, drugs, undocumented aliens, and crime, are also international problems. It is imperative that Tucsonans be informed about international events and relations so they can intelligently determine their personal responses to these problems as well as respond intelligently to public policies proposed by their local and national leaders. In an interdependent world, an international education is a necessary component in an education for basic citizenship.

2. Tucsonans will increasingly need an international education to compete for and function in jobs because: Local business is often transacted in an international market; many local businessmen need to be knowledgeable about international marketing opportunities; numerous Tucson businesses are multinational; all local businessmen are directly or indirectly affected by decisions of multinational corporations, international policy-making organizations, and by international events.

3. Tucsonans will increasingly need international education to better understand and appreciate their own local cultural mix in the face of rapid urban growth. As the population of Tucson grows, so will the size of its various ethnic and cultural groups. An understanding and appreciation of these different groups will lead to improved community relations. International education provides a broad cultural perspective and helps to alleviate cultural divisiveness that often results from cultural mixes within a community.

In summary, the global scope of contemporary problems in modern business operations and the local population mix argue for providing students with an international education.

GOALS AND OBJECTIVES FOR THE INTERNATIONAL PROGRAM

A major goal of the BEIS Office is to strengthen international education at Pima Community College.

To accomplish this goal, the office has undertaken educational activities in two areas: on-campus activities such as internationalizing the curriculum and sponsoring special workshops and seminars on international/intercultural topics; and off-campus activities such as faculty and student exchanges, study abroad programs, and international programs for business and industry. Specifically, the following four objectives were established for the international component of the BEIS Office:

1. To strengthen the international and global components of the instructional program

2. To increase the number of students who are taking courses with international studies content

3. To develop a student/faculty exchange program

4. To develop student study abroad programs

The first and second objectives are interdependent. Increasing the number of internationalized courses by modifying existing courses will result in more students receiving international studies content. This emphasis on increasing the number of *existing* courses that are internationalized through modification rather than developing *new* international courses is deliberate. According to the October–November 1979 issue of *Acquainter*, "less than 1 percent of the college age group in the U.S. is enrolled in any course which specifically features international issues or areas."[6] A curriculum modification approach, whereby international units or special topics are introduced into existing liberal arts and vocational programs throughout the college, appears to be the best way to reach the largest segment of Pima students and to meet the institutional commitment to international education. Objectives 3 and 4, exchanges and study abroad programs, are international activities that provide excellent learning opportunities for students and faculty off campus. (The college recognizes, however, that fewer students and faculty will participate in these activities than in on-campus activities.)

It is most important to note that during the fall of 1980, the faculty, the administration, and the Board of Governors affirmed the college's commitment to international education and approved the preceding goal and objectives. This affirmation gives the international studies area its major sanction. The organizational chart, figure 15.1, shows that the BEIS Office reports to the vice-president of educational services.

Program Description

The BIES Office has two areas of responsibility: the Bilingual Education Program and the International Studies Program. The bilingual component includes 150 bilingual courses offered in such varied subject areas as office education, early childhood education, accounting, history, psychology, physical education, automotive technology, economics, biology, chemistry, and management.

By enrolling in bilingual courses, students can earn an Associate of Arts Degree in Education, Early Childhood Education, and Office Education–Bilingual Secretary. The Bilingual Teacher Aide Program has a one-year basic certificate for direct employment, while the Bilingual Secretary Program has both a one-semester basic and two-semester advanced certificate. These courses, certificates, and degrees are offered through the academic subject areas in conjunction with the Bilingual Office. There are no courses or programs taught directly out of the Bilingual Office.

In 1980 the college received a two-year title VI international education grant to be administered by the BEIS Office. The grant provided in-service training to faculty to internationalize the curriculum. During each of these two years, twelve Pima Community College faculty members were paid to internationalize courses in their subject area. Participating faculty members, including two from other Arizona community colleges, represented both college transfer (liberal arts) and occupational programs. Selected faculty members were given international studies training through a workshop series conducted on five Saturdays during the fall semester. The entire college community was invited to attend the workshops. The first workshop provided an overview to internationalizing existing curriculum; workshops two and three presented content information to faculty on various geographical areas of the world; workshops four and five were writing workshops in which faculty developed their international course material using a criterion-based instructional format. Consultants were brought to the college for workshops one, two, and three. A curriculum specialist from Pima Community College and the project director conducted workshops four and five. The newly developed materials were then taught and evaluated during the spring semester. New materials developed by this means are now offered to Pima Community College students on a regular basis. The project has been enthusiastically received by faculty and students. Subsequent grant projects have followed this model.

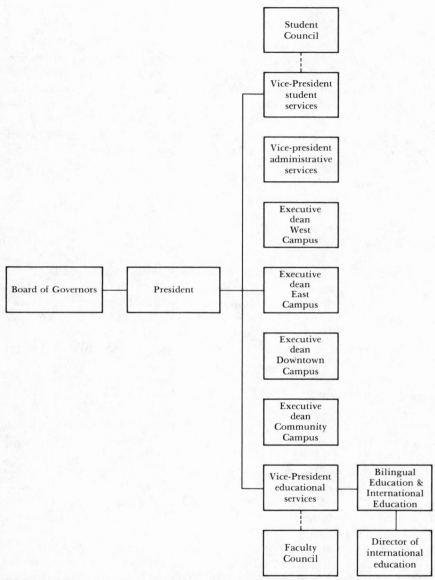

FIGURE 15.1. Administration organization of Pima Community College and International Education.

The faculty exchange program was started in 1977 and the study abroad program was first conducted in Mexico City in the summer of 1979. Both programs are still in existence though the study abroad program is now in Ciudad Obregon.

STAFF

The BEIS Office is staffed to accommodate various bilingual/international education programs. The associate dean, the secretary, and a bilingual program specialist comprise the entire full-time staff. The director of international education, a regular faculty member assigned four-fifths time to the office, reports to the BEIS dean. The director is supported by a temporary full-time secretary. In addition, a program development coordinator employed by the Bilingual Education Service of San Diego State University works out of the BEIS Office and provides technical and curriculum development services to schools with bilingual projects in the southern Arizona area.

LINKAGES WITH OTHER INSTITUTIONAL UNITS AND THE COMMUNITY

The BEIS Office works very closely with other college units. These include the Student Services and the Admissions Office, which help support the 580 foreign students on campus. Student Services also provides international/intercultural activities for all students. The Community Campus helps the BEIS Office administrator the summer abroad program and the International Business Communications Studies (IBC) Program. The ESL and foreign language departments have developed intensive language programs. The athletic department engages in exchange visitations in Mexico. In addition the BEIS Office works with numerous academic departments—humanities, writing, marketing, accounting, nursing, drafting, office education, sociology, early childhood education, history, psychology, automotive technology, biology, chemistry, and management—in coordinating international courses and bilingual classes for students. It is estimated that during the 1980/81 school year 100 to 125 full-time faculty members (about 50 percent of the full-time faculty) worked with the BEIS Office in providing internationalized academic course work for students, establishing a faculty exchange, or developing a study abroad program.

There are also many community groups and organizations with which the BEIS Office has affiliated to promote specific intercultural/international programs: the Sister City Committees, which include the Tucson–Guadalajara Sister City Committee, the Tucson–Taichung Sister City Committee, and the Tucson–Ciudad Obregon Sister City Committee; the Tucson Trade Bureau, and numerous cultural councils, including the Cultural Exchange Council and Una Noche Plateada. In addition, the office has reached out to numerous institutions of higher learning in Canada, the United Kingdom, and Mexico to establish faculty and student exchange programs. These BEIS liaisons with other Pima College offices, community organizations, foreign schools, and especially the faculty in academic departments, are an essential component of the international education program at the college.

FUNDING

In its eleven-year history the Bilingual Office has been most successful at procuring outside funding, and has received more than $600,000 from major grant awards. In 1980/81 the total budget of the BEIS Office was $189,783. Federal grant monies accounted for $138,082 of that figure. This heavy reliance on grant funds is not atypical for the office. The 1980/81 budget is a fairly accurate reflection of budgets of previous years.

Budget 1980/81

Items	Expenditures
Personnel salaries	96,889
Fringe benefits	16,333
Travel	4,888
Supplies	5,128
Programs (honoraria, faculty and participant travel costs, tuition)	66,545
TOTAL	$189,783

Obviously, it is important to spend grant funds in allocated categories. Because such a large portion of the office's budget comes from grants, there is relatively little freedom in deciding how and where the money is spent. Most of the grantor agencies allow a maximal 10 percent expenditure deviation by category. Although the college's portion of the budget is less restrictive in the amounts and kinds of money that can be transferred once allocated, careful planning and continual budget monitoring are nevertheless required. All expenditures of the office must be approved by the vice-president for educational services.

Because BEIS is heavily dependent on federal grant funds, the office must continue to seek outside funding sources, as well as to develop better ways of using Pima Community College funds. Outside funding is essential if the office is going to maintain the current level of commitment to international education.

MAJOR GROUPS SERVED BY BEIS PROGRAMS

The BEIS Office serves numerous segments of the community. Each year the office sponsors workshops and programs on various bilingual/

intercultural/international topics which are open to the Tucson and college community. The Hispanic population is served by many of the bilingual programs. The bilingual program trains a large portion of the bilingual teacher aides for three school districts in Arizona that operate bilingual programs: Tucson Unified School District, in which 27 percent of the 60,991 enrollment is Hispanic, Sunnyside Unified School District, in which 54 percent of 11,777 students are Hispanic, and Nogales School District, in which 87 percent of the 4,950 students are Hispanic.

Those Pima College students that are US citizens but do not speak English as their first language are aided by the bilingual course offerings, as are English-speaking students who take bilingual courses to improve their proficiency in Spanish. Foreign students are served by this office mainly through the ESL program. In addition, the BEIS office serves faculty members interested in internationalizing the curriculum, establishing study abroad programs, or seeking foreign exchange work with the office in order to develop new programs. Finally, the office coordinates numerous courses and programs which have been internationalized or contain international/intercultural dimensions.

Strengths and Weaknesses

Essentially, the college has two programs in the BEIS Office. The Bilingual Program is well established. Its development has been supported by top college officials and faculty and fostered by large, continuous federal grants totaling over $600,000 from 1970 to 1981. The newer International Studies Program is also supported by top college administration and faculty and has recently been awarded its first major grants. The international component works to provide an internationalized curriculum, faculty and student exchanges, and study abroad programs.

Strengths

1. A relatively decentralized approach to conducting an international education program results in the involvement of a significant portion of the college's faculty and administration. This provides a broad base of support for the programs.

2. A significant portion of the classes offered in the district have an international/intercultural dimension.

3. An institutional approach in which existing occupational/college transfer and special interest courses are internationalized rather than circumvented by the development of new courses and programs results in stronger support from existing faculty who might otherwise be concerned that new courses would draw

enrollments away from current course offerings. The approach also results in a high student involvement in international studies regardless of career goals.

4. An Office of Bilingual Education and International Studies created at a district level allows all campuses to participate and benefit from the office's programs.

5. A strong commitment to cultivating community ties helps promote the office's activities and makes it possible to cosponsor an increasing number of international/intercultural events with local organizations.

6. A sizable amount of grant money has been made available to the college to develop programs that the college would not otherwise have been able to provide.

Weaknesses

1. With such a large portion of the college involved in international/ intercultural activities, coordination is sometimes difficult. News of an activity does not always reach those who need to be involved or want to be informed.

2. Because the office is a district-level office housed on the West Campus, the office does not have as close an affiliation with faculty on the other campuses.

3. There are only two permanent full-time college-supported positions in the office. A small permanent staff makes it difficult to undertake many new projects. Often there is insufficient staff to support existing programs to the fullest extent.

4. Heavy dependence on grant funds makes future planning difficult and pressures the office to be looking constantly for a new source of funding. With such a small staff, time is often taken from supporting existing programs to researching new funding possibilities.

This decentralized approach to administering an international studies office works if the following conditions exist.

1. A strong philosophical commitment of the college to internationalize education.

2. A faculty motivated to develop international or multicultural course materials for their students. Much of the development in international education at Pima College has been initiated by

individual instructors who have received no compensation for their work.

3. A multicultural community that supports international/multicultural courses.

4. A staff that is committed to international education and willing to work with faculty and students to create international classes and programs.

Strategies for the 1980s

Pima College and the BEIS Office will continue to offer to students and faculty both on-campus and off-campus activities in international education. On-campus activities will include workshops and seminars as well as faculty development programs that will encourage faculty to internationalize their courses and programs. Students will be urged to take courses with an international component. Off-campus activities will include student and faculty exchange programs and student study abroad.

In order to serve the needs of business and industry in the Tucson area, more attention will now be focused on the possibility of offering short-term courses to train industry personnel for overseas assignments and/or for assignments in international departments. The college will develop programs and courses to respond to this need. On the basis of a needs assessment study done in the summer of 1981, the college also will provide training in English and American culture to foreigners who are on long-term assignments with Tucson businesses. Local businesses have also requested course work for their employees who return from long-term overseas assignments to help prevent "reverse" culture shock.

In addition to developing the course work mentioned above, the college is planning to conduct workshops, conferences, and seminars for businesses to help them locate overseas markets, and to provide information on how to conduct business overseas.

The major threat to the program in the 1980s undoubtedly will be inadequate funding. As grant funds dry up, the office must rely increasingly on international programs and activities that can be carried on with a relatively limited budget, or undertake only those activities that will be essentially self-supporting.

The citizens of Tucson will increasingly need an international/intercultural education to understand and cope with local and national problems, to compete for jobs and function in them, and to understand and appreciate their own local cultural mix in the face of rapid urban growth. This need, combined with the community's and college's commitment to international education, indicates strongly that the college will continue to support international education in the years to come. It will be the responsibility of the BEIS Office to find new and innovative means to develop and strengthen the program and, equally important, to find ways to finance these programs.

Notes

1. Pima Community College Master Plan 1980–1985, p. 23.
2. Pima Community College: Accomplishments, Growth, and Development, 1972–1977: A Basis for Planning, 1978–1983. (Prepared for the Pima County Community College District Governing Board, December 1977), p. 10.
3. Pima Community College Master Plan 1980–1985, p. 21.
4. Ibid., p. 66.
5. Pima Community College Catalog, 1981–1982, p. 23.
6. *Acquainter* (Newsletter published by the Council for Inter-Institutional Leadership, University, Alabama), October–November 1979.

CHAPTER 16

Bergen Community College

LYNDA ICOCHEA

Institutional Description

Bergen Community College (BCC) is located in Paramus, New Jersey, in the northeasternmost county adjacent to New York City. The college provides quality, community-based postsecondary education for adults through more than fifty credit and noncredit programs on and off campus, and serves the needs of a diverse citizenry. The college's formal commitment to international education is documented in the following mission statement: "To develop in the student an understanding and appreciation of our own and of other nations' and peoples' historical and cultural heritages and their implications for the present technological age."

Bergen Community College was founded in 1965 with an initial student enrollment of 300. In 1980/81, 11,500 full- and part-time students were enrolled. In addition, 17,000 residents were served by programs provided by Community Services. The College has significantly expanded its offerings in liberal arts and sciences as well as in the occupational curricula. College financial, physical, and human resources to meet student needs include a $23,157,956 operating budget for 1981/82 and nearly 5.5 million square feet of facilities on a 167-acre campus.

Faculty development has always been a priority at BCC. Each year the college expends funds for faculty to travel to professional meetings and for faculty tuition expenses incurred through educational enrichment, sabbatical leaves, and released time, thereby encouraging creative instructional development. In addition to workshops and staff development programs, a Center for Instructional Research and Development has been established to foster faculty and institutional vitality by providing internal support for curriculum development projects. The college's Library and Learning Resources Center, including 80,000 volumes and 22,000 units of audiovisual material, has excellent facilities to meet faculty, staff, and student needs.

FACULTY

The college has sought to employ faculty from diverse academic backgrounds who could meet the challenges of an innovative community college curricula. Many international faculty members' experiences living here and abroad add an intercultural aspect to their courses and extracurricular activities. Countries represented by these faculty members include, Egypt, Iran, Cuba, Italy, France, Mexico, India, Japan, Germany, Russia, Taiwan, Denmark, England, and Puerto Rico. In addition, since 1978 the college has hosted faculty from Taiwan and Israel.

A survey to assess existing resource persons in international studies among the academic divisions was conducted in 1979. The results showed that the following disciplines were staffed by faculty who had academic background and/or a strong interest in international/intercultural studies: Anthropology, Business Administration and Technologies, Computer Technology, Data Processing, English Language Arts and Literature, Foreign Language and Literature, Economics, History, Philosophy, Psychology, Political Science, Ethics and Religious Studies, Sociology, Mathematics, Biology, and Early Childhood Education.

STUDENTS

The students, 11,500 full-time and part-time, are mostly Bergen County residents and are quite varied in terms of income, ethnic background, and age. The average 1981/82 student was 27, and women make up well over 50 percent of the student population. There are no housing facilities on campus and most students work part-time. Approximately 1,000 foreign-born students from the following countries attend the college: Bahamas, Brazil, Cuba, Cyprus, Dominican Republic, Ecuador, Egypt, El Salvador, France, Greece, Guyana, Hong Kong, Iran, Italy, Jordan, Lebanon, Mexico, Nigeria, Pakistan, People's Republic of China, Peru, Poland, Saudi Arabia, Syria, Trinidad, Turkey, Venezuela, and West Germany. Because of the increased foreign-born student population, the college employs two full-time international student advisors who are responsible for academic and personal counseling of all international students.

COMMUNITY

The community served by the college is multiethnic. The county planning board's data revealed that approximately 42.1 percent (378,259) of the residents are international. Industry has grown at a rapid rate during the last ten years and an increasing number of international firms have moved their corporate headquarters to Bergen County. During the 1980/81 academic year, the Center for International Studies identified 2,000 companies that are dealing in international trade. More than 3,000 companies in Bergen County will join the international trade market in the next five to ten years.

Because of the student and community composition, Bergen Community College is mandated to pursue a strong and cohesive plan for practical international studies programs.

Historical Development of International Programs

Since 1965, the college's six divisions have offered a wide range of courses and programs with intercultural dimensions. These courses serve the interests and objectives of both the American and international students attending the college and fulfill the college's mission statement to "offer relevant, quality, varied, and lifelong educational programs and opportunities at the lowest possible cost and with a minimum of barriers to all motivated persons with the potential to benefit." Its mission is also to provide leadership in meeting the changing economic, educational, cultural, recreational, and social needs of individuals and the community.

The Modern Language section of the college's Humanities Division is a leader among such divisions in community colleges. Bergen Community College continues to require modern languages in all Associate of Arts and many Associate of Science degree programs. These curricula require the study of one of seven languages: French, German, Modern Hebrew, Italian, Japanese, Russian, or Spanish. More than 50 courses are offered in language skills, culture, literature, history, mathematics, and business administration in languages other than English. In addition to these offerings, more than 100 intercultural courses are offered at the college.

In September 1979, the dean of instruction approved the formation of an International Studies Task Force. Members represented all disciplines and were charged with assessing the college's resources and potential for a centralized international/intercultural program.

During the 1979/80 academic year the Task Force accomplished the following activities:

1. Surveyed faculty in order to assess interest and resources in international education. More than 50 faculty members showed an

active commitment to international education by virtue of their major scholarly interest in international and global issues.

2. Prepared a successful proposal to fund the services of a foreign curriculum consultant from Israel.

3. Formed the International Trade Round Table Association.

4. Actively participated in local and national international studies consortia.

5. Designed an active agenda for the college, including plans for the development of curricula for degree programs in International Studies, International Marketing, and Import/Export Management. Commitment on the administrative level is one of the key factors to the rapid success of the college's international studies program. The Center for Institutional Research and Development Committee, chaired by the president of the college, declared international education to be a priority in 1979. This committee awarded a small grant to the International Studies Task Force chairperson in May 1980 in order to assess the international business educational needs of county industries. Due to the positive responses of the survey and the articulated needs by industry for seminars, workshops, and courses, the president of the college approved the formation of the International Trade Round Table. The Round Table was initiated with twenty company members and doubled its membership in four months. This direct contact with local leaders in industry enabled the International Studies Task Force to document the need for international studies in the language, culture, and business areas.

6. Coordinated publication of the existing study abroad programs to Spain, France, and Puerto Rico sponsored by the college, as well as the programs to over thirty countries sponsored by consortia to which the college belonged.

7. Coordinated cultural activities among the college's eight internationally focused student organizations.

8. Researched existing international studies models on both national and international campuses.

9. Identified local resources in the New York metropolitan area in terms of guest speakers, consultants, curricular materials, and international/intercultural organizations.

Each month, the Task Force chairperson submitted progress reports to the dean of instruction and presented periodic reports to the Center for Institutional Research and Development Committee. The task force was encouraged by the administration to continue its endeavors and to seek external funding, for the college was entering a period of budgetary constraints. In September 1980, the chairperson was awarded six hours release time per semester by the dean of instruction to coordinate college activities in the international education area.

During the 1980/81 academic year the International Studies Task Force worked closely to prepare a proposal requesting federal funds under title VI, which provides funding for international undergraduate programs. The task force was ready to develop and implement a comprehensive program for internationalization of the college's curricular and extracurricular activities. Federal funding was awarded in July 1981 and the Center for International Studies was established.

The Center for International Studies

The director of the Center for International Studies reports directly to the president, just as the associate deans of other academic departments do. Reporting to the director of International Studies are the coordinator for study abroad, the part-time curriculum development coordinator, and several assistants. In a community college setting, this administrative link is essential.

Administrative support is a key factor to the program's success, but divisional support from the dean and faculty is equally significant. Since the center is an autonomous body, it can truly serve as a catalyst for institutional activities in international education. Every division and faculty and staff member has the opportunity to work with the center in a nondepartmental atmosphere, affording the participants the feeling of institutional cooperation for a common goal.

GOALS AND OBJECTIVES

The center's guiding philosophy has been that it is no longer enough for community college students to know that countries and people are different. Students need to know how and why these cultures and people are different and how the differences will effect cooperative efforts to achieve desired objectives among nations. In order to implement a workable international program throughout the college, the center established the following goals in spring 1981, to be accomplished by June 1983.

    I. To ensure that the Center for International Studies serves as a catalyst for new initiatives and provides leadership for all international/intercultural activities

A. To work with divisions to develop international courses
B. To work with faculty and staff to foster international/intercultural activities
C. To provide lists of guest speakers and curricular materials
D. To publicize international events on and off campus through a quarterly newsletter

II. To internationalize the general education program by creating cross-cultural teaching modules, defined as six to twelve hours of instructional units, based on a thematic approach to global interdependence
   A. To provide encouragement, direction, and evaluation for participating faculty
   B. To assist in design and acquisition of required supplementary curriculum materials
   C. To provide funding to support faculty development
   D. To institute an International Resource Center in the college Library Learning and Resource Center, displaying foreign language and cross-cultural arts and crafts exhibitions, books, periodicals, and lectures for cross-cultural teaching units

III. To enhance faculty understanding of global perspectives and stimulate interest in international studies
   A. To provide a sequence of monthly faculty development workshops
   B. To assist faculty with international travel opportunities
   C. To encourage and assist divisions with faculty exchange and group study abroad programs
   D. To involve faculty with visiting international scholars
   E. To involve faculty with recruitment and design of study/travel abroad programs

IV. To enhance student understanding of global perspectives and stimulate interest in international studies
   A. To publicize intercultural events in student newspaper and campus media
   B. To assist students with international travel programs and identify sources of funding and overseas work/study programs
   C. To coordinate student seminars focusing on global interdependence themes
   D. To enhance library acquisition in international/intercultural areas and publicize new acquisitions
   E. To coordinate intercultural events such as arts and crafts exhibitions, concerts, and theatre excursions

V. To create new courses and coordinate new curricula
   A. To provide funds to support faculty who are developing new courses for the International Marketing and International

Studies areas of concentration and the Import/Export Certificate Program
  B. To provide consultation sessions for faculty with expertise in these areas
  C. To provide evaluation models for faculty
  D. To apprise faculty of similar endeavors at other institutions and provide bibliographies
  E. To be responsible for appropriate faculty and administrative approval of new courses and new curricula
 VI. To enhance the international dimensions of the community and state
  A. To sponsor monthly seminars and workshops on international business themes
  B. To sponsor a community forum series on international/intercultural themes
  C. To involve international visitors (professors and students) with community organizations and agencies
  D. To serve as a referral service for the private and public sectors in terms of language translation needs, study abroad opportunities, and international courses available
VII. To expand participation in local, national, and international organizations
  A. To continue active participation in consortia whose main objective is the promotion of international/intercultural studies such as the New Jersey Collegiate Consortium for International/Intercultural Education, College Consortium for International Studies, Consortium for Development, International/Intercultural Consortium of the American Association of Community and Junior Colleges
  B. To continue to cooperate with, share resources with, and benefit from relationships with organizations dedicated to global studies and issues such as the Asia Society, Hispanic Concerns Staff Organization, International Consulates, World Trade Center, International Trade Administration of the US Department of Commerce, World Federalist Organization, and Global Learning Associates

The 1980/81 operating budget of the Center for International Studies is summarized in Table 16.1.

Program Components

CURRICULUM DEVELOPMENT

A comprehensive survey was sent to the faculty in 1979 to determine which courses had international aspects and to assess faculty interest in

TABLE 16.1. 1980/81 Operating Budget of the
Center for International Studies

Expenses	Federal	Nonfederal
1. Salaries and fringe benefits	21,838	36,348
2. Stipends and travel expenses to consultants	3,200	
3. Stipends for faculty for curriculum development	6,200	1,200
4. Faculty participation in conferences and off-campus visitations	2,000	1,000
5. Library and curricular acquisitions for curriculum development	2,500	1,500
6. Communications (telephone, printing, copying, newsletter, postage, and office supplies)	1,300	1,450
7. International Trade Round Table (honoraria, printing, postage, indirect expenses)		3,000
8. Indirect costs	2,962	1,640
TOTAL	40,000	46,130

internationalizing the curriculum. The survey revealed that, although the college offers many courses that are international in nature, the theme of global interdependence was not totally developed nor were these courses effectively organized. The survey results also showed that most faculty members wanted to expand course content and instructional techniques to include a global dimension, but lacked direction.

The Center for International Studies was established to provide this direction in curriculum development. The center, therefore, decided to dedicate its faculty and budgetary resources to three activities: (1) revising courses within the core curriculum by preparing teaching units based on themes of global interdependence; (2) creating new courses that would reflect cross-cultural themes; and (3) developing new curricula.

Specifically, the center has addressed these areas in the following manner in the first semester of its establishment.

1. *Revising core courses.* Twenty-seven cross-cultural teaching modules, defined as six to twelve hours of instructional units, were developed between September and December 1981. These modules will be integrated into required and/or high enrollment courses during the spring 1982 semester. After the modules are modified and evaluated, they will be disseminated to all faculty. Some of the developed modules are: Themes in Cross-Cultural Music Appreciation; A Global Look at Contemporary Health Problems: Stress, Divorce, Alcoholism; Introduction to Computers: A Cross-Cultural Comparison of Educational Methodology; Japanese Business Principles.

2. *Creating new courses* (listed specifically in the "Faculty Development" section of this chapter).

3. *Developing new curricula.* New courses have been and will continue to be developed for the International Marketing Concentration,

Import/Export Certificate Program, and International Studies Concentration. The college decided to offer these new curricula because:

- International trade competition and economic interdependence are a part of most modern business enterprises.
- The county's business community has expressed specific needs for well-trained personnel in international marketing, import, and export management skills.
- At least 60 percent of BCC's students major in business/career programs.
- The need for an area of concentration in International Studies is well documented. With the increasing complexity of international issues and the ever-present provincialism evident in American colleges, students need a program integrating foreign language skills, the study of different cultures, and international issues.

Although the career programs did not previously include the study of a modern language other than English, the new curricula will require this component.

FACULTY DEVELOPMENT

In order to enhance faculty understanding of global perspectives and to stimulate interest in international studies, the center provides faculty development workshops, coordination, evaluation, and funding stipends for curriculum development, and funding for off-campus participation in conferences, workshops, and conventions. Specifically, these three services have been implemented in the following ways.

Workshops. The center sponsors monthly sessions with qualified workshop leaders concerned with global awareness and the international curriculum.

Faculty who develop modules and courses in conjunction with the center are especially encouraged to attend the workshops. Participants are informed of current approaches and learn to present their subject matter in an international/intercultural framework.

Curriculum development. Faculty are encouraged to develop modules and new courses. When the course or module is approved by the director and the dean of instructional services, faculty work with the center's director and curriculum coordinator and receive stipends for their efforts.

The center approved twenty-seven modules and six course development applications during fall 1981. Other modules in addition to those listed previously were developed, and six new courses were developed as part of the International Marketing Concentration:

- Fundamentals of International Business
- International Finance and Insurance
- International Trade Documentation
- Conversational Spanish for Business Professionals
- Conversational French for Business Professionals
- Conversational Italian for Business Professionals

Off-campus conferences.   Faculty are invited to submit applications for conferences and workshops that focus on global issues and international/intercultural education. During the fall 1981 semester, the center funded travel expenses and registration fees for fifteen faculty members. Participants are required to submit written reports which are then distributed throughout the college.

Participants are also invited to make presentations at regularly scheduled meetings of the International Studies Task Force. It is essential that faculty be kept up to date on current developments in international education.

Contacts made at conferences and workshops are invaluable in terms of identifying future consultants or workshop leaders and, in general, allowing faculty to share experiences and materials. By maintaining interinstitutional contact, internationalists can modify and adapt existing material for their particular discipline and approach.

STUDY ABROAD

Faculty have organized study/travel programs since 1963. Until fall 1981 these programs were administered on an individual basis. The college commitment to international education was clearly manifested when a coordinator for academic study abroad programs was appointed in August 1981. This program involves making arrangements for accommodations, transportation, specialized courses, insurance, and orientation to the following countries for short-term programs: Spain, France, Italy, Mexico, England, Puerto Rico, Israel, and the Dominican Republic. A full-time director accompanies each group, as well as instructors who teach intensive language and culture courses.

Most of these programs require fifteen hours of contact study at the college and a minimum of thirty contact hours in the host country. Occupational courses are also offered abroad. For example, a criminal justice seminar conducted in England involved the study and comparison of international systems of law enforcement, and a retail management seminar conducted in Mexico allowed participants direct contact with the Mexican retail industry.

VISITING SCHOLARS

International scholars have been hosted by the college since 1970. In that year, the college was fortunate to enjoy the services of Dr. Zafrira Ben-David from Israel, who was sponsored by the Fulbright program. Dr. Ben-David taught two Conversational Modern Hebrew courses and the seminar *Israel Today*. The interaction between Dr. Ben-David and the college community served to heighten interest in intercultural studies and to stimulate a college commitment to host a visiting scholar each year.

In 1980, the college president traveled to Taiwan with other presidents through the Community College Cooperative for International Development. As a result of this visit, four Taiwanese educators spent the 1981 spring semester at Bergen Community College. The participants taught and observed classes and shared their resources with faculty and students.

Professor Ken Fang from the China Marine College in Taiwan is being sponsored by the college during the 1982 spring semester. The Center for International Studies is coordinating Dr. Fang's activities, including an in-service program in college administration; guest lectures in classes in every discipline and at gatherings of community organizations; seminars for students focusing on Taiwanese social issues and other seminars for the community.

As part of the college plan to sponsor a visiting scholar every year, the center prepared a proposal to host an International Business educator from Japan for the 1982/83 academic year. Contingent upon federal approval, the plan calls for the Japanese scholar to serve as a curriculum consultant for the International Marketing, Import/Export Management, and Asian studies curricula. The consultant will also be involved with the International Trade Round Table and other noncredit programs in international trade.

GRANT DEVELOPMENT

As mentioned previously, the center depends on federal support for two-thirds of its operating budget. Therefore, personnel work closely with the institutional development grants officer to identify sources of federal, state, and local funding.

In addition to the first approved grant proposal through the Office of Education in Washington (title VI—International Undergraduate Programs), which helped establish the center, and the Fulbright proposal for a Japanese curriculum consultant, the center is preparing three proposals at present: group study abroad in Spain and Africa; visiting scholar— Carribean specialist in behavioral sciences; and mini-grants from the

College Center for Institutional Research and Development for curriculum development.

Individual faculty members of the International Studies Task Force are encouraged to initiate funding proposals. These proposals are prepared under the direction of the center and the college grants officer. Eleven members of the Task Force successfully applied for funding of module development in September 1981 through the college's Center for Institutional Research and Development.

INTERNATIONAL BUSINESS PROGRAMS

In May 1980, the director of the Center for International Studies received funding to assess the needs of local industry for international studies. Four hundred and fifty Bergen County companies dealing in international trade were identified. A survey was sent and the 170 responding companies expressed needs for seminars, workshops, courses, and an International Trade Round Table Association. In September 1980, the director received release time to implement these programs. The center continues to devote 50 percent of its resources to practical programs for focusing on international business.

INTERNATIONAL TRADE ROUND TABLE ASSOCIATION

In September 1980, twenty companies sent representatives to the first Round Table Association seminar. By December 1980 the association enjoyed a membership of forty international trade companies. The 1981 membership list showed seventy companies. This rapid growth indicates the high level of interest and the need for an open forum for northern New Jersey companies to discuss timely international trade issues.

The Round Table meets monthly at the college for a luncheon/open discussion session. Experts in international business are invited as guest speakers to make presentations; a question/answer period follows. The director of the International Studies Center coordinates this association. A member of the Round Table is selected each year to serve as chairperson, thus creating a direct link between the center and local industry. Some of the topics that have been discussed at meetings include: Export Marketing, Japanese Perspective on Insurance Practices, Doing Business with Argentina, The ABC's of Importing, Export Pricing, and many others.

The Round Table has been invaluable to the center's operations. This direct contact with business leaders has enhanced the college's efforts to design practical and sophisticated programs in international trade for students and industry employees who wish to upgrade their skills.

CUSTOMIZED COURSES

Industry has requested specialized courses in international trade for employees. The center works with the Division of Community Services and has offered courses on campus and on company sites. Some authorized courses have included Conversational Spanish for Business Professionals, A Practical Approach to Letters of Credit, and Importing Techniques and Documentation.

Instructors have included members of the International Studies Task Force and the International Trade Round Table. The Round Table members are periodically surveyed and the center will continue to design programs to satisfy articulated needs.

WORKSHOPS

The center designs monthly noncredit practical workshops on various international business issues. In many instances, the workshop is a follow-up to a International Trade Round Table presentation. Companies are normally represented by high-level management at Round Table sessions, whereas midmanagement employees normally attend the followup workshop. An average of forty representatives have attended programs whose topics have included: Freight Forwarding, The Arab Boycott Issue, Marine Insurance, and Export Pricing.

The center has identified 2,000 companies in Bergen County dealing in imports and/or exports. Data from the US Department of Commerce reveals a list of 3,000 companies in northern New Jersey who will enter the international trade area within the next five years. The center is, therefore, enthusiastic and feels encouraged to continue its workshops, seminars, and courses in international trade. These activities focus on business topics as well as language and cultural themes. Dialogue with industry leaders has revealed that their employees need language skills courses and programs dealing with cultural practices that affect business transactions.

INSTITUTIONAL LINKAGES

The success of comprehensive international programs depends largely on institutional support and cooperative efforts between the Center for International Studies and three key groups: individual faculty members, division personnel, and students.

The center publicizes its events through faculty and student media in an effort to create support and stimulate interest and, above all, to create a "community" spirit at the college. International education activities must be centralized at an institution, and the activities must become an integral component and source of permanent value for all college divisions.

FACULTY INVOLVEMENT

The International Studies Task Force, which began in 1979, has expanded to include faculty from almost every discipline. At present, thirty-two faculty participate in the Task Force. The faculty and staff serve as a major center resource. Their participation and support has ensured success for each program component.

Faculty involvement strengthens the center's efforts in four major ways. First, essential faculty support is gained through approval of new initiatives by collegewide faculty committees such as the curriculum and senate committees. Second, faculty participation in the center's workshops and planning committees ensures input from all disciplines and stimulates interest in international education. Third, as more and more disciplines are identified with the center, international education becomes a collegewide concern, not just an issue to be handled by the three center faculty members. The fourth and key factor is that the participation of dedicated, qualified, and innovative faculty is necessary for successful curriculum development.

DIVISIONAL INVOLVEMENT

Support from other divisions in the college is necessary for successful implementation of international programs. At BCC, faculty report directly to assistant deans of divisions. Divisional deans are kept up to date on center activities and the progress of their division representatives who work with the center. Deans are invited to attend International Studies Task Force meetings and are asked for input in the center's programing.

The center attempts to direct appropriate material to divisional deans in an effort to maintain close contact with them. Within the institutional structure, the divisional deans are responsible for approval of curriculum development, release time, faculty scheduling, and, in general, faculty participation in projects outside of their appropriate divisions. Therefore, the center must cultivate a positive relationship, not only to foster cooperation but also to ensure that the center's activities coincide with college priorities.

STUDENT INVOLVEMENT

The business of any college is people. The center's goals and objectives were designed to provide practical programs for students and to prepare them for a complex global community. Student response to the center's activities, after all, will be the prime indication of success.

The Student Government Association sponsors eight internally focused clubs, under the guidance of faculty advisors. Approximately nine hundred students actively participate in these organizations each year. These clubs serve as support groups for their international student members as well as the US students who want to enhance their cross-cultural experiences. The center has made a concerted effort to meet with the eight organizations in order to publicize its activities and to offer support as cosponsors of events.

The director of the center is also faculty advisor of the Spanish Club. The advisors of the International, French, German, Japanese, and Social Awareness Clubs are members of the International Studies Task Force. It has been very easy to gain support from student clubs, which welcome the opportunity to expand their activities in cooperation with the Center for International Studies. Details of some of the center's student activities follow.

Seminars. The center cosponsors monthly "International Awareness" seminars with an individual club to discuss topics from an intercultural point of view. Student volunteers serve as moderators for seminars, which have included the themes of Academic Life, Music as a Cultural Expression, and Dating and Marriage Customs, among others.

Artistic Presentations. The center cosponsored three presentations during the 1981 fall semester with student clubs: a concert, "The Dance of Spain and the Classical Dances of Japan: A Unique Cross-Cultural Experience," and two expositions: "African Artists and Their Works" and "New Values: Latin American Artists' Expose."

Translation and Counseling Services. The center serves as a referral source for international students. These students also use the services of the center for the translation of documents and academic and personal counseling. Translators are available in Spanish, French, Italian, German, Russian, Modern Hebrew, Chinese, Japanese, Arabic, Hungarian, Yoruba, Hindi, Polish, Portuguese, and English.

INTERINSTITUTIONAL INVOLVEMENT

The college encourages faculty members to participate in interinstitutional meetings to foster cooperative relations and articulate curricular regulations and programing. The center actively participates in local and national consortia and organizations that focus on the promotion of international/intercultural education. A partial list of organizations and the role of the center follows.

New Jersey District Export Council. The director of the center is an active member of this committee. The council's purpose is to coordinate export-related activities in northern New Jersey. During monthly meetings, groups coordinate workshops and seminars and share the names of prospective consultants and speakers. The Export Council cosponsors many workshops and seminars with the Center for International Studies. In addition, many council members serve as consultants for faculty members developing international business curricula. Membership on this council has allowed the center to be directly involved with local industry and representatives from the US Department of Commerce. Most significantly, this relationship has allowed the center to remain attuned to industry needs and has enhanced its ability to schedule activities focusing on timely issues. Because the college enjoys flexibility in scheduling events, a workshop can be designed and scheduled in a matter of weeks or days if the director is aware that a certain issue needs to be addressed. Thus, workshops deal with timely issues and satisfy immediate needs.

New Jersey Collegiate Consortium for International-Intercultural Education. The center's director is the chairperson of this organization. The consortium was organized in 1979 to plan strategy for promoting and strengthening global dimensions in curricular and extracurricular activities throughout the New Jersey educational system.

The Center for International Studies has been a leader in the consortium in terms of sharing resources and programing events. The director conducted a workshop on behalf of the consortium at the 1981 New Jersey Education Association convention on the topic "Internationalizing the Business Curriculum."

Members of the consortium have participated in faculty development workshops and consultation sessions at Bergen Community College. In addition, many member institutions have benefited in their efforts to internationalize their own institutions through center activities.

Teaching/Learning Task Force of the New Jersey Community College Consortium. The center's director is the cochairperson of this organization, whose members are appointed representatives of the seventeen community colleges in New Jersey. The commitment of Bergen Community College to international education has benefited Task Force members who want information about how to implement international studies programs on their campuses. The center has sponsored a workshop on Comprehensive International Studies Programs and has provided Task Force members with lists of consultants and materials appropriate to each institution. Association with the Task Force has highlighted the feasibility and necessity of international programs on a statewide community college level.

Although the Center for International Studies is in the early stages of development, staff personnel consistently monitor the results. External consultants and participating faculty and students evaluate activities to modify, delete, and improve programing.

Strengths

1. Administration has made a commitment to the goals and objectives of the center as manifested by the support of board of trustees, president, and divisional deans.

2. Center is not directly responsible to any particular division; director reports to the president; thus the center can serve as a true catalyst for all divisions.

3. Director is aided in responsibilities by two coordinators who implement activities dealing with study/travel abroad and curriculum development. This staff delegation allows the center to design and implement programs effectively and rapidly.

4. Involvement by qualified and dedicated faculty representing diverse disciplines adds the required perspectives for a comprehensive and interdisciplinary approach.

5. Modules that will integrate global dimensions into every curriculum have been developed successfully. These units have been introduced in one section of all required courses. In addition, this method allows for maximum exposure since courses traditionally defined as "high enrollment" courses will also include modules.

6. Faculty interest and attendance at workshops have fostered positive campuswide relations and have encouraged other faculty to attend.

7. Interested international business community members have made their needs evident to the center. They have supported activities that satisfy their expressed need for services.

8. The culturally diverse composition of the community is a strength to the center. The community welcomes and supports efforts to design service-oriented programs that address ethnic groups.

9. The strong commitment of the college to provide matriculation and special services for international students has made it easier for the center to carry out additional services for these students.

10. Well defined relationships with consortia, organizations, and other institutions have allowed the center to share resources for curriculum development.

11. College commitment to the advancement of study/travel programs has made the college a leader among New Jersey institutions.

12. Flexibility in scheduling activities has allowed the center to address timely issues immediately.

Weaknesses

1. Budget cutbacks and fiscal restraints mean that the center relies heavily on "soft money" and therefore must devote strong resources to grant development. The unsure status of federal and state funding for international education makes long-term planning quite precarious.

2. Insufficient physical space for staff personnel reduces the role of the center as a centralized resource facility. Overcrowding limits the opportunity to serve more people inside the office.

3. A comprehensive program requires more full-time staffing. Each program component needs one staff member, backed up by part-time personnel.

Strategies for the 1980s

The goals and objectives for 1981–83 have been outlined and discussed in previous sections. The commitment of the center to strengthening global dimensions and creating a comprehensive international program is obvious. In addition, the center sees a need to address the following issues.

1. Curriculum development in areas such as allied health, police science, criminal justice, banking and finance, and cooperative education options.

2. Expansion of overseas opportunities in student–faculty exchanges and study/travel programs.

3. Enhancement of library and curricular materials in languages other than English.

4. Expansion of cultural activities such as concerts, theatre presentations, and arts and crafts exhibitions.

5. Recruitment of students for the International Marketing, Import–Export Management, International Studies, and Modern Language curricula.

6. Identification of international speakers residing in nearby locations for the purpose of addressing classes and student clubs.

7. Enhancement of faculty development workshop programing.

8. Identification of diversified sources of funding for the center, such as funding from industry, state, and private sources.

9. Continuing articulation with public and private sector agencies that are aware of future trends and can assist in planning timely events.

10. Design of in-service programs for faculty members who will train on-site at import–export companies in order to have firsthand knowledge of what constitutes a practical international trade program.

11. Design of in-service training programs for faculty who will train on-site at internationally focused organizations and agencies, such as immigration service or diplomatic and consultant agencies in order to design practical courses for students.

CHAPTER 17

Rockland Community College

HOWARD A. BERRY

Institutional Description

Rockland Community College (RCC) is located thirty miles north of New York City, in a setting that is suburban and rural, yet has access to the cultural, educational, and international resources of New York and the surrounding metropolitan region.

RCC was created in 1959 as the culmination of a five-year effort on the part of many educators, officials, and lay citizens throughout the county. RCC is an affiliated unit of the State University of New York and is a comprehensive two-year college. From its inception, the college has worked to serve the needs of the community by offering a diversity of programs and emphases, ensuring that quality education remains affordable without the burden of long-distance travel and housing away from home.

As a result of RCC's success in offering affordable, quality learning, the college has been enriched by attracting a student population which reflects the community at large. The college has a total enrollment of about 12,000, including early admissions students and parents returning to higher education after raising families; and it has a full-time enrollment of about 6,000, including college-aged students either primarily interested in the associate degree or planning to transfer to four-year institutions, and also adults who have come to RCC for professional training.

The student body comes primarily from the immediate area, but for special-interest programs the college also attracts students from all parts of New York and from many other states. Most come from low- to middle-income families, many are first-time college students in their families, and a majority qualify for some kind of financial aid. About 15 percent of the students speak languages other than English, of whom most are permanent residents; but the college has also deliberately attracted about 200 international students representing some forty countries. The immediate area has several extensive ethnic communities, including Hispanic, Haitian, Asian Indian, and Oriental.

The faculty consists of 140 full-time members, all of whom hold master's or higher degrees. Many have had educational and/or living experiences in other countries, and a good percentage speak or read at least one language other than English. The college makes use of several hundred adjunct part-time faculty, who are hired for the special expertise they bring to a subject.

In short, RCC is in many ways structured as a typical community college, serving a diverse clientele in a number of ways, seeking always to bring quality and innovative education to the broadest segment of the population. (The college organizational chart, Figure 17.1, shows the basic administrative structure.)

Institutional Commitment To International Education

The State University of New York, consistently and on a systemwide basis, has advocated a deliberate and structured thrust toward international education. With the support of the president, the administration, and many of the faculty, RCC has been developing a range of options for international/intercultural studies. This movement has not been ad hoc growth, but is based on definite premises about education in general, and international education in particular.

The premises, revolving around identified needs, are these:

1. The need to develop in students cognitive and effective tools for understanding and relating to people in other cultures. This calls for the development of curricular combining study and experience that allow students to participate in and observe other cultures while learning the content and discipline of the liberal arts.

2. The need for new pedagogies, particularly for a "pedagogy of experience" to meet educational needs and to suit the learning styles of the "new students." Coleman and others have argued that the present structures of society require that youth who are not conventionally literary and linguistic be given an "action curriculum" that brings them into contact with people, problems, and processes of the "real" world as the foundation of the curriculum.

3. The need to develop a populist theory and practice of international education. In a world increasingly interconnected, interactive, and, in the

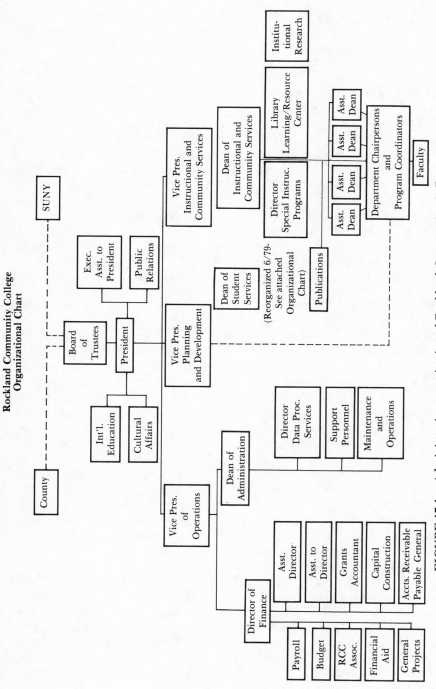

FIGURE 17.1. Administrative organization of Rockland Community College.

words of George Gerbner, "wired together so tightly that a short-circuit can fry us all," the need for international knowledge as part of general education has become imperative.

Historical Development

Rockland Community College's involvement with international education began in 1969 with the idea of shifting the traditional—and somewhat elitist—concept of the junior year abroad to the community college level. That summer a group of secretarial science students, accompanied by a faculty member, spent eight weeks in London, working in British businesses during the day and participating in academic studies in the evening. This successful demonstration of study abroad for community college students quickly began to generate further momentum.

The next year, 1970, RCC affiliated with Alvescot College, a British institution located in a rural area twenty miles west of Oxford. The idea was to have a group of American students in their freshman or sophomore year spend a semester or a year in a residential, rural British setting, studying alongside British students who were preparing for university entrance. The chronological difference in the two national educational systems allowed Americans, who had begun higher education at the community college, to participate with British students preparing for university entrance. The type and level of subjects studied was applicable to both groups. More importantly, a pattern for design of study abroad programs for community college students began to emerge. Rather than send students abroad to study subjects which could be taken equally well in America, the curriculum was designed to use the strengths of the surrounding resources while maintaining the basic quality and standards of liberal arts study. As much as possible, experiential dimensions were built into the course content. Visits to cathedrals, government offices, and historical sites were part of most courses, and practitioners from the arts, politics, and business conducted seminars with the students. This program began to shape the concept which remained consistent with later international developments: Let the country be the curriculum. That is, in study abroad programs, the entire set of experiential resources available in another culture should themselves be used as the curriculum.

With the program in England stabilized, and the pattern established, the college was ready to broaden its study abroad opportunities. In 1972 a member of the English Department faculty, following the England model, established an affiliation with a college in Jerusalem. Begun in essentially the same manner, the Israel program eventually added another dimension to RCC's study abroad approach—brokering. (Brokering is the concept of forming contacts with a variety of colleges, service organizations, communities, cultural groups, and so forth.) Affiliation with one college, as effective as it might be for starting a program, was a limiting factor, allowing only some twenty to forty students at a time to participate. With an extensive web of such contacts, made through government ministries and official representatives, American students wishing to go abroad could now be advised about the options most suited to their educational and experiential needs. In addition, brokering allowed a far greater number of students to be accommodated than did affiliation with a single institution.

At the same time that the England and Israel programs were developed, the college added another program to meet the need for more specialized study abroad opportunities. Many of RCC's students are older adults or persons enrolled in technical programs, and the semester/year time frame was either economically or programmatically not feasible for them. Therefore, the college developed a variety of short-cycle programs of two-to-three-week offerings during intersession and summer periods. Designed and led by faculty, these studies have proved popular and effective in providing study abroad opportunities for particular student needs.

Thus, by 1973, the college had implemented a full range of study abroad options available to virtually any student. Additionally, once contacts had been established, the pattern developed by the semester/year and the short-cycle programs allowed offerings to be generated in a considerable number of countries. The college was now sending almost 100 students annually on the short-cycle programs, and some 100 to 200 to the semester/year offerings.

This very success made visible another problem. Because of the numbers now involved, and the ease with which new programs could be created RCC could not alone fulfill the potential of all possible programs. In fact, programs were soon found to be competing with one another for the available student pool. If the base were to be broadened and the populist idea to be implemented, a new structure was needed. Therefore, in 1973, a consortium of community colleges for participation in study abroad programs was created. Originally called the Tri-State Consortium, it linked RCC with public community colleges in New Jersey and Pennsylvania. Structures and by-laws were worked out, allowing for membership fees and charge-back systems whereby students could remain registered at their home campus while participating in programs initiated by one of the other colleges. The idea and its implementation proved successful, practical, and attractive. Since 1973 the operation, now known as the College Consortium for International Studies (CCIS), has grown to include forty-four colleges (including some four-year units) in a number of states across the country.

Having created an extensive and sophisticated set of study abroad opportunities, RCC turned its attention to internationalizing the campus and community. If international education were to be truly an integral element of general education, an academic structure was needed to support the community dimensions and activities.

Consequently, in 1976 the resident director of the England programs, who had returned to the campus in 1972, was appointed coordinator of International College. International College is an academic division of RCC, and its major charge is to coordinate all aspects of curriculum, programs, and activities related to international/intercultural developments. Under its administration come foreign languages; English as a second language, admission of international students, and intercultural program development. Its basic function is to bring these elements together, allowing international/intercultural offerings to be an ongoing part of the campus and community.

International College supports a range of traditional, classroom-based offerings in French, German, Hebrew, Italian, Russian, and Spanish. Of greater interest, perhaps, has been the development of the Self-Study Language Service (SSLS), which offers more than forty of the so-called uncommon languages on an individualized basis through a combination of self-study materials and native-speaking tutors (many of them drawn from the college's international student population). SSLS allows students studying intercultural affairs to add a language and corporations to provide training for employees dealing with international concerns.

International College has also developed a large and sophisticated English as a Second Language (ESL) program to serve international students as well as the variety of non-English-speaking permanent residents in the area. The program serves over 500 students, at the main campus and at centers located in the communities they serve. The program presents a number of options to entering students, depending on their English language ability. They may be assigned to a full program of ESL, or to a partial program accompanied by academic courses. Specially designed "support" courses are also available to these students, providing such studies as introduction to American culture, intercultural communication, speech for international students, comparative government. Working with other departments, International College also provides advice and support to the faculty dealing with international students.

In the area of curriculum and program development, International College has been responsible for designing a two-year Associate in Arts degree program. This program fulfills all liberal arts requirements, while emphasizing intercultural studies and experiences. Supported by a three-year grant from the US Department of Education, a freshman-year "core" offering of interdisciplinary English/Social Science studies emphasizing intercultural concepts and skills has been designed. This course, Culture, Community and Communication, forms the basis for the degree program,

and, with administrative support, is projected as a collegewide requirement for general education.

International College also supports internationalization in adjunct
areas. It conducts faculty development, helping faculty design and
implement international modules within existing departmental offerings. It
works with the College's Office of Cultural Affairs to schedule lectures,
films, and cultural events for campus and community. It supports the
Global Concerns Forums, which brings speakers to the campus three or
four times a semester. It acts as coordinator for many of the activities of the
International Services Association of the Community Colleges of New
York (ISACC), a consortium of community colleges that provides
international services (curriculum development, foreign students, faculty
exchange) to the public community colleges of New York. Finally,
International College has recently been moving into the area of service-
learning. Service-learning is the linking of academic classroom learning
with experiential community services. These experiences are individualized by means of learning contracts; students have participated in
such programs in Ghana, West Africa, and in the American Southwest.

In addition to study abroad opportunities and the program offerings
through International College, the college has recognized foreign students
as an important means of internationalization. In 1978 the Center for
International Students was established to provide support services to the
college's international students. It establishes and maintains contacts with
embassies wishing to send groups of students for the technical and career
programs offered by community colleges, handles the immigration and
visa needs of these students, arranges for accommodation, provides
orientation to campus and community life, offers academic and personal
counseling, and aids students in the process of transfer to senior
institutions. The center also coordinates the use of international students as
resource persons for classroom and community groups and acts as a
channel for the ISACC colleges of New York, recommending international
students to them for programs not provided by RCC.

Finally, in addition to consortial arrangements with other colleges, the
college has developed affiliations with nonacademic groups and organizations. For example, the college's Israel program benefits from close ties
with local and national Jewish organizations interested in stimulating study
in Israel. The move toward service-learning has been greatly aided by links
with the Presbyterian church, which has opened to students the its physical
and educational resources. An affiliation with the Lisle Fellowship, which
has had much experience in providing community-based intercultural
experiences in various parts of the world to students, has resulted in the
Lisle Center for Intercultural Studies at the college. Most recently, RCC
has become a cooperating member of the Partners in the Americas

organization. Through this Washington-based group, the college and the county have become partners with a Caribbean community for cultural interchange and educational development.

Thus, in a little more than ten years the college has grown from a summer program in England to a broad-based operation that involves extensive study abroad opportunities, degree programs, international students as an accepted part of campus and community life, and numerous cultural and intercultural activities.

Administrative Organization

One of the strengths of international education at RCC is the full administrative support and visibility it receives. Sponsored by the president, and endorsed by the vice-president of instruction, deans, and other administrative offices, international education enjoys across-the-board cooperation. This integral and recognized position is a major factor in the success and scope of international studies at RCC.

Financially, all of the full-time professional staff and the support personnel occupy positions at the college that are supported by the college budget. Thus, along with its recognized administrative and academic position, international studies is a legitimate part of the college's regular financial structure and planning. All of the operations and programs of international studies are supported by student enrollment. The numbers of students participating determines the extent and stability of staffing. Adjunct funds acquired through grants, consortial membership fees, and other sources allow for pilot innovations.

The International Office is organized as a set of affiliated, overlapping, but autonomous operations. There are three divisions: Study Abroad Programs, International College, and the Center for International Students, each headed by a director or coordinator, and supplied with support staff. The direct professional staff consists of five people, drawn originally from academic departments but now performing administrative duties in supervising the programs. The various offices report to the vice-president of instruction in matters pertaining to academic or curricular affairs, to the Office of Student Services in regard to student grades, records, or behavior, and directly to the president for policies, directions, and external linkages. International studies personnel participate in meetings of the department heads, the faculty senate, and various of the college's academic and nonacademic committees.

BUDGET

RCC's international operations function in three general areas: study abroad, international students, and curriculum development, including languages and ESL. While these programs and offices are integrated and cooperative, the budgetary funding for each is somewhat separate.

Study Abroad (including consortial operations). The study abroad office functions on a minimal institutional budget, which covers only the salary of the director, office expenses and supplies, and secretarial help. The other financial needs for this program are met through consortial membership dues and administrative fees paid by students as part of the cost of participation in the programs.

International Studies. The Center for International Studies is maintained under the counseling department, which covers the salaries of the coordinator and of secretarial and paraprofessional help. Its separate budget is small and covers office supplies and expenses, plus some conference and travel allowance.

Curriculum. International College is a regular academic department, one that includes international studies, languages, and ESL, and it is therefore the most separately funded of the three offices. Aside from the salaries of its director and secretary, which are funded institutionally, it has a budget similar to that of other departments. Last year, for items such as equipment, instructional supplies, office supplies, travel, conferences, printing, and field trips, its budget was approximately $16,000.

Other Sources. Additional funding for development comes from grants. For example, during the past three years International College has received a Department of Education grant totaling about $100,000 for curriculum development at RCC and other state university community colleges.

However, funds for RCC's international programs are part of the institutional structure. Because there is broad administrative support, for example, the international operations are often able to draw on the Office of Instructional Services or the president's budget to support special ventures or pilot projects.

Finally, and importantly, as a public institution, RCC's budget is student driven, that is, there are funds only to the extent that there are students. All international programs, therefore, are self-sustaining in the sense that the students enrolled support the administrative staff, office help, support services, and developmental projects.

Program Description

Study Abroad. This office develops and administers all academic study abroad programs and also coordinates the organization and activities of the consortium of two- and four-year colleges.

Since 1970 several thousand students at Rockland Community College have participated in overseas academic programs. The Rockland Centre for International Studies (RCIS) coordinates and supervises all international activities at RCC and sends between 600 and 700 students abroad annually through a variety of programs. In addition, the centre serves as the liaison office to the College Consortium for International Studies, a group of thirty colleges that offer students sixty-five overseas academic programs in twenty-seven foreign locations. The programs range from structured, formal courses at affiliated schools and institutions abroad to service-learning and contract-independent study courses. Students may choose from winter session, short-term, semester and year programs.

Formal programs. RCIS provides formal, structured programs, lasting for a semester, a year, or two years, in Denmark, England, and Israel. Students study a full-semester program, arranged prior to their departure, at affiliated schools, institutions, colleges, or universities abroad. The subject areas range from liberal arts courses to specialized programs, such as criminal justice, languages, and human services. Many students have found their academic and personal lives enriched through a cultural experience difficult to match in a conventional two-year course of study in this country. RCIS maintains close communication with its offices in London and Jerusalem to facilitate the placement of students in qualified institutions abroad.

Contract/Independent study. The student studying independently signs with his/her mentor, who represents the institution (RCC). The student, guided by the mentor, identifies the specific learning objectives for that contract and specifies the learning activities through which these objectives are to be obtained. Learning activities may include individual and group seminars and tutorials, assigned readings, and/or formal classes. In addition, the learning contract clearly spells out the evaluation procedures to be followed: usually a combination of papers, examinations, projects, tapes, and so forth. The evaluation methods, as all contract components, are agreed upon in advance (and prior to the student's departure for his study program abroad) and can be altered or modified only by mutual agreement by the mentor and student. RCIS's contract programs provide students a chance to benefit from unstructured learning and individual guidance while studying abroad. Contract learning, particularly overseas, is a rigorous academic undertaking that requires imagination, self-discipline, planning, and foresight in addition to the usual qualities of a good student. It should be considered only by serious students.

Short-term studies. During each academic year, RCIS conducts a wide variety of winter session and short-term studies in January, during the spring recess, and in the summer months. RCC students who have been introduced to study abroad through these short-term programs, usually two to three weeks in length, often decide to study overseas for a semester or a year. The short-term courses have grown in scope as well as in number. For example, they have enabled criminal justice students to study and compare the operations of the metropolitan police forces for Amsterdam, Paris, and London. Other short-term program participants have had a chance to evaluate child welfare practices in the Scandinavian countries or compare the nursing and health care practices in Israel to those in the United States. Over the years various departments at RCC began to fashion winter session and short-term offerings in various countries according to departmental interests; at present, the Business, Criminal Justice and Public Safety, Psychology–Social Science, Human Services, Nursing, English, Foreign Languages, Science, and Art Departments are involved.

Credits, transcripts, and tuition. Students register at RCC or at one of the United States colleges in the College Consortium for International Studies and pay the appropriate tuition, which in most cases covers the instructional costs abroad. They are monitored through RCIS offices in London and Jerusalem or through individual mentors. Upon the successful completion of the formal program or after fulfillment of the contract, students receive an RCC transcript (or a transcript from the college in the consortium with which they registered) reflecting the grades achieved or the course equivalents of the work done through the contract, greatly facilitating transfer of credits to other American institutions. Students may earn up to eighteen credits per semester, leading to an associate degree. From one to six credits are given for winter session or short-term programs, depending on the time spent abroad and the instruction offered in the program.

The following programs illustrate the range of offerings generally available during one academic year.

Denmark

Institution: DIS Program, University of Copenhagen

Emphasis: Basic liberal arts, with emphasis on courses relevant to Scandinavia

Location: Copenhagen

Prerequisite: Sophomore and/or junior standing

Semester: Fall and/or spring semester

Language of Instruction: English

Egypt

Institution: American University in Cairo

Emphasis: Basic liberal arts

Location: Cairo

Prerequisite: Sophomore and/or junior standing

Semester: Fall and/or spring semester

Language of Instruction: English

England

Institution: Ealing College of Higher Education

Emphasis: Basic liberal arts, all specialized subjects, formal, service-learning, and contract/independent study

Location: London

Prerequisite: Freshman, sophomore, junior and senior standing

Semester: Fall and/or spring semester

Language of Instruction: English

Germany

Institution: Collegium Platinum

Emphasis: German Language

Location: Heidelberg

Prerequisite: Freshman, sophomore, or junior standing

Semester: Fall and/or spring semester

Language of Instruction: English

Ghana

Institution: Mampong-Akwapim Polytechnic

Emphasis: Service-learning

Location: Mampong-Akwapim (forty miles northeast of Accra)

Prerequisite: Freshman, sophomore, or junior standing; intensive orientation requirements

Semester: Fall and/or spring semester

Language of Instruction: English

India

Institution: Hislop College

Emphasis: Basic liberal arts, service-learning

Location: Nagpur

Prerequisite: Sophomore and/or junior standing

Semester: Spring

Language of Instruction: English

ISRAEL/JUDAIC STUDIES

While organizationally a part of the study abroad office, Israel/Judaic Studies is the largest overseas program and, therefore has its own staffing. Students participate in a variety of academic and experiential programs in Israel, or may concentrate on the Judaic dimension, beginning their studies at the RCC campus and then continuing in Israel.

The philosophy of international education that RCC has pioneered is that the country is the curriculum. All the resources of the country—its universities, colleges, hospitals, newspapers, hotels, agencies, and institutions—become settings where RCC students may learn. In the Israel studies program, all of Israel becomes a resource and a laboratory for learning.

Judaic Studies at Rockland Community College is an interdisciplinary program investigating the history, culture, language, and philosophical/religious values of the Jewish people and analyzing their relationships with other peoples of the world, from Biblical times to the present.

Students may receive the A.A. with an emphasis in Judaic Studies in four semesters on campus, four semesters in Israel or England, or any combination of these. RCC has the largest Israel program of its kind in the United States and can place students from more than thirty-five different institutions or programs in Israel.

Jerusalem Office. Whatever program or approach the student elects, the Jerusalem office is available as a home away from home. The office is staffed by American academics and counselors who are particularly aware of the needs of US students. Academic, personal, and transfer counseling is provided in a friendly and supportive atmosphere.

Rockland Community College offers these major programs in Israel: (1) university and college study programs, (2) specialized schools and institutes, (3) alternative study opportunities, (4) service-learning programs, and (5) individually designed study programs. Students may study at any one of Israel's major universities or colleges, including: Hebrew University, Bar Ilan University, Ben Gurion University, Haifa University, and many others. They may also select a special school, program, or institute such as Hayim Greenberg College, Gold College for Women, Midrasha, Jerusalem Torah College, or several others.

As an alternative to study at a university, college, or school, RCC can also place interested students in programs combining education and experience. These alternative study programs include:

The Jerusalem Institute (Young Judea) (full year only)

Bnai Brith Shana Program (full year only)
Institute for Youth Leaders from Abroad (Machon L'Madrichei L'Chutz) (full year only)

Kibbutz College Program (fall only)

U.S.Y. Kibbutz Ulpan Program (fall only)

Ramah Kibbutz Program (spring only)

Bnei Akiva Program

Habonim Workshop

Poale Agudath-Shaalvim Program

Givat Haviva Program

Electrical Technology Program

Service learning programs are also available. Some examples include the following:

- A student may study sociology, language, and modern Israel while living and working on a kibbutz or while living and serving on the moshavim of the Jerusalem Corridor (Matech Yehudah).

- A student may study nursing (in English) while doing clinical service in an Israeli hospital.

- A student can be placed in a learning environment that allows him or her to serve while being apprenticed to an expert in the student's major (some facility with Hebrew language required).

Individually designed study programs are appropriate for some students. Through an academic learning contract, an individual study program is created, tailored to the student's specialized field of interest.

CENTER FOR INTERNATIONAL STUDENTS

The Center for International Students provides for a centralized range of services to international students attending RCC. It maintains close relations with the Office of Student Services, the Student Activities Office, the International Club, and the academic departments in order to monitor the experience of the students while they are here.

Included among the many services provided by the Center for International Students are:

- Assistance in complying with the regulations of the US government and other agencies

- Academic, vocational, and personal counseling

- Assistance in finding satisfactory housing

- Evaluation of international student credentials

- Information about programs of study available through Rockland Community College and other units of the State University of New York

- Direct placement in two-year colleges of the State University of New York

- Information about programs offered by other US colleges and universities

- Help in learning about life in the United States

- Opportunities to act as an interpreter of one's country and culture to Americans

- Programs of special interest to international students

The multilingual staff of the Center for International Students includes faculty members and professional counselors who can provide foreign students with the full range of academic, vocational, and personal counseling services, including:

- Evaluation of students' previous academic work to determine where their academic backgrounds best fit within the American system of higher education

- Counseling, testing, and advice about programs of study available in the US

- Advice on vocational and career choices, and recommendations concerning colleges and universities that best represent those choices

- Counseling for transfer to colleges or universities offering the Bachelor of Arts degree, including professional advice as to which senior college may best suit the student's needs

- Help in applying to other colleges and recommendations to ease the eventual transition

- Continual monitoring and evaluation of the student's progress toward academic or career objectives, and special assistance when required

- Advice on career opportunities

- Assistance with personal problems that may be encountered in a new country and culture, including medical, social, or interpersonal problems

Direct placement in SUNY two-year colleges. Through agreement with the International Services Association of the Community Colleges of SUNY, the center can place foreign students in selected SUNY two-year colleges. It also maintains files on programs of study available at over 1,000 colleges across the United States, institutions that offer interested foreign students the broadest possible range of academic, technical, and skills development programs.

Assistance in complying with regulations and learning to live in the United States. In order to minimize difficulties, the Center for International Students can advise the foreign student about steps to gain admission to the United States and to US colleges and universities.

The center can also help foreign students comply with the regulations of student loan and grant or scholarship offices of agencies such as the Organization of American States and the United Nations. The center also provides details about the student's legal obligations while in the United States.

The center sponsors an ongoing series of activities to ease the foreign student's introduction into American society and culture. These activities include orientation programs for host families and newly arrived students, structured social activities, and academic courses using the arts as exposure to American life. The center also provides a handbook that offers advice on American customs and other subjects of interest.

Before arriving, each student is sent a packet of information concerning the customs, climate, and lifestyles of the northeastern United States. The packet also includes data on Rockland County and the College. During the student's stay, the Center for International Students provides:

- Orientation sessions to introduce the international student to college campus life and the general aspects of American culture.

- Access to extensive cultural affairs programs offered by the college and special trips to New York City and other points of interest. Foreign students may earn college credit by participating in cultural and travel experiences.

- Membership in the college's International Student Club, which provides companionship as well as social and cultural interaction throughout the year.

- An American student counterpart, carefully chosen, whose role will be to explain the formal and informal aspects of American life, society, and customs. This liaison provides practice in the English language and helps soften the culture shock.

The center also offers a wide range of activities designed to make the international student's stay at RCC a successful and enjoyable learning experience. These include career practicums, cooperative education, and work or community service programs.

Another service the Center for International Students offers is assistance in finding available housing. Many colleges, particularly community colleges, do not have on-campus dormitory housing. Furthermore, dormitory living does not always provide the best introduction to American life and culture.

Through a network of faculty, clergy, community agencies, and groups the center offers a variety of housing arrangements for foreign students. The center has developed community affiliations with area families who are committed to an exchange of cultural values, background, and perspectives, while providing an acceptable learning environment.

A "family stay" is usually recommended for foreign students studying in the US for the first time. However, students may also live in apartments or shared housing arrangements within Rockland County. The center maintains an ongoing list of available housing and a housing specialist is always on hand to assist students.

The college encourages incoming students to stay with American families for at least one semester. This policy is meant to facilitate the process of cultural and academic integration, allowing students to learn about American life while promoting cross-cultural communications. Family stays may be extended at the student's option. The center also provides orientation for American host families and maintains close liaison with the family and the student throughout the student's stay.

INTERNATIONAL COLLEGE

International College, the most organizationally complicated of the offices, offers students a series of emphases leading toward an A.A. degree in humanities. This degree is readily transferable to senior institutions offering the B.A. or B.S. degrees.

All International College offerings provide an international and/or intercultural approach to traditional disciplines. While studying in the chosen area of interest, the student is simultaneously fulfilling RCC degree requirements.

Divisions within International College provide full two-year programs of study that offer the options of campus-based studies, community-based experiences, and opportunities for overseas experiences.

From these studies students may continue international specialties at a higher academic level, choose to develop an international career, or simply develop a solid foundation for later studies in various disciplines. The academic offerings consist of the following elements:

1. A mentor/student relationship for individualized design of studies and experiences

2. Choice of an emphasis in one of the following categories:
   - ethnic or cultural heritage
   - religious studies
   - an area of the world
   - global problems
   - international service
   - languages

3. Practicum and community experience related to the emphasis

4. A common interdisciplinary core of English/social science studies dealing with the culture, field techniques, intercultural awareness, global problems, and world affairs

5. Language studies related to the emphasis chosen

6. Individualized special projects conducted through tutoring, learning contracts, and practicums

7. Study abroad

In International College each student is under the personal guidance of a mentor. The mentor maintains close contact with the student, helps select an emphasis, helps design studies and experiences related to the student's interests, and generally oversees the student's academic and career needs.

In addition to the mentor relationship, an important part of the academic experience is allowing the student to apply and practice the concepts and theories being studied. These experiences may include library research, working with ethnic or cultural community groups or individuals, internships with organizations concerned with international/intercultural affairs, structured and informal contact with international students, and the opportunity for study abroad.

International College has close working relations with Judaic, Irish, Italian, Hispanic, Christian, and other community and ethnic heritage organizations. Through these community groups, experiences related to the student's special interests can be provided. In addition, New York City and the metropolitan area are rich in resources and opportunities related to international studies such as the United Nations, the World Trade Center, the Asia Society, the African-American Institute, the Foreign Area Materials Center, and many others.

Among adjunct resources are full- and part-time faculty and community practitioners with special expertise and backgrounds in international affairs, cultural studies, languages, and field experience techniques. Offerings in other academic and career departments of the college related to special interests are open to students. These related resources and studies will be recommended and integrated into the student's program.

All aspects of the academic courses are transferable as general liberal arts, the basis for continued academic study at senior institutions or for work toward development of a career in international fields such as business, law, government, and languages.

Emphases/Options:

1. All four semesters may be taken at the college through a combination of regular courses and individualized studies designed according to the student's particular intercultural interests.

2. A portion of the four semesters will be spent in internship service with a local subcultural community.

3. A semester or year may be spent overseas in an area or culture related to the student's choice of special field.

English as a second language. For students whose native language is other than English, the college conducts an English as a Second Language Institute. It is part of International College, is staffed by professionals, and offers a full set of services for international students. These include testing and evaluation, English language instruction ranging from beginning to advanced, and counseling in English and all other areas of study.

All students whose native language is other than English must be tested by the institute. Based on that testing, students will be counseled into intensive English studies or into a combination of English language and other subjects. International students may take regular college offerings only with the approval and signature of the institute staff.

Foreign languages. As an integral part of its international/intercultural studies, International College offers a full range of language studies, including traditional classes in language, literature, conversation, civilization, independent study projects, bilingual courses, and self-study/tutored materials for languages not usually available. Regular classes at all levels are presented for the more common languages, including French, German,

Italian, Hebrew, Russian, and Spanish. For those wishing special studies or more advanced work in these or other languages, independent or contract study may be arranged.

Bilingual courses are available in selected areas such as business, secretarial studies, and psychology. In addition, through the full range of language offerings, students may receive the Associate in Arts degree with an emphasis on languages and linguistics.

A special feature of the language offerings is the possibility of "scarce" language study. For students, businessmen, or others wishing to pursue languages not ordinarily available—for academic, business, personal, or travel purposes—a combination of professional mentoring, self-study materials, and tutoring is offered.

Strategies for the Future

Rockland's basic international strategies for the future will, of course, be to continue to strengthen and enlarge the existing programs and organization. It will continue to maintain a holistic approach to internationalization of the curriculum, international students, and study abroad.

Specifically, however, some directions will be emphasized and supported. In regard to internationalization of the curriculum, priority will be given both to enlarging the intercultural degree program and to infusion of international/intercultural content across the general curriculum.

Secondly, much attention will be paid to increasing the number of international students, and especially to fostering campus and community interaction with them as valuable resources and translators of their culture to American audiences. This will include articulating linkages between American and international students on the campus, opening access for international students to local public schools and community groups, and forming college/community committees for intercultural interactions.

Third, with study abroad priority will be given to broadening the currently Eurocentered programs to increase opportunities for students to experience developing cultures and nations. Most especially, the idea of the "action curriculum" will be emphasized by developing service-learning opportunities in Third World areas. This idea of service in a community as an integral part of international studies will focus on the Caribbean, Asia, and Africa. Additionally, intercultural service opportunities will be opened in domestic locations—inner cities, ethnic communities, regions such as the Southwest—for those unable to participate in study abroad.

Finally, Rockland will continue creating linkages and networks with other colleges, public schools, community organizations, and businesses. This will involve academic studies and services, sharing resources, and training and technical assistance. Through these efforts the college hopes to mature its belief that institutions of higher education can be a catalyst to bring the world to the community and the community to the world.

PART IV

Conclusion

CHAPTER 18

Internationalizing the Campus: A Strategy for the 1980s

EARL L. BACKMAN

BEFORE WORLD WAR II the United States educational system demonstrated little commitment to the need for providing students with an international or global perspective. Like most Americans, educators were much more concerned with domestic growth and internal matters. Rather than acknowledge the changing circumstances brought about by new immigrant populations and increased foreign student enrollment, the educational system sought to "Americanize" their cultures and minimize any contribution they might make toward our world understanding.

The world in which Americans find themselves in the 1980s is much different from that of 1945. Today, few Americans remain untouched by events and happenings beyond US borders. The future of the United States and its people is shaped by external forces to a greater degree than ever before. Energy, environmental pollution, climatic crisis, possibilities of nuclear blackmail, starvation, the arms race, trade barriers, and inflation affect the American population every day.

The capacity of Americans to comprehend the severity of global problems, to understand the significance of world events, to work and interact with peoples of other cultures, and to obtain the requisite skills needed for new employment opportunities in foreign trade and finance depends largely on the responses of higher education and training so essential to an interdependent world. Where will business, industry, and government, for instance, recruit the cosmopolitan managers and policymakers its international operations require?

Many educators believe all the weapons in our arsenal will be inadequate if the United States fails to invest in the educational resources of this country, which serve to correct inaccurate perceptions of both Americans and other peoples throughout most of the world. Without timely exchange of knowledge, information, resources, and training, the United States will surely fail to have a significant effect on international events. If these reasons were not enough for universities and colleges to develop international studies programs, other reasons could be easily enumerated. As Rose Hayden asserts, "The first is survival. We must sustain informed connections in order to survive in a competitive and nuclear global system."[1] But survival alone is not enough; thus the second and third reasons, as she enumerates them, are "humanitarian" concerns and a need for "shared brainpower." The United States must illustrate to the desperate and starving among the world's population that Americans care about their plight. The educational system should also attempt to help Americans relate to other cultures and peoples. The role of higher education in the process of internationalizing a population is abundantly clear. In fact, it "has never been more important, the constraints never so real, and the rewards never so rich. Never have Americans so needed to reach a new level of global consciousness."[2]

In varying degrees and with differing structures, the seventeen model programs discussed in this book illustrate the process of internationalizing a campus. All have overcome five major obstacles to developing a campus-based international program. This final chapter briefly addresses these roadblocks, lists and summarizes a few of the necessary ingredients in a well integrated program, and concludes with one method of initiating and organizing an international studies effort on campus.

Obstacles to International Programing

Of the five obstacles to the establishment of an international program briefly discussed below, the first and second are particularly acute: lack of institutional commitment from top administrators and faculty opposition. In other words, the most successful campus programs develop as a result of strong commitment from the administration and with strong support from critical faculty members. Harari (1981) argues rather convincingly that all faculty do not need to be committed to a serious international program— only 25 percent or so are needed to move a campus into the international arena.

Those presidents, provosts, or vice-presidents for academic affairs who create obstacles must be enlightened and shown why an international dimension on campus is valuable. The strategies employed to "educate" such administrators depend partly on the nature of the opposition, or at least the perceived opposition. Are members of the institutional leadership opposed to an international program because they do not recognize its value? Perhaps they fail to see its relevance to the institutional mission. Maybe the perceived costs for such an effort are beyond the institutional budget. The president and other top leaders may see foreign travel and study as junkets, with no redeeming educational value. Or administrators may have the mistaken impression that faculty members are not interested. The list of reasons could go on, but the important point is that removing the obstacle, or converting the skeptics, depend on selecting the proper approaches.

Few administrators, if any, were born with a strong sense of commitment to international education; most gained this perspective somewhere during their academic experience. Fortunately, for those devoted to internationalizing the campus, there are several methods of getting committed institutional leaders. By far the easiest way is to hire administrators who have an international commitment. Faculty members often have no choice in such matters; however, when they do serve on search committees, they can urge that commitment to international education be an important criterion in the selection process.

However, if faculty leaders must work with the leadership structure already in place, other strategies may work. They might include, among others: (1) strong indication of faculty support (particularly from campus leaders); (2) campus appearances of well known individuals strongly endorsing international education; (3) working to obtain an invitation for the president to travel overseas, either alone or with a group, perhaps to deliver a speech or tour with other university presidents; (4) illustrating through documentation various approaches to internationalizing the campus that can be initiated with little or no new funding; (5) submitting examples of mission statements that similar institutions have adopted, or that professional organizations and accrediting associations (such as schools of business) strongly recommend, or policy statements that have been adopted by various education associations located at One Dupont Circle; or (6) merely articulating what is already happening internationally on the campus and expressing the desire to coordinate and direct what are currently unrelated events. In summary, if the institutional leadership is an obstacle, discover the reasons behind the lack of support, and then be innovative (and perhaps a little devious) in developing strategies to convert the president or vice-president.

A second and often more frequently encountered obstacle to the development of an international program lies within the faculty itself. Contrary to the popular notion often held by those outside the institution, when it comes to changing the curriculum, liberal faculty can be very conservative. While it is difficult to talk about changing, modifying, and adding to the curriculum without understanding how this element strengthens the entire international dimension on campus, it is the effort by faculty in their individual courses that most clearly affects the internationalizing process. Although adapting the curriculum to the changing world is clearly the most significant and far-reaching measure, this change will not, as a rule, come easily.

Removing faculty resistance to internationalizing the campus is a gradual process. As a first step, the institution needs a campuswide committee charged with making recommendations about the institution's international mission. This committee should be composed of highly respected and committed faculty drawn from many academic departments. Therefore, the plan developed becomes a program supported by faculty from its inception.

Another technique employed to convince faculty is to reward them for participating in the curriculum revision process. Such rewards can include release time for course revision; travel funds to attend workshops, conventions, and institutes; and the opportunity to participate in faculty exchange programs or to lead a seminar overseas during the summer. Such benefits are great incentives to increasing family support, not only for curriculum revision, but also for the entire process of strengthening the international dimension on campus.

Finally, it is important to assure faculty that they, and they alone, are responsible for the content of their courses. They must decide how best to impart an international dimension to their courses. Suggestions can be made, of course, but attempting to dictate specifics may lead to further entrenchment and opposition.

Faculty support for an international program is not merely desirable; it is absolutely necessary if the entire campus is to be affected. Although support of the entire faculty is not required, the broader the base of support, the more successful the international program will become. Rewards and incentives are powerful tools in accomplishing this task.

A third obstacle to the development of a viable international program is the lack of any statement of mission or goals. At many institutions international programs are launched with strong administrative and faculty support, and yet the effort flounders and proves unsuccessful in mobilizing campus support. The program may be initiated by zealous faculty members strongly committed to internationalizing the campus, or perhaps by a president who announces that there will be an international commitment. What many campuses lack, however, is a policy or mission statement that documents the support for what this commitment actually means. The purpose of the policy statement is to declare officially the institution's international mission. This statement serves as the standard to which specific goals, objectives, and actions can be compared. It offers justification for the steps the institution takes in implementing necessary changes. Such statements are approved by the faculty and administrative officers and, to increase their effectiveness, they also are adopted by trustees. While examples abound, the following policy statement adopted by Broward Community College illustrates a typical document.

> Broward Community College recognizes the importance of providing for students an international and intercultural dimension. As citizens of the United States and as inhabitants of planet Earth, today's students will be confronted throughout their lives with issues that transcent national boundaries. So interconnected is the political and economic world that some understanding of current issues and the events that shape them, as well as an appreciation for other cultures and customs throughout the world, is now basic to good citizenship. This has become an essential aspect of today's curriculum.
>
> It is further recognized that community colleges have a major responsibility in providing an international/intercultural dimension because of the increasing numbers of students for whom the community college will provide their only college-level educational experience. Moreover, the nature of the community college, and its emphasis on serving a local constituency, requires that the global agenda be addressed.
>
> It is the policy of Broward Community College to encourage and support the development of the many aspects of international/intercultural education. These would include:
>
> 1. A structured process for the involvement of the community and the college.
>
> 2. Study-abroad programs.
>
> 3. The internationalizing of the curricula.
>
> 4. Proper and effective programming of international students on campus.
>
> 5. Programs of an international/intercultural nature for the community.
>
> 6. Student, faculty, and staff exchange programs.
>
> 7. Consultant and support services with foreign institutions.
>
> 8. Staff and program development activities.[3]

Institutional structure is the fourth obstacle individuals often encounter when attempting to develop an international program. Deans and department chairpersons often view new programs, particularly those directly under the academic vice-president or provost, as a threat to their respective units. They fear loss of student credit hours through interdisciplinary courses; reduction in their budgets through allocations to a new program; loss of faculty members on short-term assignment to this new unit; and other departments supporting "their" faculty. Attempts to centralize international activities often meet with strong opposition from directors of area studies programs who prefer autonomy. In other words, even though faculty may strongly support increasing the international dimension on the campus, administrators of other units, as well as other structural characteristics, may offer opposition.

To combat structural obstacles, faculty members must work to allay fears. The president can assist in this process a great deal by illustrating his or her commitment. Furthermore, as the institutional plan unfolds, ample opportunity for input from all sectors must be given, allowing all views to be incorporated into the proposed program. To maintain the support of deans and department chairpersons (an absolute necessity for a program that depends on faculty support for success), it is important to reward these administrators through travel and funding. Time must be taken to demonstrate that the addition of an international program on campus does not threaten, but rather holds the opportunity for more faculty support, increased student credit hours, and greater faculty productivity.

The fifth major obstacle is, of course, financial. Adequate funding for support of international activities has been, and continues to be, a major obstacle. During the 1980s, reductions in federal support both to campus-based programs and to institutions will require even more innovative sources of funding. Much can be done, however, with minimal outside support. Course revisions, forums, seminars, study abroad, faculty exchange, and faculty colloquia all serve to internationalize the campus without expending great sums of money.

If part of the institution's mission is to develop and maintain a sizeable international commitment, a diversified funding base is desirable. The seventeen cases presented in this book illustrate numerous sources of funding, including: (1) institutional (most desirable and least susceptible to drastic fluctuations); (2) federal grants (most commonly mentioned agencies are Department of Education, Agency for International Development, United States Information Agency, and National Endowment for the Humanities); (3) grants from other sources (private foundations such as the Exxon Educational Fund, the Rockefeller Foundation, and the Kellogg Foundation; local community groups such as Arts and Science Councils and humanities committees; and businesses); (4) corporate contributions; (5) contracts with agencies, the US government and foreign governments and universities; and (6) sponsorship of revenue-producing programs (these might include intensive English language programs, study abroad, community travel programs, seminars for international business, or community forums). The key to long-term success is developing a strong institutional commitment based on institutional resources, and using outside funding sources to generate support for new program activities. However, relying completely on noninstitutional funding sources, while quite common, can have disastrous effects during periods of retrenchment. During the 1980s funding will be a major concern, particularly to institutions initiating their international effort.

Common Ingredients in an International Program

If the seventeen international programs discussed in this book illustrate only one point, it is that there is a wide range of international activities included under international education and considerable variation in how these activities are coordinated on a campus. Appropriate activities for one model may be inappropriate for another institution. The key to successful implementation of a campus-based international program is developing an approach, an organizational structure, and a set of activities that fit the degree of institutional commitment, level of resources, capability of faculty, and mission of the institution. Trying to increase foreign student enrollment may be disastrous if the institution is unwilling to develop the necessary infrastructure of support services. Appropriate matching of program activities and institutional mission (as defined in a policy statement) is the key to a successful campus venture.

As the cases in this book illustrate, most institutions do not try to sponsor or support all the activities that contribute to the international dimension of the campus. Collectively, these models discuss most of the ingredients found in an international/intercultural program.

Academic Program

Internationalizing the curriculum (regardless of the options selected) has the greatest long-term effect on the institution. Without a substantial commitment to an appropriate curriculum, significant internationalization will not take place. Perhaps the most far-reaching curriculum option is infusing into courses an international dimension which was previously absent. Infusion may be accomplished by adding non-Western material, which allows theories and assumptions normally made from a western orientation to be tested. Or a faculty member may decide to make a course more comparative in approach, viewing and analyzing the subject matter not only from a US perspective but from a second or third as well. In this way, faculty members can, without a major campuswide international effort, internationalize their own courses. Incentives and support given through an international program can greatly expedite the process.

Other options such as area studies, global studies, and intercultural studies require the institution to make a more substantial commitment. Faculty resources must be sufficient to offer several courses in the subject area and libraries must have adequate books and documents. Most of these options are carried out through interdisciplinary approaches, necessitating a great deal of communication and willingness to work together on the part of participating faculty and departments.

Another choice facing institutions is whether to establish a major, a minor, or a concentration. Should it be at the graduate level, undergraduate level, or both? Shall it be an international studies major or an area studies major, such as Africa, Asia, or Latin America? While the range of choices is smaller for some types of institutions than others, all campuses have some choice in the options exercised. Recently, more undergraduate institutions are opting for a concentration or a major in international or global studies, more because of a lack of necessary resources to focus on a specific area than a commitment to this approach.

While most institutions previously have concentrated their options in the humanities and social sciences, professional schools need to be emphasized much more. Schools of agriculture have been involved in international activities more extensively than any other professional program, owing to international development projects and government-sponsored agricultural contracts. Over the past few years, schools of business have increasingly indicated a willingness to adapt their curricula to the business world of the 1980s. However, much remains to be done. Far too many undergraduate business students still graduate without having taken business courses with an international perspective. Marketing, finance, and organizational theory are topics that can, and ought to be, taught from a much wider perspective.

If students are going to develop the skills necessary for them to survive in an increasingly interdependent world, they must understand the world in which they will live. To be effective, students in elementary and secondary school must develop an understanding of "worldmindedness"— a global perspective. Therefore, schools of education must train and educate teachers that are able to make sense of the impulses they receive daily from abroad. To do this, university students must take more international courses and area studies courses in their undergraduate and graduate programs. Programs on non-Western studies and global issues must also be offered to teachers in the school systems. If institutions make a concerted attempt to internationalize schools of education, the multiplier effect and its impact are obvious.

Schools of engineering are, perhaps more than any other professional school, feeling the impact of foreign student enrollment. These students want a curriculum that will give them the skills and training their respective countries need. As a result, many engineering curricula are taking on a decidedly international focus by examining problems that are particularly significant in non-Western societies. Furthermore, both community colleges and four-year institutions are developing training programs for international students, which will allow them to incorporate modern technology into development plans.

Internationalizing the curriculum is a campuswide responsibility. It involves infusing humanities and social science courses with a non-Western perspective as well as offering students the opportunity to compare and contrast issues from varying cultural perspectives. It also requires that the professional schools of agriculture, business, education, engineering, and others be aware of the international needs of the various groups they serve. However, to affect the lives and orientation of all students, merely internationalizing courses as described above, while necessary, is insufficient. As an additional step, more institutions are requiring foreign language study (an even greater number are opening up the language requirement debate once again), requiring two to three international/ intercultural/global courses of all majors (often part of a core curriculum), and developing institutional mechanisms linking foreign language and international studies in a more comprehensive manner (such as interdisciplinary courses, team-taught courses, business French, German culture and religion, for example.)

The process of internationalizing the curriculum does not just happen. It takes a critical mass of articulate faculty willing to lobby before their peers and administrators on both the need for and the design of an international curriculum. Specifically, in order to internationalize a course, individual faculty members need (1) a desire and willingness to change their courses; (2) an awareness of their discipline's literature as it relates to other cultures and societies; (3) adequate time to prepare course modifications (release time during the academic year or time off during the summer); (4) sufficient resource materials in libraries; (5) travel funds, if necessary, to conduct research and to study; and (6) a clear understanding of the goals and objectives in internationalizing their specific courses.

Although revising an institution's curricula is the most effective way to affect students, it is only one step in the process of internationalizing the campus. Many other activities, as partly exemplified in the list below, are sponsored by international programs. In some cases, all of these efforts are coordinated by one office; in others two or more administrative units are charged with implementing these activities. Regardless of the institutional structure, these activities represent the ingredients in a successful campuswide international commitment.

1. *Foreign students*, who, it is estimated, will make up 10 percent of the college population by the 1990s, add a great deal to the process of internationalizing the campus. Depending on the total number of students, an institution will need a foreign student advisor and other support systems to insure that these students receive adequate assistance in their matriculation.

2. *Student exchanges* involve sending US students overseas and receiving foreign students in this country. Most exchanges of this nature last no longer than one year. The International Student Exchange Program,

coordinated by Georgetown University, offers higher education institutions the opportunity to participate in student exchange without developing a special relationship with an institution overseas.

3. *Study abroad* opportunities, both for summer and the academic year, are sponsored by more than one thousand universities and colleges. Some institutions have only one small summer program each year, while others may provide fifteen to twenty summer programs and six to ten programs during the academic year. The larger the institutional effort, the greater the degree of coordination required. To maximize both impact and participation, these overseas activities must be related to the overall mission and goals of the institution. Therefore, the offerings should be an extension of the academic program—another setting where students are able to gain an additional perspective.

4. *Faculty exchanges* are equally important to the institution, particularly where sabbaticals do not exist. The advantage in these situations is that a faculty member receives a break from a normal routine and teaches for a year at a foreign institution. This experience gives a broad perspective and provides an opportunity for dialogue and interchange with foreign faculty members. The guest foreign faculty member on the US campus contributes to internationalizing the campus by giving seminars, teaching US students from a different cultural perspective, and interacting with American colleagues.

5. *Faculty development* activities are also sponsored by a number of international programs. Various components of this undertaking discussed in the case studies include (a) release time support; (b) summer stipends; (c) travel support for professional meetings, particularly foreign travel; (d) support for faculty exchange; (e) research grants; and (f) faculty member involvement in contracts and grants that are received from US agencies, as well as foreign universities and governments.

6. *English as a second language* is a type of program being established at a record pace in all types of higher education institutions. Not only are such programs self-supporting, but they also offer to institutions a method of monitoring the quality of foreign student admissions. Evidence illustrates that ESL programs also allow time for students to adjust to a new environment before entering a rigorous academic regimen. A high-quality ESL program is a strong addition to an international effort that wishes to increase its foreign student enrollment.

7. *Campus-based international activities* are best viewed as a catchall category in which to include the myriad of possibilities that exist. For instance, the following activities are sponsored by the international programs discussed in this book: (a) cultural events (e.g., plays, festivals, films, wine tastings, art displays, musical performances); (b) seminars and forums with outside speakers; (c) faculty colloquia using both visiting

(exchange) faculty and the institution's own faculty; (d) travelogues on various parts of the world; (e) international clubs; and (f) model United Nations sessions.

8. *Outreach activities* include those many institutional programs, designed largely for off-campus audiences, that contribute to internationalizing off-campus groups. Such activities might include, among others: (a) public forums on key international issues; (b) travel and exchange programs for the community; (c) international business seminars; (d) workshops for social studies teachers in local school systems; (e) cultural festivals; (f) international dinners; etc.

9. *Development assistance projects* cover those activities, often conducted under a contract, designed to aid either a foreign institution of higher learning or some sector of a foreign society. They might be financed through the US government (e.g., the Agency for International Development), a foreign government, or a Ministry of Education and a foreign university. Such projects often involve training, providing technical assistance, faculty exchanges, educating foreign students, and research and development. While some activities may be quite small, such as training teachers of English for a specific country during the summer, others may be of considerable size, for instance building major institutions of higher education or assisting in some aspect of agricultural production. The scope of development assistance projects if sufficiently broad to enable virtually all types of US educational institutions to participate if they view these activities as part of their institutional mission.

International activities both sponsored and coordinated by campus-based international programs are extremely varied. While most of their efforts are aimed at increasing the international dimension both on and off the campus, they also include a number of activities that assist foreign institutions, faculty, and governments. Since the possibilities are diverse, the institution must view international programming efforts as legitmate undertakings. Relating these activities to the mission of the university or college greatly assists in obtaining this legitimacy. For institutions just initiating an international commitment, it is important to begin offering a set of programs gradually, rather than attempting to do everything at once. As success begets success, it is better to be selective in the beginning and gain a positive reputation than attempt to meet all needs at once. Those activities should be chosen that can be accomplished with a minimum of support, and without threatening other constituencies. By gradually gaining support from other segments of the campus, the international effort truly becomes institutionalized.

Developing an International Program

In light of the fact that previous chapters discussed the development of seventeen different international programs, it is unrealistic to assume that there is only one way for such a program to evolve. Differing institutional structures, leadership, states of development, fiscal pressures, faculty strengths, institutional location, and differing motivations as well all affect the development of a campuswide international effort. How these factors interact at a given time and on a given campus may well indicate the best possible rationale for a certain program emphasis. However, to extrapolate from this point the theory that guidelines are useless is to fail institutions that want direction in initiating an international program. Therefore, while variations in the following approach are frequent, it does provide a framework from which to base campus deliberations. Briefly summarized, the approach presented is a composite of structures developed through a study of institutional cases. Note that it is not necessarily an ideal process, but rather one that allows any institution to structure an international set of activities appropriate for that campus.

In the case of a campus where interest has been expressed in a greater international commitment but a coordinated structure is lacking, the first step is to establish a committee. While the expression of interest may be from the faculty or the administrative structure, the most important step is the committee appointment. To be effective, this committee will be a working one, charged with several key tasks. Specifically, it should do the following:

1. Inventory course offerings to determine curriculum strengths and weaknesses.

2. Inventory the faculty to assess area strengths and weaknesses.

3. Make recommendations regarding

   - curriculum options
   - role of foreign students
   - development of study abroad
   - faculty and student exchange
   - campus and off-campus programs
   - overseas contracts and development assistance projects
   - the structure of the program desired

4. Hold open hearings to invite suggestions and comments on desired international activities.

5. Invite two to three consultants to campus to meet with the committee, other faculty, and university administrators (advice on choosing the proper consultants can be sought from education associations, the National Association of Foreign Student Affairs, the National Committee of International Studies and Programs Administrators, and from other institutions of higher education).

6. Write for descriptions of other campus programs, particularly from institutions with similar demographic characteristics.

7. Prepare a report that is thorough—one that expresses the consensus, not only of the committee, but also of other key faculty members; that is realistic, given the institution's strengths, location, and mission; and that clearly articulates the rationale behind the recommendations.

In order to complete its responsibilities effectively and expeditiously, the committee should be appointed by the president or vice president for academic affairs. In this way cooperation from the entire campus is much more likely. Second, the committee needs to be institutionwide, not located in one college or department. Third, it should be composed of faculty members with a commitment to or interest in developing the international mission of the institution. Finally, the chairman of the committee needs to be a faculty member highly respected by both colleagues and administrators—one that is knowledgeable, yet not narrow-minded, with a strong sense of responsibility and the requisite management skills to meet a timetable, allow for adequate input, and still achieve a consensus. The role of this committee, and its importance in assuring that program initiatives relate to the institutional mission, cannot be overstated. If the report is comprehensive and can stand the close scrutiny to which it will be subjected, the administrative task is made much easier. A committee appointed in the fall should complete its report in time for action in the spring.

Following the submission of the committee's recommendation, the vice-president for academic affairs should begin the process of reviewing the final report. This review process should be an administrative review and a review by the general faculty. Recommendations about curriculum must go to the normal curriculum committees of the faculty. It is important that the recommendations for establishing an international studies program be subjected to close inquiry by the entire institution. Efforts lacking this input and endorsement are likely to have difficulty in securing cooperation once established.

Once the committee's recommendation has received the support of the faculty and other administrative structures, the next step is to receive final approval by the required administrative structures. In many cases this approval involves the active support of the vice-president for academic affairs, the president, and perhaps a board of trustees or regents. Once the structure and goals of the campuswide international effort have been approved at the necessary administrative levels, the next step is to develop an institutionwide policy or mission statement. This statement reflects the campus commitment to international programs and offers a rationale for an international office. This policy statement should be approved by the president and the trustees and should be included in the catalog and other institutional literature.

The remaining steps in initiating an international studies program are a function of both the institutionally approved plan and the finances available for program initiation. Ideally, an Office of International Programs should be established. The role of this program will have been specified in the approved institutional plan. This office's responsibilities will vary considerably from institution to institution. In many cases the office will merely coordinate events, facilitating the development of a variety of international activities that may be located in other units and departments. The director of international studies should be a senior faculty member with considerable expertise in the field. Ideally this individual would direct the international office on a full-time basis, possibly teaching one to two courses a year; however, the budget might necessitate the appointment of a faculty member as a part-time director. The size of the remaining staff, both professional and support, will vary with institutional resources, outside resources, and the goals of the international effort.

The specific goals of the international office will vary considerably from institution to institution, but it typically performs the functions listed below. The following list was developed by Maurice Harari (1981) in his book *Internationalizing the Curriculum.*

1. Provide leadership to an institutionwide committee on international programs.

2. Provide a center of services, stimulation, and leadership in the international area.

3. Provide information services, and some coordination in the international area to the faculty and administration.

4. Assist in efforts to internationalize the curriculum and the institution.

5. Explore and guide international education development overseas.

6. Assist in creating faculty development opportunities in the international area in teaching, research, and public service.

7. Negotiate and implement contracts and grants.

8. Cooperate with international interests in the community, especially business, and significant regional or national associations concerned with international education.

9. Relate to or be in charge of the policy and operation of study abroad programs and foreign students on campus.

10. Prepare proposals to foreign agencies, foundations, business, and others to help implement the commitment of the institution in the international area.

These functions can be easily adapted to any institution that has incorporated into its mission the need for an international perspective. In virtually all cases, the office of international programs will be required to work closely with academic units, students services, the business office, and other support units on the campus. It will assume a major leadership role in the development of an international perspective on campus, and will also assume the responsibility to see that such activities are eventually carried out. As the funding base expands, both with institutionally appropriated funds and funds gained from other sources, program activities can be expanded. In order to maximize the expansion of such activities, close interaction with other key units on the campus is a virtual necessity.

International education in the decade ahead must take on an increased importance in American higher education. No longer should it, or can it, remain a frill; the impulses that we receive from abroad affect the world too much to be ignored. Internationalizing the institution should be a goal of every university and college, not just of the more prestigious.

The impact of political events outside the United States on international education has been considerable. The following are but a few of those events that have affected US institutions.

1. *Launching of Sputnik:* Led to massive governmental funding in the international field.

2. *Violent struggle in Vietnam and Indo-China:* Disrupted campuses, led to increased study on South Asia, presented the United States with a refugee problem. Higher education felt the impact on intensive English language programs.

3. *Political crisis in Iran:* Iranian student situation became highly tense, resulting in deportations, campus conflicts, and bills restricting foreign students introduced into legislatures.

4. *Currency fluctuation:* Causes havoc with both study abroad programs and foreign student enrollment.

5. *Conflict between People's Republic of China and Republic of China:* Affects US institutions with respect to exchange programs, contracts, English language efforts, study abroad, etc.

6. *United Kingdom triples tuition for international students:* This decision will bring thousands of Malaysians to the United States for study.

The list could be expanded; but the important point is that the higher education community in the United States must understand and be prepared to respond to the impact of external political events.

Educating Americans for the twenty-first century is one of the main goals of the higher education community. In order to accomplish this task, each institution must develop a set of policies, programs, and guidelines that will enable the campus to prepare students who will graduate with an international perspective. In order to achieve this objective, each university and college needs to examine its mission statement to determine the appropriate international commitment. This book has been designed to assist institutions in defining their respective international mission by presenting a variety of options. The need to internationalize the campus is essential; success will depend on institutional commitment, faculty support, institutionwide leadership, appropriate resources, curriculum revision, and an administrative structure to coordinate the desired activities. The process of internationalizing the campus will, as a rule, not come easily, but obstacles must not deter the higher education community from succeeding. The role that the United States plays in world affairs during the next two to three decades may well be determined by the impact international education efforts have on students and the community.

Notes

1. Rose L. Hayden, "The World and Us," *AGB Reports*, March/April 1979, p. 6.
2. Ibid.
3. William Green, "Broward Community College's International Program," *NCISPA Newsletter*, March 1982.

Bibliography

Association of American Colleges. *Toward Education with a Global Perspective.* Washington, DC: Association of American Colleges, 1980.

BACKMAN, EARL L. "The Development of an International Commitment: A Case Study." *Occasional Papers Series In International Education* 1, no. 2 (1982), pp. 1–15.

BACKMAN EARL L., and TONER, IGNATIUS. "In Lieu of Sabbaticals: An International Faculty Exchange Program." *International Studies Notes* 7, no. 1 (Spring 1980).

BARROWS, THOMAS S.; KLEIN, STEPHEN F., and CLARK, JOHN L.D. *What College Students Know and Believe About Their World.* New Rochelle, NY: Change Magazine Press, 1981.

––––––. *College Students' Knowledge and Beliefs: A Survey of Global Understanding.* New Rochelle, NY: Change Magazine Press, 1981.

BECKER, JAMES M., ed. *Schooling for a Global Age.* New York: McGraw-Hill, 1979.

BLACK, ROBERT, and BONHAM, GEORGE W. "The Council on Learning Project on Undergraduate Education: Education and the World View." *Annals of the American Academy of Political and Social Science* 449 (May 1980):103–113.

BLACK, ROBERT, and BONHAM, GEORGE W., eds. *Education for a Global Century: Handbook of Exemplary International Programs.* New Rochelle, NY: Change Magazine Press, 1981.

BONHAM, GEORGE W. "The New Necessities of National Survival: Education and the World View." *ADFL Bulletin* 11 (May 1980):34–35.

––––––. *Education and the World View.* New Rochelle, NY: Change Magazine Press, 1980.

BULLARD, BETTY M. "A Promising Agenda: International Studies in Elementary and Secondary Education." *Annals of the American Academy of Political and Social Science* 449 (May 1980):91–101.

BURN, BARBARA. *Expanding the International Dimension of Higher Education.* San Francisco: Jossey-Bass, 1980.

––––––. "Study Abroad and International Exchanges." *Annals of the American Academy of Political and Social Science* 449 (May 1980):129–140.

346

CLEVELAND, HARLAN. "The Internationalization of Domestic Affairs." *Annals of the American Academy of Political and Social Science* 442 (March 1979): 125-137.

Council on Learning. *Educating for the World View: Global Understanding and the Curriculum.* New Rochelle, NY: Change Magazine Press, 1981.

Education and World Affairs. *The University Looks Abroad: Approaches to World Affairs at Six American Universities.* New York: Walker and Company, 1965.

GARRATY, JOHN A.; VON KLEMPERER, LILY; and TAYLOR, CYRIL J. M. *The New Guide to Study Abroad: 1978-79.* New York: Harper & Row, 1979.

GRAY, AUDREY WARD. *International/Intercultural Education in Selected State Colleges and Universities: An Overview and Five Cases.* Washington, DC: American Association of State Colleges and Universities, 1977.

GUMPERZ, ELLEN M. *Internationalizing American Higher Education.* Berkeley: University of California, 1970.

HARF, JAMES E. "Undergraduate International Studies: The State of the Art and Prescriptions for the Future." *President's Commission on Foreign Language and International Studies: Background Papers and Studies.* Washington, DC: US Government Printing Office, 1979.

HARARI, MAURICE. *Internationalizing the Curriculum and the Campus: Guidelines for AASCU Institutions.* Washington, DC: American Association of State Colleges and Universities, 1981.

HAYDEN, ROSE LEE. "US Government Exchanges: The Quest for Coordination." *Annals of the American Academy of Political and Social Science* 449 (May 1980):114-128.

HAYDEN, SAMUEL L., and KOEPPLIN, LESLIE W. "International Business and International Studies: Prospects and Mutual Benefit." *Agenda for Business and Higher Education.* Washington, DC: American Council on Education, 1980.

HILL, JAMES W. "A Series of Exchanges." *Change,* May-June 1980, pp. 53-54.

KLITGAARD, ROBERT E. "Why International Studies? A Prologue." *Change,* January-Feburary 1981, pp. 281-84.

KUHNE, ROBERT J., and JORDAN, GERDA P. "Integrating International Business and Language Training." *Bulletin of the Association of Departments of Foreign Languages,* vol. 2, no. 3 (March 1980):27-30.

LAMBERT, RICHARD D. "International Studies: An Overview and Agenda." *Annals of the American Academy of Political and Social Science* 449 (May 1980): 151-164.

MYER, RICHARD B. *Curriculum: U.S. Capacities, Developing Countries' Needs.* Washington, DC: International Institute of Education, 1979.

PIKE, LEWIS W., and BARROWS, THOMAS S. *Other Nations, Other Peoples: A Survey of Student Interests, Knowledge, Attitudes, and Perceptions.* Washington, DC: US Government Printing Office, 1979.

President's Commission on Foreign Language and International Studies. *Strength Through Wisdom: A Critique of U.S. Capabilility.* Washington, DC: US Government Printing Office, 1979.

REMY, RICHARD C.; NATHAN, JAMES A.; BECKER, JAMES M.; and TORNEY, JUDITH
V. *International Learning and International Education in a Global Age.*
Washington, DC: The National Council for the Social Studies, 1975.

SANDERS, IRWIN T., and WARD, JENNIFER C. *Bridges to Understanding.* New
York: McGraw-Hill, 1970.

SCHULZ, RENATE A. *Options for Undergraduate Foreign Language Programs.*
New York: Modern Language Association, 1979.

SHANNON, WILLIAM G. *A Survey of International/Intercultural Education in Two-
Year Colleges, 1976.* La Plata, MD: Charles County Community College, 1978.

SIMON, PAUL. *The Tongue-Tied American: Confronting the Foreign Language
Crisis.* New York: The Seabury Press—Continum, 1980.

SPAULDING, SETH, and FLACK, MICHAEL J. *The World's Students in the United
States: A Review and Evaluation of Research on Foreign Students.* New York:
Praeger, 1976.

THOMPSON, RICHARD T. "New Directions in Foreign Language Study." *Annals of
the American Academy of Political And Social Science* 448 (May 1980):
45–55.

TONKIN, HUMPHREY, and EDWARDS, JANE. *The World in the Curriculum:
Curricular Strategies for the 21st Century.* New Rochelle, NY: Change
Magazine Press, 1981.

WATSON, PAUL. "Report of Survey of Postsecondary Organizational Structures for
International Studies and Programs." *International Studies Notes* 31 (Spring
1980):15–16.

WILLIAMSON, MARVIN, and MOREHOUSE, CYNTHIA T., eds. *International/Inter-
cultural Education in the Four-Year College: A Handbook on Strategies for
Change.* New York: NY State Education Department, 1977.

WIPRUD, HELEN R. *International Education Programs of the U.S. Government:
An Inventory.* Washington, DC: US Government Printing Office, 1980.

YARRINGTON, ROGER, ed. *Internationalizing Community Colleges.* Washington,
DC: American Association of Community and Junior Colleges, 1978.

Index

Notes

Notes

Notes

Notes

Notes

Notes

Notes

Notes